James A. Brander

GOVERNMENT POLICY
toward
BUSINESS
fifth edition

WILEY

Library and Archives Canada Cataloguing in Publication
Brander, James A.

Government policy toward business / James A. Brander. – 5th ed.

Includes index.
ISBN 978-0-470-15852-4

1. Industrial policy-Canada--Textbooks.   2. Canada--Economic policy—Textbooks.   3. Business and politics--Canada--Textbooks.   I. Title.

HD3616.C33B73 2013   338.971   C2013-900878-0

Production Credits
Vice President & Publisher: Veronica Visentin
Acquisitions Editor: Darren Lalonde
Marketing Manager: Anita Osborne
Editorial Manager: Karen Staudinger
Production Manager: Tegan Wallace
Developmental Editor: Theresa Fitzgerald
Media Editor: Channade Fenandoe
Production Coordinator: Lynda Jess
Permissions Coordinator: Luisa Begani
Cover Design: Joanna Vieira
Typesetting: Thomson Digital
Cover Image: ©istockphoto/SkyF

Printing and binding: Friesens
Printed and bound in Canada.
1 2 3 4 5 FP 17 16 15 14 13

John Wiley & Sons Canada, Ltd.
6045 Freemont Blvd.
Mississauga, Ontario L5R 4J3

Visit our website at: www.wiley.ca

To my daughter, Cathy

About the Author

James Brander is the Asia-Pacific Professor of International Business in the Sauder School of Business at the University of British Columbia (UBC). He did his B.A. in economics at UBC, and completed a Master's degree and Ph.D. in economics at Stanford University. Prior to taking a position at UBC, he taught at Queen's University. He has published widely in academic journals, particularly in international trade policy and industrial organization, and also in resource economics, finance, and innovation. In 1998 he won the Jacob Biely Prize, described as UBC's "top research prize." He served a four-year term as Associate Dean of the Sauder School and also served for four years as managing editor of the *Canadian Journal of Economics*. In addition, he has been active in consulting and government policy advising, particularly in areas related to international trade policy, competition policy, and intellectual property, and has been a frequent media commentator in these areas. During the 2009–10 year, he served as President of the Canadian Economics Association.

Contents

Preface and Acknowledgments

This textbook is intended for use in courses dealing with public policy toward business. It is based on my lecture notes from a course entitled *Government and Business* taught in the Sauder School of Business at the University of British Columbia (UBC). Earlier editions of this book have been widely used in business schools and have also been used for public policy courses in public administration programs, economics departments, and political science departments, and as a supplementary text for a variety of other courses.

The fifth edition of this book contains major revisions. In addition to general updating, some chapters in earlier editions have been condensed and combined, and two new chapters have been added. One new chapter is "Innovation Policy and Intellectual Property"—an area that has emerged as an important focus of government policy. This chapter deals with patent policy and other areas of intellectual property policy, and also addresses policies affecting innovation finance and the role of university research in the innovation process.

The other new chapter is "Corporate Social Responsibility." Years ago, such a chapter might have been called "Business Ethics" but the term "corporate social responsibility" (CSR) seems to have entered general usage. When the first edition of this book was published, very few large corporations had published policies or staff units devoted to such areas as "sustainability" or "social responsibility." Now, such policy statements and staff assignments are an important part of the business environment and interact with government policy in several areas, particularly regarding environmental policy.

As far as condensations are concerned, what were two chapters on international trade policy in the last edition have been condensed to one chapter for this edition, as is also true of the two former chapters on competition policy. And regulation and public enterprise have been combined into a single chapter. Much of this condensation was achieved by removing material that was very topical when the book was first published but is now of primarily historical interest. This includes such topics as the debate over the Canada–U.S. Free Trade Agreement, the development of the "new" Competition Act of 1986, and the deregulation and privatization agenda of the 1980s and early 1990s. These topics are still covered, but much of the historical detail has been dropped.

As before, the book proceeds from conceptual principles to specific policy areas. Specific policies are viewed as applications of general policy principles with a particular focus on the use of public policy to redress market failure problems. After reading the book, students should be able to readily understand new policy issues that confront them. This edition offers an up-to-date treatment of competition policy, environmental and resource policy (incliuding a discussion of sustainability), innovation and intellectual property, international trade policy, macroeconomic policy, public enterprise, and regulation. The book continues to provide a streamlined overview of the major public policies that affect business, and can be covered comfortably in a one-term course.

An important theme in the book is that policy can be viewed partly as arising from the "public interest" objectives of policy-makers, and partly as the result of competition for policy influence among various private interests. Both the "public interest" and "private interest" approaches to policy are examined at a conceptual and institutional level, and many examples illustrating both interpretations of policy are provided.

Material in this book is drawn from several areas of study, including political science, philosophy, and psychology. The underlying discipline that contributes most to the central framework of the book is, however, economics, reflecting the fact that most policies affecting the business environment are focused on economic objectives. This book is not very technical or mathematical, and it presumes only that readers have a general familiarity with introductory economics. There are a few graphs and equations, but not many. The emphasis, instead, is on the basic insights and conceptual tools of economics as they apply to business-related public policy.

I have accumulated many debts in the preparation of the five editions of this book. Earlier editions have benefited from input provided by Bruce Anderson, Paul Anglin, Trent Appelbe, Jen Baggs, Tony Boardman, Clive Chapple, Elizabeth Croft, Murray Frank, Steve Globerman, Peter Nemetz, Bo Pazderka, Asha Sadanand, Zena Seldon, Jim Vercammen, Allan Warrack, Bill Waters, and Bernard Wolf, among others. I would also like to acknowledge student research assistants who helped with earlier editions, including Anna Fok, Rick Gleason, Fred Gower, Livia Mahler, Jo-Anne McLean, Diane Wilson, and Monica Zhang. I am also grateful to my father, Stuart James Brander, who read the manuscript for the first edition and provided many helpful comments.

As for the fifth edition, I would like to start by thanking my wife and colleague Barbara Spencer, who made major contributions to the chapters on competition policy and regulation, along with many other contributions to all five editions. I also owe a particular debt to Keith Head, who made detailed comments on many aspects of the book for this and earlier editions, and whose lecture notes I benefited from in preparing the new chapters for this edition. I am also very grateful to Ed Egan, Florencia Jaureguiberry, Robin Lindsey, John Ries, Tom Ross, and Ralph Winter for valuable input. I also thank Louisa Yeung for her excellent work as a research assistant for this edition.

Finally, I would like to thank copy editor Julie vanTol and the staff at Wiley, particularly Joel Balbin and Karen Staudinger, for their patience, efficiency, and good judgment.

1

Objectives
and Overview

1.1 Introduction

This book is concerned primarily with government policies directed toward business. Such policies are an important focus of political debate and feature prominently in the business media. In addition, dealing with government policies toward business is a very important activity in the private sector, and implementing such policies is a major function of the public sector. This book is directed principally toward students in business, economics, and public policy, many of whom will deal professionally with public policy issues within either the public sector or the private sector.

Most citizens of modern developed countries expect government policy to play an important role in their lives. We expect governments to provide law enforcement, education, and a variety of other goods and services, and we accept, or at least expect, that governments will finance these activities in large part by imposing taxes. Most of us also recognize that government policy has some influence on unemployment, inflation, interest rates, and general business conditions.

Many people, however, are surprised when they discover the extent to which consumer decisions and the business decisions of private sector firms are affected by government intervention. We might wonder what all this government intervention is intended to achieve and why governments choose the policies that they do. We might also wonder whether the chosen policies are effective methods of pursuing the intended objectives. This book is concerned with these and related issues. More precisely, it offers a systematic method for analyzing government policy affecting businesses. This analysis subdivides naturally into two questions:

1. What should the role of government be?
2. What factors explain the actual conduct of government?

The first question is sometimes described as *normative* or *prescriptive*, because in answering it we are trying to suggest or prescribe what governments should do. The starting point in the analysis of this question is that government policy toward business should seek to promote the public interest. Therefore, consideration of the first question is also called the *public interest approach* to policy analysis.

The second question is *positive* or *descriptive* in that it tries to explain or describe why things are as they are. It is possible that actual policies toward business will be just as normative analysis suggests they should be. Frequently, however, actual policies coincide poorly with normative analysis, and we may conclude that the general public interest was not the major determinant of policy.

In answering the second question, we normally assume that actual policy is the outcome of a market for political influence in which politicians are pursuing political or personal advantages, public sector managers are trying to advance their careers, and special interest groups, including business lobbies, are pursuing their private objectives as well. Analysis of question two is, therefore, often referred to as the *private interest approach* to policy analysis. It is also sometimes referred to as the study of *public choice*.

1.2 The Normative Approach to Policy Analysis

We have established that normative analysis starts with the assertion that government policy should seek to promote the public interest. Unfortunately, it is difficult to say exactly what the public interest is. Conceptions of the public interest are reflections of basic values and vary over time and across social, religious, and other groups. Nevertheless, there is a well-established set of goals that are widely accepted as legitimate objects of government attention. These goals are discussed briefly below and will form the central themes of this book.

1. *Economic efficiency*: In rough terms, pursuit of economic efficiency corresponds to trying to make the per capita benefits from the consumption

of goods and services as high as possible. In a world where simple economic scarcity and poverty remain major problems, this objective is very important. In Chapter 2, the concept of economic efficiency is described more carefully.

2. *Macroeconomic stabilization and growth*: One of the most serious problems of market-based economies is that they are prone to cyclical swings in business activity and employment. After the experience of the Great Depression of the 1930s, most citizens of Western (and many other) countries came to regard stabilization of these cyclical fluctuations and provision of reliable employment opportunities as important objectives of government policy. More broadly, the objectives of macroeconomic policy are to smooth the business cycle, keep unemployment rates low and stable, keep inflation rates low and stable, and assist in promoting economic growth.

3. *Fairness*: Pursuit of economic efficiency seeks to make the overall size of the "economic pie" as large as possible. Fairness is concerned mainly with the distribution of that pie among different claimants. Canada, for example, has a system of taxation and social welfare that taxes the relatively well off and gives money and other resources to the poor. In addition to redistribution, public policy is also targeted toward other conceptions of fairness. For example, the dominant conception of fairness in Canada's health care policy is that all individuals should have essentially the same level of health care, at least for certain core medical services. There are employment laws that seek to prevent or limit discrimination by employers on the basis of age, sex, and certain other characteristics on the grounds that such discrimination is unfair in some fundamental way. Other ideas of fairness lead to public policy seeking to protect the interests of children and others judged unable to adequately defend their own interests.

4. *Other social objectives*: Governments sometimes pursue objectives that are not directly related to economic efficiency, macroeconomic stabilization, or fairness. For example, governments of many countries have sometimes tried to promote national unity or certain aspects of cultural identity as goals in themselves. Some policies, such as limitations on gambling and alcohol consumption, have their roots in a desire to promote certain values. Such policies may be categorized simply as other social objectives.

Any normative rationale for policy must be based on one of these four categories of objectives. For example, one important type of government policy toward business is environmental regulation, which, among other things, seeks to limit the damage done to the environment by various industrial activities. This policy is based primarily on the idea that unregulated business activity may cause inefficiently high levels of environmental damage. In other words, the normative rationale for environmental policy is based mainly on economic efficiency. In addition, some environmental legislation has its roots in the notion that fairness requires that certain aspects of the environment be protected for the benefit of future generations.

1.3 The Positive Approach to Policy Analysis

The positive approach to policy analysis focuses on the objectives, behaviour, and interaction of individuals and groups who influence policy decisions. Instead of focusing on what policy should be, positive analysis examines the reasons why policy takes the form it does. One important influence on policy decisions is voting. Another arises from special interest groups, including business lobbies, which spend time and money trying to influence government policies. Public sector managers themselves are an important influence, as are elected politicians.

1.4 The Major Policy Areas

Many areas of government policy affect business in one way or another. There are, however, certain policy areas that are particularly important in that they specifically or primarily target business. The largest part of the book will be devoted to a systematic discussion of these major policy areas:

- International trade policy
- Environmental and resource policy
- Competition policy
- Regulation and public enterprise
- Innovation policy and intellectual property
- Macroeconomic policy

As this list suggests, government policy influences business activity in a wide variety of ways. Some policy areas, such as regulation, are often directed toward specific firms or industries, while others, such as macroeconomic policy, address the overall economic environment.

Perhaps the best way to see the influence of government on the private sector is by way of example. The following case illustrates the important and surprisingly extensive effect of government policies on Air Canada and the airline industry.

1.5 Air Canada and Public Policy

In March of 2012, the Government of Canada passed back-to-work legislation that prevented a strike or lockout at Air Canada on the grounds that the corporation was too important to the economy to be allowed to shut down. This legislation was one of many examples of government involvement in Air Canada.

Air Canada was created by the Government of Canada in 1937 under the name Trans-Canada Airlines (TCA), which was changed officially to Air Canada as of 1965. As a corporation owned by government, Air Canada was a *public enterprise* (also called, in Canada, a *Crown corporation*). For many years, government regulation controlled both the routes and prices in the airline industry and limited the ability of other firms to compete in the market.

A major change occurred during the 1984–89 period as the government *deregulated* the airline industry, allowing unrestricted price and route competition among airlines. This change freed up private sector airlines to compete more vigorously with Air Canada. In addition, in 1988 and 1989 Air Canada was *privatized*—sold to the private sector—in sales of shares. In 1994, the government relaxed restrictions on foreign investment in domestic airlines, and Canada and the U.S. reached an agreement allowing both countries' airlines to freely serve routes between the two countries. The net effect of this deregulation, privatization, and increased international openness was a decline in airfares and more efficient route structures and aircraft types—significant benefits to consumers.

In a 1999 merger, Air Canada took over Canada's other major airline operating at that time. This merger of Canada's two major airlines required investigation by the Bureau of Competition Policy, a government agency charged with encouraging and maintaining appropriate levels of business competition in Canada.

In late 2001, Air Canada faced a crisis caused by the September 11 terrorist attacks on New York City using hijacked airliners. The resulting decline in air travel demand, combined with Air Canada's relatively high cost structure, pushed Air Canada into severe financial hardship. In April 2003, Air Canada declared bankruptcy—seeking protection from its creditors under Canada's policy on bankruptcy. While in bankruptcy, Air Canada was able to restructure its labour contracts and debts and emerged in 2004 with a more competitive cost structure. However, the global recession of 2008 once again created a need for Air Canada to reduce its costs, leading to conflicts with its unions. The Canadian government became involved in resolving these disputes, including the 2012 legislation preventing a work stoppage.

This brief history of Air Canada illustrates the importance of public policy toward business. Air Canada was started by the Canadian government. In addition, the government regulated prices and route structures, and it had a major impact on the industry through its international agreements. Restructuring the industry required the approval and participation of competition policy authorities and transport regulators, and Air Canada has been significantly affected by both bankruptcy policy and labour policy. In addition, the government continues its role in safety regulation of the airlines and has an active role in the closely related airport business. Air Canada is also affected by the broad-based policies that affect all firms, such as macroeconomic policy and tax policy. Not every firm is as closely intertwined with government policy as Air Canada, but many firms are, and virtually all firms have some significant interactions with governments.

1.6 Globalization and Internationalization

Canadian public policy and business decisions are increasingly affected by events occurring outside Canada's borders. This situation is not unique to Canada. Most national governments have found that their ability to control domestic events has weakened progressively over the past few decades due to the increasing importance of processes that are global in scope. One example of such a global process is global warming, which has already had significant effects in many areas and will probably have much greater economic effects on many countries over the next few decades. No one country can exercise much control over global warming, as it is caused by the cumulative effects of activities occurring all over the world.

Another important global phenomenon affecting business in many countries is the development of *global supply chains*—production structures in which a single final product draws on production activities carried out in a wide variety of countries. Thus, for example, a car "produced" in Canada may have significant components from a dozen or more other countries. Firms can and will readily change the source location for a particular component as local wages, taxes, or other factors change. Such potential changes reduce the control that any one government can exercise over these firms, precisely because the firms will readily move production from one country to another in the face of significant profit-reducing changes in government policy.

Similarly, the emergence of global financial markets has reduced the ability of any one government to control domestic financial events, as financial market participants in any one country can readily transact in financial markets outside that country's borders, or at least outside its control. A street corner money-changer in Moscow who, among other things, makes U.S. dollar loans (and keeps a gun handy to aid in collection) is part of a global financial market, as is a large bank making computerized trades involving perhaps ten or 12 currencies simultaneously. Many financial transactions do not really occur in any particular country at all, but occur instead in the disembodied virtual world of computerized financial networks. In general, the Internet has created a much more integrated global economy than has ever been known in the past.

The increasing significance of global processes and activities is often referred to as globalization. In essence, globalization refers to processes that transcend national boundaries. Such processes have been caused in part by technological change, particularly advances in telecommunications (such as the Internet) and transportation. Another major causal factor is worldwide population growth. As the world becomes more and more crowded, different groups of people come into more frequent contact with one another. The third major causal factor, however, is discretionary policy choice. For example, Canadian policy authorities over the past few decades have made a series of decisions, including joining the North American Free Trade Agreement, increasing immigration levels, reducing restrictions on foreign investment, and liberalizing financial regulation. These policies have increased the impact of global events on Canada. Such policies could, in principle, be reversed if a more nationalist policy stance were to re-emerge.

One should not exaggerate the importance of globalization, however, since domestic events and domestic policy control remain the main influences on the domestic economy. However, globalization provides important context for much of the discussion in this book.

1.7 Concluding Remarks and Outline of the Book

An important example of government policy toward business was described in Section 1.5 on Air Canada. Facts were reported without judgments being made about the case. Two natural questions do arise, however. First, were the government decisions reasonable; that is, was there a sound normative rationale for intervention? Second, if the decisions were not good ones from the public interest point of view, why were they made? The first question is normative; the second is positive. In this book we explore general principles that will help us answer such questions.

Part I of this book is devoted to the conceptual background of policy analysis. Chapter 2 reviews some basic economic concepts and shows how they can be applied in specific cases. Chapter 3 discusses the philosophical foundations for the role of government and the role of private enterprise in democratic societies, and it provides a more detailed overview of the normative rationale for government policy than was provided in Chapter 1. Chapter 4 discusses the role of fairness as a normative rationale for government policy. Chapter 5 examines the positive, or descriptive, theory of government. Chapter 6 is devoted to the basic economic characteristics of firms and markets, focusing on imperfect competition as a reason for government intervention, and Chapter 7 outlines some of the more important features of Canada's business environment and general economic structure. Part II of the book takes up each of the major policy areas in turn, using the tools and ideas developed in Part I.

1.8 Bibliographic Notes

The best source for current public policy information is the Internet. A good starting point for information related to the Canadian government is www.canada.gc.ca, and the various provincial governments have their own websites as well. Academic journals dealing with public policy affecting business include *Canadian Public Policy* and the *Canadian Journal of Economics*, both of which are readily available online through university and college libraries. The regulatory bodies and other organizations discussed in this text can also be found easily on the Internet.

This book will often refer to the academic literature—other textbooks, articles in academic journals (such as the two mentioned above), and other academic works. Citations for such references are listed at the back of the book in the "References" section. References to official data and reports from government bodies, international agencies, and similar institutions are also in the References section, as are references to articles in the business and popular media.

This text is related to subject matter developed in a variety of economic sub-fields, particularly international trade and investment, public finance, industrial organization, and environmental economics. Each of these sub-fields has many good and easily obtained textbooks that describe in more depth many of the topics covered in this text.

2

Four Useful
Economic Concepts

2.1 Introduction

Analysis of public policy incorporates many considerations, but four fundamental economic concepts are of particular importance: opportunity cost, marginalism, incentive effects, and economic efficiency. These concepts are discussed in this chapter.

2.2 Opportunity Cost

One of the most important and useful of all economic concepts is opportunity cost. The opportunity cost of any activity is defined as the value of the best foregone alternative. Consider, for example, a student who can either spend an evening studying or go out with friends. The opportunity cost of studying is the value or enjoyment the student would obtain by going out. If the benefits of studying exceed those of going out, then it makes sense to study. The application of opportunity cost to policy decisions means that a project or policy should be undertaken only if its value exceeds its opportunity cost. In other words, a project should be carried out only if its value exceeds those of alternative projects.

The opportunity cost principle seems so clear that one wonders why economists and other policy analysts emphasize it so much. Surprisingly, however, this idea is frequently forgotten or misunderstood at the public policy level. For example, a city council that proposes building a new recycling centre on land owned by the city because "we won't have to pay for the land" is making the mistake of ignoring opportunity cost. Suppose the land in question could be sold for $2 million. It follows that $2 million is the opportunity cost of the land. Using this land for a recycling centre has a cost of $2 million, just as if the land had been purchased on the open market, because in building the recycling centre the city loses the opportunity to sell the land for $2 million.

Part of Vancouver's successful bid for the 2010 Winter Olympics was a commitment to build a new rapid transit line called the Canada Line, the third line in the system, linking the airport to the downtown core along a heavily used commuter corridor. Both the provincial and federal governments provided significant financial support for the Canada Line, which was completed shortly before the Olympics began. Many commentators argued that the new rapid transit line should be viewed as a net benefit of the hosting the Olympics.

An economist, applying the concept of opportunity cost, sees things differently. The money devoted by governments to rapid transit could, alternatively, be used for other things, such as health care, highways, reforestation, or tax reduction. Even if, for example, the Canada Line generates significant benefits, it would not be a good investment if the money could have been used, instead, for reforestation projects with even greater benefits. If the Olympics diverted resources away from more valuable projects—causing money to be spent on rapid transit instead of more valuable alternatives—that would be a cost of the Olympics, not a benefit.

In fact, the Canada Line appears to be a far better investment than many things governments spend money on. Utilization of the line has exceeded even the optimistic early projections, and its presence has apparently increased utilization of the other lines in the system as well. The benefits, therefore, include increased revenues, reduced congestion on roads, and reduced pollution as more commuters use rapid transit rather than driving cars or using buses. The apparent success of the Canada Line was a strong argument for starting construction on a fourth line, the Evergreen Line, scheduled to begin service in 2016. While it thus appears likely that the Canada Line was a good investment, the opportunity cost insight is that the correct test for such a judgment is *not* simply whether this investment appears to generate benefits. The appropriate test is the whether the new rapid transit line generates more benefits than would possible alternative uses of the resources—whether the benefits exceed the opportunity cost.

Economists have been described as those who know the cost of everything and the value of nothing. That criticism arises in part from the emphasis economists place on opportunity cost. But this emphasis is important. Opportunity cost reasoning reminds us that concern about costs is really a concern about losing potential benefits elsewhere. The economist who criticizes rapid transit expenditures is not (necessarily) a mean-spirited individual who wants to keep people from travelling conveniently. He or she is concerned that residents of British Columbia might have been better off if they had the opportunity to spend more of their incomes on private expenditures instead of paying taxes, or if the money had been used to replenish the declining forest stock or for some other useful purpose. The opportunity cost insight reminds us that expenditures on any project leave us with fewer resources for alternative projects.

A general failure to recognize opportunity costs is often revealed in opinion polls. A quick visit to websites maintained by major polling organizations (such as Gallup, Ipsos Reid, and others) reveals that there is usually strong support for increasing expenditures in areas such as health care, education, environmental projects and the like, but very little support for raising taxes to pay for such initiatives. Clearly, these objectives are not all consistent with each other. A vote for higher expenditures on health care should be seen as a vote for higher taxes, for higher debt (and higher future taxes), or for less expenditure on other programs. Opportunity cost tells us we cannot have our cake and eat it too.

Consideration of opportunity costs often brings economists into conflict with other professionals seeking to comment on public policy. When highway engineers express a desire to make roads "as safe as possible," or when environmentalists suggest that "pollution should be eliminated," they are failing to take account of opportunity costs. Roads and highways could be made safer by doubling their width, adding bike lanes to every road, putting traffic lights at every intersection, and dramatically increasing the number of police cars as a persuasive reminder to drive safely.

But such investments would be very costly, taking land away from other uses or police away from crime prevention activities, and we judge that the benefits would not justify the opportunity costs. Given limited budgets, governments should *optimize* their expenditures, which require funding any particular activity only to the extent that benefits exceed opportunity costs.

Opportunity costs should always be kept in mind, but sometimes the measurements required are difficult. Just what is the value to society of reducing pollution or of adding more police on traffic duty? And how can these possibilities be compared with the value of an alternative project, such as increasing support for health care or lowering taxes? These are difficult judgments, but they have to be made, and even approximate valuations lead to much better decisions than those arrived at by ignoring opportunity costs.

2.3 Marginalism

A second important tool of economic policy analysis is marginalism. The *marginal* effect of any activity is the effect of doing the activity just a little bit more. For example, the marginal revenue from selling a product is the amount of extra revenue obtained by selling one more unit of that product.[1]

Perhaps the best introduction to the marginalist approach is using it to unravel one of the problems that perplexed early philosophers: *the paradox of value*. These philosophers questioned why water, which is obviously very valuable, and in fact necessary for life, was relatively cheap. Diamonds, on the other hand, contribute comparatively little to world welfare but were (and still are) very expensive. If all the diamonds in the world were to disappear tomorrow, some people would be upset, but things would go on more or less as before. If water were eliminated, however, life would cease. Why are these prices inversely related to value?

The answer is that price is determined not by total value, but by marginal value. The marginal value of water is the value of a little more water. The price that a consumer is willing to pay for a litre of water depends on the marginal value of the next litre. If water is abundant and consumers already have as much as they want, their marginal willingness to pay for an extra litre is very low. Thus the price of water is low. Diamonds, on the other hand, are comparatively scarce. The marginal value of an extra diamond is high, and this is why the price is high. Prices reflect marginal value, not total value.

The implication of marginalist reasoning for public policy is that we must always compare the marginal benefit of policy with its marginal (opportunity) cost.

> *Definition*: The **marginalist principle** states that any policy or activity should be carried out as long as the marginal benefit exceeds the marginal opportunity cost.

Consider the following statement: "Education is more important than highways; therefore, more money should be spent on schools and less should be spent on roads. We should have the best possible schools."

Statements of this sort are often made, perhaps with the environment or health care substituted for education. People who make such statements fail to apply marginalist reasoning; they have fallen victim to the paradox of

---

[1] Students familiar with calculus might recall that, from a mathematical point of view, a derivative represents a marginal effect. For example, marginal revenue is the derivative of total revenue with respect to output.

value. To an economist, the pursuit of the "best possible schools" or the best possible anything is likely to violate the marginalist principle and therefore be a poor policy, as is explained next.

The student experience in schools can be improved by providing additional teachers' aides or even individual tutors, in addition to normal classroom teachers. However, suppose that in a school of 300 students we already have 60 aides and tutors, one for every five students. The marginal value of yet another aide would be low while the marginal cost would be high. Many schools do find it valuable to have a few aides to help out with students who have particular difficulties. The marginal value of the first few aides is high. But have if a school already has many aides, the marginal value of additional aides is low.

Adding more aides in such a circumstance would not be a good policy. It does not make sense to pursue the "best possible" educational experience for students. It only makes sense to invest in educational expenditures as long as the marginal benefits exceed the marginal costs. Most of us would probably agree that, in some absolute sense, education is more important than highways. This is a statement about total value. Logically, however, the claim that more money should be spent on education has nothing to do with total value. Such a claim depends on marginal value, not total value. More money should be spent only if the marginalist principle is satisfied—that is, if the *marginal* benefits exceed the *marginal* costs. *Optimal* decision-making—making benefits as large as possible—implies that every activity should be carried out to the point where marginal benefit is just equal to marginal cost.

The marginalist principle is a basic principle of decision making. It applies to public policy and to business decisions. For businesses trying to earn as much profit as possible, the marginalist principle is captured in the idea that they should produce more output up to the point where marginal revenue equals marginal cost. If marginal revenue exceeds marginal cost, output should be increased, because revenues will rise by more than costs, and profit will increase. If marginal revenue is less than marginal cost, the firm will increase profit by reducing output. The same idea applies to public policy, except that public policy should be concerned with social benefits and costs, not just financial profits and losses.

One implication of the marginalist principle is that the best way to allocate a scarce resource between two projects is to equalize the marginal benefits. Consider, for example, the problem of allocating land in a city between residential construction (housing) and parks. Figure 2.1 illustrates the allocation decision. Land is shown on the horizontal axis, and the length

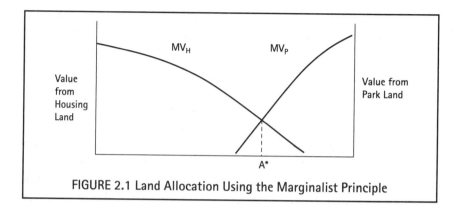

FIGURE 2.1 Land Allocation Using the Marginalist Principle

of this axis shows how much land is available. The amount of land used for housing is measured from the left, and the amount used for parkland is measured from the right. Any point on the horizontal axis shows an allocation of land between these two uses. For example, if there are 1000 hectares of land available and 700 are used for housing (measured from the left) that would leave 300 hectares for parks.

The left vertical axis measures the marginal value of additional land for housing. This marginal value depends on the amount of land devoted to housing, as shown by curve MV_H. In this case, the marginal value is declining; the value of the first unit of land is very high, but as more land is made available for housing the marginal value falls. The right vertical axis measures the marginal value of land for parks, and the curve MV_P shows this marginal value as a function of the amount of land used for parks, measured from the right. The marginal value of the first unit of park land is very high—if there are no parks, the first unit of parkland would be worth a lot—and the marginal value falls as the amount of land allocated to parks increases. The allocation of land that yields the largest possible benefit is shown by point A^* on the horizontal axis. This is the point where the two marginal benefit curves cross. At this point, the marginal value of land for housing equals the marginal value of land for parks.

If the marginal value of housing land exceeds the marginal value of park land, we should devote more land to housing and less to parks, because the extra value we gain from having more housing land would exceed the amount we lose by having a bit less park land. Conversely, if the marginal value of park land exceeds that of housing, we gain by having less housing land and more park land. Only if these marginal values are equal are we getting the largest possible benefit.

Another way of looking at Figure 2.1 is to recognize that the opportunity cost of housing land is park land. Figure 2.1 implies that we should allocate additional units of land to housing instead of parks only as long as the value of that extra unit (the marginal value) exceeds the value of an extra unit of parkland—the marginal opportunity cost.

2.4 Economic Incentives

One basic principle of policy analysis is that we expect people to follow economic incentives. Often, policy changes that affect incentives have obvious outcomes. In 2012, the Canadian government increased the *duty free* allowance—the exemption from the special taxes that are charged at the border for many goods—for Canadian residents bringing back goods purchased in the United States. In effect, U.S. goods suddenly became cheaper for Canadian visitors, creating an incentive to make more such purchases. As expected, more cross-border purchases were made in the aftermath of the policy change.

However, policy changes can induce unintended incentive effects that take policy makers and others by surprise, an example of the so-called *law of unintended consequences*. For example, the Canadian government provides support in the form of tax credits and cash subsidies for research and development (R&D) through a program called the Scientific Research and Experimental Development (SR&ED) incentive program. The intended incentive effect is to increase R&D activity in Canada. However, as described by McKenna (2011), there are also important unintended incentive effects:

> This year, Ottawa and the provinces will dispense $4.7 billion to more than 20,000 Canadian companies under one of the richest R&D tax regimes in the world. But a third or more of that cash is being wasted and paid to consultants as a result of hazy rules on what's legitimate R&D and limited government auditing resources.... The dilemma is that many claims may meet the agency's minimum filing guidelines, and yet constitute highly dubious R&D. The result, experts said, is that Canadian taxpayers are spending billions on a program that too often delivers little or no new R&D....Money is often paid out to decidedly low-tech and routine manufacturing, such as baking gluten-free cake, making injection-moulded auto parts or growing potted roses.

The problem identified by McKenna is that the SR&ED program does not just create an incentive to do more R&D; it also creates an incentive to reclassify normal production expenses as R&D. Many companies that carry out routine production activities—bakeries trying out new recipes, florists trying out slight variations in growing conditions—now have an incentive to hire a consultant to help them reclassify such activities as R&D and make a claim for a tax credit.

When the forerunner of the SR&ED program was started, the government was surprised by the cost, as the claims vastly exceeded the expected amount. Suddenly, the amount of R&D activity claimed by Canadian companies rose dramatically—too dramatically to be believable. The explanation was based on an unintended incentive: the incentive to reclassify much normal production activity as R&D.

In retrospect, this incentive effect seems obvious. The program has been modified several times to try to shift more resources to genuine R&D rather than to creative accounting. The most obvious "fix" is to devote more time and effort to auditing and evaluating claims, but this approach itself absorbs resources and often results in a tug of war between accountants and lawyers working for the government and those working for corporations seeking tax credits. Another approach is to rewrite the rules to be clearer about allowable expenses, thus reducing the scope for exploiting or abusing the system. But it is also important that the rules not be so rigid as to reduce opportunities for innovation. Getting the balance right is not easy, but properly anticipating incentive effects is crucial.

While the importance of incentive effects seems clear, it is surprising how policy makers and individuals generally fail to anticipate incentive effects in context. A good example of insensitivity to incentive effects is provided by a British Columbia tennis club. The club recently eliminated monthly dues for juniors (tennis-playing children of adult members) on the grounds that this fee did not raise much revenue and eliminating it would be helpful to families.

Many eligible children who had not previously been junior members promptly signed up. The club's capacity for juniors was quickly reached and a long waiting list formed. To the surprise and consternation of the club's directors, it soon became clear that anyone wanting to get a new junior into the club would face a long waiting list. The problem arose because, as soon as it became costless for juniors to join, every family had an incentive to enroll its children as members, whether or not the children had shown any interest in tennis so far—just in case the children might want to play someday. As a result, many of those who might have been very interested in tennis were prevented from joining by a long waiting list. After a trial period, the club restored dues for juniors.

Another good example of unanticipated incentive effects arises with early retirement buyouts. Many large corporations and other organizations, such as universities, governments, and hospitals have labour agreements preventing them from firing certain groups of workers except for "cause"; that is, unless the worker exhibits seriously deficient performance. If such an organization needs to downsize, it cannot simply dismiss workers, as very few will have poor enough performance to justify firing for cause. One approach is to use buyouts, offering employees generous payments if they quit the organization or take early retirement.

Buyout programs would seemingly increase the incentive to leave and make downsizing an organization easier. However, as described in a report by Canada's auditor general, buyout programs create perverse unintended incentives. In particular, after it becomes clear that buyouts can be obtained, "normal" quits (i.e., quits without compensation) drop sharply—why quit without compensation when, by hanging onto a job and negotiating a cash settlement, a substantial reward can be obtained?

A second perverse effect of buyouts found by the auditor general is that they disproportionately induce the best workers to quit. A poor worker in a well-paid job probably earns considerably more than he or she could get in another job. Such people have little incentive to quit. Even with a buyout, quitting is probably unattractive for such workers. On the other hand, a very good worker can probably get another good job. Such a person is close to the margin of leaving even without a buyout, and adding in a buyout then makes quitting very attractive. Thus, a commonly observed effect of buyout programs is that they tend to induce a brain drain.

The auditor general's report suggested targeting buyouts at workers the employer particularly wants to get rid of. But this, too, is a dangerous policy because it gives people incentives to become poor workers in order to attract a buyout.

Economists expect people to follow their economic interests, while non-economists often expect people to leave their behaviour unchanged despite changing economic incentives. This was true of the tennis club directors described above. It is also true of people who are surprised when unemployment levels rise as unemployment benefits rise, or when landlords operating under rent controls don't maintain their rental units.

The basic idea of incentive effects is very simple: in considering the effects of any public policy, we should expect people to follow their economic incentives. Anticipation of incentive effects will usually improve policy decisions, and an understanding of incentives will help analysts understand why a particular policy worked out the way it did. Recognition of incentive effects is fundamental to both normative and positive analysis.

2.5 Economic Efficiency

It is hard to find a discussion of business decisions or public policy in which the term *efficiency* is not freely used. Unfortunately, there are several different, although related, concepts of efficiency, and confusion can result when different notions of efficiency are used in the same discussion.

One type of efficiency is production efficiency, which means that no inputs are wasted and a given level of output cannot be produced with fewer inputs. Management efficiency (sometimes called cost efficiency) is a stronger concept, meaning that cost is minimized for the output chosen. Management efficiency requires production efficiency—that no inputs are wasted—and, in addition, that the firm use exactly the right mix of inputs to minimize the cost of producing a given output. Management efficiency focuses on the question, "Are we achieving least-cost production?" If not, they are being wasteful.

A broader concept of efficiency than either production or management efficiency is that of Pareto efficiency.

Pareto efficiency: Resources are allocated in such a way that it is impossible to make anyone better off without making someone else worse off.

Management efficiency, and therefore production efficiency as well, is a necessary condition for Pareto efficiency. Ultimately, however, the concept of Pareto efficiency, like both production and management efficiency, refers to the absence of waste. If a situation is Pareto inefficient, it is possible to improve the welfare of at least one person without harming anyone else, and it would be wasteful not to do so. Pareto inefficiency means that potential improvement to human welfare is being wasted.

The concept of Pareto inefficiency is closely related to that of deadweight loss. Figure 2.2 shows a demand curve, D, for some product. The normal interpretation of a demand curve is that it shows the quantity demanded for any price. The demand curve also shows, for any given quantity of consumption, the willingness of consumers to pay for a little more of the commodity. For example, at point A, consumers are consuming quantity Q^A and would be willing to pay price P^A for a little more of the good. A consumer's willingness to pay for the next unit of a good can be taken as a measure of the consumer's marginal benefit from consuming that good.

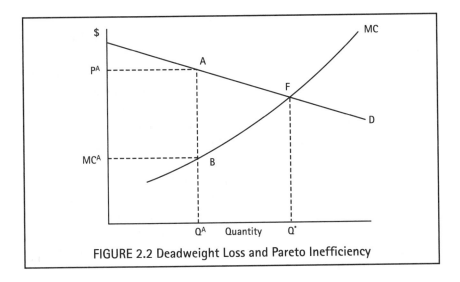

FIGURE 2.2 Deadweight Loss and Pareto Inefficiency

The curve labelled *MC* is the marginal cost of production. The marginal cost curve shows, for any given level of output, the marginal cost of producing another unit of output. The *MC* curve represents the minimum amount that owners of the factors of production would need to receive to be willing to produce a little more output. At output level Q^A, the marginal benefit (as given by the *D* curve) exceeds the marginal cost (as shown by the *MC* curve). This situation demonstrates Pareto inefficiency.

The reasoning is as follows. If an extra unit of the product was produced, consumers would be willing to pay P^A and would suffer no loss in welfare. Owners of the factors of production would be willing to receive MC^A for the extra production with no loss in welfare. This would leave a surplus of $P^A - MC^A$, which could be refunded to consumers, given to owners of factors of production, given to a third party, or a mixture of all three. In any case, the welfare of some people could be improved without anyone being worse off. Therefore, production at the original level of production, Q^A, is Pareto inefficient. The efficient level of production would be Q^*.

The triangle *ABF* is referred to as a deadweight loss. Deadweight loss represents a net gain or surplus that could be generated, without harming anyone, by moving from the inefficient allocation of resources represented by output level Q^A to the Pareto efficient allocation, Q^*. Pareto efficiency is sometimes referred to as allocational efficiency because it requires a particular allocation of scarce resources.

In Figure 2.2, the basic question is whether we are producing the appropriate amount of a particular good. If not, then the situation is Pareto inefficient. Producing the right amount of each good is a necessary condition for achieving Pareto efficiency. Note that this subsumes, or includes, the question of which goods to produce (i.e., the question, "Are we producing the right products?). If we are not producing the right products, then the production level for such goods is zero, despite the fact that surplus is available from them. Achieving Pareto efficiency would require that such activities be carried out at positive levels.

The concept of Pareto efficiency is a benchmark, or point of comparison, used by economists in evaluating policy. It is, however, important to be aware of the limitations of this concept. As a practical matter, we never achieve full Pareto efficiency. All economic systems contain many distortions, and in considering specific policies, we are always comparing one Pareto-inefficient situation to another. Thus, simply observing that a situation is Pareto inefficient is not a sufficient reason for introducing or proposing a policy change. Only when the distortion is sufficiently large would there be a strong case for action.

A related policy criterion that can sometimes be applied in instances of Pareto inefficiency is the concept of a Pareto improvement. We say that a Pareto improvement takes place if some people can be made better off and no one is made worse off. If we are in a Pareto-inefficient state, then, in principle, it is possible to make a Pareto improvement, even if full Pareto efficiency is not achieved. If we move from situation A to situation B, and no one is made worse off while some people are made better off, then we satisfy the Pareto-improvement criterion, whether B is Pareto efficient or not.

However, Pareto improvements are rare. Most policies generate both winners and losers. It is sometimes feasible for the winners to compensate the losers so that in the end everyone gains, but it is usually very difficult to ensure that all affected parties are fully compensated. An easier criterion to satisfy is that of the potential Pareto improvement, as defined below.

> *Definition*: A **potential Pareto improvement** takes place if the winners gain enough to be able to fully compensate the losers and still be better off.

Stated somewhat less precisely, a policy change creates a potential Pareto improvement if the gainers gain more than the losers lose, even if the losers are not actually compensated. If a potential Pareto improvement takes place, we say that there has been an improvement in efficiency. There are some technical difficulties associated with this concept, but it does allow us to make a connection between average levels of economic welfare and economic efficiency. Strictly speaking, however, in order to accept the idea that potential Pareto improvements are good, we must implicitly make the assumption that any resulting changes in the distribution of income are acceptable.

Particular difficulties arise in trying to apply either the Pareto-improvement criterion or the potential Pareto criterion to intergenerational issues, such as economic growth or resource depletion. Very often, the people who forego consumption and pay taxes to pay for some investment that will generate economic growth are no longer alive by the time the full benefits of the investment are realized. Conversely, when we consider the consumption of depletable resources, more current consumption may leave future generations worse off than they would otherwise be. In considering both of these intergenerational comparisons, the Pareto criterion is not helpful because it cannot be satisfied. Inevitably, one generation is made worse off to provide higher benefits for another. Focusing on the potential Pareto criterion alone does not seem sufficient to deal with the intergenerational trade-off. Therefore, we need to simultaneously consider distributional effects *and* efficiency considerations.

In this book we will use the term *efficiency* as follows:

1. If a situation is said to be efficient, Pareto efficiency is meant.
2. If a situation is said to be inefficient, Pareto inefficiency is meant.
3. If we say that one situation is more efficient than another or that there has been an improvement in efficiency, it means that the potential Pareto criterion is satisfied.
4. If management efficiency or production efficiency are being discussed, then those terms will be used explicitly. Recall that production efficiency is necessary for management efficiency, which in turn is necessary for Pareto efficiency.
5. Both allocational efficiency and economic efficiency are used as synonyms for Pareto efficiency.

Some analysts distinguish between static efficiency, which refers only to one-period analysis, and dynamic efficiency, which tries to deal with circumstances that evolve over time. The general concept of Pareto efficiency includes both static and dynamic efficiency.

It should be clear that efficiency is closely related to the marginalist principle. In fact, if social valuations of different projects coincide with individual valuations, a situation that satisfies the marginalist principle from society's point of view will be Pareto efficient.

As indicated in Chapter 1, efficiency is usually taken to be an objective of government policy, because increases in efficiency are associated with increases in per capita living standards. One of the basic dilemmas of policy is that improvements in efficiency are often damaging, or at least apparently damaging, to fairness or equity objectives. Conversely, policies intended to promote fairness or equity are often very inefficient. For this reason, some people are hostile to the economist's apparent preoccupation with economic efficiency. At the very least, however, understanding economic efficiency is helpful in allowing us, for any given equity objectives, to seek the most efficient (or least inefficient) approach.

3

The Normative
Analysis of Government

3.1 Introduction

Any normative analysis of government policy must be based on some fundamental philosophy, which provides an acceptable and consistent set of values by which proposed or actual public policy interventions can be evaluated. We cannot provide a detailed treatment of the philosophical basis of government in this book. The first part of this chapter does, however, review the philosophical perspective underlying the normative analysis of policy articulated in this text. The rest of the chapter provides a categorization of the major normative rationales for government intervention in business.

3.2 Philosophical Foundations of Government Policy

Different values will, of course, give rise to different views of the legitimate role of government policy. Anyone with even a limited knowledge of history can readily bring to mind several different sets of values underlying the role of the state. For example, in feudal Europe, the government consisted of the local feudal lord and ultimately a king or prince (occasionally a queen). In feudal systems, authority was normally based on a simple hierarchical view of human nature, which held that the natural obligation of every person was to have authority over his or her inferiors and to do the will of his or her superiors. Feudal rulers regarded themselves as having an absolute right to intervene in the economic and personal affairs of the common people.

In a *theocracy* (a religious state) the primary authority for government action is the pursuit of a particular religious agenda as interpreted by religious authorities, who regard themselves as acting on the will of God or other supernatural entities underlying their religion.

The modern philosophy of government can be seen, in part, as a reaction to feudal and theocratic forms of organization, and it draws heavily from classical Greek views on the role of government. The basic element in this philosophy is the primacy or sovereignty of the individual. Individual rights, freedoms, and well-being are regarded as the ultimate source of legitimacy for government action. Legitimate governments are those that arise from social contracts to which all (or almost all) individuals would voluntarily agree.

Many philosophers and political economists see a natural link between ideas of individual sovereignty and private enterprise. Specifically, the philosophy of private enterprise rests on two aspects of individualism:

1. Economic freedom
2. Consumer sovereignty

Economic freedom is the idea that individuals should be free to enter voluntary agreements with other individuals concerning the production, distribution, and consumption of economic goods and services. If Louisa wants to open a restaurant, hire staff, and offer meals to willing customers, economic freedom implies that she should be allowed to do so. In a country such as Canada we take such a right for granted. Opening a restaurant might require following certain rules and demand hard work, but an individual's basic right to open a restaurant is not in question. Such economic freedom did not exist in feudal and theocratic societies. Under feudalism, most people were serfs or peasants, required to work on the land, and not allowed to open businesses. In many theocratic societies, women were not allowed to open businesses at all, and many constraints were also placed on men.

An important challenge to the principle of economic freedom emerged in the 20th century as communism, built on the ideology of Karl Marx and implemented through *central planning*. In centrally planned economies, the government owns the means of production, and therefore virtually all business activity was carried out by the state, or government, with no individual right to go into business. The communist central planning experiment ultimately failed, and we have learned from experience that there are great benefits in allowing significant economic freedom. Most modern economies enjoy high levels of economic freedom.

Economic freedom sounds appealing in the abstract, but most of us would not find it acceptable as an absolute principle. For example, true economic freedom means that if one person is willing to grow poppies and produce heroin, and another is willing to buy the heroin at a mutually agreeable price, then they should be allowed to do so. Yet most societies pass laws against heroin production and consumption, and most of us agree with these laws.

Consumer sovereignty, on the other hand, means that each individual has a right to his or her own preferences and tastes for goods and services, insofar as those tastes do not impinge directly on the rights of others. The difference between consumer sovereignty and economic freedom is that economic freedom relates to what people do, while consumer sovereignty relates to how people think—to their tastes. According to the consumer sovereignty principle, the job of the government is not to question or change consumer tastes, but to create an environment in which individuals can pursue their own objectives as effectively and efficiently as possible.

Like economic freedom, consumer sovereignty is important, but is not taken as an absolute principle. It is not consistent with consumer sovereignty to have governments spending large sums of money on advertising campaigns intended to persuade people not to smoke, yet few of us oppose such policies. Governments also violate consumer sovereignty by choosing to subsidize opera, ballet, and Olympic sports while they tax gambling casinos and professional wrestling, yet most people accept such policies as reasonable. In addition, most of us accept that any right to consumer sovereignty should not be extended to certain groups, such as children and those suffering from significant mental disabilities.

While the philosophy of individual sovereignty is not an absolute, it does form the starting point for the normative analysis of government in market-based economies. There are exceptions and compromises, but such departures from the basic principles must be carefully justified. This philosophical starting point leads to political systems based on democratic principles and economic systems based on private voluntary exchange (i.e., on private markets). Thus, according to this view of the world, the role of government in business affairs is a limited one, with intervention requiring a strong case-by-case justification.

3.3 Private Enterprise and Individualism

Market-based economic systems with a limited role for government are consistent with the principles of individualism. This is not, however, the reason Canada, the United States, and many other countries have economies based on private enterprise. In fact, the converse is probably true: philosophies based on the primacy of the individual are popular because the associated forms of economic organization have performed well.

Private enterprise (or market-based) systems perform much better than the tribal, slave-based, feudal, or theocratic economic systems of the past. They also perform much better than centrally planned communism. With few exceptions, the many countries that experimented with communism and central planning have moved toward market-based systems of free enterprise—particularly Russia and China, the two pillars of 20th-century communism.

However, among the market-based economies, there is considerable range in the role of government. Of the major economies, the United States probably comes closest to the purist approach of promoting competition while allowing private enterprise to make business decisions. Other countries, such as France, Japan, and now South Korea, have developed what has been described as a corporatist approach in which the government becomes closely involved with large firms in planning major investment initiatives.

Similarly, there is considerable variety among the economic systems of former communist economies. Some, such as Poland and the former East Germany (now part of the unified Federal Republic of Germany), abruptly adopted a market-based structure. Others, such as Russia, undertook a path of gradual reform, while a few, notably Cuba and North Korea, remain resolutely anti-market communist countries. (It appears unlikely, however, that the policy stance of Cuba will survive much longer.) While it is still too early to judge the comparative economic performance of the former communist bloc countries, it seems that the countries that have taken a "cold turkey" approach to reform have performed better, despite significant adjustment costs.

China is a particularly interesting case, partly because of its position as the world's most populous country (with a population over forty times that of Canada), and partly because of its volatile policy history. China's communist revolution occurred in 1949, but by the mid-1960s some reformist elements were gaining influence. In an effort to purge such tendencies, China's leader, Mao Zedong (Tse-tung), initiated China's Cultural Revolution (1966 to 1976)[1], which ruthlessly suppressed the emergence of private markets and intellectual support for such reforms. We do not have reliable information about economic growth during this period, but it seems that per capita (per person) living standards actually fell from their already very low levels.

---

[1] The dates of the Great Proletarian Cultural Revolution are often given as 1966 to 1969. However, the economic and social policies associated with the Cultural Revolution dominated China until the death of Mao Tse-tung in 1976.

After the death of Chairman Mao and the end of the Cultural Revolution, a major market-based economic liberalization was initiated by the new leader Deng Xiaoping, beginning in 1978. The reform began in the agricultural sector and quickly expanded to other areas of the economy, particularly in the "special economic zones" (SEZs), where accelerated market-based reforms occurred. Market-based reforms have by now extended throughout the economy, although state-owned enterprises remain important to the economy. China's economic reform was not fast enough to be viewed as cold turkey for the country as a whole, but it was very rapid in some areas, and those are the areas which have achieved the most impressive economic performance. The most significant of these areas is the SEZ centred on Shanghai, often described as the "pilot area" for economic reform in China.

The result has been a very rapid increase in living standards. Between 1978 and 2011, real income per capita in China rose by a factor of more than 16.[2] China has been completely transformed in a single generation. No other economy has ever gone through such rapid economic growth, sustained over a period of such length.

Senior government leaders in China continue to call themselves communists or socialists. However, economic policy in China now has very little in common with traditional communism. China's economic transformation was achieved primarily by embracing economic freedom—allowing market-based reforms. It also seems that China's aggressive population control policy, the one child family, has made a significant contribution to rapid per capita economic growth.

3.4 Adam Smith and the Competitive Paradigm

Questions about the role of the state, or government, have a long history in philosophical debate. Plato's *Republic*, written over two thousand years ago, is still read today by many students of political science. Our modern understanding of business and government really began, however, with the publication of Adam Smith's *Wealth of Nations* in 1776. Smith was a philosopher at the University of Edinburgh in Scotland but is now regarded as the first modern economist. He is responsible for one of the major themes in economic thought: competitive private markets harness private incentives so that they serve the public interest. The following quotations from Smith (1776) illustrate his point of view:

---

[2] This data is based on the World Development Indicators maintained by the World Bank. See data.worldbank.org/country/china. This comparison is based on purchasing power parity data converted to real values.

An individual generally neither intends to promote the public interest nor knows by how much he is promoting it....By directing industry in such a manner as its product may be of greatest value, he intends only his own personal gain, and he is in this aim....led as if by an "invisible hand" to promote an end which was no part of his intention. (p.477)

By pursuing his own self-interest, the entrepreneur frequently promotes that of society more effectually than when he means to promote it. (p.477)

It is not from the benevolence of the butcher, the brewer, or the baker that we expect our dinner, but from their regard to their own self-interest. (p.18)

Whereas most people looked out into the world and saw chaos, Smith saw a remarkable degree of coordination and order. Consider the breakfast that Smith, in 18th-century Scotland, might have eaten. He might have had toast made from wheat grown in Eastern Europe, he would have spread marmalade made from oranges grown in Spain on his toast, and he would have drunk tea brought from India, sweetened with sugar from the West Indies. He might have eaten with silverware made from South American silver, and his tablecloth might have been made from American cotton and his napkins from Chinese silk.

Coordinating even such a simple breakfast at that time would be a remarkable accomplishment, beyond the capabilities of any single individual, and probably beyond the abilities of most national governments. What was the coordinating force, or invisible hand, that provided Smith with his breakfast? The invisible hand was private competitive markets. Somehow, many different individuals, mostly unknown to one another, each pursuing their own self-interest through private competitive markets, achieved remarkable results. (Note, however, that some of the firms that may have been involved with providing Smith's breakfast had substantial monopoly power, such as the East India Company.)

When we reflect on how things get done, it is natural to assume that someone must give orders to make sure the right products are produced in the right amounts and available at the right places. This is the command method followed by the army: generals give orders to colonels, who give orders to majors, and so on. It is an obvious way to get things done. It did not, however, produce Smith's breakfast. Instead, this breakfast was produced by a decentralized system of independent individuals, acting in their own self-interests, through market transactions.

Smith argued that market transactions, undertaken through the motive of self-interest, promote social welfare to a greater extent than do rival systems of organizing production, such as command systems. His main insight is very simple: if an exchange between two parties is voluntary, it will not take place unless they both believe they can benefit from it. This is the principle of voluntary exchange.

An implication of this argument is that little rationale exists for government intervention in private markets. Smith did recognize some exceptions, however. He acknowledged that the government might have a legitimate role in preventing concentrations of monopoly power, and he also believed that the government would have to provide some goods, such as national defence and roads, that would not be adequately provided by the private sector. He also recognized that for markets to function smoothly, governments must allow private property and provide mechanisms for the enforcement of private contracts and the protection of private property and personal safety.

Smith's discussion of monopoly power raises an important distinction: private enterprise can be expected to work out well, but only if markets are reasonably competitive. Modern economists and other social scientists have inherited and emphasized the notion that competition is fundamentally important. Smith's basic legacy, therefore, is the idea that private competitive markets should form the basis of business organization.

In this book, we will examine circumstances in which private markets do not perform well. These circumstances can be used to justify very substantial government influence on business affairs, but the point is that these policies will be viewed as particular cases which must be carefully justified. In other words, the basic question we will always ask with respect to any policy is, "Why can't the private sector do it?"

3.5 The Meaning of Competition

As just indicated, a crucial part of Smith's argument is that markets must be competitive. This raises the issue of what is meant by "competition." The normal use of the term, by managers and politicians, and for that matter by Smith himself, refers to the rivalry among sellers (or buyers) in a market. Competition means a conscious striving against other firms for sales, possibly on the basis of price, but also on the basis of advertising, research and development, product quality, and other business variables as well.

Economists, however, have found it useful to work with an extreme notion of competition—that is, perfect competition—which is defined by the following characteristics:

1. Buyers and sellers are sufficiently numerous that no buyer or seller has control over prices, which therefore are taken as given, or exogenous, by individual firms.

2. The product is homogeneous—each seller sells the same product.
3. Buyers and sellers have access to all information relevant to their production and consumption decisions and can transact easily (with low transaction costs).
4. There is free entry and exit in the long run.

We have in mind a market with many sellers, each selling a homogenous product, and with low transaction costs. In such a case, no one firm could raise its price without losing its market to another firm. Thus, each firm would perceive its price as being determined by the market.

Economists have been able to demonstrate that under perfect competition, and provided certain other conditions are met, private markets achieve Pareto efficiency. This is known as the first theorem of welfare economics. Furthermore, if redistributional goals are considered, then Pareto efficiency can be maintained by redistributing basic incomes and allowing markets to operate freely without intervention. This is the second theorem of welfare economics. These two theorems are the modern, abstract version of Smith's basic insight.

In addition to the theorems of abstract economics and Smith's assertions, there are some political arguments for competition. The strongest of these is that high levels of competition promote the dispersion and decentralization of political and economic power. More forcefully stated, economic competition encourages, and may be central to, the development and maintenance of democratic political institutions.

Note that the suggested relationship is between competition and democracy, not between private enterprise and democracy. There have been, and still are, many examples of countries dominated by private enterprise that are, simultaneously, very undemocratic. In fact, economic monopoly power and political monopoly power seem to go hand in hand. Political dictators frequently use their political power to concentrate monopoly power in the hands of their friends and relatives, or even in their own hands. Conversely, concentration of economic power allows a small number of individuals to use economic power for political ends.

3.6 Normative Reasons for Government Intervention

So far we have emphasized the case made by Adam Smith and his intellectual descendants for private competitive markets as the basic organizational structure for business activity. Aspects of this argument are essentially ideological, but corresponding to the ideology is a well worked out, logical structure. This structure tells us the conditions under which private markets can be expected to perform well. It also tells us, however, when private markets will fail to work effectively.

As already indicated, the inefficiency arising from monopoly power is one important reason for active government policy. There are three major types of policy response to monopoly power. One type of response is to encourage or enhance competition so that a workable level is achieved. This is, in large part, what competition policy attempts to do. A second type of response is to regulate industry directly, limiting the prices that can be charged and imposing other performance requirements. A third approach is direct government ownership, often called *public enterprise*. Some public enterprises are structured as corporations, except that they are owned by government and, in Canada, are called *Crown corporations*.

Monopoly power is not the only concern that arises about market economies. In general, as initially set out in Chapter 1, concerns about markets fall naturally into four categories:

1. Efficiency and market failure
2. Macroeconomic stabilization
3. Fairness
4. Other

3.7 Efficiency and Market Failure

Most of the specific policy areas discussed in this book draw on efficiency-based reasons for government intervention. We now recognize, based on the development of economic theory and on actual experience, that Adam Smith overstated the value of unregulated private markets. Private markets sometimes fail to achieve Pareto efficiency or even production efficiency, and these departures from efficiency can be so severe that even very imperfect governments can be expected to offer improvements. In such situations, government intervention can raise per capita living standards rather than simply redistribute wealth.

> *Definition*: A **market failure** is a situation in which private markets fail to achieve Pareto efficiency.

There are four major sources of market failure:

1. Imperfect competition
2. Asymmetric information

3. Incomplete property rights (leading to externalities and public goods)
4. Poorly designed government policies (sometimes called *government failure*)

Each of the first three items on this list is the rationale behind a major area of government policy, and each will be discussed carefully when the relevant policy areas are examined. And the fourth item, government-induced problems, has to be kept in mind to ensure that government intervention does not do more harm than good. In this section, the objective is to provide a brief explanation of each source of market failure.

3.7.1 Imperfect Competition

We have claimed above that perfect competition is efficient. Many industries, however, are not perfectly competitive. Individual firms have considerable control over market price, and there may be barriers to entry. As will be described in Chapter 6, in such circumstances profit-maximizing firms will charge prices that are too high and produce output levels that are inefficiently low. While the government cannot improve upon every minor departure from perfect competition, it does have a role in promoting competition and in regulating, or at least closely monitoring, areas where imperfect competition is inevitable.

For example, Hydro-Québec is a Crown corporation owned and controlled by the Government of Quebec. To protect the province from the problems associated with private monopolies, Hydro-Québec is part of the public sector, although continuing technological change makes market-based approaches a reasonable alternative.

3.7.2 Asymmetric Information

The perfectly competitive model of business presumes that all parties to a transaction have access to the relevant information. However, consumers are sometimes poorly informed. A consumer buying a smartphone has no way of assessing the dangers from radiation emitted by the phone. If radiation screening is expensive, and consumers cannot tell safe radiation levels from unsafe ones, then firms will have an incentive to provide insufficient radiation screening. In such cases, it is often simply better to have the government impose standards for the product.

The basic source of market failure in situations of asymmetric information is that the less-informed party will not know the true marginal benefit to be derived from the transaction as clearly as the more informed party does.

In some of these situations, although not all, there is reason to believe that government intervention is appropriate.

Markets will respond to informational market failure to some extent. In situations where the buyer finds it hard to evaluate different products, sellers will seek certification for their claims, and external sources of certification will find a market for their services. In North America, the Consumers' Union, which publishes *Consumer Reports*, is basically in the business of determining and conveying information to consumers about the quality of different products. In addition, firms will have incentives to invest in their reputations for quality so that consumers will trust the firm's products even if they (the consumers) cannot immediately distinguish quality differences among products. Both of these market responses can improve, but do not eliminate, informational market failure.

3.7.3 Public Goods

For most goods and services, property rights are defined. If Sophia owns a car, it is her property. She might sell the car to someone else, who would acquire the property right, or she might keep it, but there is no doubt about whose property is. Even with services, property rights are normally well defined. If Michael goes to a barber for a haircut, the hair-cutting service is owned by the barber who cuts Michael's hair, providing a service in return for a fee.

However, for some goods property rights are not so clear. One important class of goods that lack clear property rights are *public goods*. National defence is a public good, and so are lighthouses and public parks. A public good has the following characteristics:

1. A public good is nonrival in consumption: even though one person consumes the good, others may also consume it.
2. A public good is nonexclusive: it is impossible (or at least very costly) to exclude anyone from consuming the good.

Consider a lighthouse. The fact that one ship's captain is warned by the flashing light to stay away from dangerous rocks does not prevent other ships from receiving the same warning. Thus, lighthouse services are nonrival in consumption. Also, it is virtually impossible to keep anyone from consuming the services of the lighthouse. Anyone in a passing ship will see the light. The services of a lighthouse are therefore nonexclusive. The nonexclusive aspect of public goods causes a failure of property rights. The owner of a lighthouse cannot exercise ownership over the services provided by the lighthouse, and thus those services are not the property of the lighthouse owner.

Ordinary private goods, on the other hand, are rival and exclusive. If I consume an orange, it is gone and no one else can consume it. Furthermore, even if I do not eat the orange immediately, I can easily prevent others from consuming it. Public goods cause market failure, because private markets will not provide public goods. The basic argument relies on incentive effects. If a good is nonexclusive, no consumer has an incentive to pay for the good once it is produced. After all, he or she will be able to consume it anyway, so why pay? In other words, each consumer has an incentive to be a free rider.

Because no firm can expect to receive much payment for providing a public good, firms have very little incentive to provide such goods. The market will not provide public goods up to the point where the marginal social benefits are equal to the marginal social costs.[3] It may not provide public goods at all. Government intervention is therefore necessary.

3.7.4 Externalities

Externalities also arise because of a failure of property rights. They arise when some person or group is affected by the economic activity of others, without markets to price the effect. For instance, if a pulp mill discharges pollution that kills fish in nearby bodies of water where fishing boats operate, then the fishery is subject to a negative externality caused by the pulp mill. This externality can be viewed a failure of property rights. If the fishery had property rights over the body to water and could keep the pulp mill from emitting pollutants unless an appropriate price was paid, there would be no externality problem.

Externalities can also be positive. If Rosa lives down the street and keeps a very attractive garden that others enjoy looking at, then she is providing positive externalities. In the absence of government regulation, activities that generate negative externalities will be overprovided and activities with positive externalities will be underprovided.

3.7.5 Government Failure

In many cases, government policies are the cause of poorly functioning markets. For example, until recently, many cities in the world had rent controls, and some

---

[3] As pointed out by Coase (1974), historically there have been some private lighthouses, financed by fees paid by some ships and boats benefiting from the lighthouse services. Thus, the public good problem does not imply that no public goods will be provided. It does imply that such goods will be *underprovided*. See also Hamermesh (2010) for a discussion of firefighting as a public good.

still do. Rent controls place an upper limit on the rent that can be charged for accommodation. The objective was to help renters, many of whom had trouble affording increasing rents. However, rent controls normally had the effect of making the problem worse, not better. If the price of rental accommodation is forced below the equilibrium price, then suppliers will supply less housing, not more, making the difficulty of finding affordable housing even greater. But instead of allowing the price system to ration available housing and provide signals to suppliers to build more, rent controls just force the problem to be reflected in long waiting lists (and long waits), under-the-table payments, and general inefficiency in the housing market. In this text we will discuss many examples of government-induced market failure.

3.8 Macroeconomic Stabilization and Economic Growth

The following three basic facts about market-based economies play a major role in public policy discussions:

1. Business activity is cyclical.
2. A significant but variable fraction of the labour force is normally unemployed.
3. The price level is usually rising.

The first point refers to the idea that the pace of business activity tends to rise and fall, with corresponding increases and decreases in employment and the growth of real incomes. This rise and fall of activity is referred to as the business cycle. Since the publication of John Maynard Keynes' *General Theory of Employment, Interest and Money* in 1936, it has been generally accepted that governments have a role to play in moderating the business cycle. Ideally, the economy would always operate close to its capacity, with little unemployed labour or capital. In an attempt to achieve this goal, the government uses its control over the money supply, interest rates, exchange rates, taxes, and government spending.

The unemployment rate rises and falls as the economy goes through recessions and expansions. Even at the best of times, however, there is substantial unemployment. In Canada, the lowest monthly unemployment rate achieved in the period from 1976 to 2012 was 5.3 percent (in October 2007), and this period contained five complete business cycles.[4] There is always a lot

---

[4] Unemployment data is available from Statistics Canada's CANSIM database, Table 282-0001 at www5.statcan.gc.ca/cansim/a26.

of pressure for governments to help in the process of job creation, particularly during recessions, and public discussions of many policy issues focus on the employment consequences of the policy.

Many policies simply reallocate employment among regions or industries without increasing aggregate employment. If the Government of Canada undertakes a project in the home riding of an influential Cabinet minister so as to expand employment in that area, it is not creating employment overall but merely shifting potential employment from an alternative region where the project might have taken place. From a national point of view, there is no net gain. Many policies that are said to "create employment" only move employment around rather than expand the number of jobs. The presumption of the economic policy analyst is that unemployment problems are best tackled through broad-based macroeconomic policy that applies at a national level, not through piecemeal efforts to expand employment in a particular region or particular industry.

The rate of price increases, or inflation, has been low and stable from 1986 through 2012, averaging approximately 3 percent per year and not exceeding 6 percent in any one year. Yet in the decade of the 1970s, inflation fluctuated sharply and rose well into double digits, reaching a local peak at 10.9 percent in 1974, and a still higher peak of 12.5 percent in 1981. And inflation much higher than that is still common in many countries. However, there is considerable evidence that high and variable levels of inflation are damaging to business activity, and national governments are therefore seen to have an obligation to keep the price level relatively stable.

Keeping inflation under control in Canada is primarily the responsibility of the Bank of Canada (whose governor is appointed by the Government of Canada). Whenever the economy starts to show signs of inflationary pressure, the Bank undertakes some action to relieve the pressure—usually by raising interest rates. Normally, however, such actions slow down the economy and run the risk of inducing a recession. Ideally, the Bank would like to exercise precise enough control to prevent inflationary pressures without inducing a recession. Since the mid-1980s the Bank has maintained an inflation target of about 2 percent per year and has usually achieved it.

The cumulative path of economic recession and expansion determines the growth path of the economy, and in the long run, the overall growth path is much more important than the particular cyclical pattern underlying it. Furthermore, through the compounding effect of exponential growth, rates of growth that seem modest when quoted on a year-to-year basis can completely transform a country if continued over a couple of decades. For example, a per capita real income growth rate of 6 percent per year will cause per capita real incomes to triple over the space of twenty years. Any policy that has a significant effect on growth rates is ultimately very important. Both macroeconomic policies and the other policy areas covered in this book can have a significant impact on growth rates.

This book does not emphasize macroeconomic stabilization, but Chapter 14 is devoted to a discussion of the main concerns surrounding macroeconomic policy. When considering other policy areas, we will sometimes consider employment issues. Apart from this, however, our primary focus is on micro-economic policies–policies that address a particular firm or industry. Most such policies can be understood primarily as responses to market failure (or market inefficiency).

3.9 Fairness and Other Rationales for Policy Intervention

Fairness considerations are important in all major areas of public policy, including public policy toward business. Chapter 4 describes the role of fairness in public policy.

Other rationales for intervention are a catch-all category that includes normative or public interest objectives that do not fit into the standard rationales for policy. In popular debate, of course, one hears any number of reasons for policy intervention. On closer inspection, either most of these other reasons fit into one of the three categories we have just discussed, or they are spurious rationalizations for special interests. There are, however, some legitimate points to make here. Historically, the most important extra considerations are military. For example, many countries have taken the view that having a domestic steel industry is very important for national defence and have therefore used government policies (such as subsidies and tariff protection) to ensure that the domestic steel industry survives.

In Canada, one important non-economic influence on policy has been the desire to influence Canadian culture. Thus, Canadian policies include a variety of subsidies and local content regulations intended to foster the development of Canadian literature, music, arts, and other areas of cultural activity. Such policies have been particularly important in the effort to support and maintain French language cultural traditions in Canada. Canadian cultural policy has also sought diversity of cultural activity as part of its program of multiculturalism. Cultural policies are sometimes justified on efficiency grounds. For example, subsidies to the feature film industry are viewed by some as an investment in a potentially profitable domestic industry. However, if interventionist cultural policies really had to pay their way on economic grounds, we probably would not have many such policies.

Another important source of policy intervention is paternalism. Various censorship laws, regulations concerning drugs and alcohol, restrictions on the rights of children, and other areas of government intervention in the consumption decisions of individuals are fundamentally due to paternalism: the idea that some individuals need to be protected from themselves.

Almost all government programs consume resources. In particular, policies that seek to promote particular values typically impose significant net costs (relative to their overall size) on the government and on the economy as a whole. Canada's program of official bilingualism would be in this category, as would funding for the Canadian Broadcasting Corporation (CBC). Such social expenditures require that the economy generate a sufficiently high level of income to support them. It is very difficult for social expenditures to increase without the support of underlying economic growth. Failure to fully appreciate this fact has caused many governments to perform poorly.

3.10 Jurisdiction for Government Intervention

Many analysts have argued that, at the practical level, jurisdiction for the four basic rationales for intervention should be divided up among different parts of the government. Specifically, most government agencies and departments should focus on economic efficiency, leaving stabilization and employment concerns to the Bank of Canada and the Department of Finance, and leaving concerns about equity mainly to the broad-based tax and transfer system.

This proposed separation of jurisdiction is only partially reflected in actual practice. Most policies that surface in public debate are scrutinized for their effects on employment and their fairness as perceived by various interest groups. In any case, this separation is conceptually useful whether or not there is actual separation of function according to these four categories.

In Canada, there is also ongoing tension over the jurisdictions of different levels of government, particularly between federal and provincial governments. Canada is a federal state; that is, a state with more than one substantive level of government. The alternative is a unitary state, in which the national government has authority over all policy areas (but may delegate some of that authority to lower level governments).

Because Canada was created (in 1867) out of pre-existing political units, and because of Canada's large physical size, it is natural that Canada has a federal structure with powerful provincial governments. From a legal point of view, the power of provincial governments does not derive from delegation by the national government but is entrenched in the constitution. For example, control over health care and education resides with provincial governments, although the federal government has some involvement, primarily through its willingness to provide some funding for these areas (which derives, in turn, from its ability to tax).

We do not have space in this book to closely examine the theory and practice of federalism, but there are some general principles that should be stated. First, the general prescription for policies related to equity and redistribution is that they should be carried out by the highest level of government (i.e., by the national government), because of incentive effects. For example, with respect to old age security payments, each province would have an incentive to pay less than its neighbours, to avoid importing people who would be a net drain on the economy and to export such people to other provinces. The result would be a level of welfare payments below the level settled on at the aggregate or national level. However, old age security and the closely related Canada Pension Plan are provided by the federal government.

Policies related to national public goods and to overall economic stabilization are also most efficiently handled at the national level. However, policies related to local public goods, local externality problems, and many other (but not all) problems arising from the failure of markets to achieve efficiency are best handled at the provincial level.

3.11 Cost-Benefit Analysis

In this chapter, we have discussed the rationale for government policy intervention, but we have not discussed the techniques of policy analysis. For example, we have argued that public goods create a rationale for policy intervention, but we have not discussed how the government is to decide whether or not to provide a particular public good, or how much of the good to provide. The most important technique of policy analysis is cost-benefit analysis. A detailed discussion of cost-benefit analysis is beyond the scope of this book, but the basic idea can be easily stated. As the name suggests, cost-benefit analysis simply consists of trying to add up the costs of a project, adding up the benefits of the project, and comparing the two.

Cost-benefit analysis first became widely used in the 1930s as a method for evaluating flood control projects in the United States, and by the early 1960s it had become standard practice for a wide range of projects. In Canada, cost-benefit analysis was also common by the early 1960s, and it was formally incorporated into federal government policy analysis shortly after.

Cost-benefit analysis can be applied to projects, programs, regulations, and other government actions. Before any regulation is adopted, it is useful to consider it from a cost-benefit point of view. For example, several Canadian provinces recently experimented with large increases in cigarette taxes but found that enforcement costs were too high to make these taxes worthwhile. The basic problem was that cigarettes could be easily smuggled into a given province from other provinces and from the United States, and sold illegally. This had the effect of dramatically reducing the tax revenue earned and undermining the objective of reducing cigarette consumption. Police forces then faced the problem of deciding whether to take personnel away from violent crime investigation, traffic control, and other areas to redeploy them to deal with cigarette smuggling. Ultimately, these high cigarette taxes would not pass a cost-benefit test.

One important area of application of cost-benefit analysis is the evaluation of power projects. Suppose a government-owned power company (such as Manitoba Hydro) is considering building a new hydroelectric dam. The main output of the project would be electric power. In order to convert this output to a benefit, the electric power must be evaluated, which is normally done by determining the maximum willingness of potential customers to pay. Recall from Chapter 2 (Figure 2.2) that marginal willingness to pay is given by the demand curve. Total willingness to pay for some quantity, Q, is the area under the demand curve up to point Q. This willingness to pay is taken as the measure of benefits.

The benefit stream of the project, however, is generated through time. This introduces two complications. First, the future is hard to predict. Manitoba Hydro might have a good idea of what the demand for electric power will be next year, but there is considerable uncertainty associated with predicting demand for ten or twenty years. The normal approach, then, is to construct an expected benefit. For each year, different possible demand levels would be considered, and associated probabilities would be estimated. Based on this information, an expected benefit can be calculated for each year.

The other problem associated with time is that benefits in the future are not as valuable as benefits today. Future benefits must be discounted in some way. Normally, a discount rate is applied. Thus, for example, future benefits might be discounted at the rate of 6 percent per year, 8 percent per year, or some other appropriate rate.

Similarly, the project also generates a stream of costs. The proper measure of costs should include the opportunity costs of the factors of production used to construct the dam. Typically, the opportunity cost is taken to be equal to the market value of these resources (such as the wage rate for labour, the market price of cement, etc.). Most of the costs of the dam will be up-front costs, but there will also be operating and maintenance costs that continue through time. To the extent that these costs are uncertain, expected values would be used. For each period, we can then subtract the cost from the benefit to obtain a net benefit, and then add up all these net benefits as given by the formula,

$$NPV = (B_0 - C_0) + (B_1 - C_1)/(1 + r) + (B_2 - C_2)/(1 + r)^2 + \ldots \quad (3.1)$$

where NPV stands for net present value, B_i stands for expected benefits in period i, C_i stands for expected costs in period i, and r is the discount rate. If the NPV is positive, then we say the project passes the cost-benefit test.

The individual terms in Equation 3.1 may extend for a long time, possibly into an indefinite future. Given typical discount rates, however, terms in the very distant future will have little impact on the NPV, and as a practical matter, the NPV is normally taken over only a 25-or 30-year period. Some people have criticized this outcome on the grounds that it apparently undervalues the distant future. The future will receive more weight if the discount rate is lower. Choosing a discount rate, therefore, involves ethical judgments related to comparing future generations with the present. For this reason (as well as others), different interested parties will often disagree over the appropriate discount rate.

Often, the evaluation of benefits includes items other than the primary effect of the project. For example, a power project may have the extra (or ancillary) benefit of also providing flood control. If so, these benefits should be counted as well. Similarly, additional costs beyond the direct costs of building and running the dam may be included. For example, perhaps the dam requires construction of a reservoir that will flood recreational land, or perhaps streams used for recreational purposes will be destroyed. These are legitimate opportunity costs of the dam and should be counted in the NPV calculation. Much of the difficulty in carrying out cost-benefit analysis arises from deciding where to draw the line concerning possible ancillary costs and benefits of the project.

4

Fairness, Ethics,
and Public Policy

4.1 Introduction

This chapter deals with the philosophical foundations of fairness and ethics. The ideas developed here provide a basis for much of the analysis in later chapters on specific areas of policy, and they are particularly important in Chapter 15, Corporate Social Responsibility.

Most people have strong feelings about what they regard as "fair," but defining fairness is not easy. Dictionaries define fairness using terms such as *equity* or *justice*, but those terms are essentially just synonyms for fairness—they have almost the same meaning but do not really tell us what that meaning is.

Many philosophers regard the essence of fairness to be treating people *as they deserve*, and that is the perspective we follow in this book. Treating people as they deserve involves two important sub-cases or principles of fairness. The first one is horizontal fairness or, more commonly, horizontal equity. It means that people who are alike in all relevant respects should be treated the same way. For example, suppose that Helen and Riya have worked equally hard and have made equal contributions to a successful project. If their employer decides to give them bonuses, then the principle of horizontal equity implies that they should each get a bonus of the same size. If the employer chose to arbitrarily give Helen a larger bonus we would view that as unfair.

A second principle of fairness is vertical equity, and it holds that people who differ in relevant respects should often be treated differently. Suppose that Matthew and Olivier have been working on a successful project but that Matthew has done most of the work. The principle of vertical equity suggests that it would be fair to give Matthew a larger bonus than Olivier—that Matthew deserves a larger bonus because he contributed more to the project. Treating people the same when relevant circumstances differ is often unfair.

A somewhat more compelling application of vertical equity is provided by a recent police disciplinary problem that arose in a major Canadian city.[1] Three policemen were walking side by side on a sidewalk. A young women walking from the other direction tried to go between two of the policemen but got in the way of one of them. That policeman pushed her to the ground and the three police continued on their way without helping her, despite her difficulties in standing up. Bystanders, who had caught the incident on video, came to help the woman.

The policeman later claimed that he was surprised by the woman's actions and pushed her away because he thought she was reaching for his gun. It turned out that the woman suffers from cerebral palsy and multiple sclerosis and was having difficulty walking. In the video (which went "viral" on YouTube), there is no discernible attempt by the woman to reach for the policeman's gun. The video shows that the police were taking up a lot of space on the sidewalk. The women said her disability made it difficult for her to go around them, so she asked if she could go between them, unintentionally getting in the way. An internal police investigation found the police officer guilty of abuse of authority.

The finding might have been different if the person in question had been different. Suppose that it had been a large man who was not disabled, but was drunk. Police are often harassed by aggressive drunks or confronted by people seeking to make trouble. Pushing such people away is not unusual behaviour, rather better than pulling a gun or striking someone, and possibly the easiest way of defusing a potentially dangerous situation. What might be fair treatment of an aggressive drunk is not fair treatment of a disabled woman. Such a view illustrates the principle of vertical equity.

But what people deserve is not always obvious. In the case of an aggressive drunk, many people think the police are justified in using mild but careless force—pushing the drunk away. Other people might take a different view, expecting the police to exercise more caution. And still others might

[1] See Luk (2012).

want the police to be tougher, arresting such people and taking them into custody. Such differences of opinion reflect underlying differences in values and ethical judgments. Our views about what we think people deserve and, therefore about fairness, depend on such ethical judgments.

Ethics concerns the study of right and wrong behaviour. It is therefore closely related to fairness, but it is a broader concept. If we agree that the police are behaving ethically toward people they meet on the street, then we would presumably also agree that those people are being treated fairly. However, there are ethical issues that do not relate specifically to fairness. For example, many people believe that telling the truth is ethical and that lying is unethical. Suppose Jessica's mother asks what she is planning to do for the evening. Jessica knows that her mother wants her to study, but she is planning to go out with friends instead. Rather than tell her mother the truth and argue about it, Jessica just lies, saying that she plans to study. We would probably describe such lying as unethical but might not describe it as unfair. After all, Jessica's lie does not harm her mother, it just prevents an argument.

Most of us have strong intuitive views about fairness and ethics. However, different people and different groups often hold sharply divergent ideas about fairness. It is therefore important to have some means of assessing conflicting views over fairness and the underlying ethics and values.

4.2 Moral Relativism

General principles of ethics and fairness vary dramatically across time and cultures. In making ethical assessments of people at different times or in different cultures, do we simply apply our current ethical views? Such an approach seems rather short-sighted or even arrogant. An alternative approach is to apply moral relativism—the doctrine that individuals and organizations should be evaluated relative to the values and morality of the society in which they reside, not according to some absolute standard of behaviour.

4.2.1 Interpreting Individual Actions Using Moral Relativism

William Shakespeare (1564–1616) is widely regarded as the most important English language dramatist, but he is not without critics. During the 19th century, Shakespeare was commonly criticized for being immoral because of the sexual content of his plays. A leading editor and critic in that century, Thomas Bowdler, undertook to edit Shakespeare's works so as to remove what he thought was sexually offensive material. To us, Bowdler and others like him seem narrow-minded and unreasonable. Shakespeare simply lived in a time and place (16th-century England) characterized by relatively liberal views about sex and sexuality, at least by comparison with the more restrictive standards of 19th-century England.

On the other hand, according to the standards of the early 21st century, Shakespeare's treatment of sex may seem inoffensive, but he has been called anti-Semitic for his portrayal of the character Shylock in *The Merchant of Venice*. Shylock has many characteristics that are taken as representing negative stereotypes of Jewish communities. Should we judge Shakespeare to be a bigot? By the standards of his time (or almost any other), Shakespeare was a person of remarkable tolerance and sensitivity. At a time when most literature in most countries was resolutely xenophobic (i.e., negative toward outsiders), Shakespeare treated individuals from a variety of ethnic backgrounds with sophistication and insight. His work contains sympathetic images of homosexuality, and some of his female characters would not be out of step with modern feminists. His work does not precisely match the political sensitivities of the present, but to view him as a bigot or racist seems to get the picture very wrong. Through the lens of moral relativism, it is more correct to view Shakespeare as remarkably tolerant and sympathetic.

Other historical figures are open to more troubling criticism. What about George Washington and Thomas Jefferson (the first and third presidents of the United States)? Washington and Jefferson are widely regarded as two of the most important contributors to the entrenchment of democratic principles in the American constitution and, by inference, were very important contributors to the development of democratic traditions around the world. Yet both owned substantial numbers of slaves. By the standards of the late 18th-century United States, Washington and Jefferson were regarded as enlightened slave owners who believed that slaves should be treated with dignity and protected by the rule of law. And, after his death, Washington's will freed the 123 slaves he owned.[2]

By modern standards, however, we would be hard-pressed to imagine that anyone who tolerated the institution of slavery could be described as enlightened. How are we to judge Washington and Jefferson? The doctrine of cultural relativism offers one possibility—that we judge them not relative to our standards, but relative to the standards of their own culture.

Moral relativism asserts that the morality, or ethical legitimacy, of behaviour should be judged relative to the standards of the society within which that behaviour takes place. Such a view implies that, while ethics and values

---

[2] Jefferson's slaves, on the other hand, were sold after Jefferson's death to pay off debts owed by his estate. Jefferson did free a few of his slaves, but only a few, during his lifetime.

may differ across cultures, none are better than any other. Also, asserting that one's own values are morally superior to those of others is mere arrogance. Moral relativism leads naturally the doctrine of *conventionalism*—that it is ethically right to do what the widely held values of your immediate social environment dictate: "When in Rome do as the Romans do."

4.2.2 Problems with Moral Relativism

One may have misgivings, however, about the inherent acceptance of slavery implied by the application of moral relativism to Washington and Jefferson. A problem with moral relativism is that it seems to prevent us from criticizing what appear to be obviously unacceptable practices. Many cultures, both past and modern, regard slavery as acceptable. Cultures have been encountered in which infanticide (killing of unwanted infants) is common. Most Canadians would be unwilling to accept that slavery or infanticide represent a set of values that can be viewed as "just as good as ours."

A second problem of moral relativism is that it eliminates the concept of moral progress. Over the past century in Canada, there has been a dramatic change in women's rights and privileges. A century ago, women could not vote in federal or provincial elections or hold public office.[3] These restrictions on women have been eliminated, and most Canadians would say the current system is much more fair and superior from an ethical or moral point of view. If we accept moral relativism, however, such statements make no sense. Moral relativism tells us that we have no basis for judging values of a century ago to be inferior to our own. They are simply different, and that is all that can be said. Thus, the biggest problem with moral relativism is that it provides no basis for choosing between conflicting views, for it implies all values are equally admissible.

4.2.3 Women Drivers in Saudi Arabia

As of this writing, Saudi Arabia has a policy preventing women from driving. This rule is not part of the legal code, but various religious authorities have issued edicts banning women drivers, and traditional practice is that women are not able to obtain drivers' licences. In 1990, the Ministry of the Interior officially declared driving by women to be "un-Islamic," providing increased legitimacy to the effective ban on women drivers.

---

[3] The general right to vote in federal elections in Canada was extended to women in 1919. Women were able to vote in provincial elections before that, starting in 1916 in Manitoba. The first woman was elected to a provincial legislature in 1918 in Alberta, and the first woman was elected to the Parliament of Canada in 1921.

In June of 2011, a number of Saudi Arabian women who had learned to drive in other countries and had international drivers' licences made a point of defying the driving ban by openly driving.[4] Some of these women were arrested and taken into custody by Saudi Arabia's traffic police and by religious police. Many people in other parts of the world, including other Islamic countries, expressed outrage, viewing the ban itself and the punishments arising from it as unfair.

But were the police who made the arrests and the officials directing them being unfair? They could have looked the other way and not made the arrests—and many did. In fact, driving by women in rural areas of the country is not uncommon and is normally ignored by police. But these police and their supervisors were raised in very traditional environments. They were taught and believed that strict constraints on female behaviour were morally and ethically correct and even required by their religious values and beliefs. They believed they were acting fairly.

Few Canadians would accept that it is morally wrong for women to drive. For that matter, even in most Islamic-majority countries, women do drive. The values underlying public policy in Saudi Arabia are very different than those in Canada, and different than in many Islamic countries.

If we accept moral relativism, then we cannot judge the fairness of policies in the very traditional Saudi Arabian society based on the standards we are familiar within Canada. This, then, is a weakness of moral relativism. It provides no ethical or moral basis for policy reform.

4.2.4 Moral Relativism and Bribery

Moral relativism has been applied in evaluating apparent instances of bribery. In 2012, Walmart came under legal scrutiny in the United States for apparently paying bribes in Mexico.[5] After opening its first Mexican store in 1991, Walmart grew rapidly there, and had become Mexico's largest private sector employer by the time the bribery scandal became public in 2012. Walmart's rapid growth in Mexico required significant cooperation from many local and state governments, for business permits, zoning applications, and the like. It became apparent that this government cooperation was facilitated by bribes. Walmart is one of a very long list of American companies alleged to have routinely bribed officials in other countries, something they would not do (at least not so flagrantly) in the United States or Canada.

---

[4] See McVeigh (2012) and Sutter (2012).
[5] See Barstow (2012).

Moral relativism is a defence of such conduct. Carl Kotchian, a former chief executive officer (CEO) of the Lockheed Corporation caught bribing officials in Japan, argued before the U.S. Congress that bribery is very common in some countries, and that American firms should be able to adopt local standards, as otherwise they would suffer a competitive disadvantage relative to local rivals.

Is it unfair for U.S. courts to hold American corporations to American standards in other countries with different local standards? Is the use of bribery by such corporations unethical? In Mexico bribery is illegal but, while Mexican officials have argued that it is insulting to suggest that bribery is acceptable there, evidence indicates that bribery is relatively common. Does it follow that Walmart and other American companies should be allowed to adopt what they see as "local standards"?

Anyone taking an absolutist (as opposed to relative) view of moral or ethical standards would say that bribery and the associated dishonesty are universally wrong. Even if bribery is more common in Mexico than in the United States, and even if it is easier for Mexican government officials to get away with taking bribes than it is for their American counterparts, it is still wrong to participate in such schemes. Under this view, it is completely fair for U.S. courts to hold Walmart and other companies to account for bribery carried out in other countries.

Pragmatically, most policy analysts take an eclectic view of moral relativism in which some moral values are taken as relative and some as absolute. An example of absolute standards is the doctrine of *natural justice*, which holds that certain principles, such as the right of the accused to be heard, are fundamental and absolute. However, even in cases where we think absolute standards apply, we recognize that individuals are influenced by their environment. Thus, for example, a young child who grows up in a criminal environment where stealing and fighting are common might be inclined to view stealing and violence as acceptable behaviour. We can understand this and make some allowance for it without accepting such a value system as morally equivalent to mainstream Canadian values.

4.3 Value Conflicts or Misunderstanding?

Some disagreements over policies reflect differences in fundamental values and ethical judgments. Debates over issues such as capital punishment and abortion derive principally from differences in basic values, often influenced strongly by religious beliefs. However, conflicts over values, while fundamental, may be less significant sources of policy disagreements than is commonly understood.

Thomas Schelling, a professor at Harvard, argues that what seem to be conflicts over values are often misunderstandings.[6] He uses the example of gasoline rationing to make his point. In the past, rather than letting prices adjust, rationing has often been used as a response to perceived shortages—shortages of food, gasoline, etc. It is much less common now but is still used as, for example, in health care systems throughout Canada.

The proposed system for gas rationing is that each person gets ration coupons providing the right to a specific amount of gasoline, and no more. Schelling frequently asks his students whether they believe this system of gasoline rationing is a fair response to gasoline shortages. The students generally approve of rationing. Schelling then states that he opposes gasoline rationing and would prefer to let the market allocate gasoline through higher prices, allowing those willing to pay the most to get the available gasoline. At this point, his students infer that his basic values differ from theirs; that he is less sensitive to the needs of the poor, more committed to the market system as a process, and less concerned about the consequences of unbridled capitalism.

Schelling then proceeds to argue that, if his students like rationing, they should agree that people should be allowed to sell their gasoline ration coupons. At first, this proposal has little appeal, for it means "that the rich will be able to burn more than their share of gas, the poor being coerced by their very poverty into releasing coupons for the money they so desperately need." Eventually, however, the students recognize the point that the poor might like to be able to turn gasoline ration coupons into money. Whereas gas coupons can only be used to buy gas, money gained through the sale can be used to buy milk or groceries. At worst, the coupons can still be used by a poor person to buy gas. Clearly, anyone with the interests of the poor at heart can hardly oppose this proposal, which certainly makes the poor better off.

The next point is that, with a market for ration coupons operating, the coupons are really just like cash. If gas costs $1.00 per litre, and ration coupons sell for 50 cents per litre, then the net price of gas is $1.50 per litre, which is precisely the price that would clear the market in the absence of rationing. A gas station selling 200 litres takes in $200 in cash and $100 worth of ration coupons, which could have been sold for cash. Effectively, when a poor person (or anyone else) receives a ration coupon for 200 litres from the government, he or she is receiving the clumsy equivalent of $100.

---

[6] See Schelling (1981)

But, then, why not pay $100 directly to the poor? One could avoid all the red tape and processing costs of the ration system, greatly reducing the cost of the program, and the government would not have to give special ration coupon money to everyone but could, instead, target it to the poor. The direct costs could even be recovered by a tax on gasoline, which would be better for the poor, the non-poor, the gas stations, and the economy as a whole.

Schelling is usually able to persuade his students that their concern about gasoline fairness is misplaced. Their fundamental concern is that the poor are poor, not that the poor may consume less gasoline than the wealthy. The efficient response in this case is to give the poor more money and allow the market to do its job of efficiently allocating resources. Schelling is, if anything, probably more sympathetic to the plight of the poor than most of his students. Certainly his disagreement with them over the value of rationing does not really arise from major differences in basic values. His disagreement simply illustrates the point that popular perceptions of fairness are often biased toward favouring interference in specific markets, even when the underlying problem could be more effectively addressed in some other way.

4.4 Major Philosophical Approaches to Ethics and Fairness

Philosophers, theologians, and many other people have been thinking about principles of ethics and fairness for a very long time, but no consensus has been reached on an appropriate universal set of ethical rules. While many approaches have been proposed, all have flaws. This section reviews some of the major systematic approaches to ethics and fairness.

There are two major types of ethical theories. One type focuses only on the actions themselves. For instance, to be judged as ethical, a person must fulfill certain duties (or follow certain moral rules) that are taken to be intrinsically ethical. Such an approach is called *deontological* or *duty-based* or *rule-based*. An ethical obligation specified by most such ethical systems is an obligation to tell the truth.

A second type of ethical theory focuses on the consequences of an action rather than on the action itself. In philosophy, such an approach is called *teleological* or *consequentialist*. A consequentialist approach is based on the principle that an ethical action is one that produces good consequences, or good results.

Suppose we accept that we have a moral or ethical duty to tell the truth. If your mother has just bought some new clothes and asks how she looks, it follows that the ethical response is to be honest. If you think the clothing makes her look old or unattractive you should say so. You should *not* say, "You look great, Mom."

Using a consequentialist approach, the calculation is more complex. You might decide that there is nothing to be gained by telling the truth and you will just make your mother unhappy. If you say she looks good, your mother will feel good. Telling such a lie—a so-called *white lie*—might be the ethical thing to do if your focus is the consequences or results of your actions.

In ordinary language, the tension between duty-based and consequentialist approaches is often described as a matter of "ends versus means." Under consequentialism, it is the ends, the results or consequences, that matter. Under a duty-based or moral rule approach, it is the means or actions themselves that matter. This tension between ends and means creates some significant disagreements. One important example concerns the use of torture. Most ethical systems rule out torture, and in Canada and many other countries torture is strictly prohibited by law in all circumstances. But what if a dangerous terrorist has been caught and has information about the location of a large number of innocent hostages who will be tortured and killed unless they are quickly rescued? Would obtaining that information by torturing the terrorist be the correct thing to do? Do the ends justify the means?[7]

In following sections, we consider major duty-based and consequentialist approaches to ethics. All of these approaches imply a rejection of cultural relativism, in that each suggests a set of absolute standards or criteria by which we may judge actions to be ethical or fair.

4.4.1 The Benefits Principle

One important type of consequentialism is based on the *benefits principle*. This principle specifies the type of consequence that should be focused on. It states that in deciding on what constitutes fair or ethical behaviour we should focus on the benefits (and costs) experienced by the affected parties.

Consequences such as national glory or religious purity or an unspoiled environment would not, in themselves, qualify under the benefits principle. They would qualify only to the extent that they generate benefits experienced by affected parties. For example, if greater national glory achieved through military conquest makes some group feel good, then that positive feeling would count as a benefit. If a cleaner environment makes us healthier or

---

[7] The use of aggressive questioning was an important issue in the recent war in Iraq, in which U.S. forces were accused of using torture, which is illegal under U.S. law. Pragmatically, the main issue was one of definition—what counts as torture? We can agree that imposing severe physical pain counts. But what about sleep deprivation or holding someone's head underwater?

happier, then that would also count. But we do have to focus on the benefits (or costs) experienced by relevant parties.

A duty-based approach does not focus on costs and benefits. For example, let's reconsider the example of responding to your mother's question of how she looks in her new clothes. A proponent of duty-based ethical principles would say that costs and benefits do not matter, and lying to your mother is just plain wrong as it violates your duty to be honest. Such an approach rejects the benefits principle.

4.4.2 Utilitarianism

Utilitarianism incorporates one particular version of the benefits principle. It was first developed by David Hume, Jeremy Bentham, and John Stuart Mill in the late 18th and early 19th centuries. Each of these three philosophers, among others, offers a slightly different statement of utilitarianism. Here we focus on what might be called *strict* utilitarianism. The strict utilitarian position is that an action is good if it increases total utility or happiness. Put slightly differently, utilitarianism is based on the axiom that ethical and fair decisions are those that maximize total utility.[8]

Consider for example the problem faced by a government considering construction of a new bridge. The utilitarian position tells us that we should add up the changes in utility of all the affected parties. Such a bridge would affect drivers who would use the bridge, making it easier and faster for them to get where they are going. The bridge would also affect people who live near the proposed site. Quite possibly, the increased traffic congestion, noise, and pollution in their neighbourhoods would reduce their utility (and the value of their land if they own property). In addition, taxpayers paying for the bridge would also be affected. Calculating how the bridge would affect the utility, or the well-being, of the various parties would not be easy. However, if we could, then the method would be easy to implement. We would just add up the effects, positive for some and negative for others, and decide whether to proceed based on whether the result is positive or negative.

In practice, however, we often feel a need to modify this approach. For example, we might feel that people who live near the bridge should be given more consideration than others. In fact, many bridge projects have been blocked because of strong local resistance, even when the total benefits would

---

[8] A common but imprecise and ambiguous statement of utilitarianism is that we should *seek the greatest good for the greatest number*. This statement does not necessarily imply simply adding up utilities.

be very large. We might give local residents veto power, or possibly we could just put additional weight on local residents' utility relative to that of other affected parties. Such an approach is not strict utilitarianism, although it would still be an application of the benefits principle.

John Stuart Mill, the most influential exponent of utilitarianism, saw it as supporting a very liberal social position. For example, utilitarianism does not distinguish between the utility of a king as opposed that of a poor person. Mill regarded it as very unfair that thousands of ordinary young men would be drafted into an army and sent off to fight and die in wars whose principal objective was to secure greater glory for a king. By giving equal weight to the utility of each person, utilitarianism would of course rule out such activities. Utilitarianism is a very democratic principle because it treats everyone equally.

Mill regarded utilitarianism essentially as a doctrine that saw good in the things that gave people happiness, rather than as focused on religious or nationalistic or other moral codes emphasizing personal sacrifice as the source of virtue. Mill and other utilitarians also found in this approach a strong rationale for redistributing income from rich to poor, the basic argument being that, in general, an extra dollar of income is more valuable to a poor person than to a rich one. For example, a morsel of food likely provides more utility for a hungry person than it would for someone with more than enough to eat already. Thus, taking a dollar (or a morsel of food) from a wealthy person and giving it to a poor person would tend to raise total utility, because the poor person's perceived increase in utility would exceed the wealthy person's perceived loss. Such redistribution is therefore justified on utilitarian grounds.

Despite the appeal of utilitarianism, however, it has some serious flaws. First, it assumes that utility or happiness is comparable across individuals, something which some critics assert is impossible. Does it seem possible to declare, for example, that one person will get fifty units of utility from a new car, whereas someone else only gets forty? If such comparisons cannot be made, then utilitarianism cannot be applied.

Other critics argue that even if interpersonal comparisons of utility can be made, it is wrong to do so. In particular, utilitarianism would seem to unfairly favour people who have greater capacity for happiness or, more crudely, those who are the most efficient "pleasure machines." We all know people who seem very happy and able to derive great enjoyment from life. We also know people who are often depressed and take little pleasure in things that most of us would enjoy. Should we compound this existing asymmetry by giving even more advantages to the happier people because they are able to take more pleasure in them?[9]

Another problem with utilitarianism is that it seems to offer very weak protection for individual rights. Suppose that by sacrificing one person, everyone else benefits substantially. Is it fair to sacrifice that one person? This dilemma is a very common theme in legend and literature, and it comes up often enough in practice. Many of us have seen movies where a lifeboat has too many passengers, and sacrificing one or two people might save ten or twelve others. Or perhaps we have read about situations where a group of mountaineers are climbing a dangerous peak, such as Mt. Everest, and someone gets injured and can no longer walk. Those potentially able to carry the injured person cannot do so without greatly increasing the risk to themselves and others in their party. What should they do? That some do decide to sacrifice injured companions is reflected in the fact that there are many frozen bodies near the top of Mt. Everest. In such cases, we feel moral ambiguity, as if the utilitarian assessment to sacrifice one or two individuals to save others does not seem quite right.

Yet more extreme examples generate an even stronger discomfort with utilitarianism. Suppose some people (and they do exist) derive great pleasure from inflicting pain on others, and a large group of such people assault or "beat up" an innocent victim. Since there is only one victim but many assailants, it is possible that if we add up the utility gains of the latter, these gains could exceed the utility cost to the victim. Thus, utilitarianism could favour this action. But even thinking this way seems ridiculous. Of course, we say to ourselves, assaulting an innocent person is completely unfair no matter how much pleasure some (sadistic) people might get from it. We do not regard the pleasures obtained by sadists from harming others as a legitimate type of utility, and we believe the victim has a basic right to freedom from arbitrary assault.

These examples suggest that strict utilitarianism is not acceptable as a general principle of ethics or fairness. Some philosophers have offered more sophisticated versions of utilitarianism that seek to address these and other concerns, including the possibility of excluding certain types of utility as illegitimate, such as any utility derived from pleasure taken in harming others.

4.4.3 Rule Utilitarianism

Strict utilitarianism as we have defined it incorporates two important features. One is the simple totalling of utilities to determine the best actions. As we

---

[9] Admittedly, there are few if any public policies that take into account different individual capacities for enjoyment in deciding where to allocate resources, but as a point of principle this problem seems like a significant flaw in utilitarianism.

have seen, this feature can be modified by ruling out particular types of utility, perhaps allowing different weights for different types of utility, or putting different weights on concerns of different groups of people. The other key feature of strict utilitarianism is that it focuses on the utility consequences of a single action, such as building a bridge, telling a white lie to a friend or relative, or trying to rescue an injured mountaineer. Considering just one action at a time is called *act utilitarianism*.

The alternative to act utilitarianism is *rule utilitarianism*. Under this approach we do not assess just one act, but we assess a general rule instead. We seek to choose rules that maximize utility if the rule is always followed. For example, consider the rule, "Do not steal." We might acknowledge that, in an isolated case, utility might be raised by breaking the rule. We can imagine that a person who is hungry or in need of clothing might gain a lot by stealing some food or clothing from a wealthy person who will hardly even notice the loss. However, if we accept that theft is acceptable as a general rule, then we all end up worse off and have to spend much of our time and energy just protecting the things we have. Under rule utilitarianism, correct action means following the rule that generates the highest utility—in this case, not stealing. With rule utilitarianism, a person should not ask, "Does my action raise or lower total utility?" A person should ask instead, "Would this action raise or lower total utility if everyone acted this way—if my action is the general rule?"

However, rule utilitarianism also has flaws. We might agree that "Don't throw rock through windows" is a good rule. However, if a building is on fire and we need to break a window to get inside to save a child caught in the fire, it seems obvious that we should break the rule. Therefore, this rule is too general. Should the rule be, "Do not throw rocks through windows except in emergencies"? If so, how do we define an emergency? Ultimately, we might end up just assessing each act by itself to see if it involves a sufficient emergency, and we are not much further ahead than we were with act utilitarianism.

It is important to emphasize that rule utilitarianism is a form of utilitarianism and is, therefore, a consequentialist approach to ethics that uses the benefits principle. We assess rules based on their consequences—in terms of the effect on the utility obtained by the people involved. It should not be confused with deontological or duty-based approaches to ethics, even though those approaches are sometimes called rule-based approaches.

Whether or not it is possible to construct a reasonable theory of fairness based on utilitarian ideas is still an open question. There is no simple utilitarian principle that seems to capture all important intuitions about fairness and ethics.

4.4.4 Kant's Categorical Imperative

During the 18th century, philosopher Emmanuel Kant developed a complex but influential moral or ethical philosophy, partly as critical response to utilitarianism. Kant felt strongly, as do many others, that certain actions have intrinsic ethical or moral value quite apart from their consequences. However, rather than simply presenting a set of rules or duties that he thought were important (such as a duty to tell the truth), Kant tried to derive ethical duties and rules from a single fundamental principle that he called the *categorical imperative*. The word *imperative* means "something that must be done," (i.e. a duty), and the word *categorical* means "without exception or qualification." Kant's categorical imperative refers to a duty or obligation that people who are rational and ethical are required to follow.

The categorical imperative (or primary duty) proposed by Kant is not easy to understand. Kant expressed it in several different ways himself, and others have interpreted it in many ways. However, one widely accepted interpretation is that the categorical imperative actually has two steps. A person considering a particular act should ask the questions, a) is it logically possible for everyone to act in this way, and b) would I want everyone to act in this way? If the answer to both questions is "yes" then the action is a moral one and the person has a duty to act in this way.

Kant argued that this categorical imperative gives rise to many subsidiary duties, or moral obligations. For example, Kant sought to derive a duty to be honest. We can see that it is logically possible for everyone to be honest, and according to Kant, a rational and ethical person would want everyone to be honest. Kant also sought to derive a duty to treat other humans with dignity (ruling out slavery, for example), to work hard, and to avoid cruelty to animals, along with various other duties or obligations.

Kant's categorical imperative may seem to be related to rule utilitarianism. However, they are quite different. Under rule utilitarianism, we add up effects on utility, both benefits and costs, to assess whether particular rules are good or bad. Kant claimed that his rules or duties apply regardless of costs and benefits. They apply because of an intrinsic moral duty that is independent of outcomes or consequences.

The categorical imperative also seems similar or perhaps even equivalent to the golden rule that appears in many religious codes: People should act toward others as they would want others to act toward them. Kant, however, disagreed with this claimed equivalence. He felt that his categorical impera-tive implies a duty to others greater than that implied by the golden rule. For example, consider a proposed moral duty to help orphaned children. The golden rule instructs us to do things that would help us if others do them. An adult would not gain from the help that others give to orphaned children. Therefore, arguably, the golden rule does not necessarily imply a duty to help orphaned children. On the other hand, the categorical imperative would imply such a duty if a rational ethical person thinks it is good for people to help orphaned children as a general rule.

As with utilitarianism, Kant's categorical imperative has generated much criticism and has significant limitations as a practical guide to fairness or ethical conduct. What do you do if duties or moral rules conflict? For example, a manager may face a conflict between a duty to maintain the privacy of an employee's health records and a duty to be honest when asked about the employee's behaviour. To make a decision, the manager would first have to determine which duty is more important.

4.4.5 Social Covenants and Contracts

Kant's approach to ethics focuses on individual behaviour. The social contract approach focuses on setting up appropriate rules to guide entire societies, although such rules certainly have implications for individual behaviour. The basic idea underlying social contracts is that a fair or just system is one we would all voluntarily agree to join. Thus, the system is viewed as a social contract we have all agreed to accept. The social contract approach was first developed by John Locke and Jean-Jacques Rousseau in the 17th and 18th centuries, but the most influential modern proponent is John Rawls with his work *Theory of Justice*, published in 1972. We will focus on the Rawlsian version here.

Rawls envisions what he calls an "original position." All relevant indi-viduals are present in the original position and have a clear understanding of the way society operates and the nature of the world. However, no person knows who he or she is. Some social structure will emerge following the ini-tial position, and each of us will assume our identities at that time. Initially, however, we do not know anything about our identities: sex, intelligence level, wealth, height, level of physical attractiveness, etc. In the original position, people are behind a *veil of ignorance.*

For a rule to be part of the social contract, people in the original position must reach unanimous agreement and have a duty to follow that agreement, as with Kant's categorical imperative. Rawls argues that agreements reached behind the veil of ignorance would be fair, because the rational nature of discussion in the original position leads to a fundamentally fair process.

Rawls argued that people in the original position would choose two principles, which he referred to as *principles of justice*. The first, often referred to as the "equal liberty principle," requires that each person be granted the same liberties, such as freedom of speech and the right to vote, and that these liberties should be as broad as possible. The second principle concerns the distribution of social and economic goods, and consists of two parts: offices and positions must be open to all under conditions of "equal opportunity," and society must be ordered so as to maximize the well-being of the worst-off person, known as the "difference" or "maxi-min" principle. Rawls argues that when we are behind the veil of ignorance and do not know what our situation in society will be, we will only accept principles that make the least advantaged person as well off as possible.

Rawls points out that the maxi-min principle does not imply the equal division of well-being (or of income). Suppose we agreed there was no reason, in principle, why one person should receive more than another and, accordingly, agreed that everyone should receive the same income, irrespective of what he or she did. Total income would simply be equally shared among the all individuals. The obvious problem is that few people would work very hard under such a system. In a large population, an individual's income would be almost totally unaffected by his or her own work effort, and the resulting incentive to work would be weak. Work effort would not drop to zero, but it would be diverted into personally enjoyable rather than economically productive activities. Total output might well drop to something approaching zero. Certainly, average income and welfare would drop precipitously. In short, the efficiency costs of the equal sharing principle would be enormous. Everyone, including the worst off person, would be made worse off under such a system. In order to provide incentive effects that make everyone better off, some degree of inequality may be necessary.

Many critics, especially economists, do not find Rawls' claim that the maxi-min principle would arise from the social contract to be convincing. Suppose, for simplicity, there are 1,000 individuals behind a veil of ignorance. Suppose they are choosing between the following situations. In Situation 1, each person will get "50," which we take to be a short and hard life. In Situation 2, 999 people will get "100," which corresponds to a long and pleasant life, and one person will get only "49," which, of course, is just slightly worse than 50. You do not know which of these thousand people you will be. Would you prefer Situation 1 or Situation 2? If the maxi-min principle is correct, you should choose Situation 1. Most people, however, prefer Situation 2. They are willing to take some small risk of being marginally worse off to obtain the very likely prospect of being much better off, as is the case in Situation 2. You would have to be extremely risk averse to prefer Situation 1.

The maxi-min principle seems to put excessive weight on the very worst-off person while ignoring everyone else. In the real world, the situation of the worst-off person is hard to define. Would the worst-off person be an infant who has a very difficult and painful delivery and then quickly dies? If so, then we should devote all efforts to preventing infant mortality. No pleasures would be allowed—no food beyond the minimum necessary for efficient work effort, no nice clothes, no pleasure of any sort so long as one child died in or shortly after delivery. But even this effort would probably not be enough to prevent all infant mortality. Enormous sacrifices could be required for relatively little benefit.

Even if we reject the maxi-min principle, the social contract notion is still very interesting. The appeal of the social contract seems to be that if a group of people, with all their special interests stripped away, could voluntarily agree on social rules, then those rules would be fair. Thus, the social contract is based on the idea that fairness derives from a particular procedure that is viewed as fair. What makes this process seem fair is that people must voluntarily agree. Unfortunately, getting unanimity would be very difficult in practice. Also, while the social contract idea has appeal, it is not at all clear what a group of disembodied souls operating behind a veil of ignorance would really agree to.

4.4.6 Procedural Fairness

One important element in the social contract approach is that fairness is whatever derives from fair procedures. It therefore focuses on procedural fairness. Procedural fairness, which can also be applied without reference to a social contract, says that if we adopt appropriate procedures, or fair procedures, then we have achieved fairness, regardless of the outcomes that arise. Procedural fairness should be distinguished from distributive fairness, which focuses on the ends, or results, of some process. Procedural fairness is a deontological approach; distributive fairness is a consequentialist approach.

There is disagreement among philosophers and policy-makers over whether procedural fairness or distributive fairness is more fundamental. Rawls tried to finesse this conflict by using a notion of procedural fairness (the social contract) to derive a fundamental principle of distributive fairness—maximize the welfare of the worst-off person—but, as discussed in the previous section, there are serious criticisms of this approach.

The intuitive appeal of procedural fairness can be illustrated by the following example. Consider how we would feel if a large and healthy but poor young man snatched the purse of a frail but well-off elderly woman. There might be some differences of opinion over this transfer of wealth, but most of us would regard it as unfair on procedural grounds, despite its redistributive effect. Even if the poor young man would benefit more than the elderly woman from the money (implying that the theft would raise total utility), it seems to most of us that theft, especially when carried out under the threat of violence, is an unfair procedure that violates important basic rights of the elderly woman. Put simply, the primacy of procedural fairness is captured in the aphorism "the ends do not justify the means," while the primacy of distributive fairness is reflected in the response that "if the ends don't justify the means, what does?"

Proponents of the primacy of procedural fairness argue that society's obligation is to provide fair procedures and to focus on the idea that procedures should be non-coercive. Society's institutions should allow voluntary choices, and should avoid paternalism and coercion. Note, however, that procedural fairness described in this way does not guarantee egalitarian outcomes. Procedures that require equality of opportunity will allow some people to do better than others because of differences in fundamental (and inalienable) abilities, because of differences in luck, and possibly for other reasons as well.

4.4.7 Rights

Procedural fairness requirements are often referred to as *rights*. One possible fundamental right is that of non-coercion. Defining non-coercion precisely is not easy, but it is taken to mean that no individual can be forced to take positive action that he or she does not want to take. Thus, for example, if my neighbour's house burns down, I have no obligation to provide him or her with a bed for the night. As long as I do not actively harm my neighbour, what I do is my own business. I might choose to help my neighbour, and almost certainly would, but that is up to me and it cannot fairly be forced on me by the government.

Note that this principle of procedural fairness, or right, might drastically cut down the scope of "acceptable" redistributive activity carried out by governments. For instance, a wealthy person could not be forced to pay taxes that will simply be redistributed to the poor. The wealthy person might voluntarily choose to pay taxes in return for government-provided goods and services such as roads, police protection, etc., but might choose not to support welfare, unemployment insurance, medicare, and other redistributive programs.

One could, of course, propose other rights (or procedures) that imply highly redistributive and interventionist government programs. There have, for example, been proposals in both Canada and the United States for constitutionally guaranteed rights for a certain level of medical care or for guaranteed employment. Rights of this type would create claims on other people and would, therefore, conflict with rights of non-coercion.

For almost any set of proposed rights, it is possible to think of examples that make those rights seem less than absolute. One of the most cherished and hard-won rights in modern democratic societies is the right of free speech. But even this right should not be absolute. As has been frequently observed, it should not, for example, provide a right to yell "Fire!" in a crowded theatre.

One important and widely accepted right is the right to the control and integrity of one's person (i.e., one's own body). Thus, for example, kidnappers do not have the right to kidnap and assault an innocent victim. We feel the victim has the right of control over his or her body. Similarly, police do not have the right to torture accomplices to a crime, even if those accomplices are withholding important information.

So far, so good. But what about the hypothetical example of a woman, call her Anne, who has a unique factor in her blood that can attack and destroy HIV, the virus that causes AIDS? A serum based on her blood can cure people with HIV infection. Unfortunately, while this factor can be artificially augmented, fresh donations of blood from Anne are required to produce serum. Scientists are hopeful of producing a purely artificial version of the serum but have not yet succeeded. Doctors have told Anne about the situation and asked her for regular blood donations. Anne does not like giving blood and has a very negative view of the behaviours associated with the transmission of HIV. She therefore refuses, even though a single blood donation would save many lives. Would the government have the right to force her to give blood? Would Anne be justified in holding out for high payment for her blood? The answers to these questions are not obvious. Under current Canadian law, Anne could not be forced to give blood and could not demand payment for it.

Now suppose further that Anne goes into the hospital for some routine minor surgery. Doctors seize the opportunity to take enough of her blood to provide the basis for research focused on artificially reproducing the unique factor that kills HIV. Are doctors justified in doing this? They have certainly violated her right to control over her own body. Readers may be uncertain of what is appropriate in this case (which is based on a real example, but not involving HIV). By changing the example slightly, however, we can make a much stronger case for breaching Anne's right to control of her own body. Suppose the disease is not HIV infection, but a new, highly lethal airborne virus that threatens to kill half the population. Suppose further that only a small amount of blood is required, causing little inconvenience to Anne. We could construct an example in which it would seem fair to violate Anne's right, essentially on utilitarian grounds.

Thus, the procedural fairness approach also has flaws. First, it is far from obvious exactly which fundamental rights of fairness are appropriate. Second, it is hard to think of any rights that stand up as absolute principles in the face of careful scrutiny. As a practical matter, most democratic constitutions use some mixture of rights-based (including specific procedures) and benefits-based approaches. Thus, for example, the Canadian constitution incorporates a series of individual rights and specific procedures, but allows them to be overridden in cases of overwhelming public interest.

For our purposes, we recognize there is no simple approach to fairness that will serve as a foundation for analyzing public policy. However, it is helpful to be aware of major philosophical approaches to fairness when thinking through particular issues and examples. Thus, confronted with a particular problem, we can ask ourselves whether a proposed course of action would satisfy utilitarian requirements, whether it is something that would emerge in a social contract setting, and whether it is consistent with certain basic rights. All of these perspectives are helpful and relevant.

4.5 Individual and Group-Based Fairness

So far we have focused mainly on the individual as the unit of analysis, asking what things are fair from an individual point of view. It is, however, important to be aware that there is a distinction between individual-based concepts of fairness and what might be referred to as group fairness. Human beings seem to have a natural tendency to identify strongly with group membership and to define themselves in part by group identity: as business students, as men (or as women), as members of a particular ethnic or religious group, as part of a union or of "management," on the basis of physical disabilities, etc. It then seems natural to examine both procedures and outcomes on a group basis. In recent decades, notions of group fairness seem to have gained importance relative to notions of individual fairness. Thus, there has been, for example, increasing emphasis on whether various racial or ethnic groups are appropriately represented in universities and in certain occupational categories.

In Canada, one interesting application of group fairness principles is the Aboriginal Justice Initiative, which provides for members of Aboriginal communities to be treated differently from other Canadians in the criminal justice system.[10] This program illustrates the dilemma inherent in such an approach; on one hand, there are better outcomes for many Aboriginals, but it provides for different treatment of two people guilty of the same crime.

4.5.1 Problems with Group Fairness

Group fairness readily conflicts with individual equality of opportunity. Consider, for example, policies adopted in recent decades by the University of California at Berkeley (which are similar to policies adopted at many universities in the United States and other countries, although not in Canada). The basic policy statement of the Berkeley university administration was that the student body should "reflect the population of the state of California." Students were classified by race as Asian, black, Hispanic, native, or white, and different admission standards were applied to each group to achieve the appropriate mix of students.[11]

The net effect was that individual members with high admission scores within some groups were rejected in favour of individuals with lower admission scores from other groups. This conflicts with notions of individually based equality of opportunity. Well-meaning people have argued forcefully both for and against the policy. Partly as a response to the Berkeley case, there has been a strong backlash against policies of preferential discrimination in California, and legislation has been enacted making preferential discrimination on the basis of race or sex illegal in many situations. Berkeley, ultimately, had to modify its policies. The point, in any case, is that group fairness and individual fairness are difficult to reconcile.

There has been a significant attempt to increase female participation in traditionally male occupations, such as policing and firefighting. In a recent case, a Kitchener man, Jake, and his wife, Kim, made a formal complaint to the Ontario Human Rights Commission.[12] Jake had taken 18 months away from his job as a carpenter to take courses to meet basic academic requirements for a firefighter's position. He then took the Kitchener Fire Department's aptitude

---

[10] See www.justice.gc.ca/eng/pi/ajs-sja/his.html
[11] Such a policy was adopted by the Brazilian university system in 2012. See Romero (2012)
[12] *Macleans,* September 14, 1992, p. 23.

test, on which he scored 83 percent. His application was rejected because the cutoff for white males was 85 percent. However, the cutoff for women was 70 percent, well below the score Jake received. Jake argued that this policy constituted discrimination based purely on his sex and race. In an interesting twist, his wife Kim also argued that not only did this discrimination adversely affect Jake, it also adversely affected her and their two children.

Until recently, women were not considered for jobs as firefighters. It seems relatively uncontroversial that this discrimination against women was unfair. Given this history, fire departments have a higher proportion of men than they would have had under a fairer system. Is fairness served by trying to achieve an appropriate proportion of women by discriminating against men in favour of women at the entry level? As Jake pointed out, he was in no way responsible for past discrimination in fire department hiring. Furthermore, he had not benefited from discrimination in fire department hiring. In fact, men who had previously discriminated against women in hiring and who had presumably benefited from this discrimination were now senior fire department officials who were discriminating against him. This does seem to violate norms of fairness based on individual rights, but arguments can be constructed to justify it on utilitarian grounds or on group fairness grounds.

Many people involved in group fairness debates simply assert as a matter of ideology that group differences in choice or performance must be due to discrimination in some form or other. It is certainly true that overt race and sex-based discrimination has played an important role in relative occupational success in the past. For example, until the late 1960s, most medical schools in Canada, as a matter of policy, admitted very few women.[13] The existence of past discrimination does not imply, however, that nondiscrimination necessarily leads to equal performance or proportional representation of various groups. For example, it seems unlikely, based on what we know about occupational preferences and the distribution of physical strength across males and females, that a neutral system would give rise to equal numbers of male and female firefighters.

Most people have strong emotional reactions to particular group fairness issues but are unable to articulate consistent conceptual positions to support their emotional response. Many of us assume that we want to help people and that people with opposing views must have bad intentions, thereby allowing

---

[13] In 1959-60, women made up 9% of first-year medical students in Canada. This percentage rose modestly to 11% in 1964-65 but reached approximately 50% by the late 1980s, where it has remained. See *Canadian Medical Educational Statistics*, 1990, vol. 12, Ottawa: Association of Canadian Medical Colleges.

us to label those who disagree with us on matters relating to group fairness as racists (or sexists, or whatever). It is, for example, easy to call someone a racist for arguing that members of Aboriginal communities should be treated as different from other citizens in some fundamental way, but equally easy to call someone a racist for arguing that they should not.

Race and sex are not the only categories over which group fairness is considered. In Canada, freedom of association, intended as an individual right, has been viewed by the courts as providing fundamental protection for labour unions, including the rights of labour unions to exclude non-union workers from certain jobs. This seems to conflict with the basic individual freedoms concerning choice and it stretches the notion of freedom of association, but this was part of a political battle over union-based group rights.

In Canada, there has also been a high degree of attention paid to regional groups and considerable discussion of regional fairness. This concept has been used to justify taxing the population at large to provide income support for regions with below average incomes. Unfortunately, the poor in well-off regions also pay their share for such policies, and the greatest beneficiaries are often people who are already well-off but happen to live in poor regions. Regional redistribution is a very crude and inefficient way of trying to achieve distributive fairness.

4.5.2 The Nondiscrimination Principle

Another attempt at the reconciliation of group-based and individual-based approaches to fairness is adoption of a principle of fairness sometimes called the *nondiscrimination principle*. According to this principle, people have a right to be assessed for employment or for other economic purposes based on their individual abilities rather than on their membership in some group, such as ethnic or gender group. For example, a rule that women cannot serve in the military violates the principle of individual treatment. Relevant performance standards might be imposed, such as standards of physical strength needed to handle military equipment, which might be more challenging for the average woman than for the average man. Such a situation is, however, consistent with individual treatment. What is ruled out by individual treatment is excluding women simply because they are women.

While nondiscrimination requires that women who meet appropriate objective performance standards be allowed to serve in the military, it equally requires that women should not benefit from quotas or preferential access. An admission rule stating that 30 percent of recruits must be women or that specifies lower admission standards for women is just as much a violation of individual treatment as a rule that prevents women from serving. Individual treatment requires that each person be treated on his or her merits as an individual, irrespective of membership in a particular group.

Politicians and special interest groups can be very imaginative in creating ideas of fairness that justify their own objectives. We find that the word "fairness" enters almost every policy debate. Notions of group fairness seem to be particularly susceptible to political use. Somewhat surprisingly, economists place relatively little emphasis on fairness in analyzing many policy areas. This follows from a general presumption among economists that fairness objectives are best pursued at the broadest possible level, which is the national system of taxes and transfers (such as welfare, unemployment insurance, and old age pensions). More specific policy areas should, according to this view, focus on economic efficiency.

4.6 Trade-offs Between Efficiency and Fairness

The first point economists usually make about public policies dealing with fairness is that there is a trade-off between fairness and efficiency, principally because of incentive effects. One of the basic conclusions of most influential views of fairness, such as utilitarianism or the Rawlsian maxi-min principle, is that we would like to redistribute from the relatively well-off to help the relatively disadvantaged. In countries like Canada, we do this through a progressive tax and transfer system. Low-income people receive income from the government in various ways, including welfare, and from subsidized or free services, such as medical care. Tax rates are modest at moderate income levels and rise to fairly high levels as income rises.

Income tax rates vary by province as they incorporate both federal income tax rates, which are the same throughout Canada, and provincial income tax rates, which vary substantially. For 2012, combining federal and provincial taxes, Alberta had the lowest top marginal income tax rate—the rate paid on each additional dollar of income—at 39 percent. In B.C. the top marginal rate was about 44 percent, and in all other provinces the rate was between 40 and 50 percent.

But why stop in the 40 to 50 percent range? Why not have tax rates of 70 or 80 percent for very high income earners? Surely that would be even fairer. The problem is that if there are very high tax rates for high levels of income, the incentive for high-income earners to work will be low. Governments in many countries, including in Canada, have at times had very high marginal tax rates, on the order of 70 or 80 percent. Strangely, these high taxes collected very little revenue. Highly productive people either reduced their work effort and income, and/or increased the time and effort devoted to tax avoidance and tax evasion.[14] High-income earners were obviously made worse off by a policy of near-confiscatory taxation, but so were low-income people, as there was less money to redistribute to the poor and highly valued services were withdrawn from the economy. This high-tax policy was inefficient in the Pareto sense: it made all parties worse off.

Many such policies intended to promote fairness have efficiency costs. Free medicare is an example. If medical attention is free, trips to the doctor will be made more frequently than necessary and will sometimes be used by lonely people as a way of getting some attention. In general, there will be no incentives for efficiency.

Another anecdote illustrates this point. When James returned to British Columbia after several years in Ontario, he was, for a period of three months, not covered by the B.C. medical plan. (Medical bills were to be sent to Ontario to be reimbursed.) He was taking monthly allergy shots at the time and shortly after arriving was due for a shot. He went to the emergency ward of a hospital. His bill was about $100 (2012 dollars), and we can understand why. He had been processed by three people: a receptionist, a nurse, and a doctor. He had filled in forms that would have to be processed by others, and he had sat in an impressive hospital waiting room (for a substantial period of time) with all kinds of expensive equipment standing by. If anything, $100 was less than the cost of the visit. James then found a small clinic where, two mornings a week, a nurse gave allergy shots to all people who showed up. He came in, got his shot, waited a few minutes, paid his bill, and left. This time his bill was about $10, in keeping with the resources consumed.

The clinic was far more efficient than the hospital, but incentives to use clinics are generally very weak. If James had not been in the unusual situation of having to process his own medical expenses, he would never have discovered the difference in costs. Because most people face no incentives that bring resource costs to bear on individual behaviour, the medicare system is more expensive than it needs to be. It might, of course, still be important to have free medicare. We might decide that the fairness objectives of universal free medical care are so significant that we are willing to pay high resource costs.

Rent controls are another example. Most people who favour rent controls do so because of some sense of distributive fairness; they want to help poor

---

[14] If the tax rate is zero then revenue raised is also zero. As tax rates increase from zero, revenue increases and reaches a maximum at some point, after which further increases in the tax rate cause revenue to fall. A 100% tax rate on income would collect virtually no tax as no one would have any incentive to earn income. This pattern is often called the Laffer Curve after Arthur Laffer, who is noted for popularizing it.

tenants. Once again, the efficiency costs are large because of incentive effects. Landlords will stop maintaining controlled apartments and will not build new ones. One of the most well-established empirical regularities of economic policy analysis is that areas subject to strict rent controls end up with housing shortages, imposing large costs on anyone looking for a place to live. Landlords then screen prospective tenants on the basis of personal preferences, and the poorest tenants are frequently unable to find any accommodation at all.

Another important example is unemployment insurance. If unemployment insurance is very generous, unemployed workers will remain unemployed longer and be much choosier about the jobs they will accept. This raises the natural rate of unemployment and increases the total efficiency losses associated with unemployment. There is no easy way out. As Thomas Schelling (1981) has remarked,

> Offering 90 percent of normal pay [as unemployment insurance] can make unemployment irresistible for some...Providing only 40 percent...makes life harder than we want it to be. There is nothing to do but compromise. But a compromise that makes unemployment a grave hardship for some makes it a pleasant respite for others, and we cannot even be comfortable with the compromise.

Similarly, if benefits to unwed mothers are very generous, unmarried teenage mothers will be more inclined to keep their babies rather than give them up for adoption. This raises the overall public costs associated with raising these children, not to mention reducing their prospects for a happy life. High benefits may even reduce incentives to avoid unplanned pregnancies. However, low benefits to unwed mothers would make life much harsher for those unmarried women who have and keep their children, and, perhaps more disturbingly, would make life harder for their children as well.

All of these examples point out the fundamental problem with policies that give resources to the disadvantaged. By their very nature, these policies provide rewards for being disadvantaged and tend to reduce private incentives to avoid such circumstances. This does not mean we should always avoid such policies, but it does mean that we should recognize the associated efficiency costs.

When we argue that programs intended to promote fairness cause inefficiency, we do not mean simply that they consume resources. We expect medicare, employment insurance, welfare, and such things to consume resources. The inefficiency refers to the problem that the costs of delivering the desired results are higher than they need to be. Very often the incentive effects of social programs can be improved. The objective is to seek out least-cost methods of achieving fairness in public policy.

4.7 Improving Fairness and Efficiency

Despite the unavoidable conflict between fairness and efficiency, most economists would argue that it is possible to improve on both the efficiency and fairness of current policies. Most such improvements rely on market-like incentives. One point to emphasize is that universal social programs are suspect. Universal programs are those that apply to everyone, irrespective of income. For example, all Canadians receive free medical care for most medical needs, and all are eligible for the Old Age Pension.[15] In effect, the government taxes money and gives it back. Unfortunately, the resources consumed in the process are substantial. A more accurate description is that the government taxes $1 and gives back 75 cents. The difference is a pure deadweight loss, or waste. Inefficiencies created through taxing the well-off to give to the poor may well be justified on the grounds of fairness. However, taxing the well-off even more and then refunding a portion while consuming the rest in the process is more problematic.

In Canada, health care is a very large and important industry, accounting for over 12 percent of national output. The industry consists of private providers of health care (doctors, nurses, many hospitals, laboratories, etc.), but most payments in the system are provided by governments, not by individuals. The exact administrative details vary from province to province (since health care is a provincial responsibility), but certain aspects of the overall health care system are governed by the Canada Health Act, which is federal legislation. In particular, provinces are required to provide universal access to the major parts of the health care system (acute-care hospitals and most doctors' services) at no cost to the user.

Suppose that we want to improve the efficiency of medical care without reducing fairness. One possible modification in the system would be adoption of modest users' fees—not enough to make medical care inaccessible to people with low incomes, but sufficient to provide incentives in the direction of efficiency. In addition, substantial amounts of revenue would be collected, easing the problems associated with rapidly growing government debts. People

---

[15] The Old Age Pension system incorporates a "clawback" by taxing back some of the payments to high income recipients. This system of taxing, paying money out, and then re-taxing is inefficient as each step in the process consumes resources and creates incentives for tax avoidance.

who could really not afford even modest user fees could be given vouchers. These vouchers would function like tickets or licences, each worth a specified sum of money. Qualifying individuals would be given vouchers by the government to buy a service. The seller of the service redeems the vouchers with the government for their nominal value.

Another possibility would be to introduce an insurance system to cover the costs of catastrophic illness. Depending on how such a system was implemented, it might be similar to the health premiums that exist in most provinces now. However, such a system could also incorporate some incentive elements by linking the premium payment to certain high-risk behaviours, such as driving, smoking, or dangerous occupations.

Those who suggest modest user fees, possibly supplemented by catastrophe insurance, do not advocate complete or even substantial elimination of the current medicare system. There are benefits for everyone in some elements of universal health care. For example, we all have an interest in providing immunization for certain diseases, as this protects the immunized people, and it benefits everyone else by reducing their exposure to infectious disease.

Vouchers, also, can be used for other things in addition to medical user fees; for example, as an alternative to rent controls. If we believe that some people deserve assistance in paying for housing, we could provide them with vouchers for, say, $400 per month (or any amount) and have them compete on the open market for housing. This would increase the demand for housing and lead to a corresponding increase in supply, which would likely be more efficient than public sector housing.

Quite a few changes have been made to improve the incentive properties and fairness of the tax/transfer system in Canada, but many problems remain.

4.8 Attitudes Toward Fairness in the Marketplace

One of the difficulties in establishing policies that are both efficient and fair is that we seem to have trouble thinking consistently about fairness. This point has been demonstrated clearly by Kahneman, Knetsch, and Thaler (1986), from whom the following examples are taken.

A large (random) sample of individuals was presented with several examples of business behaviour and asked if each of the behaviours was either unfair or acceptable. Some of these situations and the responses to them are reproduced below:

1A. A company is making a small profit. It is located in a community experiencing a recession with substantial unemployment but no inflation.

There are many workers anxious to work at the company. The company decides to reduce wages and salaries 7% this year.

Acceptable 38%   Unfair 62%

1B. A company making a small profit is located in a community experiencing a recession, with substantial unemployment and inflation of 12%. The company decides to increase wages and salaries only 5% this year.

Acceptable 78%   Unfair 22%

2A. A shortage has developed for a popular model of automobile, and customers must now wait two months for delivery. A dealer had been selling these cars at list price, but now prices this model at $200 above list price.

Acceptable 29%   Unfair 71%

2B. A shortage has developed for a popular model of automobile, and customers must now wait two months for delivery. A dealer had been selling these cars at a discount of $200 below list price but now sells this model only at list price.

Acceptable 58%   Unfair 42%

3A. A small company employs several people. The workers' incomes have been about average for the community. In recent months, business for the company has not increased as it had before. The owners reduce the workers' wages by 10% for next year.

Acceptable 39%   Unfair 61%

3B. A small company employs several people. The workers have been receiving a 10% annual bonus each year, and their total incomes have been about average for the community. In recent months, business for the company has not increased as it had before. The owners eliminate the workers' bonus for the next year.

Acceptable 80%   Unfair 20%

Each pair of questions presents similar situations. For instance, situations 1A and 1B are objectively identical as far as real income is concerned as, in each case, workers are presented with a 7 percent cut in real income. Despite the objective equivalence of the situations, intuitions about fairness differ significantly for each. Imposing a 7 percent real wage cut in the presence of 12 percent inflation is judged to be fair, while offering a 7 percent real wage cut in the absence of inflation is judged to be unfair.

Situations 2A and 2B make a similar point. In each case, the car dealer raises the price by $200. The list price is, of course, completely arbitrary, and has no direct bearing on the welfare of consumers in either case. Yet raising the price $200 above list generates many more assessments of unfairness. Similarly, between situations 3A and 3B, perceptions of fairness concerning a wage cut change dramatically depending on the wording of whether or not some part of regular income is referred to as a bonus.

In general, perceptions of unfairness are very sensitive to how the situation is framed or described. Slight changes in description can produce very dramatic changes in the intuitive response of most people. People are more strongly influenced by the connotations of the description than by the economic realities of the situation.

This has three very disturbing implications. First, it means that perceptions of fairness are easily manipulated, a fact which many self-serving politicians and business people frequently take advantage of. Second, it means that individual perceptions of fairness tend to be inconsistent, which makes it very hard to determine what we mean by fairness. Third, even if people seem confident in their perceptions of fairness, we must wonder what these perceptions are based on if they are so easily manipulated.

4.9 Concluding Remarks

This chapter makes the point that concerns over fairness have a long history of analysis and still generate much disagreement and debate. In part, this is because some of the issues that arise are difficult ones that trouble us as individuals, even before considering differences in viewpoints across individuals. A person's attitudes toward fairness are strongly influenced by the culture and environment in which he or she develops and lives, and we observe that different cultures of the past and present have major differences in their conceptions of fairness and morality. One possible implication of these differences is the doctrine of cultural relativism, which holds that we have no basis for asserting the superiority of one value system over another.

While acknowledging the importance of keeping cultural relativism in mind, especially when judging individual behaviour, we considered several attempts to provide absolute standards of fairness. These attempts subdivide into two major categories. One category consists of consequentialist approaches, which focus on the consequences of different actions in order to assess their fairness. The other approaches are duty-based and focus on absolute standards of behaviour (do not lie, do not steal, etc.) that should be followed regardless of their consequences.

This chapter also noted the distinction between group-based and individual-based conceptions of fairness. It then made the important point that there are trade-offs between fairness and efficiency, but suggested that it might be possible to improve both at the same time. We then considered problems associated with assessing fairness in the marketplace in connection with framing effects.

Despite the difficulties in determining an absolute set of criteria for fairness, it is important that fairness considerations be handled rigorously in public policy analysis. One useful step that acts as a complement to the cost-benefit analysis described in Chapter 3 is identification of the likely distributional effects of proposed policies: who gains and who loses, along with an assessment of how much they gain or lose. We can then ask whether this pattern of distributional changes meets some reasonable standard of fairness.

5

The Positive
Theory of Government

5.1 Introduction

The normative analysis of government is concerned with what governments should do. It is prescriptive in nature. The positive analysis of government, on the other hand, tries to explain why governments choose the policies they do. In other words, positive analysis seeks to understand why current policies have come about and tries to predict future directions in policy. The positive theory of government is sometimes referred to as public choice theory.

It might be the case that actual policy coincides very well with normative prescriptions. If so, positive analysis need go no further. We frequently see examples, however, of policy decisions that seem hard to explain on the basis of any clear normative principle. Why, for example, have rent controls been in force in many Canadian cities despite the fact that almost all economic policy analysts agree that rent control is a bad policy? Why is it often alleged that government contracts seem to be awarded on the basis of reasons that have little to do with basic normative criteria? Why, for that matter, is there so much concern over conflict of interest in policy-making?

The answer to these questions and others like them is that politicians and civil servants are motivated by the same fundamental force that motivates private sector economic behaviour: self-interest. Politicians wish to be re-elected. Civil servants wish to do well in their careers. Sometimes these incentives lead to policies that are not in the general public interest. Furthermore, various special interest groups devote substantial effort to influencing public policy in their favour, often at the expense of the public at large.

This chapter presents a brief analysis of the forces other than normative principles that shape government policy. We focus primarily on incentive effects—the incentives facing policy-makers.

Elected policy-makers normally wish to be re-elected and therefore are influenced by voting patterns. In addition, policy-makers are subject to lobbying by special interest groups and may be influenced by such lobbying for a variety of reasons. Also, policy-makers might be influenced by their own direct economic self-interest. In this chapter, these three major determinants of the incentives confronting policy-makers are examined in turn. Section 5.2 is devoted to a discussion of voting, section 5.3 deals with special interests and the related process of transfer-seeking, and section 5.4 addresses direct self-interest.

5.2 Voting

It is obvious that voting influences public policy. Furthermore, virtually all citizens of modern democracies would argue very forcefully that voting is the operational foundation of democracy and that it should influence public policy. Most of us probably think that voting and democracy are synonymous.

However, even if we agree that voting should be the basis of policy, there are still many procedural issues that must be decided. One obvious issue is the question of who should vote. Should convicted criminals, teenagers, the mentally disabled, or the clinically insane be allowed to vote? How should immigrants and expatriates be treated in the voting process?

After resolving the question of who should be allowed to vote, the next issue is how voting should be translated into policy. There are two basic approaches: direct democracy and representative democracy. Direct democracy involves direct voting by the citizenry on policy issues. In Canada, direct democracy is common at the local level. For example, cities and municipalities often hold referendums on major civic construction projects, such as bridges and roads. The referendum contains a proposal and financial plan, and voters vote for or against it. At the provincial and national levels, on the other hand, direct democracy is very rare.

One exception has been referendums brought forward by the Government of Quebec concerning sovereignty association with Canada. The people of Quebec were asked whether they wanted the Government of Quebec to negotiate with the Government of Canada to remove itself from provincial status and establish instead a more independent association with Canada.

One referendum took place in 1980[1] with 60 percent against the proposal and 40 percent in favour. A second referendum on essentially the same question was held in 1995. In this case, about 51 percent voted no and about 49 percent voted in favour. In 2012, the Quebec provincial election was won by a party (the Parti Québécois) proposing yet another referendum on the same question, "when possible."

In 2011, British Columbia held a referendum on taxes. The choice was whether to retain the harmonized sales tax (HST), which applied sales taxes to all goods and services covered by the national goods and services tax (GST), or to return to the provincial sales tax (PST) system in place before the HST was adopted in 2009. There are several differences between the PST and HST, the most important of which was that the PST system applies sales tax only to goods, not to services, implying a smaller range of products to be taxed. Approximately 55 percent voted to drop the HST and revert to the PST system, which took effect in 2013.

Almost all policy decisions at the national and provincial levels of government (and most local policy decisions as well) are made by representatives rather than directly by the public. Canada's political system is almost exclusively one of representative democracy rather than direct democracy. There are good reasons for this. In the first place, it would be impractical, if not impossible, to have citizens vote directly on most policies. Second, representatives can make use of expert opinion and presumably make better decisions as a result, especially on technical matters. It would make very little sense, for example, to hold a national referendum over the design of military aircraft, as most citizens would be incapable of making an informed judgment without enormous amounts of time and effort. Instead, we elect representatives whom we trust to make good decisions on our behalf in accordance with general objectives that we elect them to pursue.

Representative democracy puts severe restrictions on the way in which voters can influence policy. Individuals make a host of market decisions every day, and governments make hundreds, perhaps thousands, of important decisions per year, yet voters can choose or recall their representatives only

---

[1] The first Quebec referendum was held on May 20, 1980. The question, as reported in Fitzmaurice, *Quebec and Canada: Past, Present and Future* (London: Hurst and Co., 1985, p. 301), reads, "The government of Quebec has made public its proposal to negotiate a new agreement with the rest of Canada, based on the equality of nations; this agreement would enable Quebec to acquire the exclusive power to make its laws, levy taxes, and establish relations abroad, in other words, sovereignty—and at the same time maintain with Canada an economic association including a common currency; no change in political status resulting from these negotiations will be effected without approval from the people through another referendum. On these terms, do you give the government of Quebec the mandate to negotiate the proposed agreement between Quebec and Canada?"

at infrequent intervals of several years at a time. Some important policy-makers, such as Supreme Court of Canada justices, are not elected directly but appointed by an elected government and serve until retirement, which may be a long time.[2]

The Supreme Court is called upon to interpret a constitution that seeks to entrench various rights that often conflict with each other and that allows exceptions to or limitations of these rights under very general guidelines. Supreme Court Justices have enormous latitude for decision making and are, therefore, among the most important policy-makers in the country.

The importance of the Supreme Court as a policy-maker was made very clear in 1988, when it decided that Canada's abortion law was in violation of the Charter of Rights. This decision made abortion on demand legal in Canada. This is clearly a policy decision by the Court, as the Charter, which does not address abortion directly, is open to varying interpretations. The Court did leave open the possibility of new legislation limiting abortion, but as of 2012 no such legislation has been passed. In 2012, important Supreme Court decisions[3] included determinations that pre-nuptial agreements have significant force in determining the division of assets in divorce proceedings, and that police do not require a search warrant to use infra-red imaging to measure heat arising from houses, a method of detecting marijuana "grow-ops" and other drug-related activity.

There are limited options available to a voter in making choices. A voter may prefer the position of one candidate on one issue, of a competing candidate on a second issue, and may find his or her view on some other issue totally unrepresented. Yet the voter must choose one candidate (or abstain altogether) who will then represent him or her on every issue.

It is possible to introduce elements of direct democracy into modern politics. In some states in the United States, citizens have the right to bring forward direct referendums (called initiatives) in state elections. In a typical state election, voters choose candidates to represent them and, in addition, vote directly on several initiatives. It is through this method that Massachusetts voters were able to restrict property taxes to 2.5 percent of assessed value, against the recommendations and wishes of most politicians. In 2012, two states, Washington and Colorado, passed initiatives legalizing marijuana use, potentially bringing state law into conflict with U.S. federal law. In recent

---

[2] Mandatory retirement for Supreme Court Justices in Canada is at age 75.
[3] Supreme Court decisions can be obtained by following the links on the website www.scc-csc.gc.ca.

years, some political forces in Canada have been advocating more extensive use of direct democracy.

While voting for political representatives is a very important part of the political process, a second important part of policy formulation is voting within government itself. Modern government is really government by committee, and understanding the way in which committee voting works is very important for understanding the policy-making process. Different committee voting systems have different properties. The following subsection considers properties of representative voting in more detail, and subsequent sections present a theory of party platforms and discuss surprising and interesting properties of committee voting.

5.2.1 Representative Voting

In Canada, as in all modern democracies, the public elects representatives who are then responsible for the actual formulation of policy, a system of representative democracy. It is interesting to consider how the outcome of direct democracy might differ from that of representative government. Capital punishment (the death penalty) is not legal in Canada, despite the fact that a majority of Canadians support it and have consistently done so from when polls were first taken on the issue.[4] In the United States, a majority of the population favours much stricter national gun control than is currently in place, yet gun control has made very little progress in the U.S. Congress. These are two cases where national referendums would clearly lead to a different policy outcome than has occurred with representative government.

Why does policy under representative government differ from that under direct democracy? There are at least three major reasons. First, as already mentioned, there is the matter of expert judgment. Representative governments have the capacity to obtain expert information and may therefore be in a position to make more informed judgments about some policy matters. Second, representative governments are more subject to interest-group lobbying than are private individuals. This is probably the reason why gun control has made little progress in the United States. The National Rifle Association

---

[4] A 2012 Angus Reid poll found that 63% of adult Canadian believe that the death penalty is "sometimes appropriate" and only 23% believe it is "never warranted"—Canada's current policy. See www.angus-reid .com/polls/44374/canadians-hold-conflicting-views-on-the-death-penalty/. The number favouring capital punishment was up from 42% in 2001 and 60% (in a Gallup poll) in 1990 and down slightly from 70% in favour in a 1982. In 1987, a free vote on reinstatement of capital punishment was held in the House of Commons. Reinstatement was defeated by a 148-127 margin. Capital punishment was abolished in Canada in 1976.

(NRA) is a very powerful lobby opposed to gun control that most politicians do not want to offend, and which some politicians benefit from.

Third, the representatives are different from the population at large. In general, politicians have higher incomes, are better educated, and come from more advantaged backgrounds than the average citizen. In addition, politicians tend to share certain personality traits and values, just as other occupational groups do. As a result, politicians have, as a group, a slightly different set of values and principles than the general population has, probably explaining why Canadian politicians have tended to oppose capital punishment (the death penalty) while public opinion has tended to be in favour.

Despite the examples given in the last few paragraphs, it should be emphasized that, generally, differences between policy and public opinion are not large, and certainly cross-country differences in policy are closely related to cross-country differences in public opinion. The correspondence between policy and public opinion is, however, far from perfect.

There are several ways in which representatives may be elected and governments formed. Virtually all modern democracies have a party system at the national level. Various individuals who stand for office align themselves with a particular political party and present a common platform or set of policies to the electorate. Not all party members might agree with the platform, but they find that the advantages of party alignment outweigh the costs.

In Canada, as in most countries, representatives are elected on a regional basis. Each member of Parliament (MP) must be elected from a particular riding, or area. One result of this process is that political debate in Canada includes significant regional competition for policy advantages. Each MP has a strong incentive to pursue the interests of his or her riding (or constituency within the riding) at the expense of the general public interest. For example, any MP who could persuade the government to grant defence contracts in his or her riding would face improved local re-election prospects, even if the local bidders presented higher-cost, lower-quality bids than bidders in other parts of Canada.

In part, of course, the system of regional representation has arisen because regional issues are important in Canada. However, the regional representation system reinforces the importance of regionalism.

5.2.2 Hotelling's Theory of Political Parties

It is difficult to predict the behaviour of political parties. Party platforms are based on a combination of pragmatic attempts to get re-elected and ideological commitments to particular policy agendas. One very simple theory of party platforms, first suggested by Hotelling (1929), is presented below. The basic assumptions of the theory are as follows:

1. There are two parties.
2. Each party wishes to maximize the number of votes it receives.
3. Voters are uniformly (evenly) distributed over a single left–right dimension.

These assumptions are simplifications of reality, but they allow us considerable insight into political platform formulation.

As indicated by assumption (3), voters are spread evenly over a single left–right dimension. We can represent this policy dimension with a line, as illustrated in Figure 5.1, and name the parties Party X and Party Y. Where will the parties locate their platforms along the line?

Suppose the parties begin at the polar positions: Party X at the extreme left, Party Y at the extreme right. In this situation, if each voter votes for the party closest to his or her preferred position, each party will then get exactly half the votes. If, however, Party X were to move slightly to the right, to point A on the diagram, it would gain votes. The voters to the left of point A will continue to vote for Party X, and the voters between point A and the extreme right will be evenly split between the two parties. Thus Party X will gain a majority of the votes.

In fact, the further to the right Party X moves, the more votes it gets. It can maximize its votes by moving as far to the right as it can, while still be-

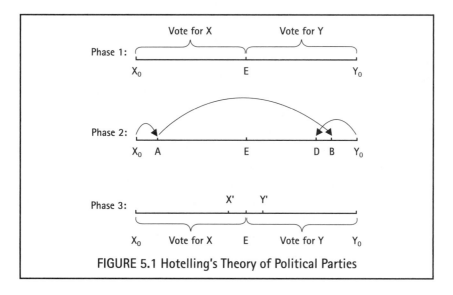

FIGURE 5.1 Hotelling's Theory of Political Parties

ing to the left of Party Y. This is (approximately) represented in the diagram by point *B*. Point *B* maximizes votes for Party X, given Party Y's position at the extreme right. If, however, Party X were to move to *B*, Party Y could then maximize its votes by leapfrogging over Party X and moving to point *D*. Party X would then move, and so on. The equilibrium, or resting point, of this process occurs with both parties beside each other at the middle of the spectrum, as represented by point *E*.

The prediction of this theory is that the two parties will cluster around the middle of the political spectrum. In practice, parties do not usually arrive at the midpoint of the spectrum by leapfrogging one another; they are more likely to approach the centre by gradually moving from an extreme position. This gradualist, dynamic path would be implied by a slight modification of Hotelling's theory. If, instead of maximizing votes, political parties were satisfied by moving just sufficiently far from their initial positions so as to gain a majority, then we would see such behaviour. In any case, the end equilibrium of the process seems to be very representative of actual party policies in countries like Canada and the United States, where there are typically (although not always) comparatively few differences of substance in overall party platforms of the major parties.

The assumption that voters are spread uniformly is unnecessary. Voters could also be spread, for example, according to a normal, bell-shaped distribution over the spectrum, or according to some asymmetric distribution. The general statement of Hotelling's theorem is that political parties will tend to cluster around the median, or middle, voter.

Hotelling's theory has two main implications. First, in a system dominated by two political parties, policy platforms between the two will not differ very much. Second, the policy platforms will closely match the preferences of the median voter. This is the median-voter principle.

Hotelling's analysis is complicated by the fact that policy issues are multidimensional rather than one-dimensional, as well as by the presence of additional parties. In addition, as already mentioned, party platforms reflect ideology as well as pragmatic vote maximizing. Despite these qualifications, however, Hotelling's principle has considerable descriptive power.

The median-voter property of the Hotelling model would seem to be desirable from a normative point of view. What is more democratic than to have the median policies adopted? One fundamental problem, however, is that voting does not take intensity of preference into account. Suppose, for example, that we have a population of one hundred people and are considering a policy that sixty people prefer. Assume that the average monetary value of the policy is $100 each to these sixty people who form the majority. Assume further that the other forty people (the minority) who dislike the policy would have their welfare reduced by $1,000 each if the policy were implemented. The policy would, therefore, generate costs to the minority of $40,000 in total, and benefits to the majority of only $6,000. The median voter, however, is one of the sixty who favour the policy. So if the median voter determines the outcome, the policy outcome would be inefficient in the sense that the costs would far exceed the benefits.

5.2.3 Committee Voting and the Power of the Agenda Setter

Consider the following problem. A committee of three Cabinet ministers must select one project to be funded out of three alternative projects. The three Cabinet ministers are the Minister of Energy, the Minister of Health, and the Minister of Transportation, and they must choose between a major energy development, a new state-of-the-art health centre, and new rapid transit lines. How can the three ministers choose?

The first voting system that comes to mind is majority voting. Suppose each minister votes for his or her most preferred project: the Energy minister for the energy project, the Health minister for the health centre, and the Transportation minister for rapid transit. Thus, each project gets one vote and no project has a majority. What should be done next? One approach is pair-wise majority voting: first deciding between one pair of projects using majority voting, and then deciding between the winner of that vote and the third project using majority voting.

To determine the outcome, we will need to know the preferences of all three committee members, as shown in Table 5.1.

This table shows that the Energy minister (in the first row) likes the energy project best, the health centre next and the rapid transit project least. The Minister of Health likes the health centre best, rapid transit next and so on.

TABLE 5.1 The Paradox of Voting

Ministry	Energy	Health Centre	Rapid Transit
Energy	1	2	3
Health	3	1	2
Transportation	2	3	1

The person who sets the agenda (the order of votes) can, in this situation, determine the project to be selected. For example, suppose the agenda setter favours the energy project. He or she should set up the first vote between the health centre and rapid transit. In this first vote, the health centre gets votes from the Minister of Health and from the Minister of Energy and wins by a vote of 2–1. The health centre project is then put up against the energy project. In this vote, the Minister of Energy and the Minister of Transportation both vote for the energy project and it wins by a vote of 2–1. Thus, the energy project is the overall winner.

Imagine now that the agenda setter had wanted rapid transit to win. In this case, the first vote would have been between the energy project and the health centre, which, as we have just seen, is won by the energy project by a vote of 2–1. The energy project would then be put up against rapid transit. This time, according to the preferences given in the above table, both the Ministers of Health and Transportation vote for rapid transit and it becomes the overall winner. The reader can verify that it would also be possible for the health centre to emerge as the winning project, depending on the order in which pair-wise votes were taken.

In this case, the agenda setter has great power. Note, however, that the agenda setter does not always have power. If all three ministers liked the energy project best, the order of pair-wise votes would not matter: the energy project would always win. Thus, the power of the agenda setter depends on the preferences of the committee members. In a wide range of circumstances, however, an agenda setter can exercise considerable influence.

There is no best voting procedure. As we have seen, overall first-choice voting may produce no winner, and pair-wise voting is subject to manipulation by the agenda setter. If each alternative is put up against each other alternative in round-robin fashion, this process may cycle endlessly, with no project emerging as the winner. This phenomenon is sometimes referred to as the paradox of voting.

Another voting scheme for committees is approval voting, in which each member of the committee votes for all the alternatives of which he or she approves, with the winning project being the one with the most approval votes. Still another voting method is point voting, in which each member of the committee is given a certain number of points to be allocated among the alternatives as he or she sees fit. This method takes intensity of feeling into account. Someone who is almost indifferent may divide up the points more or less evenly. Someone who cares passionately about a project may give all his or her points to that project. The project with the most points wins.

Each method of voting has advantages and disadvantages. The voting method deemed "best" will vary according to a number of factors, including the number of committee members, the number of alternatives, the importance of the policies, and other issues as well. We do not have space here to go into the properties of committee voting in detail. However, the reader should be aware that different voting systems will generally produce different policy outcomes.

5.2.4 Vote-Trading

As already indicated, individual members of a government will not, in general, fully support the platform of the governing party. Similarly, each member of a committee will normally have their own set of policy objectives within the many issues about which policy must be formulated. One member of a government or a committee may be very sensitive to environmental protection, another may be very interested in fishery enhancement, and a third might be very concerned about the pricing of natural gas, and so on. How are actual policies decided upon? One process, first described by Downs (1957), is referred to as vote-trading or logrolling.

Vote-trading occurs when different members of the policy-making group form coalitions to support one another's policy proposals. For example, a city council member who cares about creating more park space may agree to support another city council member's proposal for building a bridge, in return for a positive vote on park development. Downs argues that this vote-trading (or influence trading) process has certain desirable properties. However, the outcome of this process may easily differ from the policies prescribed by pure normative analysis.

5.2.5 The Normative Significance of Voting

A lesson that most people absorb from childhood is that voting has considerable normative significance. Thus, people will often argue that a particular policy is good simply because it won popular support, or that a political party has legitimacy because it was elected. Because we accept the process of voting as a good process, we accept the outcome as normatively appropriate (i.e., what should be done) even if as individuals we prefer a different alternative.

For example, the 1988 Canadian general election was fought largely on views of whether or not Canada should enter into the Canada–U.S. Free Trade Agreement (FTA), the forerunner of the North American Free Trade Agreement (NAFTA). Debate over the issue was vigorous, but when the party favouring the FTA (the Conservatives) won the election, there was general, though far from universal, agreement that the FTA should be implemented. The other political parties (the Liberals and the NDP) had sought to obstruct the FTA's progress prior to the election but cooperated in its speedy implementation after the election.

This approach could be used to establish principles of fairness. We could say that fair policies are those that are products of the political process. In practice, we do not take a position as extreme as this—we do not assume that all policy outcomes arising from voting are fair. In part, this is because we recognize that there is no best electoral system, and electoral outcomes depend on the details of the system. For example, if either the Australian electoral system, in which second place votes count, or the German system, in which a significant share of seats are allocated on the basis of overall popular vote, had been in place in Canada in 1988, the Conservatives and therefore the Canada–U.S. Free Trade Agreement would have been defeated.

Furthermore, we often find that something is unfair, despite the fact it is the result of a voting process. For example, many observers have claimed that a 2012 vote in favour a new Egyptian constitution entrenching a number of Islamic principles is unfair to Christian and other non-Islamic minorities.[5] More generally, minority ethnic groups and minority religious groups have often been seriously disadvantaged by majority voting. Therefore, while electoral legitimacy has some significance, we also think that factors beyond simple majority voting outcomes are important in assessing fairness.

5.3 Special Interest Groups and Transfer-Seeking

We have argued that voting is a major influence on policy and policy-makers. A second major external influence on policy-makers is interest-group activity. While the influence of voting on policy is obvious and relatively uncontroversial, the influence of interest groups is both subtle and a cause for concern.

It is worth distinguishing between two types of special interest groups: those concerned primarily with their own economic self-interest, and those trying to promote particular moral or social values. We will refer to these as economic interest groups and social interest groups, respectively. Sometimes a single interest group will undertake both kinds of activities. For example, the Canadian Labour Congress, a coalition of Canadian labour unions, is a strong proponent of policies that will benefit its members directly, but it also supports a variety of social policies that have little to do with the direct economic welfare of its members. Similar statements could be made about

---

[5] See, for example, Kirkpatrick and Fahim (2012).

the Canadian Federation of Independent Business (CFIB). For example, the CFIB lobbies for policies such as lower taxes on small business, a policy that directly affects its members, but its activities also promote values favouring free enterprise.

Despite this dual focus of some interest groups, most can be classified fairly easily as falling within one of the two categories. So-called pro-life (anti-abortion) and pro-choice (pro-abortion) groups, for example, are focused on a fundamental conflict of values that has relatively little to do with the economic self-interest of the people involved.

Some obvious economic interest groups include individual unions, specific industry lobbies, professional associations, and regional lobbies. It should be noted, of course, that even the most purely self-interested groups will usually claim, in public at least, that they have the overall public interest at heart.

5.3.1 Transfer-Seeking

Transfer-seeking (also called rent-seeking) is the process of devoting resources to trying to obtain or retain economic benefits through the redistribution of the wealth of others, rather than by creating new wealth. When the CEO of a major corporation spends his or her time and the company's money trying to persuade the government to provide special grants to the CEO's firm, this is transfer-seeking. The CEO is trying to redistribute wealth from taxpayers to the firm, and is using up resources in the process. Litigation in court is an example of transfer-seeking. When one corporation sues another for damages, the corporation bringing the lawsuit is trying to redistribute wealth from the other party to itself. No new wealth is created, and significant resources are used up in the process, including the time and effort of lawyers and other participants in the legal process.

An even more obvious form of transfer-seeking is theft. A thief is trying to redistribute wealth from the victims to himself, and all the resources consumed in the process represent net losses. Consider a thief who breaks into a car, causing $1,000 worth of damage to the car, in order to steal a stereo worth $400, which will perhaps be sold for about $200. The $1,000 in damage, the value of the thief's time, and the value of the victim's time used getting repairs to the car and buying another stereo are all pure losses.

The more resources are devoted to transfer-seeking, the more potential output we lose. If we spent all of our time transfer-seeking, nothing would be produced and we would all be very poor. Transfer-seeking is essentially a parasitic activity, but it can be very attractive from an individual point of view. An individual faces the choice of how best to allocate his or her resources in pursuing various objectives. If bringing a lawsuit or lobbying the government or theft will lead to a higher return than working in some wealth creating or productive activity, then the individual has a clear incentive to undertake the transfer-seeking activity.

Transfer-seeking has three major consequences:

1. Resources consumed in transfer-seeking are wasted from the social point of view.
2. There is a wealth transfer from society at large to the transfer-seeker.
3. The policy induced by transfer-seeking usually has pure waste associated with it.

One classic example of transfer-seeking is the firm seeking to obtain a monopoly franchise for some service. Such a franchise would be worth a substantial amount in expected future profits, and a company would be willing to use up a lot of resources in the process if it thought it could obtain such a franchise. Several companies may compete for this right, and the resources consumed in this process are costs, as indicated by the first point, above. Second, once a company has a franchise, it can charge a monopoly price. This illustrates the second point; the outcome of the transfer-seeking is a transfer from one group (consumers) to another (the firm). Finally, there will be a deadweight loss from the resulting monopoly power, as indicated by the third point.

Transfer-seeking greatly increases the cost of monopoly power, as is illustrated in the monopoly situation shown in Figure 5.2. The demand curve, *D*,

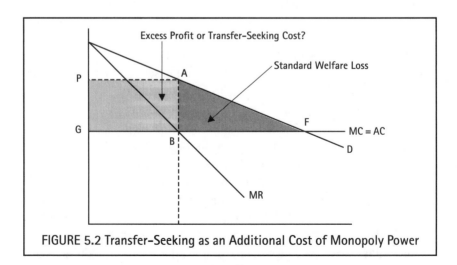

FIGURE 5.2 Transfer-Seeking as an Additional Cost of Monopoly Power

shows the quantity demanded for any possible price. The average cost *AC* and marginal cost *MC*–the cost of producing another unit of output–are assumed to be constant, which implies that they are both the same. Marginal revenue is shown by the curve *MR*. The monopolist wishes to maximize profit, and the marginalist principle for profit maximization by the monopolist implies that it should choose price (and output) so that marginal cost is just equal to marginal revenue.

As described further in Chapter 6, there is an efficiency loss, or welfare loss, associated with the monopoly. This loss is represented by triangle *ABF* and arises because a monopolist restricts output to a point at which consumers' willingness to pay (as shown by the demand curve) exceeds marginal cost. Thus, society is foregoing consumption that would generate a net surplus. This lost surplus is the efficiency loss, or deadweight loss, due to monopoly.

Consider the rectangle *PABG*. It is equal to the price-cost margin times the quantity sold. Costs are assumed to include all direct costs plus a normal return on capital, risk-taking, and entrepreneurial ability, so the price-cost margin represents a pure or above-normal profit per unit. The rectangle *PABG* therefore represents the total above-normal profit earned by the monopoly.

In the standard monopoly situation, area *ABF* is the resulting inefficiency, or deadweight loss. The socially efficient outcome is to produce where price equals marginal cost, which occurs if the firm produces at point *F*, charging price *G*. By charging the monopoly price *P*, the monopoly reduces consumers' surplus by area *PAFG*, of which area *PABG* is transferred to the firm as profit (resulting from a price above average cost). Consumers might not like the transfer of area *PABG* to the firm, but it does not appear to be inefficient. Consumers lose this amount but shareholders of the firm apparently gain this amount. Only the deadweight loss triangle *ABF* is an efficiency loss, since it is a loss to consumers that no one else gets.

This argument demonstrates the standard welfare cost of monopoly. Tullock (1967) argued, however, that area *PABG* is also likely to be a welfare loss, once transfer-seeking is considered. Tullock points out that there is competition to become a monopolist, especially in cases where monopoly power is created by government policy. Potential monopolists will lobby the government and fight with each other for the right to exploit consumers. How much will be consumed in the process? Tullock argues that approximately all of the potential above-normal profits will be consumed in the monopoly-creation process. After all, if there is a large supply of people wishing to be monopolists, and if their opportunity cost is the normal rate of return, then they should compete the value of the monopoly rents, net of transfer-seeking costs, down to the normal return.

A closely related transfer-seeking situation is created by import quotas, which are described in Chapter 8. Import quota licences allow certain importers to import goods but not others and restrict the total amount imported. This creates quota rents, since the scarce supply of the desired product allows importers to charge considerably higher prices for sales than they have to pay for goods on the world market. The competition for these quota rents will, however, use up much of the potential returns in transfer-seeking costs.

In Canada, as in most developed countries, quotas and the associated quota rents are a relatively minor business phenomenon. In many other countries, however, the creation of quota rents is very important. Many economists argue that the pervasiveness of transfer-seeking activities is one of the greatest barriers to economic development in a significant number of countries.

Transfer-seeking situations are common. In many cities, entry into the taxi business is restricted by local government, creating large rents and large transfer-seeking costs. As already mentioned, litigation is an example of transfer-seeking, as are theft and other economic crimes. In recent years, considerable controversy has arisen over insider trading in financial markets. This is largely a transfer-seeking activity, since insiders transfer wealth from shareholders of firms to themselves. Business lobbying is mainly a transfer-seeking activity, as are strikes in the workplace. The ultimate transfer-seeking activity is war.

The costs of transfer-seeking are high. The direct economic costs are substantial, but there is a secondary cost as well. If the general perception is created that rewards in society are a return to special privilege created by lobbying or dishonesty, then the motivation to succeed through the creation of new wealth (i.e., through productive activities) is very much reduced. If auto industry pioneer Henry Ford or telephone inventor Alexander Graham Bell had decided to lobby for government grants before proceeding with their commercial enterprises, we might all be walking to work and communicating mainly by writing letters.

Two final points should be made about transfer-seeking. First, service provision should not be confused with transfer-seeking activities. Services such as health care, education, and financial advising are productive even though no physical output is produced. It is true that most transfer-seeking activities appear in national income accounting under the services category, and the value of services is therefore overstated in gross domestic product calculations. However, most services are productive in the sense that they add to the stock of things that make people better off.

The one category of services that probably is largely transfer-seeking is legal services, since most legal activity involves attempts to redistribute income and wealth. Magee (1991) argues that litigation imposes a significant burden on the U.S. economy. He states,

> The costs of litigation-specific economic predation include the failure to accumulate capital because of the erosion of property rights, the time wasted fighting spurious claims, the economic loss of engineers, doctors, and executives who become redistributive litigators, and the discouragement of innovation because of excessive product liability.

Magee is not hopeful about legislative change, however, because so many legislators and the entire judiciary are members of the interest group that benefits most from litigation—the legal profession itself.

The second concluding point is that, even if we could, we do not want to eliminate all transfer-seeking activity. While it is true that transfer-seeking is economically inefficient, the transfers of wealth created by transfer-seeking may, in some cases, be beneficial from a broader point of view. The court system is one example. If Ms. Sparks is careless in using her barbecue and sets her neighbour's house on fire, we regard it as appropriate that the neighbour be able to seek redress in court, even though the costs to the government and the parties involved may well exceed the magnitude of the settlement. While the court system is an extremely inefficient way of making transfers of income, it is probably necessary that it be available for settling disputes, thereby maintaining certain principles of fairness, and to avoid even more costly methods of settling disputes, such as resorting to violence.

A second example of possibly beneficial transfer-seeking involves some charitable organizations. When the Canadian National Institute for the Blind lobbies governments to provide money for training guide dogs, it is transfer-seeking. Donation requests are also transfer-seeking, but not many of us would speak out in opposition. The general point is that most people would approve of the wealth transfers created by some transfer-seeking activities on equity grounds, even if some economic inefficiency is created.

Despite the possibility that the transfers caused by transfer-seeking might be socially worthwhile in some cases, it should be emphasized that the equity effects of most transfer-seeking activities are seen by most as undesirable. This is because those who already have substantial influence are in the best position to undertake successful transfer-seeking activities. This strengthens the basic presumption against transfer-seeking. It has even been argued by some that the basic success of a society is closely related to its ability to keep transfer-seeking institutions to a minimum so that as many resources as possible are devoted to productive pursuits.

5.3.2 The Transitional Gains Trap

One interesting phenomenon related to transfer-seeking is the transitional gains trap. The argument is that successful transfer-seeking by an interest group will lead to only transitional gains. This idea is best illustrated by some examples.

In many North American cities, taxi drivers are required to have special operating licences. In New York City, these licences are called "medallions." The number of medallions is fixed at well below the number that would emerge in a competitive market. As a result, taxi cabs can charge higher fares, and drivers and taxi companies can earn above-normal profits. And getting a medallion is not cheap. Medallions must be purchased from someone else, and they are valuable, for they confer the right to monopoly profits. The market price of medallions should equal the present value of the stream of monopoly profits arising from ownership of the medallion. In 2012, the average price for a single medallion in New York City was approximately $700, 000—more than double the price of only ten years earlier.

From the driver's point of view, the cost of the medallion offsets the monopoly rent he expects to earn. Therefore, his overall return is only the amount he would have earned without the medallion system—the opportunity cost, which is quite low, of those people willing to be taxi drivers. If one objective of the medallion policy was to increase the income of taxi drivers, then the gain of the medallion system is only transitional: only early recipients of the medallions experience a gain, much of which is realized when they sell their medallions. Once medallions are priced to fully reflect the monopoly rents created by the medallion system, drivers who buy medallions earn no more than they would have earned without the system. Many medallions are purchased by taxi companies who then just hire drivers at their (relatively low) opportunity cost. In addition, there is now deadweight loss arising from the monopoly power created by the policy.

The basic problem is that the monopoly profits created by the medallion policy are *capitalized* in the cost of gaining entry into the protected group. Having paid the entry cost, the net returns to entrants are at the normal level, the level of the entrant's opportunity cost. At least, this is what we expect if there is a competitive supply of people wishing to get into the protected group. This makes it very hard to undo the policy, for removing the policy will cause the expensive medallions that the drivers regard as valuable assets to suddenly lose their value, thus reducing the net returns of the protected group to below-normal levels. The original beneficiaries of the policy, the first entrants, earned windfall rents, and their benefit is not taken away. From the policy point of view, however, the benefits are only temporary because soon there is a new group of taxi drivers earning low incomes, and people looking for taxis have trouble finding them.

In Canada, a good example of the transitional gains trap in action is the national dairy quota system initiated in the early 1970s by the dairy industry. The objective was to raise the incomes of dairy farmers, and the policy was effective in that quotas reduced output so that higher prices could be maintained. In effect, the policy created monopoly power in a previously competitive industry.

Current dairy farmers must buy or inherit quotas from the people who received the quotas originally or bought them subsequently. The value of monopoly rents created by the quota system is capitalized in the price of quotas, so the net effect of the quota does not raise the overall income of a farmer who must buy the quota to be allowed to produce and sell output. Consumers pay high prices for milk but the current farmers earn only normal returns. Society as a whole still suffers and incurs costs of a system that created only temporary gains more than forty years ago. As of early 2013, the cost of a quota granting the right to produce and sell dairy products containing one kilogram of butterfat per day was approximately $40,000 in British Columbia and Alberta; $30,000 in Saskatchewan and Manitoba; and $25,000 in Ontario, Quebec, and the Atlantic provinces.[6]

5.3.3 Economic Interest Groups

Economic interest groups have a major influence on public policy toward business. Unfortunately, it is hard to determine the extent of interest-group activity in Canada. One useful measure is maintained by Canada's Commissioner of Lobbying. In Canada, organizations and individuals who lobby elected or unelected government officials are required to register with the commissioner. Over just a seven-year period, 2005 through 2012, the number of registered active lobbyists increased dramatically, from 3,294 to 5,162 between

---

[6] See www.dairyinfo.gc.ca/index_e.php?s1=dff-fcil&s2=quota&s3=qe&page=intro.

August 2005 and August 2012.[7] Some lobbyists are corporations, some are unions, some are trade associations, and many are hired consultants who will lobby on behalf of various clients who pay for their services. The leading lobbying areas are international trade, government procurement, and regional economic development.

The registry applies only to federal government lobbying. There is also an enormous amount of lobbying at provincial and local government levels. Furthermore, large corporations typically have a significant staff, headed by a senior executive, devoted to business–government relations. In total, all this lobbying activity represents a very substantial amount of transfer-seeking.

Not all lobbying is transfer-seeking, however. Lobbyists actually do produce something of value: information. A successful lobbyist is one who can provide Cabinet ministers, members of Parliament, and senior public servants with useful information. This information is offered as a return to the policy-maker for spending time with the lobbyist. A lobbyist who offers very biased or inaccurate information or who has nothing to offer will not have much access to senior policy-makers. It might be the case that the amount of useful information produced by lobbyists is small compared to the total amount of resources consumed in lobbying, in which case we would assume that lobbying is mostly transfer-seeking, but it is possible to make a case that lobbying has a significant productive component.

A second argument that can be made for the value of economic interest-group lobbying is that it helps to offset some basic public policy biases. In fact, business lobbies and consumer lobbies can often be found arguing for policies that are closer to those suggested by normative policy analysis than are the policies offered by politicians. For example, business lobbies have argued for trade liberalization, reducing the government budget deficit, removing rent controls, and generally restricting the role of government in the economy. In the absence of such lobbies, it is argued, governments would be even more tempted than they already are to try to gain short-term political advantage by adventuring in policy areas where they do very little good and often do net harm.

This argument may be too generous to lobbyists. Certainly much, and probably most, lobbying is pure transfer-seeking that acts to the detriment of the public interest at large. However, the extent of lobbying and the analysis

---

[7] Lobbying statistics and much other information about lobbying can be found at the website of Canada's Commissioner of Lobbying at https://ocl-cal.gc.ca/eic/site/012.nsf/eng/h_00000.html.

of many examples suggest that economic interest-group lobbying is very effective. Why?

Lobbying is effective because a small, well-organized group with a lot at stake has much more incentive to get involved in the political process than does a broad, diffuse group. For example, the CEO of a major corporation has a strong incentive to lobby the government for grants or special protection. If successful, he or she may earn hundreds of thousands, possibly millions, of dollars in higher income. The losers in the deal are taxpayers. Most taxpayers will not even be aware that the deal is proceeding, and the liability for any one taxpayer is small—perhaps a few dollars and rarely more than a few hundred dollars. No one is likely to pay the airfare to Ottawa and other travel costs to argue over a few dollars or even over a few hundred dollars. Interest groups are effective because the benefits of lobbying are concentrated and the costs are diffuse. Therefore, the beneficiaries have an incentive to get involved; individual losers do not.

5.3.4 Examples of Business Lobbying

In 2012, one of the major lobbying stories in Canada concerned a possible Northern Gateway pipeline to run from Bruderheim, Alberta, (near Edmonton) to Kitimat, British Columbia. The pipeline would carry output from the Alberta oil sands to the port of Kitimat for transport to Asia via oil tankers. The project would be developed by Enbridge Inc., an oil pipeline company based in Alberta.

Enbridge devoted a large effort to lobbying the federal government to obtain regulatory approval for the pipeline, but largely neglected the B.C. government until significant resistance in that province became apparent in 2012.[8] Enbridge then shifted its efforts to B.C., seeking to influence the provincial government, Aboriginal communities that would be affected by the pipeline, environmental groups, and general public opinion.

In the United States, the passage of expanded health care legislation in 2010 (the Affordable Health Care Act) led to enormous lobbying campaigns by interested parties to modify the legislation. The debate over health care policy was taken up in Congress, in the Supreme Court, and in state governments throughout the country. Ultimately, a Supreme Court decision in 2012 and Barack Obama's 2012 presidential election victory settled many of the issues.

---

[8] See Dene (2012).

It is difficult to assess the total amount spent on lobbying over the Affordable Health Care Act, as partisans on both sides exaggerate expenditures by the other side and understate their own, and there is no reliable nonpartisan accounting. Certainly, however, hundreds of millions of dollars were spent. Lobbying organizations included the health insurance industry association (AHIP), the American Hospitals Association (AHA), AARP (formerly the American Association of Retired Persons), chambers of commerce, drug companies, and labour unions, along with other interested parties.

There is no doubt that business lobbies and other economic interest groups have been and continue to be important influences on public policy, but it is increasingly difficult for such groups to be successful through a case based on direct self-interest. A request for a public policy change is more likely to be successful if it is based on carefully argued normative rationales for such changes.

5.3.5 Social Interest Groups

Social interest groups also have a major influence on policy and have proven quite effective in changing the political centre of gravity. Most Americans are not opposed to abortion and support the idea that birth control is very important in improving the economic circumstances of less-developed countries. Nevertheless, U.S. anti-abortion groups were successful in the 1980s in eliminating U.S. contributions to international birth control agencies that include the option of abortion. Some contributions were subsequently restored, but even in the early 21st century, this remains an important issue in funding international family planning organizations.

In Canada, organized lobbies on both sides have made abortion a very sensitive issue. Environmental lobbies have made politicians very concerned about environmental issues. Relatively small humanitarian, religious, and ethnically based interest groups have had a large impact on immigration policy.

Why are social interest groups more effective than their numbers alone might suggest? One reason is that members of social interest groups are often one-issue voters. They will vote for the candidate coming closest to their position on the issue they care about, regardless of other issues. This affects a candidate for office in a clear way, as the following example shows.

Suppose there are one hundred voters, twenty of whom feel strongly that activity A should be outlawed, and who will vote for any candidate taking their position. Suppose the other eighty voters see nothing wrong with activity A, but are concerned about a variety of issues, so that a candidate who opposes activity A has only a 10 percent chance of losing any particular voter in this group. Under a system of direct democracy, an up or down vote over activity A would result in a landslide in favour of legalizing the activity. A candidate in an election for a representative government would, however, have an incentive to oppose activity A. By doing so, he or she will gain twenty votes for certain and will lose an expected vote total of 10 percent of eighty, or eight votes, producing a net gain of 12 votes.

There are other reasons for the effectiveness of social interest groups. They make life difficult for policy-makers because they are prepared to spend their own time taking up the time and energy of busy politicians and government officials. In addition, they put elected officials in an adversarial position in the news media, which is very damaging to political fortunes, and they make campaign contributions. As a result, there are strong incentives for policy-makers to be very sensitive to the demands of social interest groups.

It is not clear whether the power of interest groups is good or bad. Many people resent interest-group lobbying, feeling it leaves ordinary citizens under-represented in the political process. But any citizen may join (or create) a social interest group. Interest groups are one way in which intensity of preference is taken into account in the political process. If 10 percent of the population feels passionately about something, while the other 90 percent feels only a slight preference for the opposite policy, is it obvious which policy direction is appropriate?

There have, of course, been some disastrous policy outcomes from the interest-group process. Perhaps the most striking example was the Prohibition period in the United States. In 1919 (until 1933), alcohol consumption was made illegal in the United States. This was largely as a result of the efforts of organized lobbies, particularly the Anti-Saloon League and the Women's Christian Temperance Union. A clear majority of Americans at the time occasionally drank alcohol, and a substantial minority continued to drink alcohol despite Prohibition.

The resulting flagrant violation of the law by many citizens, including police, judges, and politicians, caused a general decline in respect for the law. The costs of trying to enforce Prohibition were enormous. In addition, there was a substantial loss of tax revenue because the alcohol industry was forced underground. Perhaps most importantly, the profits from illegal alcohol distribution allowed organized crime to establish itself as a major force in the United States. The point here is not to argue that alcohol is good or bad. The point is simply that a small, focused interest group can have considerable influence despite disagreement by the majority and despite the high costs of the policy advocated by the interest group.

The power of social interest groups suggests that an organized minority can be very effective in exploiting or at least controlling a disorganized majority. Nevertheless, political scientists have traditionally been more concerned with the possible exploitation of a minority by a majority, and certainly there have been some terrible examples of this, including the treatment of Jews in Nazi Germany. However, in modern democratic societies, organized minorities often have substantial influence over policy. Some political scientists have coined the term "minoritarianism" to describe situations of apparent bias in favour of organized minorities in the public policy process.

5.3.6 Interest Groups and Financing of Political Parties

One potentially important way for interest groups to obtain influence is through campaign contributions. A significant fraction of campaign funding is provided through government programs (i.e., paid by taxpayers). Tax credits and direct subsidies by the federal government to political parties, combined with publicly funded contributions to individual candidates, have accounted for about 40 percent of total expenses in recent elections. The other 60 percent comes from other sources, raising the question of whether interest groups are heavily involved in campaign financing.

In Canada, as of 2012, the maximum allowable individual political contribution was $1,100 per year.[9] An individual may, in a given year, give this amount to a political party, an electoral district association, a candidate for a party nomination, a leadership candidate, *and* an election candidate. Thus, an individual could, in principle, give several thousand dollars to political contestants in a given year. However, typical individual contributions are fairly small, and relatively few people actually make donations. Most contributions by individuals are on the order of $100 to $200, and only just over one percent of the Canadian population makes contributions to political parties. Since 2007, corporations and labour unions have no longer been allowed to make contributions to political parties or candidates.

In Canada, each significant contribution to a political party or candidate must be disclosed. In addition, parties are limited in the amount of electronic media advertising they can buy during election campaigns. The advertising limits for a party are based largely on its success in the previous election. Overall, although there are some concerns about campaign financing, it seems that campaign contributions do not act as a major conduit of interest-group influence in Canada.

---

[9] Information on campaign contributions is provided on the Elections Canada website at www.elections.ca.

As Canada has reduced interest-group influence on election financing, the United States has gone in the opposite direction. A controversial Supreme Court decision in 2010 (*Citizens United vs. Federal Election Commission*) largely removed the restraints then in place on campaign finance in the United States, thereby allowing unlimited spending by "independent" groups in election and nomination campaigns. Thus, an organization (often called a political action committee, or "PAC") can be set up to act in parallel with the candidate. As long as the PAC remains legally independent, its actions are essentially unlimited. The 2012 general election in the United States cost well over $4 billion,[10] vastly more per capita than is spent on elections in other democratic countries.

5.4 Direct Self-Interest

So far, we have considered the two major external sources of pressure on policy-makers: voting and interest-group lobbying. These external pressures are important because they affect the self-interest of policy-makers. Politicians will be sensitive to voting pressures, and they will be sensitive to interest-group lobbying. In addition, however, policy-makers are subject to direct self-interest. Decisions they make affect their own welfare directly, leading to conflicts of interest, and at the very least, policy-makers can be expected to take advantage of the perquisites of their positions. We will focus separately on unelected government officials (the bureaucracy) and on elected officials.

5.4.1 The Theory of Bureaucracy

Strictly speaking, a bureaucracy is a non-elected government body characterized by a hierarchical system of specialization that formulates and implements government policy. It has also become common for any complex hierarchical system of organization, especially if associated with fixed rules and "red tape," to be referred to as a bureaucracy, even in the private sector. In this book, however, the term "bureaucracy" is used in the strict sense and refers only to government. It is used synonymously with the terms "civil service" and "public service."

The history of literature owes much to bureaucracy. The earliest known literature, that deriving from ancient Egypt, was dominated by rules of conduct for young officials in the imperial bureaucracy. The Chinese imperial bureaucracy of eunuchs has been immortalized in the writings of many

---

[10] See Christensen (2012) in Sources.

Chinese scholars, including Confucius, and both Plato and Machiavelli wrote their best-known works on the subject of bureaucracy. Much of this literature is very critical of bureaucracy, although usually employing a subtle and ironic style.

In some countries, such as Japan and France, employment in the senior bureaucracy is accorded the highest status and is regarded as appropriate for only the most able and intelligent. In Victorian (19th century) England, the senior bureaucracy in the Foreign Office and the Colonial Office were drawn from the highest ranks of society. The domestic civil service was next in status, with employment in the universities, professions (law and medicine), and business ranking much lower.

In North America, however, as in most of the modern world, the bureaucracy is viewed with suspicion, and government managers are often viewed as inferior to their business counterparts. In Canada, senior bureaucrats are often described in unflattering terms, although they are probably accorded more respect than in the United States.

Our question is, "What do bureaucrats do?" One extreme but influential answer is provided by Niskanen (1971), who presents what might be described as a Leviathan theory of bureaucracy. The elements of Niskanen's theory are as follows:

1. The bureaucracy carries out valuable programs that society at large and the elected government are willing to pay for.
2. The bureaucracy will maximize its own welfare, which is directly correlated with slack—the difference between the budget it receives for a program and the minimum cost of carrying out the program. This slack is consumed by the bureaucracy in various ways: thick carpets, large staffs, generous expense accounts, etc.
3. The bureaucracy knows the true cost of its programs much better than elected officials do. As a result, the government will pay the budget asked for by the bureau, as long as the benefit of the program exceeds the budget cost. The main implication of this theory is presented in Figure 5.3.

In Figure 5.3, there is a demand for the service provided by the bureau, denoted by D. The average cost and marginal cost of production are equal and denoted by the line $MC = AC$. The normatively efficient outcome would be to offer amount Q^* of the program at a cost equal to AC times Q^*, as represented by the shaded area under the average cost curve. If the good could

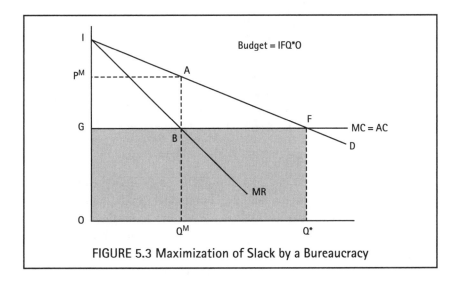

FIGURE 5.3 Maximization of Slack by a Bureaucracy

be provided by a monopolist on a price-per-unit basis, the monopolist would supply output Q^M and charge price P^M, leaving consumers with surplus IAP^M.

Under Niskanen's theory of bureaucracy, the bureau is able to set both the quantity of service and the total budget. The political authority is assumed to accept the total budget offer as long as the total budget does not exceed the total (gross) benefit of the service. If the bureau wishes to maximize slack, it will offer amount Q^* for a budget almost equal to the entire area under the demand curve, up to Q^*. In other words, it will ask for a budget equal to the minimum cost, plus almost all the surplus associated with the program. As long as there is some residual surplus, the government will accept the bureau's offer, and taxpayers will wind up with almost no surplus from the program. The outcome is worse for taxpayer-citizens than if the service were provided by a private monopoly.

This theory is an extreme and inaccurate version of bureaucratic behaviour. Even Niskanen would not say it is accurate. Many government programs are carried out efficiently and effectively by the civil service. In addition, the theory assumes that the bureaucracy merely implements policy (i.e., produces desired services) and does not formulate it. However, a growing literature stresses the role of bureaucrats as architects of policy. Niskanen's theory does, however, illustrate two important insights. First, bureaucrats have an incentive to create slack in government programs because they are not subject to market discipline. Second, a bureaucracy has even more potential monopoly power than a private monopoly. These insights contain a lot of truth and explain much of what we see. The real world is not as extreme as Niskanen's model, but the model does contribute to an overall understanding of bureaucracy.

These ideas were well-expressed by Sir Humphrey Appleby, fictional permanent secretary of the fictional U.K. Department of Administrative Affairs:[11]

> The Civil Service does not make profits or losses. Ergo we measure success by the size of our staff and our budget. By definition a big department is more successful than a small one.... This simple proposition is the basis of our whole system. Nobody had asked the NW controller to save 32 million pounds.... Suppose everybody started saving money irresponsibly all over the place?

In defence of bureaucrats, it should be pointed out that the foreign and colonial bureaucracies of Victorian England and many modern civil servants are widely regarded as very good managers. Part of what is needed for bureaucratic success is a sense of professionalism and esprit de corps. In addition, a set of analytical tools that can aid in making good decisions, and more importantly, an incentive structure that encourages good performance are also necessary. In most bureaucracies, salary is related to the importance of the task, as measured by the number of people under one's supervision and the size of the budget being managed. This creates an incentive to maximize slack. It would make more sense to give bonuses for carrying out tasks at lower cost, as in the private sector.

5.4.2 Conflict of Interest and Self-Interested Politicians

Perhaps the most obvious explanation of why actual policies might differ from normative prescriptions is simply that a policy-maker has enriched him or herself through the use of government policy. A government official may accept bribes or kickbacks in return for awarding contracts to certain firms rather than to others. Or the official might make policy decisions intended to improve the profitability of firms owned by friends and family.

All countries, including Canada, have a long history of such corruption in public office. In many political jurisdictions in the world, including some U.S.

---

[11] Lynn and Jay (1984), p. 59.

cities and states, bribes are an expected part of an elected official's income. It should be pointed out, however, that the increased frequency of conflict of interest cases in Canadian politics in recent decades reflects increased scrutiny of public officials and higher standards of integrity, rather than an increase in self-interested behaviour. This elevation in scrutiny and in standards has very likely reduced the use of political office for personal financial gain. Furthermore, while such activity is not likely to disappear any time soon, corruption and abuse of power in Canadian policy-making is very much the exception rather than the rule.

6

Firms and Markets

6.1 Introduction

In Chapter 3, we established the basic idea that competitive free enterprise is an effective form of economic organization. However, if markets are not very competitive, we cannot be nearly so confident about the benefits of private enterprise. As argued in Chapter 3, imperfect competition is an important rationale for government intervention. Most markets will not be perfectly competitive, so the real questions become, "Is there a workable or reasonable level of competition?" "What happens in markets where there are only a few firms?" and "How do public policies of various types affect markets?" An essential step in answering such questions is understanding the basic characteristics of firms and markets. The objective of this chapter is to provide an overview of the theory of the firm and the theory of markets. The study of firms and markets is often referred to as industrial organization.

6.2 The Firm

Markets are composed of firms, and these firms determine the performance of each market. Firms produce most of what is consumed and are the basic unit of organization in modern market-based economies. Firms vary tremendously in size and scope. Many employ only one or a few workers and carry out highly specialized tasks. On the other hand, very large firms, such as Toyota and Microsoft, employ thousands of people and have budgets larger than many national governments. Most firms are specific to one location in their operations, but some operate in hundreds of locations.

Corporate fortunes can change quickly. Apple, started in the garage of Steve Jobs' home in the 1970s (displacing his father's old car parts), became the most valuable company in history in 2012, beating out the record set by Microsoft, another company that went from being a small start-up to a corporate giant in a short time. Google grew even faster, starting out in 1997 as a hobby program created by two Stanford University graduate students using university computers. In addition to becoming an enormous corporation, surpassing Microsoft to become world's second-largest tech company in 2012, Google even created a new verb in the process—as in, "to google" a subject on the Internet.

In Canada, most large firms are corporations, meaning they are legally incorporated and have limited liability: shareholders of the firm cannot be held personally liable for the firm's debts beyond their own investment in the firm. However, a large majority of firms are small, and most of those are not incorporated but are sole proprietorships or partnerships that do not have limited liability. Such a firm is basically an extension of the individual or partners who own the firm, from a tax and financial liability point of view. Table 6.1 offers a list of Canada's largest corporations, ordered by revenue.

TABLE 6.1 Canada's Largest Corporations in 2011 (in 2011 dollars) by Revenue

Rank	Company	Industry	Revenue ($billions)
1	Manulife Financial	Insurance	50.1
2	Suncor Energy	Oil and Gas	39.6
3	Royal Bank of Canada	Banking	35.8
4	Power Corp. of Canada	Financial	32.9
5	George Weston/Loblaw	Grocery	32.4
6	Imperial Oil	Oil and Gas	30.5
7	Magna International	Automotive	28.9
8	Toronto–Dominion Bank	Banking	27.2
9	Bank of Nova Scotia	Banking	26.7
10	Onex Corp.	Financial	24.4

Source: The *Financial Post* 500 at www.infomart.com/2012/06/19 /top-12-companies-in-canada-fp500-database/.

This list is interesting in several respects. First of all, it is dominated by traditional companies in traditional industries, particularly the financial sector. The fifth company on the list, George Weston Ltd., might not be familiar to readers at first glance, but it is the parent of the Loblaw supermarket chain, which includes the Superstore chains in western and Atlantic Canada and the Provigo chain in Quebec.

Despite the great diversity of the business world, there is one unifying principle: private sector business firms of all types are in business to earn profits. (Government-owned firms are likely to have objectives other than the pursuit of profits.) The basic activity of any firm is to acquire inputs, use them in some productive process, and market the output. The inputs are normally either purchased from sellers or provided by the owners of the firm. The revenue of the firm is the output quantities multiplied by the prices at which the outputs are sold. Costs can be divided into two categories: contractual costs, which are the costs of purchased (or rented) inputs, and noncontractual costs, which are the opportunity costs of the factors provided by the owners of the firm, including their own labour. The firm's economic profit is revenue minus total costs. Thus, an economic profit of zero includes a return to the owners of the firm equal to their opportunity cost. This opportunity cost paid to the firm's owners is sometimes referred to as *normal* profit.

Accounting statements do not directly report economic profits. One problem is that it is difficult to measure normal profits and include them as a cost. Another problem is that even contractual costs and revenues can be hard to measure. For example, if the firm buys a computer that will last for several years, how should the cost of the computer be assigned? Ideally, costs should be assigned in accordance with economic depreciation. For example, if a new computer comes to market rendering the purchased computer obsolete and reducing its market value to zero, then that computer should, from an economic point of view, be written down to zero immediately. However, accounting conventions operate differently. There are, of course, conventions for dealing with almost any situation that might arise, but these conventions do not (and cannot) coincide exactly with economic fundamentals.

Accounting statements report a variety of calculations related to economic profits, two of which are the rate of return on assets and the rate of return on equity. A sample calculation of these rates of return is shown in Table 6.2.

Note that the total assets and the total of liabilities and shareholders' equity are the same. This relationship arises due to the fact that shareholders' equity is the difference between assets and liabilities. If liabilities equal assets, then shareholders' equity drops to zero.

TABLE 6.2 Loblaw Companies 2011 Rates of Return

Assets	($billion)
Credit card receivables	$2.101
Inventories in stores	2.025
Other current assets	2.336
Fixed assets	8.725
Other assets	2.241
Total	17.43
Liabilities and Shareholders' Equity	
Current liabilities	4.718
Long-term debt	5.493
Other liabilities	1.210
Shareholders' equity	6.007
Total	17.43

Net earnings = $0.769 billion
Rate of return on equity = Earnings/Equity = 0.769/6.007 = 12.8%
Rate of return on total assets = Earnings/Assets = 0.769/17.43 = 4.4%

Source: *Loblaw Companies Limited Annual Report 2011*, p. 47.

The rate of return on equity is a useful measure of profitability, provided measured costs and measured revenues coincide reasonably well with actual economic costs and revenues. A firm acting in the interests of its current shareholders should, other things being equal, try to maximize this rate of return. Shareholders might also be interested in the risk characteristics or variability of the rate of return.

Another commonly used measure of financial performance is the rate of return on assets. As assets are equal to liabilities (debt) plus equity, the return on assets reflects the return to all financial investors in the firm, including bondholders and others creditors, in additional to shareholders. A firm earning normal profits should be able to provide a rate of return on equity equal to the competitive rate of return on financial capital for shareholders.

Both high earnings and rates of return on equity allow the firm to pay out higher dividends to shareholders or retain the earnings in the firm. Over the long run, a firm that pays no dividends but reinvests earnings in new projects should have faster growth in the value of shares than a comparable company that pays out its earnings in dividends. From the shareholder's point of view, it is better to have the money paid out in dividends if the shareholder can make better use of the money than the firm can.

An important aspect of the modern corporate world is that the owners of the firm, the shareholders, rarely control the firm. Firms are controlled by top management and, to some extent, by boards of directors, who are supposed to represent the shareholders. However, the interests of boards of directors, top management, and shareholders may diverge substantially, introducing an important possible source of market inefficiency. Government regulation is increasingly concerned with controlling and correcting such market failures.

Because of the problems created by this separation of ownership and control, many people have questioned whether modern corporations really do maximize profits. It has been argued by Jensen and Meckling (1976), among others, that the modern corporation is best viewed as a complex mesh of contracts between self-interested individuals. The managers are, in effect, the agents of the shareholders and bondholders, so the analysis of principal and agency relationships subsumes the theory of the firm as a special case. Managers would be expected to maximize their own welfare, which will coincide only partially with maximizing the profits of the firm.

The agency approach to the theory of the firm contains many valuable insights, but for a variety of reasons, the traditional idea that firms strive to maximize profits has proved to be very robust. One reason is the survivor principle: firms that fail to maximize profits will tend to disappear or at least diminish. In this book, we treat the idea that firms maximize profits as the main unifying element in the theory of the firm.

We should, however, keep in mind that firms are much more than profit-maximizing automatons. They are complex organizations that are similar in many ways to other organizations. Furthermore, to say that firms are in business to make a profit does not really answer the question of why firms exist or why they take the form they do. We do not address such questions here, but the reader should be aware that a significant literature on the firm as an organization does exist.

6.3 Market Structure

The next useful step in industrial organization is classification of markets into five distinct market structures: monopoly, dominant firm, oligopoly, monopolistic competition, and perfect competition. This ordering ranks market structures from the least to the most competitive. In examining the different market structures, we will use a different ordering. The natural starting point for analysis is the theory of perfect competition. Monopoly is the next easiest market structure to understand, and the dominant firm structure is a small modification of pure monopoly. Monopolistic competition is considered next, leaving the most difficult and most interesting market structure, oligopoly, until last.

6.3.1 Perfect Competition

Perfect competition was defined in Chapter 3 and that definition is repeated here. It requires the following four conditions:

1. Buyers and sellers are sufficiently numerous that no buyer or seller has control over prices, which therefore are taken by individual firms as given or exogenous.
2. The product is homogeneous; that is, each seller sells the same product.
3. Buyers and sellers have access to all information relevant to their production and consumption decisions and can transact easily (with low transaction costs).
4. There is free entry and exit in the long run.

Chapter 3 also stated that perfect competition is efficient. Figure 6.1 illustrates this assertion using the cost curves of a competitive firm. In the figure, the price is taken as constant, as illustrated by line *PP*. For a purely competitive firm, marginal revenue—the extra revenue from selling one more unit of output—is equal to price. Because price is constant, marginal revenue is just equal to the price; there is no price decline to be concerned about. Marginal cost is shown by curve *MC* and average cost by curve *AC*. As is customary in economic analysis, the costs represented by these curves are assumed to include opportunity costs in the form of normal profits to owners of the firms.

The marginalist principle for the profit-maximizing firm requires that the firm set marginal cost equal to marginal revenue, which in this case is the price. The firm will therefore produce where the marginal cost curve crosses the price line. In addition, free entry implies that no above-normal profits be earned in the long run (at least for marginal firms). If above-normal profits were being earned, more firms would enter the industry and price would fall until profits were reduced to their normal level. This implies that, in the long run, price must equal average cost. Furthermore, it is a property of

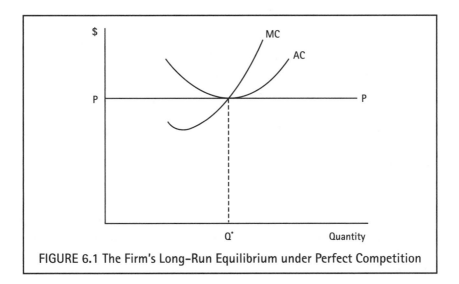

FIGURE 6.1 The Firm's Long-Run Equilibrium under Perfect Competition

marginal and average quantities that marginal cost must cut average cost at the minimum point of the average cost curve. Figure 6.1 illustrates all this. In long-run equilibrium, the following condition holds:

$$P = MC = AC = Min\ AC$$

where *P* stands for price, and *Min AC* denotes minimum average cost.

The basic efficiency comes about because market price is, as described in Chapter 2, a measure of society's marginal benefit from consuming a little more of the good. Thus, marginal cost and marginal benefit are equated, satisfying the marginalist principle from the social point of view and implying that no potential Pareto improvements are possible.

In the real world, most industries are not perfectly competitive, but some important examples exist, particularly in agriculture. There are thousands of wheat farmers, and no one farmer has any control over price. Price is determined by market conditions, and any single farmer can sell all he or she wants at that price. Entry into the industry is relatively free, so there is little reason to expect above-normal profits.

There are many highly competitive industries, such as restaurants and retail trade, but individual sellers have some control over price in most of these industries. As a result, they are better described by some other market structure, such as monopolistic competition.

6.3.2 Monopoly

The polar opposite of perfect competition is monopoly, where there is a single seller in the market. Unlike a perfectly competitive firm, a monopolist confronts a downward sloping demand curve. In fact, the monopolist faces the industry demand curve. Because demand is downward sloping to the firm, the firm recognizes that if it wants to sell more output, it must (other things equal) charge a lower price. This means that the marginal revenue curve lies below the demand curve (i.e., marginal revenue is less than price). Marginal revenue consists of the extra price obtained by raising sales by one unit of output, minus the value of the price reduction for all other units sold.

Furthermore, because it is not confronted by the entry of new firms, it is quite possible for the monopolist to earn above-normal profits in the long run. These above-normal profits are sometimes referred to as monopoly rents. The price and output configuration that maximizes profit is obtained by choosing an output level so that marginal revenue is equal to marginal cost. The monopoly solution is illustrated in Figure 6.2.

As shown in Figure 6.2, there is an inefficiency, or deadweight loss, associated with monopoly. The socially efficient level of output is Q^c, which is the output level at which the marginal cost of production just equals the price, or marginal benefit, to consumers. This is the output level that would emerge under perfect competition. The competitive price would be P^c. The monopolist charges a higher price, P^M, and produces a lower quantity, Q^M,

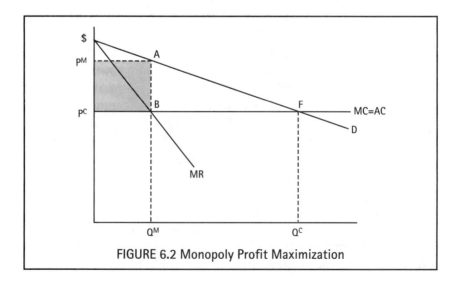

FIGURE 6.2 Monopoly Profit Maximization

creating an efficiency loss represented by triangle *ABF*. This diagram is similar to Figure 2.2, with a similar inefficiency shown.

The above-normal profit of the monopolist is shown by the shaded rectangle. This rectangle is the markup of prices over average cost (inclusive of normal returns to the shareholders), times the output. This above-normal profit is a transfer from consumers to the owners of the firm. This transfer is not inefficient in itself, although it may be viewed as undesirable from an equity standpoint. A monopoly may have other effects as well. A monopolist may fail to achieve management efficiency—so costs would not be minimized for the output chosen, as if the entire cost curve were shifted up. The failure to minimize costs is sometimes referred to as X-inefficiency.

Monopolies may arise for several reasons. One important reason is increasing returns to scale. Increasing returns to scale (IRS) refers to the advantages of producing large quantities of output. Strictly speaking, IRS is defined as occurring if a proportionate increase in inputs leads to a more than proportionate increase in output. Thus, for example, there are increasing returns to scale if a doubling of inputs causes output to more than double. If a firm's input prices remain constant, then increasing returns to scale are reflected in a downward sloping average cost curve: average cost falls as output rises.

Constant returns to scale (CRS) arise when a proportionate increase in inputs causes output to increase by the same proportion. In this case, if input prices are fixed, the average cost curve would be flat. Decreasing returns to scale (DRS) occur if output increases by a smaller proportion than inputs, and it would tend to make the average cost curve slope upwards if input prices were fixed. The term *economies of scale* refers to downward sloping average cost and *diseconomies of scale* refers to upward sloping average cost. Thus, increasing returns to scale are the main cause of economies of scale.

Most production processes have increasing returns to scale over some range of output, then experience decreasing returns. Therefore, a typical firm will have a U-shaped average cost curve that is declining over some range of output, then turns upward. However, the long-run average cost curve may also slope downwards and then become approximately flat—roughly described as "L-shaped." Both U-shaped and L-shaped cost curves are illustrated in Figure 6.3.

The lowest output at which the firm reaches an average cost that is as close as possible to the minimum average cost is called the minimum efficient scale (MES). Monopoly arises when the MES is very large relative to

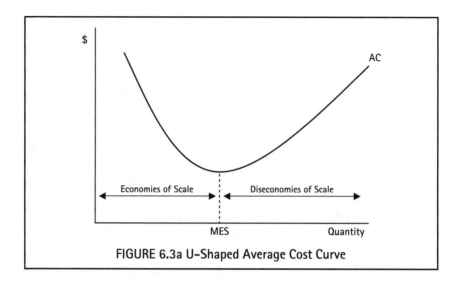

FIGURE 6.3a U-Shaped Average Cost Curve

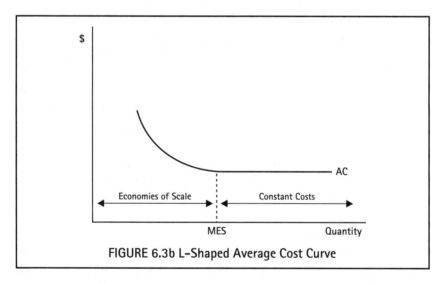

FIGURE 6.3b L-Shaped Average Cost Curve

market demand. If the MES lies outside the demand curve, then monopoly is the natural outcome. If, however, the MES is very small relative to market demand, then the market is likely to be highly competitive.

Definition: A **natural monopoly** arises when economies of scale are such that any feasible level of demand can be met at a lower average cost by a single firm than it can be by two (or more) firms.

In addition to natural monopolies, monopolies can be created by other means. One important type is legal monopoly—monopoly created by law. Most countries have patent protection, which gives the developer of a new product the right to be a monopolist for a certain period of time—twenty years from the date of filing in Canada and the United States for most products. In addition, governments may create monopoly franchises. This was common in earlier times. For example, the Hudson's Bay Company was given a monopoly franchise by the King of England to be the monopoly fur trader in British North America. In some less-developed countries today, it is not uncommon for monopoly franchises to be given to friends or relatives of government leaders.

A monopoly may be created by the amalgamation of firms in an industry, in combination with the creation of barriers that prevent entry by new firms. Such situations were relatively common in the late 19th and early 20th centuries but have been reduced by competition policy in Canada and its equivalent anti-trust policy in the United States. In Canada and most other countries, significant natural monopolies are either closely regulated or owned outright by the government.

One development in the concept of monopoly is the contestability hypothesis, in which potential entry is the focus. Basically, under this hypothesis, a single firm in an industry, or a few firms, may still take on competitive-type behaviour because of potential entry. More specifically, if new firms are able to enter the industry whenever industry prices exceed the minimum average cost, then the incumbent firm or firms will be unable to charge prices above the minimum average cost. The importance of this idea rests on whether exit and entry are sufficiently easy. Many observers feel the contestability hypothesis is not likely to be a reliable guide to industry behaviour in very many (if any) cases. As indicated above, if entry is restricted in some way, then we expect monopoly price markups to emerge.

6.3.3 Dominant Firms

The dominant firm structure is closely related to monopoly. In such markets, there is a single firm that controls a large share of the market (usually 50 percent or more) and a competitive fringe consisting of several or even a large number of small firms. The large firm has market power and acts much as an ordinary monopolist, except that its behaviour is constrained by the presence of small rivals. The small firms act more or less as perfect competitors, taking market conditions as set by the dominant firm. If the dominant firm sets a price that is very high, then the small firms, taking that price as given, will produce and sell a lot of output.

The dominant firm acts as a monopolist on what is called the residual demand curve–the industry demand curve net of what is supplied by the competitive fringe. The dominant firms occasionally undertake predatory actions (such as reducing price with the intent of driving some of the smaller firms out of business) if firms in the competitive fringe become too aggressive. Such actions are, however, in violation of competition policy in Canada and anti-trust policy in the United States, and are therefore not very effective as a disciplining device on competitors.

Some of the major examples of dominant firm industries are computer operating systems (Microsoft), ketchup (Heinz), and canned soups (Campbell Soup Company). Apart from the Canadian subsidiaries of U.S.-based dominant firms (such as Campbell Company of Canada), there are not many true dominant firms in Canada. Most large Canadian firms are in oligopolistic industries.

6.3.4 Monopolistic Competition

Just as the dominant firm structure is similar to monopoly, monopolistic competition is close to perfect competition. This is the market structure associated with industries such as restaurants, corner grocery stores, clothing retailers, movie theatres, and hotels. As in perfect competition, entry and exit costs are relatively low. Also, minimum efficient scale is reached at output levels that are low relative to total market demand. Each firm has only a small share of the total market, and any consumer has a wide range of choices available.

Typically, there is considerable product differentiation, with each firm offering its own, sometimes unique, product qualities. As a result, each firm faces a demand curve that is slightly downward sloping; that is, its sales will rise if it lowers its price, and fall if it raises its price. Firms' demand curves are, however, very elastic, or price sensitive. Large increases in price will drive most consumers away because there are many close substitutes in the market. Still, the key difference between perfect competition and monopolistic competition is that, under the latter, individual firms perceive they have some control over the price they receive, whereas under perfect competition, firms simply take price as given.

Firms feel the general competitive pressure of the market, which keeps prices within certain bounds. Thus, movie theatres cannot depart very far from the going price for movie seats, and restaurants that fail to offer quality commensurate with price soon go out of business. In the long run, because of free entry, profits are driven to their normal level, with price equal to average cost. The long-run equilibrium of monopolistic competition is illustrated in Figure 6.4.

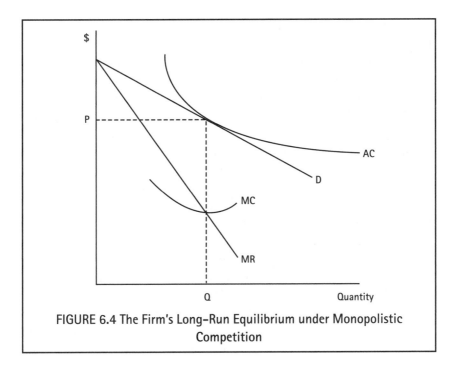

FIGURE 6.4 The Firm's Long-Run Equilibrium under Monopolistic Competition

In Figure 6.4, we can see that the equilibrium under monopolistic competition implies that firms will be producing on the downward sloping portions of their average cost curves. This can be compared with perfect competition, under which firms produce at the minimum points of their average cost curves.

This market structure is important and expanding, because it is the natural market structure for many service industries that are growing in importance. Monopolistic competition is very rarely a target for competition policy or price regulation because of its highly competitive nature.

6.3.5 Oligopoly

The most interesting market structure for public policy considerations is oligopoly. Oligopoly literally means few sellers. In practice, however, the number of firms can be fairly large. Oligopolistic industries may have as few as two firms in the industry or as many as ten or more. The main characteristics of oligopoly are as follows:

1. Each firm, or each major firm, faces a downward sloping demand curve.
2. Firms are in a strategic position relative to one another.

The second characteristic is important, because it means firms recognize that the fortunes of any one firm depend very much on what its rivals do. For example, the performance of General Motors depends on pricing and product decisions made by Ford, Toyota, and other rivals. In other words, the firms are highly interdependent. This can be contrasted with monopolistic competition, where firms compete in some general sense but no single rival is particularly important.

It is, of course, hard to draw a strict line between oligopoly and monopolistic competition, and some industries may be on the border between the two. Over time, oligopoly structures may merge into monopolistic competition situations or vice versa. Nevertheless, it is conceptually useful to distinguish between the two market structures.

Oligopoly can also be contrasted with the dominant firm structure, where firms on the competitive fringe take market conditions as given, rather than viewing themselves as important strategic players in the market. In the computer software applications industry, Microsoft is close to being dominant, along with two or three other large firms, including Oracle and Adobe. But the software industry as a whole is on the borderline between dominant firm structure and oligopoly. The same could be said of Intel and the computer processor industry.

In oligopoly, entry barriers may or may not be important, and there may or may not be high levels of product differentiation. Most major manufacturing and resource industries could probably be described as oligopolistic; for example, oil refining, automobile manufacturing, and steel manufacturing, as well as most mining, semiconductor manufacturing, and consumer electronics industries. In Canada, banking has traditionally been a major oligopoly, although recent regulatory changes have increased competition in the financial service industries.

Firms in an oligopoly face conflicting pressures. On the one hand, there is an incentive to collude. Successful collusion can in principle replicate monopoly outcomes, with correspondingly high profits for the firms involved. As a result, there are many examples of formal collusive arrangements (called cartels) in jurisdictions where they are allowed, and informal collusive arrangements in jurisdictions where cartels are illegal (such as in Canada).

There is, however, a very strong conflicting incentive to cheat on the collusive agreement. If a group of producers has restricted output to the monopoly level and a high price is available, the incentive for any one producer to sell more output at a slightly lower price is very strong. Consequently, collusive arrangements are notoriously unstable. One prominent example is

TABLE 6.3 Oil Prices: Dubai Crude Oil Spot Price, US$ per Barrel

Year	Price	CPI*	Real Price (US$2003)
1972	1.90	22.7	8.36
1973	2.85	24.1	11.81
1974	10.41	26.8	38.81
1975	10.70	29.2	36.59
1980	35.69	44.8	79.70
1985	27.53	58.5	47.08
1990	20.38	71.0	28.69
1995	16.10	82.8	19.43
2000	26.20	93.6	28.00
2005	49.35	106.2	46.45
2010	78.06	118.5	65.87
2011	106.18	122.2	86.86

* Consumer Price Index

Sources: BP Statistical Review of World Energy, www.bp.com; U.S. Bureau of Labor Statistics.

provided by the OPEC oil cartel,[1] whose effects on the world price of oil are illustrated in Table 6.3.

OPEC first flexed its muscles in 1973 when it made the decision to restrict supply, limiting each member of the cartel to a strict quota. This restriction on supply was initially very successful in raising prices, resulting in a 1974 price that was more than four times as high as the 1972 price. And in 1979, OPEC tightened supplies again, resulting in another price surge. However, the price by then was so high that many countries within OPEC faced strong incentives to "cheat" on the agreement, producing more than the quota they were allocated and contributing to subsequent declines in price.[2]

The OPEC oil cartel is an attempt by producers to act cooperatively in determining quantities. While this is legal in the OPEC countries, most countries—such as Canada, the United States, the European Union countries, and most of

---

[1] OPEC stands for Organization of Petroleum Exporting Countries and consists of twelve member countries (as of 2013), the most important of which are Saudi Arabia, Iraq, Iran, Kuwait, Nigeria, and Venezuela.

[2] Other factors affecting oil prices over the period shown include the business cycle (which affects demand), production by non-OPEC countries, and substitution away from oil due to changing consumption patterns and technological progress.

Asia–do not allow such collusion within their borders. Firms in an oligopoly position in such countries cannot legally collude; they must act independently or non-cooperatively. The first formal description of how such an oligopoly might behave is a model originally proposed by Cournot in 1838.

6.3.6 The Cournot Model of Oligopoly

The simplest version of the Cournot model has only two firms–the case of duopoly. The basic setting is two firms producing a homogeneous product. The two firms make simultaneous decisions concerning how much output to produce in a given period. Cournot used the example of two firms producing bottled water from mineral springs. Readers who have consumed Perrier or Evian bottled water will notice that this industry is no less fashionable today than it was 175 years ago.

The firms act independently or non-cooperatively, but they recognize their interdependence. For Firm 1, its profit-maximizing output depends on the amount that Firm 2 produces. For example, suppose industry demand is given as a linear function of the form $P = 100 - Q$, where P is industry price and Q is industry output. If we let q_1 be the output of Firm 1 and q_2 be the output of Firm 2, then $Q = q_1 + q_2$. Suppose that Firm 2 produces 50 units of output. It follows that the demand facing Firm 1 is given by $P = 100 - 50 - q_1 = 50 - q_1$. Firm 1 will then take this demand curve and figure out its profit-maximizing output, setting marginal cost equal to marginal revenue. It therefore determines its best response to Firm 2's output of 50 units. We assume that Firm 1 determines its best response to every possible output of Firm 2. Thus, we can think of Firm 1's desired output as a function of Firm 2's output. This function is called a best-response function. Firm 2 also determines its best-response function in relation to Firm 1's output. Best-response functions for each firm are illustrated in Figure 6.5.

Cournot proposed that the equilibrium, or expected outcome, would occur where the best-response functions cross.[3] This is the Cournot equilibrium. At this point, each firm is choosing the best output it can, given the output chosen by the rival. At any other point, at least one firm is dissatisfied with its output choice and would like to change it.

---

[3] More formally, if we let demand be $P = a - Q$, then revenue for Firm 1 is $R_1 = (a - [q_1 + q_2]) q_1 = aq_1 - q_1^2 - q_1 q_2$. The associated marginal revenue (given by derivative dR_1/dq_1) is $MR_1 = a - 2q_1 - q_2$. If we assume marginal cost (MC) is a constant equal to c, then the profit-maximizing choice of output by Firm 1 is given by $MR_1 = MC$ or $a - 2q_1 - q_2 = c$. Rearranging this so as to isolate q_1 yields the best-response function for Firm 1: $q_1 = (a - c)/2 - q_2/2$. Firm 2's best-response function can be derived in the same way and is therefore $q_2 = (a - c)/2 - q_1/2$. Solving these two linear equations in two unknowns simultaneously yields the Cournot equilibrium, which in this case is $q_1 = q_2 = (a - c)/3$.

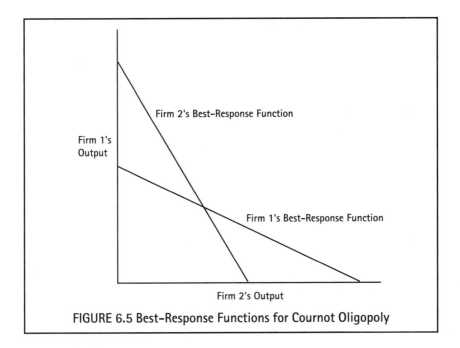

FIGURE 6.5 Best-Response Functions for Cournot Oligopoly

The Cournot model has several plausible features that can be outlined here. First, the combined output level will exceed the monopoly level, and total profits (summed across the two firms) will be less than the monopoly level. As more firms are added, total output rises, price falls, and total profits fall. Thus, the industry gets more competitive as more firms enter. As the number of firms becomes very large, the industry approaches the perfectly competitive state.

The Cournot equilibrium is a special case of a Nash equilibrium, which is defined as follows.

Definition: A **Nash equilibrium** arises in a strategic game when each player selects a strategy that maximizes that player's payoff, given the strategies chosen by the other players.

From this definition, we can see that the Cournot equilibrium is a Nash equilibrium for a game in which each player simultaneously chooses its output as its strategy choice. More realistic oligopoly games in which firms choose research and development (R&D) levels, investment levels, advertising levels, prices, or other variables can be studied using the Nash equilibrium. In a sense, all of these models build on the Cournot model.

One very simple modified version of the Cournot model arises if, instead of assuming that firms move simultaneously, one firm moves first. This leader firm is then in a position to anticipate the follower's reaction. In particular, the leader realizes that for any output it chooses, the follower will choose its best response—an outcome that will be somewhere on the follower's best-response function. The leader can then simply choose the point on the follower's best-response function that is best for the leader, and select the corresponding output. This is called the Stackelberg model. More detailed analysis of the Cournot model and related models of oligopoly can be found in most intermediate microeconomics textbooks, and in industrial organization textbooks.

6.3.7 Oligopoly and the Prisoner's Dilemma

Strategic situations form the subject matter of game theory. While formal game theoretical modelling is beyond the scope of this book, there is one very simple game theoretical structure that captures the basic oligopoly incentive problem very well. This structure is the prisoner's dilemma. Consider a two-firm industry (a duopoly) in which firms may charge either a high (collusive) price or a lower price. Note that this setting is different from the Cournot model in two respects. First, firms choose price rather than quantity. Second, their choice is discrete in that they have only two prices to choose from. In the Cournot model, firms can choose any one of a large number of possible quantities. Despite these differences, however, the incentive structure of this game is similar to that of the Cournot model.

The strategy of charging a high price is referred to as cooperation; a lower price is a defection. If both firms cooperate, or charge high prices, both will do well, essentially sharing in the monopoly profits. If one firm charges a high price and the other defects, the defector takes most of the sales in the market and does very well, and the other firm does very poorly. If both firms defect, both make modest profits. This payoff structure is illustrated in the following box or matrix.

		FIRM 2			
		Cooperate		Defect	
FIRM 1	Cooperate	40	40	0	70
	Defect	70	0	20	20

The first element in each cell is Firm 1's profit (or payoff); the second element is Firm 2's profit. Combined profits are highest under the strategy of mutual cooperation. If, however, Firm 1 believes Firm 2 intends to charge the collusive price, then Firm 1 has an incentive to defect, for by defecting it can raise its profit from 40 to 70. Furthermore, even if Firm 1 believed Firm 2 was likely to defect, then the best strategy would be to defect also, for by defecting Firm 1 gets 20, while if it remains true to the agreement, it will get nothing. Similar reasoning applies to Firm 2. Thus, for each firm, no matter what the other does, its best strategy is to defect. A strategy that is best no matter what the rival does is referred to as a dominant strategy. It is likely, therefore, that mutual defection will be the outcome, even though the firms could earn twice as much by colluding. Note that mutual defection is a Nash equilibrium—given the strategy chosen by the rival, each firm is doing the best it can.

The original version of the prisoner's dilemma dealt with two suspects in a crime, rather than two firms. In that version, each prisoner was induced to confess (defect) in the hope of getting a lighter sentence, even though both suspects would do better if neither confessed.

If firms (or prisoners) had to make single, once-and-for-all choices, it is hard to believe they would do anything other than defect. If, however, the interaction between the firms is repeated, there is a much better chance of maintaining cooperation. In a repeated game, there is an incentive to co-operate if the firms believe that cooperation in this period will bring forth cooperation from the rival in the next period, while defection today will induce defection by the rival in the next period. Thus, cooperation may be maintained in a repeated game, although if one firm believes it may not be around next period, or if the one-period gains from defection are very high, then defection is likely to result.

It is a fortunate thing for consumers that oligopoly situations have a prisoner's dilemma aspect to them, for this is what maintains reasonably vigorous levels of competition, even when only a few firms are involved. We cannot say in general how much competition is enough, but as indicated above, even industries with only a few firms can be highly competitive. There are, however, several alternative theories of how oligopolies behave, each of which is useful for some industries but not others.

6.3.8 Modes of Rivalry

Firms do many things to compete with each other. Most of these strate-gies are relevant, principally, in oligopoly situations, but they may arise in other market structures as well. The first, and most obvious, area of competition is price and quality. Perfectly competitive firms, oddly enough, do not compete over price. They simply bring their output to market for sale at what they take to be the going price. In all other market structures, firms recognize they can affect their sales by changing price. Even under a monopoly, although the monopolist does not face direct competition from firms producing similar outputs, the monopolist is in competition for the consumer's dollar with firms producing other products. For example, if the price of tickets to sporting events gets high enough, consumers will turn to other forms of entertainment.

In addition to price and product competition, firms compete with advertising and other marketing practices, through research and development, and they may undertake predatory actions to deter or prevent entry. For example, firms may carry excess capacity to deter other firms from entering an industry, or they may engage in the occasional price war to convince potential entrants that entering the industry would be a poor idea. In our discussion of competition policy in Chapter 11, we will examine public policy responses to these and other strategic actions that firms might undertake.

6.3.9 Market Structure and Public Policy

The main concern of (normative) public policy toward business is the performance of an industry. Performance means the extent to which the industry achieves allocational, or Pareto, efficiency both at a point in time and over time. Unfortunately, it is very difficult to measure performance directly.

Because measuring performance directly is difficult, public policy and academic research in industrial organization have made use of the structure-conduct-performance (SCP) approach. This approach is based on the idea that market structure is the fundamental determinant of the conduct (or behaviour) of firms, and that conduct is in turn the fundamental determinant of performance. For example, the theory of market structure suggests that an oligopoly consisting of two or three firms is likely to engage in certain forms of conduct, such as collusion, that in turn lead to (socially) inefficient performance. Therefore, public policy might focus simply on the market structure and either regulate or break up small group oligopolies accordingly, rather than try to measure the actual performance of the industry.

The key requirement for the application of the SCP approach is a measure of structure. Typically, a measure of seller concentration is used. One could, for example, look at the four-firm concentration ratio, which is simply the market share of the largest four firms in an industry. Both the four-firm concentration ratio and the eight-firm concentration ratio have been commonly used. A slightly more sophisticated measure of concentration is the Herfindahl index, which is the sum of squared market shares for all firms in an industry. Thus, if there are three firms with shares of 0.5, 0.3, and 0.2, the index would be $(0.5)^2 + (0.3)^2 + (0.2)^2 = 0.38$. The index must lie between 0 and 1. Under a monopoly, the Herfindahl index is 1, while if there are many small firms, the index would approach zero.

Another central focus of concern in SCP analysis is barriers to entry, particularly if those barriers are deliberate strategic devices. For example, it has been argued that brand proliferation in the breakfast cereal market has been used as an explicit barrier to entry, which might explain why a handful of companies dominate a market that would seem ideal for substantial competition. Carrying excess capacity is another strategic barrier to entry, because the excess capacity signals to potential entrants that incumbent firms can easily increase production in the event of entry, making life difficult for an entrant. In essence, if an industry has a high concentration ratio and has apparent strategic barriers to entry, it is a natural candidate for policy investigation.

6.4 The Legal Environment

6.4.1 The Rule of Law

So far we have discussed the role of firms and markets without paying much attention to the underlying legal environment. In fact, however, the legal environment is crucially important for the efficient operation of market economies. Adam Smith's invisible hand, discussed in Chapter 3, consists of private incentives operating under competitive conditions. Chapter 3 noted that the invisible hand provides for very effective economic performance under certain circumstances. However, this invisible hand relies on the principle of voluntary exchange: economic transactions must be voluntary, not coerced. Therefore, the invisible hand cannot produce a good outcome under anarchy, where coercion and outright theft are the norm. To operate effectively, competitive markets require what is often referred to as *the rule of law*.

The term "rule of law" used by legal scholars, political scientists, and economists incorporates several important ideas. First, it implies that there must be a legal system in place to govern economic, political, and social actions. In a lawless environment (where a legal system is absent), the strong take from the weak, random violence is common, and most people spend much of their time and energy protecting what little they have rather than in creating new wealth. Economic activity is very inefficient in such a context.

The second important idea associated with the rule of law is captured by the assertion that the hallmark of civilization is "the rule of law, not of men." This means that laws should be clear, well-understood, and applicable to everyone. No individual, not even a king, president, or prime minister is above the law. Thus, for example, most legal systems prohibit theft. Under the rule of law, this prohibition applies to a king or president just as much as to anyone else. Even the government itself is subject to the law and has its actions constrained by an independent judiciary. The law can of course be changed through the actions of government, but this change itself is subject to "due process" and should operate sufficiently slowly and incrementally that the legal system has clarity, predictability, and consistency.

Economists emphasize two other features that are often taken as fundamental to the rule of law: protection of private property through *property rights* and *enforcement of contracts*. It is possible to imagine a rule of law that incorporates only weak property rights and contract enforcement, but the evidence strongly suggests that economic growth and efficiency depend heavily on rigorous application of these two concepts.[4] Protection of private property allows people to benefit from economic investments. For example, someone who starts a business is willing to invest in the business only if he or she can anticipate enjoying the profits or other benefits from that investment. If the person expects confiscation by the state or theft by other individuals, he or she would not make the initial investment, and much potential economic benefit would be lost.

Contract enforcement is also very important as it allows for intertemporal transactions—transactions that involve different time periods. Evan might borrow money from a bank today in order to purchase a home, signing a contract to pay back the loan (plus interest) in future periods. If Evan could then simply refuse to honour the contract, the bank might be unwilling to make the loan in the first place. Because legal contract enforcement requires Evan to either pay back the owed money or suffer significant negative consequences, the bank feels comfortable making the loan. This allows Evan to actually buy the house. In regimes where loan contracts are not legally enforceable, some loans still occur but enforcement is through private and often violent means, and interest rates tend to be so high as to rule out most

---

[4] There are substantial research agenda underway focusing on assessing the importance of the rule of law for economic growth and on the relative performance of different legal regimes.

potentially beneficial loan agreements. In general, business investment would be severely curtailed if the contracts specifying the terms of future returns to the investors could not be enforced.

The efficiency of competitive markets is based on the principle of voluntary exchange. In order for people to be willing and able to enter into voluntary exchanges, they must have secure control over the item they plan to exchange, and they must expect to keep or use the item they receive in return, free from significant fear of expropriation or theft. In other words, they must have property rights over the components in the exchange. In addition, they must be able to anticipate that the other party to the transaction will fulfill any future contractual obligations. The efficiency of private competitive markets that Adam Smith emphasized is, therefore, a relatively fragile outcome. It depends on the rule of law incorporating property rights and contract enforcement.

6.4.2 Broad and Narrow Views of the Rule of Law

The view of the rule of law given in the previous subsection is a relatively narrow view, focusing mainly on procedural attributes of the law such as the requirement that it apply to everyone, that it enforce contracts, etc. Many legal scholars and practitioners advocate a broader conception of the rule of law that incorporates statements about the substantive content of the law. For example, we might seek to include basic principles such as free speech, freedom of association, and prohibitions against slavery or exploitation of children into the rule of law.

The narrow view of the rule of law includes the idea that contracts should be enforced. But what about a contract where a person sells himself or herself into effective slavery, or sells his or her children into slavery? Most will agree that we want to exclude such contracts. Similarly, the rule of law implies that the law should apply to everyone. But how do we feel about a law that makes it illegal to criticize government policy? Simply having such a law apply to everyone is not much of a consolation for the apparent harm it might do.

In essence, the question of whether we should use a narrow or broad definition of the rule of law is a semantic issue. Most scholars find it useful to have a term—the rule of law—that specifies a particular procedural approach. They acknowledge that procedures are not the only important aspect of the legal system and that the substantive content of the law is also important. However, it is useful to have terminology allowing us to distinguish between procedural issues and substantive issues. Therefore, the term "rule of law" is often used in a fairly narrow or procedural sense, even by people who believe strongly in other fundamental principles, such as freedom of speech and prohibitions on slavery and child labour.

This semantic issue has relevance to ongoing efforts by international agencies to promote legal reforms based on the rule of law.[5] The definition of the rule of law used in these efforts determines how ambitious such reform projects will be.

6.4.3 The Corporate Legal Form

The previous section established the overarching principle that a legal system incorporating property rights and contract enforcement is vital for economic efficiency and economic progress. At a more detailed level, there are, in addition, important specific aspects of the modern legal environment to consider. One significant legal innovation of modern economies is that of the corporate form of business organization.

The modern corporate form has two particularly important characteristics: limited liability and the recognition of the corporation as a legal entity distinct from the owners or senior managers. The modern corporate form is the product of a range of imaginative private contracts, incremental legal rulings in various political jurisdictions, and explicit legislation. Prior to the 19th century, the corporate form was very rare and existed only as a result of special government dispensation. In the absence of this special permission, business firms were viewed as extensions of their owners. Small firms were normally "sole proprietorships" and larger, more complex firms would be organized as partnerships among the providers of the firm's equity capital.

During the 19th century, the corporate form took shape and grew very rapidly in importance (particularly in the United States), largely taking over from partnerships. It has been argued that one reason for the very rapid economic growth of the United States relative to the rest of world in the 19th and early 20th centuries was the development of the corporate business form.

Partnerships had two great disadvantages. One disadvantage, shared by sole proprietorships, was unlimited liability. If a partnership took on debts, the partners would be liable for those debts as individuals. If the partners' investments in the firm were insufficient to pay off a company's debts, partners

---

[5] For a discussion of recent reform efforts see, for example, "Economics and the Rule of Law," *The Economist*, March 13, 2008, at www.economist.com/node/10849115.

would be obligated to use their personal assets to repay those debts, even if those assets had no connection to the firm. Thus, an individual could be ruined by an unsuccessful business investment. This was a strong disincentive to investment, particularly to arm's length investments where investors would, in effect, be liable for the actions and decisions of people they did not know. In the corporate form, the most an investor can lose is what he or she puts into the corporation.

A second great disadvantage of a partnership is the possibility that the firm can be dissolved due to the private activities of a single partner. For example, one of the first major multinational corporations was Singer, the world's leading producer of sewing machines, which was incorporated in 1863. Prior to 1863, the Singer Company was a partnership owned by Isaac M. Singer, the inventor of the Singer sewing machine, and Edward Clark, a lawyer who handled Singer's original patent application and who was largely responsible for the development of the company. Clark had become very concerned about Singer's private life, as Singer had fathered children with at least four different women, only one of whom was ever his legal wife. He had two children with his wife, eight children with another woman, and several more children with at least two more women. Clark was concerned that claims by these many potential beneficiaries to Singer's estate would cause dissolution of the company. Possibly one or more of Singer's children or female companions could make a contentious claim during Singer's life, and almost certainly the beneficiaries would have claims when he died.

Under the partnership form, these claims would very likely be far more than the Singer Company could pay while still continuing to operate. A judge overseeing such claims would normally order liquidation of the company to pay the beneficiaries whatever was due to them. Once the company became a corporation however, it was an independent legal entity that could not be dissolved due to personal claims against Isaac Singer. He, of course, owned very valuable shares in the company, but any legal wrangling by his dependents or heirs would be over ownership of those shares, not over the physical assets of the corporation. Among other benefits of incorporation, Singer's heirs would be better off with shares in the Singer Corporation as a going concern than with the cash payout from a liquidated company. Clark and the firm's employees and customers were certainly better off under the corporate form. Also, in moving to the corporate form, Clark arranged for senior managers to acquire equity positions in the company, and this had desirable incentive effects on those managers.

The corporate form encourages investment by allowing limited liability, and it insulates a company from personal problems of individual investors which, among other things, allows firms to pursue projects with long time horizons and to pursue large projects that require many investors. Partnerships and sole proprietorships still exist, as do certain hybrid forms of business organization, and limited liability has been extended to these various business forms to some extent. However, the corporate form is the dominant business form in Canada and in most other parts of the world, especially for large scale and complex business activities.

The advantages of limited liability have, in recent years, persuaded governments in many countries, including the United States, to extend limited liability to sole proprietorships and partnerships that request it and that satisfy certain basic requirements. Such firms are called limited liability companies (LLCs). Canada has not yet gone very far in this direction, although limited liability partnerships are available for certain occupations, such as accountants, doctors, and lawyers.

6.4.4 Corporate Governance

The development of the corporate form of business organization gives rise to the need for a legal environment that defines how corporations are to be governed. The modern corporation often leads to a separation of ownership from control. In a large modern corporation such as Apple or Disney there are thousands of owners with varying amounts of stock. The vast majority of these owners have no role in making corporate decisions. Actual control of the corporation rests in the hands of the senior executives.

The relationship between shareholders and senior executives falls into the general class of *agency* relationships. We can think of the senior executives as the agents of the shareholders. Because the senior executives know much more about the company and about their own actions than shareholders do, this situation gives rise to the possibility that the executives will act in their own private interests rather than in the interest of the shareholders.

The primary response in law and in practice to this agency problem is the board of directors. Directors are elected by the shareholders to monitor the decisions of the senior management. The board has primary responsibility for corporate governance and has various legal responsibilities to shareholders, including the *duty of care* and the *duty of loyalty*. Another response of public policy and the exchanges on which shares are traded has been the adoption of laws or rules requiring auditing and disclosure of various financial statements and other pieces of information associated with widely held corporations.

Despite the safeguards associated with boards of directors, auditing requirements, and disclosure requirements, a number of scandals involving conflicts of interest at major corporations have surfaced in recent years. The study of how best to deal with potential agency problems inherent in the corporate form of business organization while retaining the advantages of the modern corporation is a very active area of business research at present.

7

The Canadian Business Environment

7.1 Introduction

Public policies toward business operate in a complex environment. Good decision making in government or business requires an understanding of this environment. This chapter provides a brief, selective survey of Canadian economic structure and other aspects of Canada's business environment. Section 7.2 considers population and demography, and section 7.3 focuses on recent macroeconomic trends. Section 7.4 is devoted to industrial structure, and section 7.5 examines the role of government. Finally, section 7.6 briefly discusses Canada's place in the world economy.

7.2 Population and Demography

The population of Canada was 28.1 million at the 1991 census,[1] rose to 31.0 million as of 2001, and was just over 34.5 million in 2011. By international standards, Canada is a country with only a modest-sized population. In 2011, China, the world's most populous country, had a population of approximately 1.3 billion, India was second at about 1.2 billion, and the United States was a distant third with a 2011 population of 312 million, close to ten times that of Canada. Other countries with large populations include Indonesia (about 240 million), Brazil (about 190 million), Pakistan (about 180 million), and Nigeria

---

[1] Census information is available from the Statistics Canada website, at www.statcan.ca.

(about 166 million). The entire European Union, consisting of 27 countries, had a 2011 population of 502 million, led by Germany (82 million), France (65 million), and the United Kingdom (62 million).

Most of Canada's population is concentrated in Ontario and Quebec, which account for 39 and 23 percent of the population, respectively, although western Canada has been growing in relative importance. British Columbia accounts for about 13 percent of the country's population and Alberta for about 11 percent, while Manitoba and Saskatchewan together account for about 7 percent. The Atlantic provinces, as a group, make up about 8 percent of the population, while the Yukon, Northwest Territories, and Nunavut together account for less than 0.5 percent of the total. One of the striking features of Canada's population is that it is concentrated in a narrow strip of land adjacent to the U.S. border. Canada is, from a demographic point of view, a long, thin country.

A very important demographic factor for public policy analysis and strategic planning in business is the age structure of the population, which is determined in part by the pattern of birth rates over time. Figure 7.1 shows the pattern of births over the period 1950 to 2011. These data illustrate an important phenomenon known as the baby boom. Between 1947 and 1961,

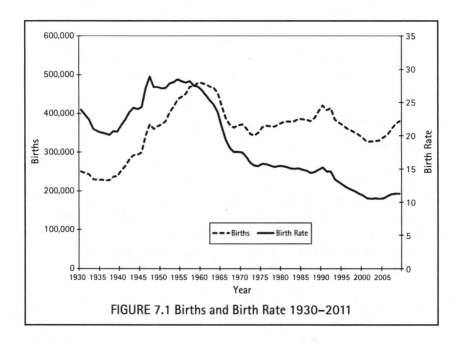

FIGURE 7.1 Births and Birth Rate 1930–2011

the baby boom period, the annual birth rate was high, at close to 30 births per 1000 people through this period. The number of births per year rose quickly at the start of the baby boom and remained high through this period. Then a dramatic reversal took place as the birth rate first fell sharply through the 1960s and then more slowly after that, to about 11 births per 1000 by 2011.

Since the end of the baby boom, Canada's population has continued to increase, but more slowly. Canada's main source of population growth is now immigration. At current fertility rates, Canada would, in the absence of immigration flows, move to a situation of zero population growth or very close to it by the middle of the 21st century.[2] However, if current immigration levels are maintained or increased, Canada will have a growing population for the foreseeable future.

The baby boom generation has had a major impact on business and on public policy. During the 1950s and early 1960s, child-related businesses such as the diaper and baby food businesses did very well. As this generation grew into childhood and adolescence, much public policy emphasis was placed on education, first in the school system and then at the post-secondary level, as new schools and then universities sprang up in all major population centres in Canada.

In the 1970s and 80s, the flood of baby boomers into the labour market, along with the increasing labour-force participation of women, taxed the capacity of the economy to absorb new workers. Now, in the second decade of the 21st century, the baby boom generation is starting to retire, putting upward pressure on the ratio of non-working to working people (the dependency rate). An increasing dependency rate strains the ability of the economy to support the elderly while meeting the aspirations of younger Canadians. It seems likely that the average retirement age will need to rise, reflecting the growing size of the elderly population and increased life expectancy. And as this generation enters old age and needs more medical care, pressures on health care facilities will continue to increase.

Another demographic phenomenon requiring emphasis is the increasing labour-force participation of women. Table 7.1 reports women's labour-force participation for the period 1965 to 2011. As this table shows, very significant increases in female labour-force participation occurred during the decades of the 1960s, 70s, and 80s. In the 1990s and the first part of the 21st century, female labour-force participation has continued to increase,

---

[2] This projection can be calculated by assuming net migration flows of zero, applying current age-specific birth rate and mortality rates, and simulating the resulting population dynamics.

TABLE 7.1 Labour-Force Participation Rate of Women 1965-2011

Percentage of Females Age 25+ in the Labour Force

1965	31%
1970	35
1975	40
1980	46
1985	52
1990	57
1995	57
2000	59
2005	61
2010	62
2011	62

Source: Statistics Canada CANSIM Table 282-0002.

but more slowly. At present, labour-force participation of women is double what it was in 1965.

It is important to view this evolution in female labour-force participation in perspective. Women have always made major economic contributions. In the past, however, most of these contributions were in the form of household production, particularly cooking, cleaning, making clothes, taking care of children, gardening, and, in rural households, farming. Throughout most of history, women's duties in and around the household have been a full-time job.

In recent times, technological innovation in the household appliance, clothing, and food processing industries have greatly reduced the labour required to achieve a given level of household production. Washing machines (and dryers), dishwashers, vacuum cleaners, televisions, and the availability of ready-made clothing and food have reduced the demand for labour in the household. As a result, women have shifted their economic activity outside the household and into the formal labour market. Increasing urbanization (itself caused mainly by technological innovation in agriculture) has also played an important role in moving women into the formal labour market.

As is typical with social attitudes, attitudes toward working women have tended to follow economic incentives. In 1960, only 5 percent of Canadians answered "yes" to the question "Do you think married women should take a job outside the home if they have young children?" Even after the expansion of the modern feminist movement in the 1960s, only 13 percent answered "yes" in 1970. A 1987 Gallup poll[3] reported that 47 percent of Canadians answered "yes" to the question—a dramatic change in attitudes over a single generation. Gallup has not asked this question since 1987, in part because it ceased to be a controversial issue. If the question were asked today it seems likely that a large majority would answer "yes."

One significant population trend is the increasing preponderance of elderly women, because women are outliving men by about four years. In 1931, life expectancy for Canadian men stood at 60 years and for women at 62 years. By 2009, the life expectancy of women had risen to about 83 years, while for men it had risen to about 79 years.

The educational attainment of Canadians continues to evolve significantly. Table 7.2 shows the recent history of educational attainment in Canada. Virtually 100 percent of children between the ages of 6 and 11 attend elementary school, and close to 100 percent of those aged 12 to 17 are in secondary school. As of 2011, almost 25 percent of the adult population (25 and over)

TABLE 7.2 Highest Educational Attainment (Percentage of Population Age 25 and Over)

	0–8 Years of School	High School		Post-Secondary		
		Some	Graduated	Some	Certificate/ Diploma	Univ. Degree
1961*	46.0%	29.0%	11.0%	5.0%	4.0%	5.0%
1991	16.1	19.4	20.9	7.1	23.6	12.8
2001	10.8	13.5	19.5	7.1	30.8	18.3
2011	6.8	9.8	19.3	5.7	34.1	24.3

Source: Statistics Canada CANSIM Table 282-0004.
* The 1961 numbers are approximate only.

---

[3] *The Gallup Report*, Monday, March 23, 1987, The Gallup Poll of Canada.

had a university degree, up from only about 5 percent in 1961 and about double the proportion in 1991. And almost two-thirds of the adult population had some post-secondary education in 2011. Education levels have risen dramatically over the last generation. Slightly more women than men now attend university in Canada, but men continue to significantly outnumber women in graduate programs.

7.3 Macroeconomic Trends

The environment of business is determined largely by macroeconomic conditions (the state of the business cycle). As discussed in Chapter 3, moderating the business cycle and controlling the macroeconomic environment are important functions of government policy. The macroeconomic environment refers mainly to three variables: unemployment, inflation, and per capita real gross national product (GNP), or the closely related gross domestic product (GDP).[4] Interest rates and exchange rates are also important influences on these three variables and are important to business in general, and they therefore also receive a lot of attention in macroeconomic analysis.

The objectives of macroeconomic policy are to keep the unemployment rate low, to keep the inflation rate low, and to promote growth in real incomes, usually measured by per capita GNP or GDP. Table 7.3 reports the recent history of these three variables.

Perhaps the most important piece of information in Table 7.3 is the increase in real per capita GDP, which is a measure of general living standards. Real living standards more than doubled between 1965 and 2011, as annual real GDP rose from just under $22,000 per person to almost $51,000 per person. Furthermore, average living standards rose at least slightly in almost every year, with GDP per capita only failing to grow in sharp recession years. This means that living standards today are much higher than they were 40 or 50 years ago, and significantly higher than they were even 20 or 25 years ago. By historical standards, this is remarkably good performance. This strong sustained economic performance is often forgotten in the general day-to-day concern over economic fluctuations.

Real GDP is not, however, a perfect indicator of living standards. GDP is the total value of goods and services produced in Canada, measured at

---

[4] Gross domestic product (GDP) and gross national product (GNP) differ slightly from each other. GDP measures the total amount of economic product produced in Canada. It is therefore the best measure of total activity and is the appropriate variable for describing economic activity. A small (but growing) part of GDP is due to foreign-owned factors of production, so not all GDP corresponds to earnings of domestic factors. When earnings due to foreign factors are subtracted from GDP, and foreign earnings of domestic factors are added, the result is GNP. GNP is therefore the appropriate measure of the earnings of domestic residents.

TABLE 7.3 Unemployment and Inflation Rates in Canada, 1965–2012

Year	Unemployment	Inflation	Real per Capita GDP (2012 dollars in '000s)
1965	4.0%	2.4%	21.71
1970	5.7	3.3	25.32
1975	6.9	10.8	28.62
1980	7.5	10.2	32.87
1985	10.5	4.0	35.25
1990	8.1	4.5	39.03
1995	9.5	2.2	39.52
2000	6.8	2.7	45.55
2005	6.8	3.7	49.10
2010	8.0	2.1	49.59
2011	7.4	3.4	50.59
2012	7.4	1.0	50.82

Source: Statistics Canada CANSIM Table 282-0002, 326-0021.

market prices. It includes much activity of questionable value, including various types of transfer-seeking; it does not properly include subtractions for environmental damage; it cannot cope very well with product innovation; and it does not account for the value of household production or of leisure. Nevertheless, it is the best widely available measure we have of aggregate economic performance.

Even accepting per capita GDP at face value, there are some causes for concern. First, the growth rate has slowed markedly since the 1960s. Growth rates for the past 20 years have been modest by the standards of the 1950s, 1960s, and 1970s. The parents of most university-age children are, on average, much better off than their own parents were, who were, in turn, much better off than their parents. It is not clear, however, that current Canadian university students will be better off than their parents. Also, even moderate unemployment rates reflect a lot of individual frustration. Inflation has been kept in check for a long period of time, but it remains a potential concern.

TABLE 7.4 History of Provincial Unemployment Rates, 1976–2011 Age 15 and Over

	Canada	Nfld. and Labrador	P.E.I	N.S.	N.B.	Que.	Ont.	Man.	Sask.	Alta.	B.C.
1976	7.1%	13.4%	9.3%	9.2%	11%	8.7%	6.1%	4.7%	3.8%	3.9%	8.4%
1980	7.5	13.3	10.5	9.7	11.1	10.0	6.9	5.5	4.3	3.9	6.7
1985	10.5	20.2	13.5	13.4	15.2	12.2	7.9	8.3	8.1	9.8	14.3
1990	8.1	17.0	14.4	10.7	12.1	10.4	6.2	7.4	7.0	6.9	8.4
1995	9.5	18.0	14.8	12.2	11.4	11.5	8.7	7.3	6.7	7.8	8.5
2000	6.8	16.6	12.0	9.1	10.0	8.5	5.7	5.0	5.1	5.0	7.2
2005	6.8	15.1	10.8	8.4	9.6	8.3	6.6	4.8	5.1	4.0	5.8
2010	8.0	14.4	11.2	9.3	9.3	8.0	8.7	5.4	5.2	6.5	7.6
2011	7.4	12.7	11.3	8.8	9.5	7.8	7.8	5.4	5.0	5.5	7.5

Source: Statistics Canada CANSIM Table 282-0008.

Even though the business cycle has been moderated by macroeconomic policy, it is still sufficiently strong that it creates costly uncertainties in business planning and individual lives.

One important feature of Canada's business environment is the extent to which it varies from region to region. Some parts of the economy are traditionally depressed, such as much of Atlantic Canada and parts of Quebec. Table 7.4 gives some indication of this regional variation by reporting the recent history of regional unemployment rates.

There is also significant variation in regional incomes, with Alberta, British Columbia, and Ontario having higher per capita incomes than the other provinces. Before-tax incomes in the wealthier provinces are about 35 percent higher than in the poorest provinces (Newfoundland and Prince Edward Island). However, once government taxes and transfers are taken into account, average provincial incomes are considerably more equal, and once differences in housing prices are factored in, average real income is quite similar across the provinces.

7.4 Industrial Structure
7.4.1 Sectoral Shares of Business Activity
The objective of this section is to provide some understanding of the relative importance of different parts of the economy. Business activity can be divided into two broad categories: *goods* and *services*. The goods sector can be further subdivided into primary and secondary industries. Primary industries, including agriculture, fishing, energy, mining, and forestry make direct use of major natural resources. The secondary sector consists mainly of manufacturing and construction. The service sector includes the financial industry, health care, education, government administration, personal and business service industries, and retail and wholesale sales.

Historically, Canada has been viewed as a producer of primary products. Even today, one sometimes hears that Canadians are mainly "hewers of wood and drawers of water." This view of Canada is very misleading. Table 7.5 shows the employment share of the major sectors of the economy. We can see that as of 2011 only a small share of employment, less than 5 percent, was in the primary sector. Most of the Canadian economy consists of services. If you think about the occupations you and your friends aspire to—as accountants, financial managers, doctors, lawyers, teachers and so on—you will realize that most of these jobs are in the service sector.

Table 7.5 clearly shows the movement, from 1976 through 2011, away from employment in the primary and secondary industries toward occupations in

25

TABLE 7.5 Employment Share (Percentage) by Sector and Industry, 1976–2011

	1976	1981	1986	1991	1996	2001	2006	2011
GOODS								
Primary (agriculture, forestry, fishing, hunting, mines, oil) and utilities	8.5%	8.1%	7.3%	6.9%	6.2%	4.8%	4.9%	4.5%
Construction	7.0	6.3	5.5	5.7	5.3	5.5	6.5	7.3
Manufacturing	19.1	18.4	16.9	14.8	14.3	14.9	12.8	10.2
Total	34.6	32.7	29.7	27.4	25.8	25.2	24.2	22.0
SERVICES								
Retail and wholesale trade	16.1	15.6	16.4	16.0	15.6	15.9	15.9	15.4
Transportation	5.8	5.6	5.2	4.9	5.1	5.2	4.8	4.9
Finance and related services	5.4	5.8	6.0	6.6	6.4	5.9	6.3	6.3
Professional and business services	4.2	5.4	6.1	7.2	8.4	10.2	10.8	11.5
Educational and health services	15.1	14.6	15.5	16.9	17.2	16.8	17.9	19.1
Accommodation and food services	4.2	5.5	5.7	5.9	6.3	6.3	6.2	6.3
Other	14.6	14.8	15.4	15.1	15.2	14.5	13.9	14.5
Total	65.4	67.3	70.3	72.6	74.2	74.8	75.8	78.0

Source: Statistics Canada CANSIM Table 282-000811, 13.

the service sector, continuing a trend that started earlier in the 20th century. The service sector is slightly less important in terms of total output than it is in employment numbers, reflecting the relatively high capital-to-labour ratio in the primary and secondary sectors.

Table 7.6 shows the share of national output, as measured by gross domestic product (GDP), accounted for by the major sectors. The GDP shares indicate a strong shift into services, although not quite in proportion to the shift indicated by the employment data. Some people have expressed concern over the decline of the primary and secondary sectors and the expansion of the service sector. This phenomenon is sometimes referred to as de-industrialization. Concern about de-industrialization is related to the physiocratic idea that physical or material things are the source of value. According to this reasoning, somehow we are worse off if more time is spent producing services and less time is spent producing physical goods.

Like many misleading ideas, this physiocratic view contains a half-truth. Many socially unproductive activities of the transfer-seeking type are included in the service component of GDP. Movement of a greater fraction of economic activity into transfer-seeking reduces the welfare of society as a whole. For example, the service component of GDP includes the incomes earned by lawyers who may have spent the entire year arguing divorce cases or patent infringement cases against each other—arguing over the distribution of wealth rather than producing anything of net value. In this example, each lawyer's services are of value to his or her client, of course, but the net value is zero in the sense that the lawyers cancel each other out.

Police and prison services are also included in the service sector. Police services are very valuable, but if an increase in police services reflects an increase in crime with a corresponding increased need for police, we can hardly argue that society is better off. In 1962, there were 1.41 police per 1000 persons, but by 1975 it had increased to 2.06 per 1000, after which it remained relatively stable, and stood at 2.03 in 2010. A deduction should be made from GNP to account for criminal and noncriminal transfer-seeking activities and for the resources that go into controlling such activities. The appropriate deduction would be much larger for the United States than for Canada.

The point that should be emphasized, however, is that services can be just as valuable as material goods. If a consumer is willing to pay $25 for a haircut, then the service of cutting the consumer's hair is just as valuable as a $25 pizza the consumer might also be willing to buy. There is nothing wrong with services, and there is nothing wrong with having the service sector of

TABLE 7.6 GDP (Percentage) by Sector and Industry, 1976–2011

	1976	1981	1986	1991	1996	2001	2006	2011
GOODS								
Primary (agriculture, forestry, fishing, hunting, mines, oil) and utilities	12.5%	14.0%	11.5%	9.6%	10.7%	10.8%	12.7%	9.5%
Construction	8.3	7.7	6.1	6.3	5.0	5.3	6.5	6.0
Manufacturing	8.0	17.5	17.7	15.2	17.4	17.4	13.6	12.6
Total	38.9	39.2	35.4	31.1	33.1	33.4	32.8	28.1
SERVICES								
Trade	11.4	10.4	11.2	11.1	10.4	10.4	11.0	11.7
Transportation	5.6	5.6	5.5	4.8	4.8	4.7	4.7	4.7
Finance and related services	13.5	15.3	17.0	19.0	19.4	18.9	18.5	21.0
Professional and business services	3.1	3.7	4.2	5.1	5.6	6.7	7.2	7.3
Educational and health services	11.2	10.8	11.4	13.0	12.0	11.0	11.1	11.8
Accommodation and food services	2.7	2.6	2.5	2.5	2.4	2.3	2.2	2.2
Other	13.5	12.3	12.8	13.4	12.2	12.4	12.5	13.2
Total	61.1	60.8	64.6	68.9	66.9	66.6	67.2	71.9

Source: M.C. Urquhart and K. Buckley. 1983. *Historical Statistics of Canada*, 2nd ed. Toronto: Macmillan Co.; *Canadian Economic Observer*, Statistics Canada Catalogue No. 11–210; Statistics Canada CANSIM Table 379–0017.

the economy increase in size, provided those services represent net value creation, not transfer-seeking.

In fact, the increasing share of services in the economy reflects increasing wealth. Overall, consumption of services is income elastic: as income rises, consumers tend to spend a greater fraction of it on services and a smaller fraction on the consumption of physical materials. For example, food consumption varies little by income class in Canada. The relatively wealthy consume about the same amount of food per capita as the relatively poor. Instead of using higher incomes to buy larger quantities of food, people spend extra money on services, such as those provided by restaurants (which are part of the accommodation and food services sector). Note also the growth of the financial sector, reflecting in part the increased attention to investment-related activities by individuals with enough wealth to justify obtaining help in making investments.

The increasing relative importance of service occupations also reflects labour-saving technological innovation in the primary and secondary sectors. Services, by their very nature, are labour intensive and have less scope for substitution of physical capital for labour. Labour has been released from the primary and secondary sectors and absorbed by the service sector. We have just as much physical production as before, and in addition, we have more services to consume. This process is a major reason why per capita living standards in Canada have risen to their current very high levels.

One final point to make is that there is considerable variation in industrial structure by region. In general, the western provinces are more closely linked to primary resource-based industries, while a relatively larger share of economic activity in Ontario and Quebec is devoted to secondary manufacturing. All regions have large service economies.

7.4.2 Market Structure

In Chapters 3 and 6, we emphasized the importance of market structure to economic performance. Market structure refers mainly to the degree and type of competitiveness in a particular industry. It is difficult to directly measure competitiveness, but one commonly used indicator of market structure is the concentration ratio, which shows the share of an industry accounted for by the largest firms in that industry. For example, a four-firm sales concentration ratio would show the share of sales accounted for by the largest four firms in that industry.

It is, of course, not clear what we mean by an "industry." Is tennis shoes an industry, or is it part of the athletic shoes industry or simply part of the footwear industry? In general, the higher the level of aggregation (i.e., the broader the definition of an industry), the lower we expect the concentration ratio to be. There are several categorizations of industries, corresponding to various levels of aggregation. These categories are described by the North American Industrial Classification System (NAICS) used by Statistics Canada and comparable bodies in the United States. The industry breakdown used in Tables 7.5 and 7.6 largely corresponds to the two-digit level of aggregation. A finer subdivision of industries is given by the three-digit level of aggregation, a still-finer level by the four-digit level, and so on, down to the six-digit level where industries or products are identified by six-digit numbers.

7.5 The Role of Government

The objective in this section is to provide an overview of the role of government in the economy. Governments affect the economy in many ways, including through the various policy areas described in subsequent chapters of this book. This section is devoted mainly to data describing the size of government and the evolution of the public debt. These issues are taken up in more depth in Chapter 14. Table 7.7 shows how the ratio of government expenditures to income has changed since 1935.

TABLE 7.7 Total Expenditure of all Government Levels as a Percentage of GNP, 1935–2011 ($millions, current dollars)

Year	Expenditure	GNP	% of GNP
1935	$ 1,093	$ 4,301	25.4%
1945	5,029	11,863	42.4
1955	7,498	28,865	26.0
1965	16,531	56,928	29.0
1975	68,454	170,967	40.0
1985	223,567	470,638	47.5
1995	373,760	781,876	47.8
2000	432,399	1,048,545	41.2
2005	526,066	1,348,097	39.0
2010	684,235	1,596,394	42.9
2011	706,964	1,688,828	41.9

Source: Statistics Canada CANSIM Tables 385-0001, 380-0030.

Table 7.7 indicates that the government's share in the economy rose significantly in the middle years of the 20th century but has been fairly stable since the 1970s.[5] This growth of government was accompanied by a tendency of governments to spend more than they took in, leading to deficits and a build-up of debt, as illustrated in Table 7.8.

The striking feature of Table 7.8 is the extent to which deficits grew between the mid-1970s and mid-1990s. During the late 1990s, the federal government was able to eliminate the federal deficit and move to a surplus position, but with a large accumulated debt. Other levels of government (provincial and local) run occasional net deficits, with significant current problems in Quebec and Ontario. As of the early part of the 21st century, the government sector in Canada is not far from an overall balanced budget position and, importantly, the debt-to-GNP[6] ratio has been trending downwards. As will be described in Chapter 14, stabilization macroeconomic policy suggests that the government should run deficits in recessions, and that these deficits should be offset by surpluses during periods of economic expansion.

During the 1970s, generous social programs in education, social services, and health care were entrenched, and during the late 1970s, interest payments on the debt began to grow sharply. None of these areas of expenditure could be easily reduced. The ratio of deficits to GNP (and debt to GNP) grew until the 1990s, when governments of the day made significant structural changes in expenditure patterns. Concerns about government debt forced the possibility of restructuring of social programs onto the policy agenda, although many of the reforms were valuable in their own right, quite apart from their fiscal impact. As of the early part of the 21st century, the government budget position is relatively healthy—making Canada an outlier among high-income countries—and this has been achieved even while income tax rates were reduced. However, significant pressures on public expenditure are looming on the horizon, especially in the area of health care.

7.6 Canada in the World Economy

So far this chapter has focused on domestic issues. It is important, however, to give some indication of Canada's place in the world economy.

---

[5] The year 1945 was an outlier because of the Second World War.

[6] Tables 7.7 and 7.8 use GNP rather than GDP. The two are very similar but GNP is more relevant in this case as it provides a slightly better indicator of the ability of domestic residents to pay for debts.

TABLE 7.8 Deficits, Debt Service, and GNP, 1935–2011 (all levels of government, $millions in current dollars)

Year	Total Revenue	Total Expenditures	Surplus/(Deficit)	% of GNP	Interest on Debt (% of GNP)	Interest on Debt (% of Revenue)
1935	$ 922	$ 1,093	$ (171)	−4.0%	6.5%	30.4%
1945	3,338	5,029	(1,691)	−14.3	4.3	15.3
1955	7,458	7,498	(40)	−0.1	2.3	8.9
1965	16,688	16,531	157	0.3	3.0	10.0
1975	64,170	68,454	(4,284)	−2.5	3.9	10.2
1985	191,031	233,567	(42,536)	−9.0	8.7	21.0
1995	321,073	373,760	(52,687)	−6.7	7.9	19.1
2000	468,669	432,399	36,330	3.5	5.7	14.5
2005	559,782	526,066	33,716	2.5	4.6	11.2
2010	625,042	684,235	(59,193)	−3.7	3.8	9.6
2011	659,546	706,964	(47,418)	−2.8	3.7	9.5

Source: Statistics Canada CANSIM Table 385–0032.

7.6.1 International Trade Flows

Chapter 8 is devoted to international trade policy, but it is worth noting here the importance of international trade to Canada. The size of Canada's trade flows vary from year to year, based in part on the business cycle, but in recent years Canada has exported between 30 and 40 percent of its GDP,[7] mostly to the United States. Table 7.9 reports the relative importance of Canada's major trading partners.

The United States consumes more of Canada's GDP than any single province, except Ontario. The U.S. economy is clearly a very important part of Canada's business environment. Trade with eastern Asia, especially China, is growing and will soon displace Europe as the second most important trading area for Canada.

7.6.2 World Living Standards and Population Growth

On the whole, the picture painted in this chapter is a relatively rosy one. Canadians are, generally, very well off, and there are no acutely threatening features in the domestic business environment. Along with a handful of other market-based economies, Canada has a relatively high standard of living and relatively low population growth, along with democratic government and relatively little violence.

Table 7.10 shows some cross-country comparisons of growth rates in living standards and population. The countries are listed in order of 2011 per

TABLE 7.9 Merchandise Trade by Principal Trading Areas, 2012 (first 3 quarters)

Country	Exports (%)	Imports (%)
United States	74.5	50.9
United Kingdom	4.3	1.9
China	4.2	10.7
Japan	2.4	3.3
Mexico	1.1	5.4
All Other Countries	13.5	27.8

Source: Canadian International Merchandise Trade Database, Statistics Canada.

[7] Based on Statistics Canada CANSIM table 380-0064.

TABLE 7.10 Changes in Population and Living Standards, 1975–2011

Country	Population Increase	Real Per Capita GDP Increase
Norway	23%	119%
Japan	14	104
United States	44	90
Hong Kong SAR*	59	381
Canada	49	75
Australia	63	90
France	21	70
Mexico	91	54
Brazil	82	66
China	47	1,705
Egypt	106	229
India	100	278
Pakistan	158	228
Nigeria	149	41
Congo (D.R.)	243	−66

Source: World Bank *World Development Indicators* database tables.
*Hong Kong is part of China, but is shown separately here.

capita GDP. The change in per capita GDP is adjusted to reflect changes in real purchasing power. Thus, for example, the amount an average person in Norway could buy rose by 119 per cent over this period—more than doubling. The numbers also show the percentage change in population between 1975 and 2011. This table illustrates the "big picture" concerning real income comparisons. As expected, there are wealthy countries and poor countries. It is hard, however, for people living in places such as Canada to comprehend the desperate circumstances of the poorest countries.

A striking fact shown by the table is the stunning growth in per capita income of China in the past 35 years. Per capita living standards in China are still modest compared to the wealthiest countries, but they have improved dramatically, by a factor of 17, since the late 1970s when China began its transition from a centrally planned economy to a market-based economy. India has also been growing rapidly in recent years, and for similar reasons relating to market-based reforms. The improved performance of China and India, which together accounted for about one-third of the world's population in 2012, has lifted a significant fraction of the world's population out of poverty.

Economic performance in Africa continues to be disappointing. Nigeria has performed better than most African countries, as many have had little improvement in living standards over the past 35 years. Living standards in some countries have even declined, including in the Democratic Republic of the Congo, whose disastrous experience over the past few decades has left it as one of the world's poorest countries, along with several nearby countries in sub-Saharan Africa. These impoverished African countries have the world's highest population growth rates, contributing to their poor economic performance and increasing the number of people living in desperate circumstances.

The path followed by the rest of the world is very important for Canada's business environment. Economic development in other parts of world means markets for Canadian products, opportunities for Canadian-based multinational firms, and sources of supply for imports. However, the increasing gap between rich and poor in the world economy along with the problems created by excessively rapid population growth in low income countries could easily foster violent conflict and ecological decline. These concerns loom as major considerations for public policy at the international level, and as possible influences on domestic policy.

8

International Trade Policy

8.1 Introduction

International trade is a very important part of Canadian business activity. In recent years, exports have accounted for 30 to 35 percent of Canadian gross domestic product (GDP) on an annual basis,[1] a greater share than in earlier decades and a high trade share by international standards. In addition, many firms producing for the domestic market compete with imports, and many other firms are dependent on imports of inputs for their own production. In total, well over 50 percent of private sector activity in Canada is closely connected to international trade. Public policy toward international trade is therefore very important in Canada, one of the few countries in the world where international trade policy has frequently dominated political debate.

Most of Canada's trade (more than 60 percent) is with the United States, but U.S. dominance in Canadian trade flows has diminished in recent years, as is shown in Table 8.1.

The table shows Canada's trade partners in current order of importance. The U.S. is still dominant, but it is interesting that China has emerged as Canada's second-most important trading partner, from being virtually negligible as recently as the mid-1980s.

---

[1] See Statistics Canada CANSIM table 380-0106.

TABLE 8.1 Major Canadian Trading Partners Share of Total Trade, 1926–2010 (Exports plus Imports)

	1926	1955	1970	1985	2000	2005	2010
U.S.A.	49	67	67	75	76	71	62
China	0	0	0	0	2	4	7
Japan	0	1	5	5	3	3	3
United Kingdom	28	13	7	3	2	2	3
Other	23	19	21	17	17	20	25

Sources: M.C. Urquhart and K. Buckley. 1983. *Historical Statistics of Canada*, 2nd ed. Macmillan: Toronto; Statistics Canada CANSIM Table 380-0106; Statistics Canada *The Daily*, April 7, 2011, Table 1.

Canada is a trading nation. However, the extent of trade varies from province to province and region to region within Canada, with some regions heavily involved with trade, and others more self-sufficient. Western Canada exports a large quantity of resource-based products to Asia (including agricultural products), whereas southern Ontario's trade is more focused on the United States and is mostly in manufactured products.

This chapter focuses on the theory, vocabulary, and main concepts of international trade policy. This discussion falls naturally into the following categories. Section 8.2 deals with the basic economics of international trade, including the theory of comparative advantage. It also emphasizes the relationship between industrial organization and international trade. Section 8.3 surveys the major instruments of trade policy, and 8.4 reviews the normative reasons for trade policy. A positive analysis of international trade policy is undertaken in 8.5. Section 8.6 describes the major institutions governing international trade in the global economy, and section 8.7 focuses on Canada–U.S. trade relations and the North American Free Trade Agreement (NAFTA). Section 8.8 contains concluding remarks.

8.2 The Basic Economics of International Trade
8.2.1 Comparative Advantage
Consider the following problem. You are a senior manager in a multinational corporation, Hi-tech Inc., producing a specialized high-technology product. Each finished product contains components that must be produced and assembled. Thus, a given employee might work in either component production

TABLE 8.2 Output per Worker per Month

	Components	Assembly
Canada	4	4
Caledonia	2	1

or assembly. Your firm has production facilities in two countries: Canada and Caledonia. Canadian workers are somewhat more productive than Caledonian workers. One Canadian worker can produce enough components for four products per month or, given the components, four finished products per month. In Caledonia, one worker can produce enough components for two finished products per month or can actually assemble one final product per month. These basic data are illustrated in Table 8.2.

At the moment, you have 120 workers under contract in Canada and 240 under contract in Caledonia. No workers can be laid off in the short run. Assuming the costs of transporting components are minor, how should production be allocated between Canada and Caledonia to maximize output per month?

One possibility is to have the production facility in each country produce complete products, doing both production and assembly. In this case, the Canadian plant would allocate 60 workers to components and 60 to assembly, producing 240 finished products per month. In Caledonia, 80 workers would be allocated to components and 160 to assembly, yielding an output of 160 finished products per month. The firm's total output over both countries would be 400 products per month.

A second possibility is to have Caledonia specialize in component production. If all workers in Caledonia produced components, they could produce enough for 480 final products. If these components were then transported to Canada, they could be assembled by the 120 Canadian workers, yielding a total output of 480 products per month. This second allocation of labour, involving specialization and trade, is in fact the allocation that maximizes output. The gain over *autarky*—the no-trade case—is 80 products. These 80 extra products represent the gains from trade.

The pattern of specialization is important. If Caledonia were to specialize in assembly, then 60 Canadian workers would produce 240 sets of components per month for export to and assembly in Caledonia, enough to keep the workers there fully occupied. The remaining 60 Canadian workers would be divided into a group of 30 workers producing components for assembly in Canada and 30 assembling finished products. Thus, 120 finished products

TABLE 8.3 Total Production

	Total Production
Autarky (no trade)	400
Caledonia specializes in components	480
Caledonia specializes in assembly	360

would come from the Canadian plant and 240 from the Caledonian plant, yielding a total of only 360 finished products, which is actually less than the production under autarky. This production information is summarized in Table 8.3.

Why are there gains from Caledonia specializing in component production? It cannot be that Caledonian workers are better at producing components than Canadian workers, because Canadian workers are in fact twice as efficient in component production as Caledonian workers are. The answer is related to opportunity cost. In Canada, moving one worker from assembly to component production means that components for four extra products can be produced, but four fewer units are assembled. The opportunity cost of the extra components is one less product assembled per additional set of components produced. In Caledonia, on the other hand, the opportunity cost of an additional set of components is only one-half that in lost assembly. Because the opportunity cost of component production is lower in Caledonia than it is in Canada, it is to the firm's advantage to have Caledonia specialize in components. In other words, Caledonia has a comparative advantage in component production.

> *Definition*: A country is said to have a **comparative advantage** in the production of X if the opportunity cost of producing more X is lower in that country than it is in other countries.

A dentist who is very good at cleaning patients' teeth would still be better off hiring a dental hygienist to do cleaning and focusing his or her time on more sophisticated dental work. The opportunity cost of cleaning teeth is just too high from a dentist's point of view. Cleaning teeth is not a dentist's area of comparative advantage, even if the dentist is very good at it. The dentist has a comparative advantage in sophisticated dental work, and will earn more income by specializing in such work. Similarly, it pays for a country to specialize in its areas of comparative advantage.

The idea of comparative advantage was first described early in the 19th century by an English stockbroker and economist named David Ricardo. Ricardo's famous example involved England and Portugal. Ricardo first assumed that England was absolutely more efficient in producing cloth than Portugal was, and that Portugal was absolutely more efficient in producing wine. Under these circumstances, there are obvious advantages to having England specialize in cloth production, exporting it to Portugal, while Portugal specializes in wine and exports it to England.

Ricardo then imagined that England was not only more efficient in cloth production, but also in wine production. Suppose, for example, that each English worker could produce four units of wine per time period or, alternatively, four units of cloth, and that each worker in Portugal could produce two units of wine or one unit of cloth. Suppose, before trade, that each country is producing both products. Now consider the following thought experiment. Move one worker in England from wine production to cloth production. This reduces wine production by four units and increases world cloth production by four units. Simultaneously, transfer three workers in Portugal from cloth to wine. This increases wine production by six units, more than compensating for the reduction in English production of wine. In addition, cloth production falls by only three units, less than the gain in England. In aggregate, the gain is one unit of cloth and two units of wine.

This thought experiment demonstrates the gains from trade. Portuguese workers need not fear being undercut by more efficient English workers, and English workers need not fear cheap Portuguese labour. Both groups can be made better off through specialization (according to comparative advantage) and trade.

It is true, of course, that real wages in each country will depend on absolute productivity levels and that English workers will be better off than Portuguese workers because they are more productive. If productivity levels in Portugal increase, then workers in Portugal will earn higher real wages. Regardless of absolute productivity levels, however, both sides can gain from trade.

The Ricardian model of comparative advantage is a very simplified view of the world. It ignores the costs associated with moving workers from one industry to another, which may be substantial. It also ignores potential complications created by imperfect competition and increasing returns to scale. Nevertheless, it powerfully illustrates the most important idea in trade policy: there are gains from trade.

An implication of the theory of comparative advantage is that countries trade with each other because they are different. If the nature of production and demand were the same in each country, there would be no comparative advantage because the opportunity cost of each good would be the same in each country. There are several reasons why production possibilities are different in different countries. Most importantly, different countries have different basic resources, or factor endowments. Also, climate, education levels, consumer tastes, and technology all contribute to differences in comparative advantage across countries. Thus, the theory of comparative advantage explains why Canada might export forest products to China and import coffee from Brazil.

8.2.2 Comparative Advantage, Competitive Advantage, and the Exchange Rate

In policy debates, one often hears the terms "competitive advantage" and "competitiveness." From the point of view of an individual firm, having a competitive advantage means being able to produce a product of given quality at a lower cost than your rivals, including your international rivals. It is less clear what a national competitive advantage might be, and it certainly does not follow that policies which would make firms more internationally competitive are necessarily in the national interest.

The most obvious way for a firm to improve its competitive advantage is to lower its costs directly by paying lower wages and lower taxes. While the firm itself would certainly benefit from such cost reductions, it would not necessarily be good for the country as a whole. We could always be more competitive by lowering real wages, but the cost would be a lowered standard of living. Similarly, firms would be more competitive if they did not have to pay taxes, but that would mean giving up the socially provided services those taxes pay for. Arguments that Canadian policy should do something to offset the competitive advantage of relatively low-wage or low-tax countries such as the Philippines or Mexico are highly questionable.

A firm could also become more competitive by improving its productivity. This might come about through having more productive workers, a more stable and predictable political environment, better infrastructure (roads, communications systems, etc.), or for other reasons. A competitive advantage derived from increased productivity is in the national interest. In fact, high productivity is precisely what allows Canadian workers and citizens to have high wages and high standards of living.

Among the short-run influences on competitive advantage, exchange rate movement is probably the most important. The exchange rate is the rate at which one currency can be exchanged for another. In this book, we refer to the exchange rate as the foreign currency price of a unit of domestic currency. For example, if one Canadian dollar can be exchanged for $0.98 (or 98 cents) in U.S. currency, then the exchange rate is US$0.98. When an exchange rate appreciates, it means the foreign currency price of one unit of the domestic currency is rising. For example, if the Canadian dollar were to rise from US$0.98 to US$1.02, we would say that the Canadian dollar had appreciated. Conversely, if the value of the Canadian dollar fell to US$0.95, we would say that the dollar had depreciated, or that the exchange rate had fallen.

Exchange rate appreciation increases the purchasing power of the domestic currency on world markets. It is therefore good for consumers, especially if they are planning foreign vacations. However, an increase in the exchange rate also tends to reduce the competitive advantage of Canadian producers. Canadian firms require a certain price, in Canadian dollars, to cover their Canadian-dollar costs. If the value of the Canadian dollar rises, that price translates into a higher foreign currency price than before. This makes it easier for foreign producers to undercut Canadian producers.

Suppose, for example, that a producer of Canadian plywood can produce one standard-sized sheet of plywood for C$5.00. If the U.S. exchange rate is 90 cents, then a price of US$4.50 would cover these costs. Suppose now that the Canadian dollar appreciates to "par"—to a value of US$1.00. To cover costs of C$5.00, the firm would now have to charge a price of US$5.00 in the U.S. market, making it more vulnerable to U.S. competition.

Short-run movements in the exchange rate are influenced by many factors, including a variety of government policies. In the long run, exchange rate movements reflect comparative advantage. Consider the example of England and Portugal in the previous section, and suppose that, initially, England could produce both wine and cloth more efficiently (in labour time) than Portugal. Suppose further that at the initial exchange rate England was able to sell both wine and cloth more cheaply than Portugal. In other words, a Portuguese importer could take escudos (the historical Portuguese currency now replaced by the euro), exchange them for British pounds, buy British wine (or cloth), and save money over what it would have cost to buy the wine or cloth in Portugal.

Such a situation would not persist. The process of buying British pounds with Portuguese escudos would bid up the price of English pounds (as measured in escudos). The appreciation of the pound-escudo exchange rate would continue until importing English wine into Portugal was no longer profitable, and wine would be exported from Portugal to Britain instead. In the long run, the exchange rate will adjust so that domestic producers of the good in which a country has a comparative advantage have a competitive advantage over foreign rivals in world markets.

If Portuguese productivity were to improve drastically so that Portuguese firms could undersell British firms in both wine and cloth, the exchange rate would eventually have to adjust. The higher levels of Portuguese productivity would be reflected in an appreciation of the Portuguese currency. This appreciation would mean that Portuguese workers could then buy more goods on world markets, an increase in their real wages.

While we will not discuss exchange rates in any detail here, one problem is that short-run fluctuations of the exchange rate can temporarily create a competitive disadvantage in an industry in which a country has a long-run comparative advantage. There is often pressure on governments to do something to protect the industry in question. One approach is to use domestic monetary policy (as described in Chapter 14) to move the exchange rate toward what is believed to be its long run level.

On balance, it is reasonable to be concerned about competitiveness at the national level, as long as we keep in mind that competitiveness is not an end in itself. If we become more competitive as a result of productivity improvements, then living standards will rise, which is good. However, if instead we become more competitive by lowering wages, then all we do is lower living standards. Such adjustments might sometimes be necessary, but they are not a cause for self-congratulation.

8.2.3 Increasing Returns to Scale

Ricardo's reasoning assumes constant returns to scale. If labour is the only factor of production, this means that output per worker stays the same no matter how much is produced. More generally, with many factors of production, we say there are constant returns to scale if a proportionate increase in all inputs yields the same proportionate increase in output. Real production processes, however, are often characterized by increasing returns to scale, which means there are advantages to producing large quantities of output. At the level of the individual firm, increasing returns to scale are reflected in a downward sloping average cost curve: average cost falls as output rises, at least up to some limit.

Not all production processes have increasing returns to scale, but many do, especially those with large fixed overhead costs. For example, it is frequently argued that automobile production has increasing returns because of the high costs of getting an assembly line set up for a particular model. Once an assembly line is set up and calibrated, it is relatively easy to produce additional cars. Thus, good performance in automobile production requires long production runs. The production of electric power is another industry with substantial economies of scale.

International trade may result from increasing returns to scale. Furthermore, the presence of increasing returns to scale expands the gains from trade. Consider a small country, such as Chile. Left to itself, such a country could not economically produce certain goods, such as jet aircraft, an industry with very substantial increasing returns to scale. The small market size of Chile means that only a small demand for jet aircraft exists. Therefore, if jet aircraft were produced for just the Chilean market, they would be produced at a very high average cost. If, on the other hand, one firm were to produce jet aircraft for both Chile and a second country, say Argentina, that firm would achieve a lower average cost per jet than in the case of autarky. Thus, there are incentives for a firm in one country to produce jet aircraft and export some of its production to another country.

In the real world, both Chile and Argentina take part in a much larger trading community and both countries benefit by being able to import jet aircraft from low-cost producers in other countries. The point is that increasing returns to scale lead to advantages from specialization and trade, even if countries are very similar. Increasing returns to scale are therefore an important cause of trade.

The motor vehicle industry in Canada and the United States illustrates the importance of increasing returns to scale in Canada's trade. The enormous volume of trade in motor vehicles and parts across the Canada–U.S. border has accounted for about 15 percent of Canada's total merchandise trade in recent years, with both parts and assembled vehicles going in both directions.

However, it is hard to tell which country has a comparative advantage relative to the other as the economics of automobile production are very similar in Canada and the United States. Normally, comparative advantage is determined in part by relative factor endowments. Thus, for example, we expect countries with large relative supplies of unskilled labour to have a comparative advantage in producing goods that use a lot of low-skilled labour, and countries with substantial natural resources to have a comparative advantage in production of resource-based products. However, Canada and the United States have relatively similar factor proportions as far as relevance to the motor vehicle sector is concerned, so factor-based explanations cannot explain the large volume of motor vehicle trade between the two countries.

This trade between Canada and the United States in automobiles is not based on comparative advantage; it is based on economies of scale. Some

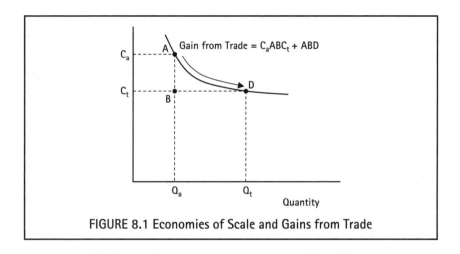

FIGURE 8.1 Economies of Scale and Gains from Trade

models are produced in Canada for the entire North American market, such as the Lexus RX 350 produced by Toyota. Other models are produced in the United States and exported to Canada.

Figure 8.1 illustrates how increasing returns to scale (or economies of scale) generate gains from trade. This figure has a downward sloping average cost curve. Before trade, the firm is producing at low levels of output as indicated by Q_a (the subscript "a" stands for autarky). Its average cost is high, as indicated by C_a. After trade, output expands to Q_t and average cost falls to C_t. This decline in average cost may generate gains for the firm in the form of higher profits, for consumers in lower prices, or for workers in higher wages and salaries.

The downward movement along their average cost curve that results when firms engage in international trade is sometimes referred to as rationalization. At a practical level, it is important to know where scale economies arise and how significant they are. Most Canadian economists have emphasized product-specific, plant-level scale economies. This suggests that gains do not come so much from having large, diversified firms as from longer production runs on the factory floor.

8.2.4 Market Structure

One other implicit assumption of Ricardo's reasoning, in addition to constant returns to scale, is that markets are perfectly competitive. If markets are perfectly competitive, then prices equal marginal cost (as described in more detail in Chapter 6). Therefore, prices will be high if costs are high, and such goods will be imported if they are produced more cheaply abroad (as they will be if foreign countries have a comparative advantage in this good).

If, however, foreign production is controlled by a monopolist, then it is no longer true that price will equal marginal cost, as the price will also include a monopoly markup. Before trade, the price of the good in the foreign country might be higher than the domestic price, even if a comparative advantage in production is enjoyed by the foreign country. The domestic country might, under such circumstances, end up exporting this good, and foreign consumers will then benefit from lower prices arising from higher levels of competition in their markets.

This example illustrates two points. First, market structure (reflecting the degree of competition) itself influences trade patterns. Second, one consequence of trade is increased competition, because firms in different countries are induced to compete with each other. Some firms may lose profits in this process, but the more efficient firms will often gain, and consumers will benefit. The net benefits will exceed the losses to the less efficient firms, leading to additional gains from trade.

8.3 Types of Trade Policy

Having discussed the basic economics of international trade, we are now prepared to discuss trade policy more directly. The next step is to go over the main instruments of trade policy. The most common objective of trade policy is to restrict imports. Such policies are referred to as "protection" because they protect the domestic industry from foreign competition. It is also fairly common for governments to attempt export promotion, or encouragement of exports, often by using subsidies.[2] In addition, policies seeking to discourage exports or encourage imports are possible, but relatively rare. Our discussion of trade policy will focus primarily on protection—restricting or reducing imports.

8.3.1 Import Restricting Policies
Protective policies include the following:

1. tariffs
2. quotas (or quantitative restrictions)

---

[2] Although the World Trade Organization (WTO) and the North American Free Trade Agreement (NAFTA) now prohibit export subsidies, governments manage to provide disguised subsidies in some cases. A more innocuous method of export promotion is through trade missions, where government officials and business executives take trips to foreign countries to promote exports. However, as shown by Head and Ries (2010), such missions seem to be of little value.

3. government procurement polices
4. administrative barriers to trade
5. other regulations

8.3.2 Tariffs

Definition: A **tariff** is a special tax levied on an imported good or, more rarely, on an exported good.

Tariffs may be expressed in *ad valorem* terms, meaning as a percentage of the price. Alternatively, they may be expressed as specific tariffs, which are fixed sums independent of the price, such as $1 per unit. Historically, tariffs are by far the most important type of trade policy. The earliest tariffs no doubt predate recorded history, and even today, tariffs exercise an important influence on trade flows and government budgets. Tariffs are attractive to governments in part because they raise revenue for the government, and they are also popular with domestic industries competing with imports. An important example of tariffs in Canada is in the area of textiles and clothing, where significant tariffs are applied to many products originating outside the North American Free Trade Area (NAFTA) region, consisting of Canada, Mexico, and the United States.

8.3.3 Quotas

Quotas, or quantitative restrictions (QRs), are fixed limits on imports. Quotas are usually implemented using licences. Thus, for example, a licence may be obtained from the government of an importing country by an exporter in another country to export up to some specific number of units of the good. Quota licences are sometimes sold to exporters, or to importers, creating revenue for the government. However, more commonly, quotas are simply given away and therefore generate no government revenue. Import-competing domestic industries tend to prefer quota protection to tariff protection. Quite a few products are subject to both quotas and tariffs.

One interesting special kind of quota is the so-called voluntary export restraint, or VER. This is a quota voluntarily agreed to by the producers and monitored and controlled by them. A VER is no different from an ordinary quota in its effect on the consumer. Unlike ordinary quotas, however, VERs cannot raise revenue for the government, nor can they be given to domestic importers. Furthermore, VERs can be a tool to facilitate collusion among exporters. VERs allow exporters to restrain competition among themselves by, in effect, acting as a cartel agreement limiting the output of each firm.

Ries (1993) presents evidence that a VER on Japanese automobiles exported to the United States and Canada resulted in significant increases in profitability for Japanese exporters.

8.3.4 Government Procurement

When it comes to government procurement of goods and services, most countries give preference to domestic producers. This means that a domestic government will give preference to a local supplier, even if a lower price could be obtained elsewhere. The United States claims that Canada's Crown corporations (corporations owned by government) follow strong "buy Canada" policies, especially in telecommunications and transportation. Such policies create an incentive for domestic suppliers to quote higher prices than they otherwise would. The extent to which such preferential purchasing causes prices to rise depends on the level of local competition.

8.3.5 Administrative Barriers to Trade

The term "administrative barriers" refers to the cost of filling in forms, lining up at customs offices, waiting to get permission to export, and all the other administrative procedures that make it harder (and more costly) to export rather than to produce and sell locally. While it is difficult to measure the effects of administrative barriers to trade, many small businesses argue that such barriers are a serious impediment, especially for Canadian producers hoping to sell in Asia.

8.3.6 Regulatory Barriers

Governments regulate many aspects of economic activity. Such regulations normally focus on a nontrade objective, such as making sure the food supply is safe or that monopoly power is not abused. However, regulations can have an important impact on trade flows. For example, safety regulations are often used to prevent imports deemed to be unsafe. Such interventions are sometimes legitimate but at other times seem to be merely an excuse to engage in protectionism—protecting domestic producers from foreign competition.

In Canada, probably the most important regulatory structures affecting international trade are agricultural marketing boards with supply management power. Such boards, which are particularly important in dairy products and eggs and poultry, have the power to determine who is allowed to sell and how much they can sell in Canada (or in a specific province in Canada). Such marketing boards normally use their power to exclude foreign products.

8.3.7 Interprovincial Trade Barriers

Our discussion of trade policy generally refers to national trade policies pursued by sovereign governments, especially the Canadian government. In Canada, however, provincial governments also carry out policies that affect interprovincial and international trade. Strictly speaking, the federal government in Canada has exclusive jurisdiction over international trade policy, so provinces are unable to impose tariffs or quotas. Provinces do, however, use preferential purchasing, administrative barriers, and regulatory barriers in an effort to assist local producers and to discriminate against producers from other provinces and countries. Interprovincial barriers to trade are considered by many to be a significant source of economic inefficiency in Canada.

8.4 Normative Reasons for Trade Policy

8.4.1 Overview of Reasons for Intervention

In our discussion of the economics of international trade, the main point is that there are gains from trade. The apparent policy implication is that the best policy is one of free trade. In other words, countries should not use tariffs, quotas, preferential procurement policies, export subsidies, or other interventions in business activity associated with international trade. This is, in fact, the prescription made by Ricardo, and this prescription is widely accepted by modern economists.

There are, however, a few complications. First of all, even if we agree that free trade is the best policy for the world as a whole, it does not follow that every country faces a unilateral incentive to avoid trade barriers. In fact, much of the international conflict over trade policy reflects an attempt by one country to gain from interventionist trade policy at the expense of other countries. From the nationalist public interest point of view, it might be normatively defensible to pursue a policy whose principal effect is to transfer benefits from other countries, leading to trade policies of the beggar-thy-neighbour variety.

Second, the prescription that free trade is the best policy does not apply to all situations. There are potential benefits to intervention in some instances, especially in the presence of economies of scale and imperfect competition.

Normative rationales for trade policy include the following:

1. raising revenue
2. non-economic objectives (e.g., military or cultural objectives)
3. exploiting market power in world markets
4. the infant industry argument

5. profit-shifting
6. domestic redistribution
7. increasing employment ?
8. improving the trade balance ?

Of these eight reasons for trade policy intervention, the most politically important are probably the last two, and particularly item 7: increasing employment. It is a rare discussion of trade policy that does not dwell on employment effects. There are, however, question marks after both the employment and trade balance rationales for trade policy intervention, as most existing evidence and most theoretical analysis suggest that interventionist trade polices do not increase aggregate national employment or improve the trade balance. In other words, most economists would argue that the employment and trade balance rationales for policy intervention are spurious. Each of the rationales for intervention is discussed below.

8.4.2 Raising Revenue

Historically, the most important reason for tariffs and trade policy intervention in general is simply to raise revenue for the government. There is general agreement that governments have some legitimate functions. It follows that these functions must be paid for in some way. Virtually any source of finance has efficiency costs associated with it. For example, personal income taxes reduce work incentives, corporate income taxes reduce corporate activity, money creation creates an inflation tax, government borrowing reduces private investment and raises long-term liabilities, and so on. Application of the marginalist principle suggests the appropriate way to raise revenue is to impose taxes in such a way that the marginal efficiency loss is the same on all taxes, including tariffs. This will imply positive tariffs.

In the past, tariffs were a relatively efficient form of taxation, because collection costs were much lower than for other taxes. It was relatively easy to identify goods coming from overseas, because such goods would come through the dock areas of port cities. The customs official could stand near the dock and collect duties as goods came ashore. Land borders were a bit harder to monitor, but still much easier than other transactions. Collecting income taxes or business taxes was much more difficult than collecting tariffs. For one thing, citizens and businesses would have incentives to lie about their incomes and there was little a government could do about it. Income taxes did not become an important source of revenue until the 20th century.

Nowadays, tariffs contribute only a small fraction, less than 2 percent, of federal government revenue in Canada, and they contribute nothing to provincial government revenues. Over the last few decades, trade liberalization under the WTO has dramatically reduced the importance of tariff revenues for most countries. NAFTA has further reduced tariff revenues in Canada by essentially eliminating tariffs between Canada, Mexico, and the United States. In some countries, however, tariffs and sales of quota rights remain an important revenue source.

8.4.3 Non-Economic Objectives

National governments can use trade policy to pursue military, cultural, or other objectives not directly related to the economic criteria of efficiency, macroeconomic stabilization, or fairness. For example, many countries use tariffs and quotas to protect a domestic steel industry for military reasons, and in Canada, trade policies are used to promote Canadian culture.

8.4.4 Exploiting Market Power

It is quite possible for one country to have potential market power in a particular industry even if underlying producers are small and highly competitive. Consider, for example, Brazil's position in the world coffee market. Brazil is a large enough producer to affect the world price of coffee; if Brazil has a very good crop, world prices fall. Each individual Brazilian producer, however, is much too small to have any influence on world prices. Therefore, individual producers are perfect competitors, and, in the absence of government intervention, they would not earn any above-normal profits from the world coffee market. If, however, the government imposed an export tariff on coffee, it would raise the world price toward the monopoly level, and the government would earn the equivalent of cartel profits (profits based on market power) from the tariff revenue.

Similarly, if a country is a large enough buyer of a particular product, it could use an import tariff to take advantage of its market power. Obvious opportunities to exploit market power using an import tariff are not very numerous, but opportunities for export tariffs are fairly common.

Nevertheless, market power arguments for tariffs are rarely heard in political discussion, even in private, and they are never heard in public political debate. The reason is that export tariffs are not very well-received by producers, since they (the producers) do not benefit directly, and in fact may lose. Producers would prefer a policy of quantity restrictions, without export taxes, so that they earn the market power rents. Since producer groups are effective special interest groups, supply restraint is more common than export tariffs.

8.4.5 The Infant Industry Argument

The revenue-raising motive for tariffs is probably as old as international trade itself. The infant industry argument is not that old, but it has been around for a long time. In Canada, for example, it was used in the early days following Canada's Confederation in 1867 to justify a national policy of high tariffs against U.S. manufactured goods.

The argument for infant industry protection runs as follows. In general, free trade is the best policy. A country might not, however, be able to achieve its natural comparative advantage, especially if other countries are already well-established in the relevant industries. For example, Canada might potentially be a successful producer and exporter of high-technology computer hardware, but forced to compete with U.S. giants such as IBM, Hewlett-Packard, and Apple, the Canadian industry might never have a chance to get going. A potential entrant must be prepared to suffer large losses while it trains its labour force, acquires a consumer base, and so on. The infant industry argument suggests, therefore, that such industries be given protection (or subsidies) in their early years, or infancy, to allow them a competitive advantage in the domestic market until they can compete internationally. It is argued that Japan and South Korea have followed successful infant industry policies in areas such as consumer electronics.

This argument is related to the concept of learning by doing, which refers to the idea that, for some types of production, experience is important in improving productivity. This certainly sounds persuasive. We all know it takes time for a firm to become efficient and profitable. If we know it, however, bankers, investors, and entrepreneurs should know it too. If computer hardware is a potentially profitable industry for Canadian firms then investors should be willing to accept short-term losses in return for long-term gains. Private financial markets exist precisely for the purpose of providing financial support for firms with good investment opportunities. If it can be argued that private financial markets are not doing their job and that there is some market failure in financial markets, then infant industry protection might be appropriate. The point to be emphasized is that there must be some market failure for the infant industry argument to make sense. Thus, market failure in financial markets is a possible justification for infant industry protection.

Another possible market failure justification for the infant industry argument is based on positive externalities. Suppose the domestic country has a potential comparative advantage in some industry. Suppose further that there is no labour with the appropriate skills, and if one firm did train workers they would soon quit to start up their own firms. Thus, any firm would confer benefits on other firms that it could not capture for itself. In such a situation, a potentially valuable industry might never get going—it might fail to achieve *critical mass*. It could be reasonable to get the industry started using an infant industry tariff.

One practical problem with the infant industry argument for protection is that there are currently some very old infants around, and some industries are in their second childhood. Even a very good set of policy analysts in government will not pick winners 100 percent of the time and probably not even 50 percent of the time. It must be expected that some attempts at infant industry protection will not be successful. The problem is that it becomes politically very difficult to abandon an industry that needs protection in order to survive. The cost of supporting industries that pass from infancy to old age without any intervening period of maturity must be set against the benefits of any successes.[3]

8.4.6 Profit-Shifting

The profit-shifting argument for interventionist trade policy focuses on the presence of imperfect competition in international markets. The basic idea is that government policy can be used to increase the domestic share of the above-normal profits that may be available in imperfectly competitive industries.

The simplest case of profit extraction involves imposing tariffs on imports from a foreign firm with monopoly power. Such a tariff will divert some of the monopoly profits into the domestic treasury. It will also act in part as a tax on consumers, but, on balance, the country can gain from the appropriately chosen tariff. A more interesting case arises when there is a domestic firm in the market as well, or if there is a potential domestic entrant. The outcome of a tariff depends on the way in which firms interact, but the tariff can be expected to damage the competitive position of the foreign firm, shifting profits from the foreign firm to the domestic firm.

In a slightly different form of profit-shifting, profits in world markets are the target. In this case, subsidization of a domestic firm may enhance its competitive position and increase its profits sufficiently for there to be a net gain to the domestic economy, at the expense of rivals. This analysis

---

[3] A very interesting attempt to estimate the effects of infant industry tariffs is presented by Head (1994).

TABLE 8.4 Profits without Government Subsidy

		Airbus			
		Enter		Not Enter	
Boeing	Enter	−5	−5	100	0
	Not Enter	0	100	0	0

derives from Brander and Spencer (1985) and is presented in very clear terms in Krugman (1987).

Suppose two countries are capable of producing a particular good. For concreteness, let us call the good a 300-seat passenger aircraft and let us call the countries America and France. Also, assume there is one firm in each country that can produce the good. We will call the firms Boeing and Airbus, respectively. Suppose the internal market for this product is small in both countries, and most consumption of the product is in other countries (as it might well be for a particular type of aircraft). We can then take the profit earned as the appropriate measure of national benefit from this product for each of the two countries.

We assume each firm must choose either to produce the product or not. We also assume the market is profitable for one firm if it is the only entrant, but the market will be unprofitable if both firms enter and must share the market. The profits or payoffs are shown in Table 8.4. The first number in each cell is the payoff to Boeing (and America), while the second number is the payoff to Airbus (and France).

Given this payoff matrix, the outcome is indeterminate. If either firm enters, the other would prefer not to. If, for example, Boeing entered while Airbus did not, then Boeing would earn a return of 100 and Airbus would earn nothing. If Airbus did enter, its return would be -5, so it would prefer not to enter. Similarly, if Airbus enters and Boeing does not, then Boeing would prefer not to enter. What can government policy do? Suppose the European government offers a subsidy of 10 to Airbus if it enters. The new payoff structure is shown in Table 8.5.

In this case, the outcome is clear: Airbus will enter and Boeing will not. The basic reason for this outcome is that the subsidy makes entering a dominant strategy for Airbus. Entering is the best strategy for Airbus no matter what Boeing does. If Boeing enters as well, Airbus still earns 5, which is better than

TABLE 8.5 Profits with Government Subsidy

		Airbus			
		Enter		Not Enter	
	Enter	−5	5	100	0
Boeing					
	Not Enter	0	100	0	0

the zero it gets if it does not enter. If Boeing does not enter, then Airbus gains 110 by entering. Thus, Airbus should certainly enter. Knowing that Airbus will enter for certain, Boeing should not enter, for it will lose 5 for certain. Thus, Airbus will earn 110 and Boeing will earn nothing. This policy has ensured a net benefit of 100 (110 minus the subsidy of 10) to France. Profits have been shifted to Airbus, hence the term "profit-shifting."

8.4.7 Domestic Redistribution
One major aspect of trade policy is that it can be used to redistribute income and wealth within a country. For example, tariff protection for an industry located in a particular region will tend to raise the income of that region at the expense of other regions. More directly, tariff protection for a particular industry will tend to raise the incomes of people involved in that industry.

Trade policy can also affect the distribution of income between different types of workers or between workers and owners of capital. It now seems that trade liberalization in the world as a whole has put downward pressure on the incomes of low-skilled workers in high-income countries such as Canada and the United States. Trade liberalization appears to be part of the story behind the increasing income inequality in Canada, the United States, and other high-income countries that has occurred in the past 20 years.

Would it make sense for a government in such a country to try to use trade policy to offset this change? If we wanted to make the distribution of income more equal in Canada we could, for example, provide tariff protection to industries that employ many low-income workers. However, most analysts would claim that trade policy is a very poor tool to use in pursuing redistributional objectives.

The trade liberalization that has occurred in the past few decades has generated significant net gains. Some of those gains have gone to high-income earners in in high-income countries. In countries such as China, India, and

Korea, it seems that people at all levels of income have experienced gains from trade. Low-income workers in high-income countries have been hurt, but economists would argue that if we want to help such people it would make more sense to use other policies, such as reducing their taxes, providing better training and education, or possibly by making transfers to them. Such policies would allow for the efficiency gains of trade liberalization while providing compensation to those who would otherwise lose.

8.4.8 Employment

Politically, the most important rationale for trade policy intervention is employment promotion. Almost every discussion of trade policy focuses on the employment consequences of the policy under consideration. For example, during the debate in Canada and the United States leading up to ratification of NAFTA, former U.S. presidential candidate Ross Perot became famous for asserting that tariff reductions under NAFTA would give rise to a "giant sucking sound" as jobs and factories moved from the United States to Mexico.

Despite the attention paid to the employment effects of tariff and quota protection, the main conclusion of economic analysis is that protection in the form of tariffs and quotas (or in any other form) has little effect on employment. To the extent that there is an effect, it tends to be negative. In short, the employment argument for protection is spurious. The conclusion that protection does not promote employment is based partly on historical experience. During the Great Depression of the 1930s, many countries increased tariffs in an attempt to protect industries damaged by the decline in business activity. The net effect was apparently a further reduction in employment, making the depression worse. Conversely, the trade liberalizations of the postwar period seem to have boosted employment and economic activity.

There are good reasons why protection is likely to damage rather than help aggregate employment. Before looking at these, however, it is important to observe that protection certainly does increase employment in the protected industry. If tariffs in the textile industry (polyester, cotton, wool, etc.) were removed, it is probable that many Canadian workers in this industry would lose their jobs.[4] And higher tariffs or re-introduction of strict quotas would expand employment in the industry. The problem is that protection in one industry, such as textiles, is damaging to employment in other industries.

---

[4] The textile industry is a standard example of protection in Canada. However, even in this area, tariffs have fallen significantly. As of 2012, there are no tariffs on textile imports from the United States or Mexico (due to NAFTA) and tariffs of 10% to 12% on most textiles from other countries. See www.apparel.ca/textile_tariffs.html. Textile quotas in Canada were largely eliminated in 2005.

There are at least five reasons why protection for one industry reduces employment in other industries:

1. Because of protection, prices will be higher for the output of the protected industry. This means industries using that output as an input for their production will face higher costs and have lower employment. Textiles, for example, are used as an input in the clothing and apparel industry and in various other industries.
2. Because of protection, employment will be higher in the protected industry. Some of this higher employment will simply be in the form of workers bid away from other industries, rather than in the form of workers taken from the pool of unemployed workers. If the industry in question has higher than normal wages, workers might even prefer to wait in an unemployment queue for these high-wage jobs, rather than work in lower-paying jobs elsewhere. (The textile industry is not a high-wage industry, but many protected industries are.)
3. Other countries are likely to retaliate, reducing employment in export industries.
4. Even if protection is successful in reducing net imports, there will be adjustments in the exchange rate that tend to induce a corresponding decrease in exports. This is the least obvious but most important reason why protection does not increase aggregate employment.
5. Finally, protection will normally have net economic costs, resulting in a reduction of average living standards. This effect will be small for protection in any one industry, but, to the extent that it occurs, there will be a depressing effect on aggregate economic activity.

For all of these reasons, employment created in one industry due to protective trade policy tends to be offset by employment lost in other industries. The case is not absolutely clear cut, however. It is possible that by protecting very labour-intensive industries while output declines in more capital-intensive industries, aggregate employment might be slightly raised. However, such a policy would reduce average capital intensity in the economy, effectively reducing productivity and real wages.

The main conclusion of this section is that protection can be very effective in redistributing employment among regions or among industries, but it is not likely to increase aggregate employment. Because of the large amount of supporting evidence, this view of trade liberalization is widely accepted by economists.

8.4.9 The Trade Balance

It is sometimes argued that protection can be used to improve the balance of trade (exports minus imports). The first problem with counter-argument is that it is not clear why having a positive balance of trade should be a policy objective. Second, protection will generally not improve the trade balance. Protection will decrease imports, but it will also tend to decrease exports. The balance of trade is determined mainly by considerations other than the cost of imports. Like the employment rationale for protection, the trade balance rationale is spurious.

8.5 The Positive Theory of International Trade Policy

Despite the long list of normative reasons for activist trade policy, the conclusion at the end of Section 8.4 is that the case for trade policy intervention is not very strong. Raising a little revenue with a tariff may be appropriate, but the other rationales would apply in, at most, a small number of cases, and the employment and trade balance rationales are viewed by most economic analysts as invalid. Why then is interventionist trade policy so common and important? The answer probably lies in the positive analysis of policy.

A positive analysis requires an understanding of who the gainers and losers are from any policy. Consider the textile industry. The beneficiaries of protection are the workers who are able to keep their jobs and the owners (shareholders) of firms in the industry. Furthermore, regions in which this industry is concentrated also benefit from protection.

The losers are harder to identify. Consumers of clothing, which includes all residents of Canada, are certainly losers. They pay higher prices for clothing and other products made from textiles than they otherwise would, and the range of choice is more limited. When quotas were in force (prior to 2005) the low-income consumers were the most seriously affected, because the effects of quotas are most strongly felt in the low-quality, low-price segment of the market. This is due to the fact that suppliers restricted by a quota tend to substitute high-price, high-value items for low-price items. This is the so-called quality upgrading effect of a quota. Other losers are people who might have found jobs in related industries, particularly export industries, if there was less protection in the textile industry. It is hard to identify those affected by this "what if" scenario; all we can say for sure is that there would be such people.

Note that there is a major asymmetry between the losers and the gainers from protection. The gainers know who they are, the issue is very important to them, and they are represented politically by well-organized lobbies.

Furthermore, the gainers are geographically concentrated and represented by elected politicians whose major policy objective is often to maintain or increase protection in the industry. The losers, on the other hand, are geographically dispersed, so they have no political representation. Neither are they represented by any organized lobby. And the costs of the industry protection, although very high when added up for all losers, are not all that high for any one consumer, so no single consumer has an incentive to buy airline tickets to Ottawa to lobby for his or her views. Most importantly, most losers do not even know that they have lost something. Certainly, potential beneficiaries from expanded employment in other industries cannot identify themselves, and most consumers are not aware of the existence of tariffs in the textiles industry that result in unnecessarily high prices for their clothing and other goods made from textiles.

Trade policy in textiles is explained very well by the principles of transfer-seeking described in Chapter 5. More generally, trade policy seems to be very responsive to special interest groups. In addition, support for active trade policy also stems from a misunderstanding about the so-called general equilibrium effects of trade policy described in connection with the employment rationale. Politicians and individual citizens see that protection can save jobs in any one industry, but there is very little recognition that it reduces jobs in others. However, despite such perceptions, the general case for trade liberalization has been increasingly widely accepted over the past few decades and trade barriers in the global economy have fallen significantly.

8.6 The Global Trading System
8.6.1 The General Agreement on Tariffs and Trade
The present-day global trading system has its origins in the General Agreement on Tariffs and Trade (GATT), which went into effect in 1947. Initially, GATT had 23 signatory countries, including Canada, along with the United States and a range of other countries. GATT was developed primarily as an aid to the re-establishment of commercial relations among the nations emerging from World War II. At the time, GATT was thought to be a temporary device to assist in trade liberalization, pending the formation of a permanent international agency for the regulation of international trade.

It took a long time for a permanent international agency to be developed—until the World Trade Organization (WTO) was established in 1995. From 1947 until 1994, GATT functioned both as an international agreement *and* as an international institution. It had a physical presence in the form of a small, permanent secretariat in Geneva. As an agreement or contract among the countries involved (which were referred to as the contracting parties), GATT provided a common set of rules for the conduct of international trade.

GATT also had two other important functions. First, it provided an independent forum for monitoring, discussing, and settling trade disputes. Second, it served as a sponsor for multilateral negotiations on trade policy that worked to reduce tariffs and other trade barriers, allowing for a dramatic liberalization of international trade. GATT was generally viewed as a great success, and by the end of 1994 the number of signatories had risen from the original 23 to 128.

8.6.2 The World Trade Organization

In 1995, the World Trade Organization took over the institutional functions of GATT (and took over its offices and its employees). Most of the GATT signatories immediately became members of the WTO, and by 2012 the WTO membership had grown to 157 member countries, including almost all of the world's significant trading nations.

The case of China is particularly interesting. It was one of the original 23 signatories to GATT, but following the communist takeover in 1949, China abandoned any attempt to meet GATT obligations, and its membership was converted to inactive status. In the late 1990s, China sought to reactivate its GATT membership. China's readmission to GATT and membership in the WTO were the subject of difficult negotiations over a variety of issues, especially intellectual property rights and human rights issues. However, these issues were resolved, or at least put aside, and China became a full member of the WTO in 2001.

GATT continues to exist as a treaty within the WTO. Although GATT is called *an* agreement, it actually contains many agreements on many issues. In addition, the WTO also incorporates two other major treaties—a trade-related intellectual property rights (TRIPS) treaty and the General Agreement on Trade in Services (GATS) treaty dealing with trade in services. Both of these treaties also contain many specific sub-agreements.

8.6.3 Current Issues in WTO Negotiations

Negotiations on trade policy issues continue within the WTO. There is a long list of agenda items, but the most important at present are intellectual property, contingent protection, and the environment.

Intellectual property agreements covered in TRIPS require that patents and copyrights in all member countries be honoured in accordance with specific rules similar to those in force in North America and Europe. Despite this agreement, compliance in most low-income and some middle-income countries is poor. Most of the major producers and owners of intellectual property (such as drug patents, other new product patents, and computer software) are in the wealthiest countries. These owners of intellectual property seek to earn as high a return as possible on this property, and have therefore sought action against the many unlicenced producers of copycat products operating in low-income countries. For example, products such as Chanel perfume, Rolex watches, and Apple iPhones, among others, are copied by producers in countries such as China and Indonesia, and sold without any licence fee being paid to the corporations (such as Rolex or Apple) that own the trademarks and patents associated with these products.

The problem is different with respect to drugs, as it is relatively easy to control production of drugs and prevent copying. And users do want authentic products. The problem with drugs is that many poor countries are virtually priced out of the market. This has become a major issue with respect to AIDS drugs, which are very effective at prolonging and improving the lives of people with AIDS but are relatively expensive. Only a very small fraction of the infected population in Africa is able to obtain such drugs. Some low-income countries are seeking changes in intellectual property regimes, allowing them to obtain low-cost AIDS (and other) drugs.

However, drug companies are reluctant to inexpensively sell, give away, or set up local production of these drugs in poor countries without rigorous monitoring of distribution systems. One major problem is that provision of low-price drugs would create a very strong incentive for those who control local distribution of the drugs to sell them for high prices in wealthier countries, rather than distribute them locally.

Contingent protection, another agenda item, refers to temporary trade measures, including countervailing duty actions, anti-dumping actions, and "safeguard" actions undertaken by governments of importing countries. Such actions are normally initiated based on a complaint from a domestic producer in competition with imports. The complaint is investigated by domestic government authorities who may then impose temporary tariffs to offset the alleged problem. In several high-income countries, especially the United States, companies have taken to launching legal complaints in these areas as a deterrent to foreign rivals. Such complaints may be made to domestic authorities or to the WTO itself. Complaints to domestic authorities have tended to become highly politicized in a number of countries, especially the United States, leading to decisions that often seem to be based on pure transfer-seeking (as described in Chapter 5) rather than on the merits of the case.

Countervailing duty actions arise from instances of export subsidies in violation of the WTO agreement that governments are not supposed to offer export subsidies to specific firms or industries. A wide range of other subsidies, even if not directly targeted at exports, are also "countervailable." In the case of such subsidies, if they are beyond a certain size, and if they actually confer benefits on subsidized firms, then exports from those firms are subject to countervailing action by the government of the importing country. Such action is normally in the form of a special tariff, referred to as a countervailing duty, levied on the subsidized products.

Anti-dumping actions deal with dumping, which occurs when a firm underprices its products. Formally, dumping is defined to occur if an exported product is sold in the export market for a price below its cost of production, or if it sold for a price below its normal home market price. If dumping is identified, then the country where the product is being dumped is entitled to impose an anti-dumping duty. Anti-dumping duties are therefore similar in principle to countervailing duties. The principal difference is that anti-dumping applies to an action taken by foreign firms (i.e., dumping), whereas countervailing duties are to offset an action taken by foreign governments (i.e., subsidies). Anti-dumping and countervailing duties have sunset clauses. Such duties expire automatically after five years, although they can be renewed after a new investigation.

Safeguard actions are those designed to offset a "temporary import surge" happening for unspecified reasons. The logic is simply that it might sometimes be necessary to offset a temporary phenomenon that might otherwise damage a domestic industry. For example, a foreign producer may suddenly decide to liquidate a large inventory and temporarily flood the market. However, critics suggest that the safeguard provision in the WTO is just a loophole that allows governments to impose protection for political convenience.

Environmental issues have become a major agenda item in the WTO. The world is becoming an increasingly crowded place with increasing pressures on natural resources and other aspects of the environment. Much of the world is already facing serious water shortages, and fish stocks are in decline in many major fisheries of the world. And, most importantly, global warming remains a very high-profile issue and is an increasingly serious problem.

Second, various groups of countries have enacted environmental agreements. There are well over 200 international environmental agreements in place between various groups of countries. One very successful multilateral environmental agreement is the Montreal Protocol of 1987, which successfully limited use of chlorofluorocarbons (CFCs) in order to slow and eventually stop ozone depletion. At present, there is considerable discussion regarding the Kyoto Protocol of 1997, which restricts "greenhouse gas" emissions in an effort to slow global warming. The countries of the European Union, Canada, Russia, Japan, and a variety of other countries have ratified the agreement. However, the two most important countries, the United States and China, have not.

Environmental issues have come up in the WTO because of a potential link between environmental policies and trade policies. Specifically, many environmentalists favour using trade sanctions to punish countries that fail to maintain appropriate standards of environmental protection. At a minimum, trade sanctions could be used (and sometimes are used) against goods produced using methods that are excessively damaging to the environment.

8.6.4 The International Monetary Fund

The WTO is one of three international organizations forming a triumvirate for the global regulation and coordination of international trade and investment flows. The other two are the International Monetary Fund (IMF) and the World Bank.

The IMF and the World Bank both arose from the same set of international negotiations that gave rise to GATT (and ultimately to the WTO). The IMF came into formal existence in 1945 with 44 members, including Canada. By the end of 2012 its membership had risen to 188 countries. The basic purpose of the IMF is to support and promote the world trading system by providing relief for short-run balance of payments problems and by promoting the smooth operation of international currency markets. In essence, the WTO deals with flows of goods and services across countries, while the IMF deals with financial flows used to pay for those goods and services.

The most important article of agreement in the IMF is the requirement that member countries maintain currency convertibility for current international transactions. This means that each country agrees to allow importers to exchange their local currency for the currency required to buy products from other countries, and to allow exporters to exchange foreign currency for domestic currency at the same exchange rate (apart from transaction costs). In addition, each country stands willing to redeem its own currency from foreign central banks in return for appropriate assets (such as other currencies).

For example, the Bank of Canada agrees to provide, at a market exchange rate, euros to Canadian importers who wish to import European automobiles. In addition, the Bank of Canada stands ready to buy euros, at (roughly) the same exchange rate. Suppose, for example, the exchange rate is C$1.29 per euro. If the Bank of Canada accumulates an excess of euros, it can then sell them to the European central bank for Canadian dollars at the rate of C\$1.29 for every euro.

Currency convertibility is very important, for without it international trade would be very difficult. In fact, imports are limited in many countries simply by not allowing importers to purchase foreign currency, or by charging very high rates for foreign currency.

The IMF also makes loans to countries to facilitate the solution of international balance of payments and debt problems. For example, in recent years the IMF has made significant loans to Greece. The IMF intends to get its money back, but it is willing to provide short-term credit to struggling governments. Usually, however, the IMF attaches conditions to these loans concerning the domestic macroeconomic policy and exchange rate policy it expects the country to follow. This is referred to as IMF conditionality, and it has been an important cause of market-based economic policy reform in much of world.

8.6.5 The World Bank

The World Bank, as the third member of the international economic triumvirate, provides development funding to governments and private sector participants in a range of countries (mostly low-income countries) to promote economic development. Like the IMF, it came into existence in 1945, with the same set of 44 member countries, and it had the same 188 member countries as of 2012.

The World Bank actually consists of five components. The largest of the five is the International Bank for Reconstruction and Development (IBRD), which lends money on commercial terms to national governments. The International Finance Corporation (IFC) is a second organization, set up to promote direct private investment in developing countries. It takes equity positions in some projects (i.e., it owns shares in the projects) and it also makes loans to the private sector.

The third organization, set up in 1960, is the International Development Association (IDA), which provides loans on very favourable terms (essentially interest free) for periods of 35 to 40 years. These loans are made to governments in the very poorest countries, for financing specific projects. The operations of the IDA provide a net subsidy to poor countries. These subsidized loans were separated from the IBRD loan portfolio so the IBRD could maintain its overall creditworthiness by normal commercial standards.

The fourth organization is the International Centre for Settlement of Investment Disputes (ICSID). As its name suggests, it provides facilities for

mediating and arbitrating disputes between governments and foreign investors. It is a small operation, dealing with a handful of cases per year. Finally,
the most recent addition to the World Bank portfolio of organizations is the
Multilateral Investment Guarantee Agency (MIGA). It provides insurance against
noncommercial or political risks in low-income countries, and insures foreign
investors against such contingencies as war, revolution, and expropriation.

As described so far, the World Bank seems to combine the functions of
a commercial bank (IBRD), an investment bank (IFC), an insurance company
(MIGA), and an arbitrator (ICSID), with some direct foreign aid (IDA) added on.
But the World Bank also has an important role in economic policy development
and implementation. Part of its policy role is to provide skilled supervision
of projects. The more important aspect of its policy role is that it often ties
loans to economic policy reforms in the debtor country. For example, the
World Bank might require trade liberalization or a reduction in public sector
control in return for a loan. In addition, the World Bank has a substantial
research capacity that it exercises on a variety of relevant topics. Much of
this research is published through an active publication series.

The IMF and World Bank overlap to some extent and sometimes cooperate,
as with recent loans to Greece. In principle, however, there is a conceptual
difference between the two organizations. The IMF focuses on short-run loans
to governments to deal with balance of payments problems and temporary
liquidity problems. The World Bank focuses on long-term loans and equity
investments that support specific economic development projects, and lends
money to the private sector as well as to governments.

The organizational structure of the World Bank is much like that of a
private sector corporation, except that its shareholders are the member countries. Countries get some voting power just for being members, but most of the
voting power is allocated in proportion to a country's financial contribution
to the World Bank's portfolio. As of 2012, the United States was the most
important country with about 16 percent of the voting power, followed by
Japan with about 7 percent, a group of countries with about 4 percent each
(China, Germany, the United Kingdom, and France) and many other countries
with smaller shares, including Canada.

8.6.6 The United Nations

There is one additional international institution that should be mentioned:
the United Nations (UN). The UN maintains an ongoing organizational unit
referred to as the Conference on Trade and Development (UNCTAD) to deal
with trade policy issues. The UN also recognizes and has loose affiliations

with the IMF, the World Bank, and the WTO, but at a practical level, all three of these institutions run completely independently of the UN. The main point concerning UNCTAD is that it has very little influence on international trade policy. Most textbooks on international trade, international business, or international finance do not even mention UNCTAD.

The reasons for UNCTAD's lack of significance are worth understanding, for they apply to many UN activities. All international agencies, institutions, tribunals, courts, treaties, and agreements suffer from one great defect—they have no sovereign power to support them. If the Government of Canada chooses to levy taxes on income, residents of Canada must pay those taxes or be carted off to jail (at least suffer some penalty severe enough to induce compliance). The Canadian government has sovereign authority over residents of Canada, and can back up that authority with physical force. International agencies, in contrast, can only obtain voluntary compliance. The IMF might decide to impose a tax on member countries, but it has no way of requiring payment, and very little recourse if payment is not made, short of ejecting a member nation from the IMF, which it is not likely to do.

An international agency can offer financial or other incentives for compliance with its principles—as the IMF, the World Bank, and even the WTO do—and that is where much of their influence comes from. Someone or some country must, however, voluntarily supply the resources used to provide incentives. In the World Bank and the IMF, policies are controlled by those who pay the bills, which, for the most part, are a handful of developed democracies consisting principally of the United States, Japan, Germany, Britain, and France. China has also become a significant force in the World Bank and IMF, reflecting its recently acquired status as the world's second-largest economy (after the United States).

As a result, the principles formulated by the WTO, the IMF, and the World Bank have been in line with the views of the major trading nations, and these nations have therefore been willing to comply reasonably closely with WTO principles. Other countries in turn then have an incentive to abide by these principles, so as to have the benefits of access to the markets and productive capacities of the influential countries.

The UN operates, instead, on the one country, one vote principle. Needless to say, powerful countries like the United States and China have more influence than smaller countries, but UN and UNCTAD resolutions are dominated by the large number of relatively small low-income countries, and therefore do not have as much significance as WTO or IMF or World Bank policies.

8.7 Canada–U.S. Trade Relations

8.7.1 The Auto Pact and the Canada–U.S. Free Trade Agreement

Given the dominance of the United States in Canada's international trade and investment flows, Canada–U.S. trade relations play an important role in Canadian public policy. Both Canada and the United States were founding signatories to GATT and were founding members of the IMF and the World Bank. And both countries have actively promoted trade liberalization in those forums. In addition, Canada and the United States have a long history of important bilateral economic trade agreements—agreements between the two countries.

In 1965, Canada and the United States signed a special bilateral agreement sanctioned under GATT, known as the Auto Pact. The Auto Pact removed tariffs and quotas on wholesale flows of North American–made motor vehicles and motor vehicle components, subject to certain safeguards. This agreement generated substantial gains from trade, since each country was able to specialize in particular models and realize greater economies of scale.

This Auto Pact agreement was the forerunner of a much broader bilateral agreement that extended similar trade liberalization (removal of tariffs and quotas) to most of the economy. This broader agreement was the Canada–U.S. Free Trade Agreement that was signed into law in 1988 and went into effect in 1989. Mexico subsequently joined the agreement, which was renamed the North American Free Trade Agreement (NAFTA). The expanded agreement went into effect in 1994. From 1994 through the present, the trade policy environment has been relatively stable, with no major changes to the policy framework.

8.7.2 NAFTA

The most central and important part of NAFTA was the gradual elimination of all tariffs and quotas on movements of qualified goods between the three countries. Qualified goods are those produced or substantially produced in the three countries. Many tariffs were eliminated ahead of schedule, as allowed under the agreement. The exempt goods consisted of a few agricultural products. Tariffs remain in effect for some of those products, but efforts are underway to eliminate them. As of 2012, the vast majority of trade flows between Canada, the United States, and Mexico were tariff free.

The restriction to free trade only for *qualified* items is to eliminate the re-export of goods originating from outside the three countries. Thus, for example, the United States would not be able to import low-cost textiles from Sri Lanka and re-export them to Canada without paying normal Canadian tariffs for such goods. The rules determining whether goods qualify as "substantially produced" in NAFTA are referred to as "rules of origin." The rules of origin are quite complicated, but the basic principle is that goods with at least 50 percent of their value added arising from NAFTA countries qualify, subject to a few exceptions.

The energy component of NAFTA was one of the more controversial aspects of the agreement, at least in Canada. NAFTA establishes what has been referred to as a continental energy market. More specifically, the agreement eliminates import and export restrictions on energy products. Furthermore, all countries are required to treat energy consumers (and producers) roughly equally, regardless of which country they are based in.

It is this latter provision that concerns economic nationalists. For example, many nationalists would like Canada to provide energy at low cost to domestic users and impose extra taxes on U.S. users. Such policies are ruled out by NAFTA. Prices in the two countries may differ, but only as long as the price difference comes from normal commercial practice rather than as a result of government policy. Similarly, in the event of an energy shortage, the Canadian government may take action to reduce energy consumption, but is expected to do so on a proportional basis: consumption of Canadian oil, for example, would be expected to fall by the same proportion in both countries. Canada could not adopt a "Canada first" policy.

Most economists would argue that NAFTA commits Canada to a policy that makes sense. One advantage is that it will prevent economically wasteful domestic subsidies to energy consumption of the type sometimes implemented in the past, as with the ill-fated National Energy Policy of the late 1970s.

U.S. investment in Canada has been a contentious issue in the past. NAFTA requires *national treatment* for new businesses. This means American, Canadian, and Mexican investors starting up new businesses in Canada would be subject to the same rules. The rules in the United States might be different from the rules in Canada, but whatever they are, they apply equally to American, Canadian, and Mexican investors. The agreement also establishes national treatment for U.S.- or Mexican-owned firms operating in Canada and for Canadian-owned firms operating in the other two countries, with no restrictions on the repatriation of profits.

One of the key aspects of NAFTA concerns the resolution of trade disputes. If NAFTA did not exist, disputes would be resolved by unilateral government decisions in each country. Appeals to the WTO are possible, but WTO findings do not have the force of law in any sovereign country, such as Canada, the United States, or Mexico. Previous GATT findings (prior to the establishment of the WTO) were quite frequently ignored. The fact that trade policy disputes were decided nationally was of much more concern to Canada than the United States, because the United States is a much larger share of the total market than is Canada. Therefore, a unilateral U.S. decision could have a major impact on Canadian producers and on Canada in general, whereas a Canadian decision would have, at most, a small impact on the United States.

NAFTA contains formal dispute settlement procedures that have the force of law in all three countries. There is still the possibility of a conflict between U.S. (or Canadian) law and a NAFTA ruling, just as two laws in the same country may be inconsistent with each other. Such conflicts would ultimately be decided in court. Since NAFTA went into effect, many trade disputes have started but only a fraction of those go all the way to dispute resolution panels. Neither country is completely happy with the resolution system, but it does seem to be preferable to the previous system.

The big question arising from consideration of NAFTA is whether it has been good for Canada (and for the other two countries) overall. In the first few years after the agreement went into effect, there was a great deal of public rhetoric about it. Various groups that had strongly opposed it, such as the Canadian Labour Congress (CLC) and the New Democratic Party (NDP), argued strenuously that the effects were very negative. On the other hand, groups that had supported the agreement, such as the Business Council of Canada and the Conservative government, argued equally strenuously that NAFTA was having very positive effects. Both sides used a similar methodology: pick out all the bad things (or all the good things) that happened after the agreement and attribute them to NAFTA.

Careful econometric analysis has shed light on the role of NAFTA in Canada's recent economic performance. A typical view among economists who have studied the effects of the agreement is that it had a modest but significant positive effect.

8.7.3 Other Issues

Given the importance of interactions between Canada and the United States, it is not surprising that many issues have arisen over the years. Recently, much debate has occurred over the proposed Keystone pipeline that would transport synthetic crude oil from the Alberta oil sands in Canada to multiple destinations in the United States. However, most disagreement and debate has NOT occurred between representatives of the governments of the two countries. Instead, argument has been generated in both countries between environmentalists, who tend to oppose the pipeline, and potential beneficiaries of the pipeline, who tend to support it.

Perhaps the most longstanding specifc trade policy conflict in modern history is the Canada–U.S. softwood lumber dispute. The basic argument made by the United States is that Canada provides a subsidy to exports of softwood lumber to the U.S. Such a subsidy would be a violation of both WTO and NAFTA agreements. In Canada, most softwood lumber is harvested from government-owned land. The lumber companies are allowed to harvest wood from the land and are charged a "stumpage fee" to do so. The U.S. argument is that this stumpage fee is too low, below market levels, and is therefore a subsidy of the type not allowed under NAFTA or the WTO. Canada argues, in essence, that the stumpage fees are not too low and therefore do not constitute a subsidy. And there are many other legal complications that have been raised on both sides.

This dispute pre-dates NAFTA and still continues. It has, at times, been the subject of specific time-limited treaties between the two countries that resolve the problem temporarily. It has gone through NAFTA panels, and it has gone to private arbitration proceedings, but still the issues always seem to resurface.

8.8 Concluding Remarks

International trade policy is very much a success story for the economics profession. For much of the 20th century, major barriers to international trade existed. Some of these barriers were based in ideology—the communist countries with centrally planned economies hardly traded at all, for example. And even in market-based economies, substantial trade barriers were the rule rather than the exception for most of the 20th century.

Ever since Adam Smith (1776) and David Ricardo (1817), most economists have made the case for free trade and have argued against protection. This view has finally become political orthodoxy and is widely accepted across the political spectrum and around the world. There are of course alternative points of view, but they are very limited in their influence compared with earlier decades.

The record of trade liberalization appears to be very positive and is an important contributing factor, along with market-based reforms more broadly, underlying the recent dramatic improvement in living standards in China and India (the world's two most populous countries) and elsewhere. However, it is important to recognize that the benefits of international trade do not eliminate the need for government intervention in some areas, and they do not eliminate the need for extensive international coordination. The world trading system is very much a managed system, not anarchy or "laissez-faire."

9

Environmental Policy and Externalities

9.1 Introduction

In Canada, there is a vast array of regulations and government programs designed to protect the environment. Yet many Canadians believe governments in Canada are not doing enough to ensure a clean environment for future generations. In addition, there are major environmental problems that are global in scope, requiring coordinated action by many governments if we are to avoid significant future environmental damage. In this chapter, we focus on business practice and government policy affecting the natural environment.

Major environmental problems include air and water pollution, global warming, and waste disposal. In the next chapter, we take up the closely related problem of managing major natural resources such as fisheries, forests, oil, and land. Much of the debate over environmental and natural resource issues has become ideological, with strong emotions on both sides of many issues—emotions that may cloud understanding of the underlying economic and scientific principles. A useful first step in analyzing environmental issues is to examine the market failure basis of environmental problems, which requires an understanding of externalities.

9.2 Externalities: Definition, Analysis, and Examples

9.2.1 Defining Externalities

An *externality* can be defined as arising when a consumer's well-being or a producer's productive capacity is directly affected by the actions of other consumers or producers. An effect that operates indirectly through prices is not an externality. This definition can be illustrated by an example. Suppose Justin lives in an otherwise quiet neighbourhood but likes to host monthly parties at which he plays loud music that keeps his neighbours awake. Justin's action, playing loud music, has direct negative effects on the well-being of his neighbours. Furthermore, this interaction between Justin and his neighbours is not mediated by any market, as Justin does not pay his neighbours for the right to play loud music. Justin's actions therefore impose a negative externality on his neighbours.

Externalities might also be positive. Suppose Lily is another neighbour who maintains a beautiful rose garden. Other neighbours often stop and admire her garden, which, in other circumstances, they might be willing to pay to see. Lily is conferring a benefit on her neighbours for which she receives no payment. This non-priced benefit conferred on others is a positive externality.

These two examples do not have much to do with the world of environmental policy and corporate strategy, but such neighbourhood effects are very important in the lives of most people. Furthermore, externalities are also very important in the business world, and represent the key to understanding environmental problems.

One example of an environmental externality problem is acid rain. Acid rain in North America is caused mainly by emissions of sulphur dioxide (SO_2) generated by burning coal to produce electricity. Burning other fossil fuels, such as natural gas and petroleum, to generate electricity and for other purposes also generates some SO_2. In the air, sulphur dioxide interacts with other compounds to form sulfuric acid that coalesces with water vapour to form slightly acidic raindrops.[1] Normal rain is neutral, not acidic, and is essential for most animal and plant life in the natural environment. Acid rain, on the other hand, is harmful to a variety of plants and animals, particularly to forests and fish.

Acid rain in Canada first became a major issue in the 1970s when it was recognized that acid rain due mainly to coal-burning electric utilities in the United States and southern Ontario was damaging the forests and lakes of

---

[1] A second source of acid rain is emissions of nitrogen oxides, which lead to nitric acid in rain. Nitrogen oxides are also caused mainly by burning fossil fuels.

Ontario and Quebec. The production of electricity using coal and other fossil fuels therefore had direct, unpriced negative external effects on producers of forest products and on inland fisheries because of acid rain.

Various policies designed to reduce acid rain were enacted in the 1970s, 80s, and 90s, including plans to phase out most of Ontario's coal-burning power plants. By 2011, annual SO_2 emissions in North America had fallen more than 70 percent from their peak levels in about 1980.[2] However, acid rain is still a significant problem in Canada and is a growing problem in other parts of the world, particularly in China and India, where coal-based electricity generation is increasing to help meet the energy demands of rapidly expanding economies.

Other forms of environmental pollution are also important examples of negative externalities. Such pollutants include car exhaust, airborne emissions from waste incinerators, waterborne emissions of chemical waste from many industries, and radiation from accidents in nuclear power plants. All of these pollutants have significant negative health effects on humans, wildlife, and plants.

9.2.2 Externalities as Market Failure

Externalities cause market failure: they cause private markets to be inefficient. Market failure can be understood by noting that externalities cause a failure of the marginalist principle for social efficiency—that social marginal benefit should be equated with social marginal cost. A negative externality results in a marginal cost of an activity (such as playing loud music or burning coal) that is not borne by the firm or person undertaking the activity, but is borne instead by others. A profit-maximizing firm generating an externality will equate its own private marginal cost to the marginal benefit of the activity, but will ignore the marginal costs imposed on others.

For example, suppose a coal-burning electric utility in Ohio can choose between high-sulphur coal, which produces a lot of acid rain, and more expensive low-sulphur coal, which produces less acid rain. Left to itself, it will choose the lower-cost, high-polluting coal, even if the extra costs imposed on others are far higher than the savings to the utility. The result is an inefficient outcome: total costs to society (including the externality costs) are higher

---

[2] U.S. data is available at from the Environmental Protection Agency database at ampd.epa.gov/ampd/. SO_2 emissions fell from over 17 million tons in 1980 to under 5 million tons as of 2011. Canadian emissions followed a similar pattern, as indicated by Environment Canada data at www.ec.gc.ca/inrp-npri/default .asp?lang=En&tn=F98AFAE7-1. See also Weiss (2012).

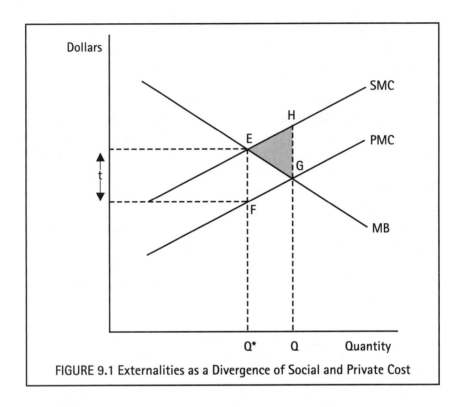

FIGURE 9.1 Externalities as a Divergence of Social and Private Cost

than necessary for producing electricity. Figure 9.1 illustrates the inefficiency associated with externalities.

In Figure 9.1, the curve labelled *MB* is the marginal benefit of some activity (such as producing electricity using high-sulphur coal). The curve labelled *PMC* is the private marginal cost, and *SMC* is the social marginal cost. In this example, the *PMC* and *SMC* curves are drawn as linear and parallel to each other for convenience. In general, they need not be either linear or parallel.

Because of the negative externality, the social marginal cost exceeds the private marginal cost. The difference is called the marginal external cost. A socially efficient outcome would involve carrying out the activity up to point *Q**, where the social marginal cost is just equal to the marginal benefit. However, private producers would choose to carry out the activity up to point *Q*. The efficiency loss is given by area *EGH*.

We can apply this diagram to competitive markets. In a competitive market the *MB* curve is the demand curve. At any given quantity, it shows the price or marginal willingness to pay for the next unit of output. In a competitive market, profit-maximizing firms will produce where price equals private marginal cost (Chapter 6), which is where the *PMC* curve intersects the demand curve given by *MB*. Thus, a competitive market would generate activity level *Q* instead of the socially efficient level *Q**. In Chapter 3 we described the first theorem of welfare economics–competitive markets are efficient. This theorem assumes that externalities are not present. If externalities are present then competitive markets are not efficient, as shown by Figure 9.1.

More generally, this diagram illustrates two important points. First, activities with negative externalities will be carried out at too high a level if left to private incentives. Second, the socially efficient level of the activity in question is above zero. These points seem elementary when presented in connection with Figure 9.1. However, they seem to escape many participants in public policy debates over environmental pollution.

In particular, environmentalists often talk about seeking to eliminate or minimize pollution. This is misleading. The public interest would not be served by minimizing pollution, and certainly not by its elimination. Literal elimination of pollution would require stopping most human activity. Pollution should be reduced only so far as the costs of doing so are less than the benefits.

9.2.3 The Simple Economics of Pollution Abatement

Figure 9.1 illustrates a situation where some economic activity has a fixed external cost associated with it. The activity might be driving, producing pulp used to make paper, using high-sulphur coal to produce electricity, or doing something similar. In this case, carrying out the activity is assumed to necessarily cause external damage. This is often the case, at least in the short run. If so, then the only form of externality reduction or abatement is to do less of the activity. Thus, for example, if a firm operates a pulp mill, the only immediate way to cause less pollution is to run the mill less, and therefore produce less pulp.

In the long run, however, it is often possible to undertake other forms of pollution abatement. The firm could install scrubbers on the mill to remove pollutants, install new and cleaner machinery, or take other actions to reduce pollution. A diagrammatic analysis of pollution abatement is shown in Figure 9.2.

This diagram gives a very similar message to that of Figure 9.1. In this case, however, the horizontal axis measures abatement activity (e.g., extra scrubbers in pulp mills). The problem here is that the private marginal benefit of abatement is much less than the social marginal benefit of abatement. A private, profit-maximizing firm has an incentive to undertake abatement

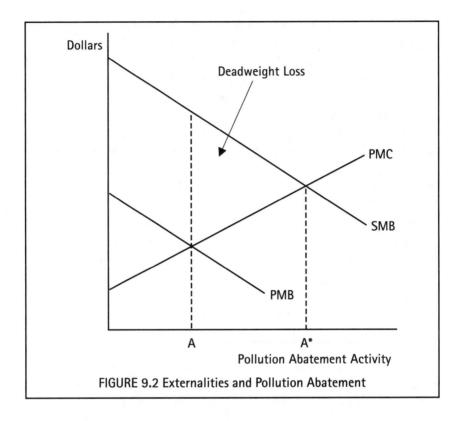

FIGURE 9.2 Externalities and Pollution Abatement

only up to the point where the private marginal benefit of abatement equals the private marginal cost of abatement, which occurs at point *A*. From the social point of view, these private incentives lead to too little abatement. The socially efficient level of abatement occurs where the social marginal benefit equals the social marginal cost, at point *A**.

Abatement generates positive external benefits in that it results in benefits that are not captured by the party undertaking the abatement activity. As with any activity that generates positive externalities, pollution abatement will be underprovided if left to private incentives.

9.2.4 Technological and Pecuniary Externalities

Externalities arise because one economic agent has an impact on another that does not operate through the price system. Suppose National Paper Inc. produces paper but discharges fish-killing pollution as a by-product. The actions of National Paper have a direct negative effect on the production capabilities of the fishing industry and on the welfare of fishery employees and shareholders. These actions are not priced and are therefore externalities. Sometimes we use the term *technological* externalities to describe such effects.

There is a similar idea that sometimes causes confusion. Suppose that wheat farmers increase their demand for fertilizer used in wheat production, causing the price of fertilizer to rise. Flower producers who also use fertilizer would therefore experience higher costs and lower profits. The actions of wheat producers in seeking to buy more fertilizer have therefore affected the welfare of another party: flower producers. People are often tempted to refer to this phenomenon as a *pecuniary externality*–an externality caused by price effects. This example is, however, *not* a case of market failure, as pecuniary externalities do not cause market failure. Effects on other parties arising from the normal operation of the price system do not cause inefficiency, and do not create a rationale for government intervention. Most so-called pecuniary externalities are merely examples of the marketplace allocating resources to efficient uses.

It is, of course, possible that some underlying market failure might be reflected in prices. For example, furniture consumers might pay more for furniture if the cost of wood increases due to the negative effect of acid rain on the supply of high-quality wood. In this case, the negative externality arising from acid rain is reflected in inefficiently high prices for furniture. We might say that consumers of furniture are negatively affected by acid rain. However, the essential point is that the market failure is caused by the underlying technological externality due to the negative impact of acid rain on wood production. The effect is transmitted through prices but there is no separate "pecuniary externality" that causes market failure.

9.2.5 Transaction Costs and Incomplete Property Rights

Why do externalities exist? Two fundamental causes of externalities are high transaction costs and incomplete property rights. Consider once again Justin, the noisy neighbour who regularly plays loud music at parties. If the music bothers neighbours, why don't they just offer to pay Justin not to throw parties? If the neighbours offer him enough money, presumably he would stop or rent some other facility in which to hold parties. In principle, this could solve the noise pollution problem. If the benefits of getting Justin to stop hosting noisy parties, as measured by his neighbours' willingness to pay, exceed the costs (the minimum amount he would accept to stop), then he will stop (or move) his parties. This would satisfy the marginalist principle and restore efficiency. This solution involves, in essence, the creation of a market for loud music.

In principle, the creation of markets for previously unpriced external effects can solve externality problems. Externalities are interactions between people (or firms) that are not priced because they occur outside of markets. In short, externalities arise precisely because certain markets fail to exist. But why do certain markets fail to exist? Why are loud music externalities ever a problem if markets can spontaneously spring up to price the external effect? There are two basic reasons: high transactions costs and the absence of natural property rights.

Consider transaction costs first. In order to create the market for Justin's loud music, his neighbours have to negotiate with him. This is time-consuming for all parties involved. In this case, the costs are not prohibitive, but in many cases they are. Consider instead the problem of trying to set up a market for pollution caused by automobile exhaust. Are we to gather all polluters in a given region and all people affected by pollution in that region (i.e., everyone who breathes) together to negotiate how much money will induce drivers and other polluters to install pollution abatement equipment? The transaction costs would be prohibitive. If the transaction costs of operating a market are high compared to the potential gains from trade in the market, then the market will fail to exist.

The second issue concerns property rights. It may have struck many readers as unfair that Justin's neighbours should have to pay him to stop playing loud music at his parties. Perhaps Justin should be required to pay his neighbours before being allowed to throw such parties. The ambiguity here illustrates that there are no natural property rights over loud music.[3] It is not clear whether Jason's neighbours have a basic property right to quiet or whether Jason has a natural right to loud music—and it is unlikely that Jason and his neighbours would agree on who has the property rights.

9.2.6 The Coase Theorem

If the only issue underlying an externality problem is incomplete property rights (i.e., if transaction costs are not an issue), then the externality can be solved or removed by establishing property rights. Consider, for example, the case of a pulp mill discharging waste into a lake, killing fish and reducing the profits of a fishery operating on the lake.

Suppose there are three possibilities. If the pulp mill does not operate the fish are healthy and the fishery earns a daily profit of 500. However, if

---

[3] Most cities have noise by-laws that create some implicit property rights. Such rights are, however, hard to enforce.

the mill operates it earns a daily profit 400, but its waste discharge damages the fishery and reduces the fishery's daily profit to 100. A third possibility is for the mill to use expensive filters that reduce the discharge. In this case the mill earns 300 per day and so does the fishery. This option, using filters, is efficient as its combined profit of 600 is more than under the other two possibilities. However, without agreed-upon property rights, the pulp mill might operate normally and earn 400, the fishery would earn 100, and the combined return would be 500. The reduction, from 600 to 500, in combined profit is the inefficiency due to the externality in this case.

However, suppose the government grants property rights over the lake to the fishery. Therefore, if the pulp mill discharges waste into the lake it would need pay the fishery for a permit. What would happen in this case? If the fishery refused to allow any discharge, the mill would not operate and the fishery would earn 500. But if the fishery wanted to maximize profit, it would allow the mill to operate and require it to use the expensive filtering technology. With the technology in place, the fishery would earn 300 from its own operations and the mill would earn 300 before paying whatever fee was charged by the fishery. The fishery could charge the mill anything less than 300: perhaps 250. The fishery would earn 300 plus the discharge fee of 250 for a net profit of 550—more than it would earn by shutting down the mill. The mill would earn a net return of $300 - 250 = 50$, which is better than nothing, which it would get if it cannot operate. The combined return is $550 + 50 = 600$. This is the efficient outcome—the highest possible combined return.

Now suppose that instead of giving the property right over the lake to the fishery, the government gives it to the pulp mill. The mill could operate normally, earn 400 from its own operations, and charge the fishery any amount up to 100 to fish on the lake: perhaps 50. But the pulp mill would do even better by offering to install expensive filters and then charging the fishery 250 for the right to fish. In this case, the mill gets 300 from its own operations and 250 from the fishing license for a total of 550—more than it gets if it operates normally. The fishery earns a gross return of 300, pays the fee of 250, and is left with a profit of 50, which is better than nothing, for a total of 600.

Regardless of who has the property rights, we get an efficient outcome. The expensive filter is used and combined profits are 600. Assigning property rights eliminates the externality. The waste from the mill still hurts fish, but that effect is now priced.

As was first pointed out by Coase (1960), as far as achieving efficiency is concerned, it does not matter who gets the property rights, as long as someone gets them. This insight is called the *Coase Theorem*: if there are no transaction costs, then bargaining between economically rational parties over an externality will lead to an efficient outcome, provided property rights are clearly defined and enforced.

Assignment of property rights does, however, affect the distribution of benefits between the parties. The fishery owners are better off if they get the property right rather than if the property right is given to the pulp mill, and vice versa.

The Coase Theorem is helpful in understanding the nature of externalities, but it is rarely applicable in practice. In most important externality examples it is not feasible to assign property rights. We cannot, for example, assign property rights over the atmosphere or the ocean. And even when we can assign property rights, the transaction costs of bargaining can easily become prohibitive. In the case of the pulp mill and the fishery, we can imagine that the two parties might bargain efficiently. But what if there are other uses of the lake: swimming, boating, hiking, and so on? If the discharge into the lake affects these activities, the affected parties need to be part of the negotiation as well, and the transaction costs would soon become a major problem.

9.3 Policy Solutions to Externality Problems

There are four basic policy solutions to market failure caused by externalities:

1. Internalization of the externality
2. Quantity controls and standards
3. Taxes and subsidies
4. Cap and trade systems

9.3.1 Internalizing Externalities

One response to externalities is to internalize them, which means placing both the economic agent generating the externality and the parties affected by it under one management. For example, if a pulp mill damages a fishery, having the pulp mill's owner acquire the fishery would internalize the externality. The single owner would then have an incentive to reduce the emissions from the pulp mill to the efficient level.

However, in most important cases internalization is not feasible. For one thing, the private sector spontaneously undertakes most efficiency-improving internalizations, leaving no particular role for public policy. The remaining cases are those where internalization itself has very high costs. For example, to internalize the acid rain externality it would be necessary to place most of the coal-based electricity generation in the northern part of the United States and in Canada under the same management, along with the steel industry, the auto industry, and other emitters, and along with responsibility for fish, forests, and wildlife in these areas. Aside from not being politically feasible, this kind of proposal would generate enormous costs of various types, including coordination costs and creation of market power. The costs of internalization would greatly exceed any likely benefits.

Although it is difficult to solve externality problems by internalization, it is possible to create externality problems by what might be called "externalization." Land tenure rights for logging in Canada provide one such example. In much of Canada, substantial areas of forest are owned by government but are leased to forest products companies for logging. It is often argued that the level of reforestation carried out on such land is too low. This is not surprising, because the forest products companies cannot reasonably assume that they will benefit from the reforestation they carry out, especially as leases approach expiration and they have no certainty of obtaining new ones. The company cannot be sure the land will not be leased to someone else or given up to an aboriginal land claim instead. The long-run benefits of reforestation are potentially "externalized" from the point of view of the company. Thus, reforestation has the character of a positive externality. It raises the value of the land and will confer benefits on others—on the government and on future users of the land. Private incentives lead to underprovision of activities with positive externalities. Therefore, we would expect reforestation to be underprovided.

9.3.2 Quantity Controls and Standards
The most common solution to externality problems is to use quantity controls and standards. Factories are constrained to limit themselves to certain levels of pollution or to install specific types of pollution abatement equipment. It is possible, in principle, to achieve the efficient solution through quantity controls. In Figure 9.1, the efficient solution could be obtained simply by setting the activity level at Q^*. When acid rain is discussed, the suggested policy approach is to set targets for emission reductions, such as a 50 percent reduction by a particular date. Emission standards are widely used in Canada, the United States, and much of the world.

9.3.3 Taxes and Subsidies
Most economists would prefer to see less reliance on standards and quantity controls and more on taxes and subsidies. The appropriate response to a negative

externality is to tax it. In Figure 9.1, when the activity is taxed at rate t, then the private marginal cost rises (inclusive of the tax) until it coincides with the social marginal cost at the efficient point, yielding activity level Q^*. Subsidies are used for activities with positive externalities.

In Figure 9.1, taxes and quantity controls standards look like equivalent ways of achieving efficiency. Why, then, do economists favour taxes while policy makers (and the public) tend to prefer quantity controls? Economists favour taxes because of the incentive effects. If pollution is taxed, this gives the polluting firm a continuing incentive to reduce pollution. Taxes are a market-based solution; they exploit market-based incentives. In addition, taxes generate revenue that can be used to pay for environmental programs or for other purposes. On the other hand, standards are like a central-planning approach. When standards are used, even if they are enforced, the firm has an incentive to conform to the standard but go no further. Economists are also suspicious of the ability of policy makers to set appropriate standards. It is very difficult to determine what the appropriate standard should be. A tax approach requires assessing the marginal external cost which, while not easy, is more likely to be estimated with reasonable accuracy. Finally, obtaining compliance with pollution standards can be difficult.

Canada has had emission standards for pulp mills since 1971. However, despite frequent noncompliance with standards, pulp mills have largely avoided sanctions or penalties. Criminal-based sanctions for noncompliance are politically difficult to impose and convictions are legally difficult to obtain because of the reasonable doubt standard of proof. Governments in Canada are worried about employment in towns where pulp mills are major employers, and they do not want to be in an adversarial position with such pulp mills. Furthermore, industry regulators tend to be close to the industry itself. Thus, when noncompliance occurs, as it often does, it is politically much easier to get the firm to promise to try to do better in the future than it is to impose penalties.

From the firm's point of view, the marginal incentive to comply is weak. Given that reducing emissions is costly, it may be more attractive to hope that bargaining with governments will protect the firm from prosecution if their violation of emission standards comes to light. The advantage of taxes is that they are imposed *ex ante* and simply become a normal cost of business. Firms might not like taxes, but there is much less scope for avoidance than there is with standards. Taxes also provide a more level playing field than do standards that are commonly violated. Standards can, however, be effective in some areas. For example, while far from perfect, auto emission standards have substantially reduced emissions, at least on a per car basis.

It is not entirely clear why politicians and most other people tend to favour standards. One possibility is that simply taking the taxes and allowing a firm to pollute is regarded as equivalent to selling the right to pollute, and as morally wrong, much like selling the right to commit assault or murder would be morally wrong. Politicians and others think quite naturally in terms of right and wrong, good and bad. If pollution is bad, we should try to reduce it, not sanction it. Julia Langer, executive director of the Ottawa-based Friends of the Earth, made the following statement: "[it is] the wrong signal to give. If you say you can buy the right to pollute, then people will buy it. They won't strive for perfection."[4] Others have noted that many people believe clean air and water is a right, and that making it a marketable commodity is dangerous—setting a price on a right. A desire to recast a complex world in terms of simple absolutes, such as a right to clean air or water, is understandable but is often an ineffective approach to complex problems.

It is also likely that most people do not trust or appreciate the power of market solutions. They imagine that if pollution is taxed, then firms will simply pay the tax, pass the costs on to consumers, and continue to pollute. This is a misconception, as the appropriate tax would reduce pollution by exactly the right amount. Pollution taxes have not been used extensively in Canada, although Quebec and British Columbia became the first Canadian provinces to impose carbon taxes—taxes on the carbon content in fossil fuels—in 2007 and 2008, respectively. Pollution taxes have been widely uses in Europe for many years, particularly in the Netherlands, where effluent charges were first imposed in 1969. Initially opposed by both business and environmental groups, effluent charges in the Netherlands are high and increasingly used. They have resulted in a dramatic decline in effluent emissions and have raised substantial revenues for environmental programs.

9.3.4 Cap and Trade Systems

Cap and trade systems, sometime called *tradable pollution permit* systems, seek to combine quantity controls with market incentives. One component of a cap and trade system is the *cap*—a maximum allowable quantity, or quota, of a pollutant, such as sulphur dioxide (SO_2). This quota is divided into *permits* that grant the right to emit a certain amount of the pollutant per year. Sometimes, the permits are given to polluters in proportion to the amount

---

[4] John Fox, "Credit system could make pollution fight pay," *Financial Post,* April 23, 1990, p. 1.

discharged annually prior to the imposition of the cap. For example, emitters might get permits equal to 70 percent of their previous annual emission. If each emitter simply used its permits, then each would have to reduce SO_2 emissions by 30 percent.

An alternative to giving out permits is for the government to auction them off to emitters. Whether permits are given away or auctioned or distributed in some other way, the holders of the permits are then allow to *trade* them—to sell them at whatever price they can obtain in a market for the permits.

The United States and other countries use cap and trade systems in a number of areas. It was the primary policy tool used to reduce acid rain due to SO_2 emissions in the United States. The advantage of a cap and trade system is that it minimizes the cost of achieving a given pollution target.

To see this, suppose that we have two electric utilities, Shocking Electricity Co. and Power is Us Co., operating in a particular area. Each company currently releases 50 tons of SO_2 per year—100 tons in total. Shocking Co. has a newer plant and can install and operate SO_2 filters relatively easily, incurring an annual cost of $400 per ton to reduce SO_2 emissions. Power Co. has an older plant with many more leaks in its chimneys and therefore incurs annual costs of $800 per ton to reduce SO_2 emissions.

Suppose that a policy calling for a combined reduction from 100 to 60 tons for the two plants comes into effect. One approach is to simply require each plant to drop from 50 to 30 tons per year in emissions, a reduction of 20 tons per plant. Such a system would impose an annual cost of $400 $\times$ 20 = $8,000 on Shocking Co. and $800 $\times$ 20 = $16,000 on Power Co. The total cost would be $24,000 per year.

Alternatively, suppose that the government gives each utility permits for 30 tons of emissions per year and allows the companies to trade. Shocking Co. then sells permits for 20 tons to Power Co., keeping only permits for 10 tons for itself. Power Co. would then not need to reduce its emissions at all and would therefore not incur any costs aside from buying the permits. Shocking Co. would have to reduce its emissions from 50 tons to 10 tons, a reduction of 40 tons, at a cost of $400 $\times$ 40 = $16,000. This is a much lower total cost for reducing pollution than the $24,000 cost resulting from a pure quota system.

What about the cost paid by Power Co. for the permits? This is a pure transfer between Power Co. and Shocking Co. It does not add anything to the net cost of the SO_2 reduction. We cannot be sure what price Power Co. would pay for the permits. Any price less than $800 allows the company to save money by purchasing a permit rather than undertaking abatement. On the other hand, any price above $400 generates profit for Shocking Co. A price of $600 would "split the difference." At that price, Shocking Co. can sell a one-ton permit for $600 and reduce emissions by one ton at a cost of $400, making a profit of $200 on the transaction. By paying $600 per ton to buy permits, Power Co. is able avoid paying $800 per ton to reduce its own emissions, saving $200 per ton. Thus, both firms gain $200 per ton if the price is $600. However, any price between $400 and $800 will give both firms an incentive to trade.

The economic benefits of correcting such externalities can be enormous. The U.S. Environmental Protection Agency estimated the annual benefit of acid rain reduction in North America to be about $122 billion per year as of 2010, while the annual cost was about $3 billion per year—a benefit-to-cost ratio of about 40 to 1.[5]

A related system allows firms to earn credits that can be used as permits in other areas. Thus, for example, a firm achieving pollution reductions above some mandated level in one production facility might be allowed to treat the difference as a credit, offsetting excess pollution in another plant. Usually, these credits are not tradable but must be used by the firm that earns them. Credit systems are being tried in Australia, Germany, and the United States. Such systems have some valuable properties, but they would be even more efficient if the credits could be traded. The use of both credit and tradable-permit systems is still in its early stages. Some cap and trade systems have been used in Canada, but they have been small in scope.

9.4 Global Warming

The extent and causes of global warming have become areas of contentious political debate in a number of countries, particularly in the United States and, to a lesser extent, in Canada. The scientific evidence is much clearer than the political debate, although there are some uncertainties.

The earth has gone through many warming and cooling cycles in its history. At present the earth is warming. Relatively accurate temperature measurements have been available since about 1880. Since that time, the average surface temperature of the earth has risen by about one degree Celsius. This is a seemingly small amount, but even this small change has had important effects, causing significant melting of polar ice caps and other glaciers, and marked increases in sea level (about 22 cm since 1880).[6] Although the measurements

---

[5] See www.epa.gov/capandtrade/documents/benefits.pdf.

[6] There are several standard sources on such climate change data, including NASA at climate.nasa.gov/key_indicators.

are not precise, the basic facts that the earth has warmed, glaciers have lost mass, and average sea level has risen are not in scientific dispute.

The relative importance of the possible causes of global warming is slightly more uncertain as year-to-year variations in temperature are influenced by several factors, including changes in ocean currents and solar activity. However, a consensus among scientists has emerged that global warming over the past century has been caused mainly by an accumulation of greenhouse gases in the atmosphere. The major greenhouse gases are water vapour, carbon dioxide, and methane, and other gases also contribute.

Greenhouse gases work like a real greenhouse. Energy from the sun comes to earth over the entire radiation spectrum, but mostly in the form of visible light, which travels through the atmosphere and warms the earth's surface. This warmth is then emitted from the surface in the form of the long wavelength, infrared radiation, much of which is trapped by the greenhouse gases in the atmosphere and reflected back to earth. Greenhouse gases do not stop visible light from coming in but they do stop some of the resulting heat (infrared radiation) from getting out. This greenhouse effect increases the net warming effect of the sun. As greenhouse gas concentrations have risen, the greenhouse effect has increased and temperatures have risen, and they will continue to rise until a new equilibrium is reached. The basic science of the greenhouse effect is not in dispute.

It is possible that some of the increase in greenhouse gas concentrations is due to natural phenomena such as forest fires rather than to human activity. However, there is no doubt that a large share of this increase is due to burning fossil fuels—oil, natural gas, and coal. Other major contributions to greenhouse gas emissions include the digestive processes of large herds of livestock and the burning and decomposing of garbage. Overall therefore, from a scientific point of view, it is clear that most of the global warming that has occurred over the past century is due to a build-up of greenhouse gases arising mainly from human activity.

The major uncertainties associated with global warming relate to the future. We do not really know what a new equilibrium temperature will be. Possibly, global warming will slow down or even stop entirely before catastrophic harm is done. Furthermore, it is possible that some warming will do net economic good. While there is no question that global warming has already caused significant harm in some areas, other areas have benefited. For example, in countries with relatively cool climates, such as Canada, Russia, and the countries of northern Europe, more land has become suitable for cultivation as warming has occurred.

It seems likely that the biggest single problem caused by global warming is rising sea levels. Although average sea level has risen by only about 20 cm in the last century, the rate of increase has accelerated, and current estimates suggest a sea-level increase on the order of one metre (100 cm) over the next century.[7]

Large parts of entire countries (e.g., Bangladesh and the Netherlands) are within one metre of sea level. Canada is much less vulnerable to rising sea levels, but significant parts of Atlantic Canada and some heavily populated parts of Greater Vancouver are at risk. In densely populated urban areas, a one metre increase in sea level can be defended at a high but feasible cost using dikes, but large agricultural areas could not be saved, and flooding would become more frequent and more costly in all areas. Greenhouse effects also cause greater variability in weather patterns, resulting in more floods and droughts, etc.

Global warming caused by greenhouse gases is an externality problem. As we drive our cars or use electricity, we get full private benefits from such activities. We also impose global warming effects (i.e., negative external effects) on the entire world. Thus, we bear only a negligible share of any global warming costs related to our personal activity.

It has been suggested that carbon taxes could be used to address the greenhouse effect, but there is little reason to be optimistic about attempts to reduce greenhouse gas emissions. At the international level, the externality problems are too great, given the central importance of energy production in economic development. At present, the greatest producers of greenhouse gases tend to be the world's largest economies. According to the U.S. Environmental Protection Agency, the top four countries for greenhouse gas production are, in order, China, the United States, India, and Russia. Together, these four countries account for over 50 percent of global greenhouse gas emissions, and all four, for different reasons, are doing very little to reduce or limit greenhouse gas emissions.

9.5 Hazardous Waste and the NIMBY Problem

One of the most intractable current environmental problems involves locating hazardous waste facilities, ordinary waste facilities, and waste incinerators. The most extreme aspect of this problem is the storage of nuclear waste, but

---

[7] Estimates of the increase in sea level are being adjusted upwards as a better understanding of the process has emerged. The widely cited IPPC report of 2007 suggested an increase of only 20 to 50 cm between years 2000 and 2100, but, using new and better information, in 2012 the U.S. Academy of Sciences estimated a range of 50 to 140 cm over the 2000-2100 period. See dels.nas.edu/Report/Level-Rise-Coasts/13389.

storage and treatment of toxic chemical waste is a larger, more immediate concern. The traditional method of storing toxic chemical waste was simply to dump it into landfills on private or public land. Starting in the 1970s and continuing to the present, strong evidence has emerged that communities close to toxic waste landfills suffered significant negative consequences, including higher than expected rates of birth defects, leukemia and other cancers, and various other health complaints.

While scientific and legal controversies continue over the exact links between toxic wastes and health hazards, various regulations have been passed in many countries, including in Canada and the United States, governing the disposal and treatment of toxic waste. In addition, public concern and awareness over toxic waste has risen enormously, giving rise to the so-called NIMBY problem.

NIMBY stands for "*not in my backyard*," and refers to the fact that communities will usually strongly resist local placement of hazardous waste dumps or other facilities that might generate negative externalities. In the United States, some four years of work and $1.5 million were spent on a proposed (and much needed) treatment and storage facility for chemical waste in Sand Canyon, Los Angeles. However, the facility was abandoned in the face of seemingly insurmountably negative public opinion. Construction of hazardous waste storage facilities remains inadequate to meet "need," with the result that waste is being stored in unsuitable locations.

Hazardous waste needs to go somewhere. At the government policy level, it is possible to decide on relatively good locations for hazardous waste. The facilities should be in geologically stable areas, away from major population centres, and easily and safely reachable on major transportation routes. Inevitably, however, proposed waste facilities are near someone, and these people are not usually persuaded by arguments that it is in the social interest for them to bear whatever risks are associated with hazardous waste facilities.

A fairly natural economic response would be to financially compensate local communities for increased risks associated with hazardous waste, but such approaches do not seem to go very far toward solving the NIMBY problem. In particular, many people view locating hazardous waste as an all-or-nothing issue, and they are not amenable to discussing market-like transactions associated with hazardous waste. Second, in cases where a compensation approach has been tried, levels of compensation demanded tend to be prohibitively high. Even if compensation can be used, there is a question of who should pay. Applying economic principles, the payment for waste disposal should be incorporated in the price of the products whose production gives rise to the waste. This is, however, hard to implement, giving rise to externality problems.

It should be noted that the NIMBY problem also applies to areas other than toxic waste disposal, and it explains some of the operations of local government. Locating halfway houses for paroled prison inmates, drop-in centres for drug users, and low-income housing projects are, for example, all subject to the NIMBY problem. Many people think such projects are good ideas in the abstract but do not want them in their own backyard.

9.6 Traffic Externalities

As population centres become more crowded due to population growth, externalities become more important. In rural communities people live relatively far apart and have little impact on one another. They can play loud music without disturbing each other and travel around their local communities without getting in each other's way. Life is very different in densely populated urban areas, however, where it is hard to do anything without having an external effect on someone else.

Externalities caused by crowding and getting in other peoples' way are often called *congestion externalities*. Perhaps the most obvious congestion externalities in urban areas relate to traffic. And traffic also generates other negative externalities, including pollution due to exhaust emissions. The traffic externality problem has been extensively studied. See, in particular, Lindsey (2010) and Anas and Lindsey (2011) for a more in-depth discussion of many of the points covered here.

The externality problems of traffic are clear. When Liam considers how to get to work he considers his own cost of transportation. If he wants to drive he will need to buy (or lease) a car and pay for insurance, gas, repairs, and parking. He will also have to consider the time he spends driving and his risk of injury or other health problems. However, he will probably not consider the costs he imposes on others. For example, if he has to make a left turn at a busy intersection, he might easily delay five or six drivers (or more) behind him by a minute or so each, but he will not take that cost into account in deciding whether to drive. By the time he actually gets to work he might easily impose cumulative time costs of an hour or more on other drivers. He will also cause wear and tear on the road, and increase the risk of injury to cyclists, pedestrians, and other drivers. He will emit pollution into the air, contributing to local health problems, acid rain, and global warming. If he drives during peak periods in a major city, the costs he imposes on others (the negative externality) will almost certainly exceed his own private costs.

This negative externality implies that people drive too much. They do not bear anywhere near the full marginal cost of their decision to drive (even taking gasoline taxes into account). The efficient solution would be to charge people for driving, using tolls.

The cost of congestion delays while commuting in Canada's major urban areas is well into the billions of dollars per year.[8] It not necessarily optimal to reduce congestion delays to zero, but it is clear that negative externalities due to traffic are a major cost that is much bigger in economic magnitude than most issues city governments spend time on.

Other negative externalities due to traffic are of comparable magnitude. While tolls have often been used to cover construction costs for highways and bridges, their use to correct congestion and other externalities has not been common. At one time, transaction costs might have been an issue, as setting up toll booths and collecting tolls is costly, although far from prohibitive. With modern technology, however, road pricing is much easier. For example, placing communication devices (transponders) in cars would allow for automatic electronic billing. Ideally, the system would incorporate peak-load pricing—charging the highest prices at the busiest times—and it should adjust for weight of the vehicle, as heavy vehicles impose much more wear and tear on roads, generate more emissions for a given distance driven, and are much more dangerous to other road users.

Most economists regard road charges as an obvious policy tool for crowded cities. In addition to reducing congestion and inducing more efficient transportation choices, they would also raise revenue and could be used to reduce other taxes, reducing the inefficiencies causes by those taxes. However, there is great consumer (and voter) resistance to road pricing. If urban road pricing does become more widely used in Canada and the United States, it will likely be a slow process. Experience with road pricing in Europe and Asia indicates that support for the policy increases after such prices are put in place, especially if consumers can see the revenues being used for activities they value.

---

[8] Canada's six major metropolitan areas are Toronto, Montreal, Vancouver, Ottawa, Edmonton, and Calgary. The average commute time for drivers and public transportation riders in those six metro areas exceeds 30 minutes, of which more than a third is delay due to congestion. In these areas, there are well over 5 million commuting trips per day by car or bus. The aggregate congestion delay exceeds 1 million hours per day. Studies by Transport Canada suggest valuing commuting time at about $25 per hour, which implies that the annual time cost of congestion delays in these urban areas is many billions of dollars per year.

9.7 Cost-Benefit Analysis and Discounting for Environmental Projects

In evaluating possible environmental policies, cost-benefit analysis is often used. Consider, for example, the problem of sewage treatment. Private incentives for sewage treatment are too weak, because each individual household bears only a small fraction of the total cost of its untreated sewage. Thus, individual households rarely invest in household-level sewage treatment technology, even though such technology does exist, unless forced to do so by governments. In large cities that lack sewage treatment, water supplies are excessively contaminated with the bacteria that reside in human waste, causing excessively high levels of disease. Thus, there is a strong externality-based rationale for public provision of sewage treatment, possibly financed by mandated sewage connection charges or general taxes.

Suppose a local city government is contemplating expanding its sewage treatment facilities. It could use cost-benefit analysis, as described in Chapter 3. It would add up the costs and benefits and see whether the total value is positive or negative. With construction projects such as sewers, the costs of the project come long before the major benefits. The main costs come during the years of construction, but the benefits do not even begin until after construction is completed, and then continue for a long time. Thus, in comparing costs and benefits, the principal trade-off is between current costs and future benefits.

In comparing costs and benefits that arise at different times, a discount rate is used. For example, suppose our project is a very simple one, involving current costs and benefits that arise after ten years. The net present value of the project would be

$$NPV = -C + B/(1 + r)^{10}$$

where r is the discount rate. Suppose C (the cost) is 100 and B (the benefit 10 years hence) is 250. If $r = 0.1$ (or 10 percent), then $(1 + r)^{10} = 2.59$, and $NPV = -100 + 250/2.59 = -3.5$. The value is negative, implying the project should not be undertaken. However, even a slight decline in the discount rate to, say, 9 percent would make the value positive and lead to a positive recommendation. Thus, the choice of the discount rate is very important. The longer the time horizon, the more important the discount rate will be. The selection of the discount rate is particularly important in the analysis of environmental projects, where we often consider projects that will have impacts for decades or even centuries.

How is the discount rate selected? One influential idea in public sector discounting is that the discount rate should equal the opportunity cost of capital, which is taken to be the pre-tax rate of return on investment projects in the private sector. The basic rationale for using the opportunity cost of capital as a discount rate is the assumption that the project (in this case the sewer) would replace an alternative private sector investment. Suppose, for instance, that the pre-tax annual rate of return is 10 percent. We imagine that if we do not build the sewer, an alternative private investment with a 10 percent return will happen instead. Therefore, if we did not build the sewer, we could put the initial amount of 100 into the private investment and let it accumulate returns at the rate of 10 percent per year. At the end of 10 years, the value would be $100(1 + 0.1)^{10} = 259$, which exceeds the environmental benefit of 250. Thus, if the people who would have received the environmental benefit of 250 instead could get the private benefit of 259, they would choose the private sector investment. We should only opt for an environmental project that yielded more than 259. This implies that using a discount rate of 10 percent would lead to the right decisions.

While this argument has relevance in some cases, it is far from complete. Most significantly, the argument for using the opportunity cost of capital rests on the assumption that the true alternative to the public project is a private sector investment. If, instead, the true alternative is to spend the money on a big party (or some other form of current consumption), then the private return on capital is not relevant. In such a case, the appropriate discount rate is determined by the willingness of consumer/taxpayers to trade off future benefits for current consumption. This possible discount rate is referred to as the consumer rate of time preference. The consumer rate of time preference is normally much lower than the private pre-tax rate of return on capital, perhaps on the order of 5 percent instead of 10 percent.

There is another complication. Over 10 years there will be some turnover of consumers: some people will move away while others move in. Now we have a distributional issue to consider. Those current consumers who will not be here in 10 years would prefer current consumption, since they get no benefit from the project. Future consumers who are not current taxpayers prefer the project because they do not pay the cost but do receive the benefits. In this case, the discount rate is determined by the relative weights we put on future and current consumers. For projects with a duration of only 10 years, this intergenerational problem seems relatively minor as the turnover in consumers would be small. But for projects that will last 50 or 100 years, the intergenerational conflict is the key issue. If the government is the guardian of the future, it should place some weight on future genera-tions. This implies a further reduction in the discount rate, below current consumer's rate of time preference, at least for projects whose opportunity cost is current consumption.

A third point is that private sector returns may incorporate a risk pre-mium. The private sector investment has an expected return of 10 percent, but is risky—it might yield nothing. The high expected yield of 10 percent is needed to offset the risk. The sewer benefits, on the other hand, are not very risky. Even if the return on the sewer is less than 10 percent, it might be preferred to the risky private investment because of risk aversion. In general, the appropriate risk premium that should be incorporated in public sector discounting is less than the risk premium embodied in private sector returns. If so, then this is another reason for using a discount rate that is lower than the private return on investment.

There has been much debate over appropriate discount rates. In Canada, the official standing recommendation for public sector discounting derives from a 2007 Treasury Board document that suggests using a (real) discount rate of 8 percent, down from the previous recommended rate of 10 percent which had been in place since 1976. However, as the analysis here suggests, no single discount rate can be applied to all situations. The appropriate discount rate depends on the nature of the project. In particular, it depends on whether the alternative use of resources is a different investment or cur-rent consumption. More precisely, it depends on the entire time path of the alternative consumption stream. The appropriate discount rate also depends on the duration of the project, because this determines the extent to which intergenerational equity considerations arise, and it should depend on the riskiness of the project.

For long-run environmental projects, a real discount rate of 8 percent is too high. Lind (1982) suggests 3 or 4 percent as reasonable discount rates for such projects. Harvey (1993) has made the sensible and interesting sugges-tion of using a declining discount rate (called *hyperbolic* discounting). For instance, the first few years might be discounted at a rate of 8 or 10 percent, but a lower rate would be used for more distant years.

9.8 Jurisdiction for Environmental Policy

Some environmental externalities are primarily local in nature, such as urban air pollution or sewage treatment, whereas others are global in their effect, such as global warming. There are, in addition, environmental issues with an intermediate scope, such as acid rain. This variation in the scope of

environmental externalities and problems suggests various levels of government might reasonably be involved in environmental policy.

It is not surprising therefore that jurisdiction over environmental policy
in Canada is divided among all three major levels of government: local,
provincial, and federal. At the federal, or national, level a government
department, Environment Canada, has jurisdiction over environmental policy.
Most provincial governments also have separate environment ministries.

The global nature of many environmental problems creates tensions at
the international level, especially since there is no single international body
that coordinates and adjudicates international environmental disputes. Environmental issues are considered to some extent in the North American Free
Trade Agreement (NAFTA), the World Trade Organization (WTO), the World
Bank, and the United Nations, among other international bodies. Thus, some
supra-national institutions dealing with environmental issues are emerging.

10

Natural Resources and Sustainability

10.1 Introduction

This chapter is devoted to a set of environmental issues associated with natural resource use. We normally distinguish among three major types of natural resources: renewable resources (such as forests and fish stocks), nonrenewable resources (such as oil and natural gas), and land. These resources are important parts of the natural environment. In recent years, increasing concern has been expressed over the management of these resources. Of particular concern is whether current patterns of resource use are sustainable—whether such resource use can be maintained into the future—or whether we are doing irreparable harm to the resource base, thereby reducing future well-being.

Furthermore, in Canada, a significant part of business activity is based directly on natural resources, including the forest products industry, oil and gas, agriculture, mining, and fisheries. And even tourism in Canada is due largely to the natural environment. In this chapter we consider some important principles of resource management, public policy toward natural resources, and the role of sustainability.

10.2 Management of Renewable Resources

A *renewable resource* is one that can replenish itself naturally over a relatively short time period. The major renewable resources are fish stocks; forests; animal species; and, less obviously, soil. These resources regularly

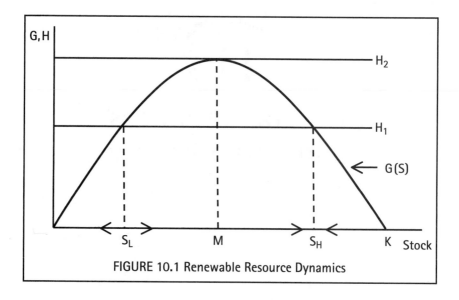

FIGURE 10.1 Renewable Resource Dynamics

renew themselves through natural, primarily biological, processes, thereby fully or partially replacing resources harvested for current use. The amount of natural growth in the resource normally depends on the size of the stock in place. One possible relationship between a resource stock and its growth rate is shown in Figure 10.1.

The horizontal axis in Figure 10.1 measures the stock, S, of the renewable resource. The curve labelled $G(S)$ represents the growth of the stock. Assume that the resource stock under consideration is a species of fish. As drawn in the diagram, the growth of the fish stock is zero if the stock itself is zero: if there are no fish to breed, then no fish will be added to the stock. If the stock is small but positive, the fish will breed and add to the stock, leading to positive growth. As the stock increases from low levels, the growth rate also increases since more fish are available to breed. At the point indicated by stock level M, however, the fish stock is large enough to induce significant crowding effects, since newborn fish must compete with a large existing stock of adult fish for food, reducing opportunities for survival. Thus, the growth rate of the stock declines with further increases in the stock. Left to itself, the fish stock would reach its maximum size, indicated by stock level K in the diagram, where growth would be zero. This point is the carrying capacity of the fishery and represents the maximum stock level that can be supported.

A commonly used mathematical function capturing this pattern of growth is the logistic function, which can be written as follows.

$$G(S) = rS(1 - S/K)$$

Inspection of this equation shows that if $S = 0$ the growth of the stock is zero. Similarly, if $S = K$, the growth of the stock is also zero. For intermediate levels of stock, growth is positive, and it is maximized at $S = K/2$. The logistic function is often used in modelling renewable resources, although it is only an approximation, and actual growth functions will differ for particular resource stocks. A common variant of the logistic growth function is one for which growth drops to zero at some positive stock level.[1] This would happen if some minimum positive stock is needed to ensure successful breeding—the minimum viable stock. However, the general pattern exhibited in Figure 10.1 does capture the essential character of most renewable resources.

If harvest rate H is precisely equal to growth rate G, then the stock does not change in size, because the amount being harvested is exactly equal to the amount of growth. Thus, if $H = G$, we would say the stock is in steady state and the harvest is *sustainable*. The horizontal lines H_1 and H_2 in Figure 10.1 are potential harvest rates. If we consider harvest rate H_1, we see it can be sustained at a stock size of either S_L or S_H, the levels where the harvest line intersects the growth function. At either of these stock levels, $H = G$. Given harvest level H_1, stock S_H is what we refer to as a stable steady state stock, meaning that if the stock moves slightly away from S_H, it will tend to return. Consider, for example, a slight increase in the stock above S_H. This will cause the growth rate to fall slightly—below the H_1 harvest rate. Since harvesting now exceeds growth, the stock will shrink in size and return toward S_H. Similarly, if the stock fell below S_H, the growth rate would rise above the harvest rate, leading to a self-correcting increase in the stock, moving it back toward S_H.

Similar reasoning shows that stock S_L is an unstable steady state. Specifically, consider what happens if the stock is at level S_L and the harvest rate is H_1. This is a steady state, in that growth of the stock exactly replaces the harvest as time proceeds. Suppose, however, some shock lowers the stock slightly. Now the harvest rate exceeds the growth rate, so the stock gets

---

[1] The formula for this variant is $G(S) = r(S - V)(1 - S/K)$ were V is the minimum viable stock. With this variant, growth falls to zero if S falls to level V, implying that the stock must exceed V for growth to occur.

smaller. As the stock gets smaller, the excess of harvesting over underlying growth increases and the stock declines even more rapidly, until extinction occurs. Similarly, if we start at stock S_L and then the stock rises slightly, the stock will continue to grow and never return to S_L, provided harvest level H_1 is maintained. Thus, S_L is unstable in the sense that slight disturbances are not self-correcting. If the stock deviates from S_L, it quickly moves even further away, and never returns.

The possibility of unstable steady states has some interesting policy implications. It clearly does not make sense to try to manage a resource at an unstable steady state, even if this appears to be desirable, because a slight mistake can bring disaster. It is important to manage the stock with a considerable margin for error, especially if there is uncertainty about key variables, such as the harvest or the precise size of the stock.

The maximum sustainable harvest (called the maximum sustainable yield) is H_2, and is possible at stock size M. Consider what would happen, however, if the stock happened to fall below M and harvesting continued at rate H_2. Now the harvest rate would exceed the stock growth rate and the stock would fall. In the next period, the harvest, still H_2, would exceed the growth rate by even more, and the stock would fall even faster. Eventually, the stock would be extinguished. However, an increase in the stock would be self-correcting. Stock M is a semi-stable steady state. As with the unstable steady state, it would be risky to try to manage the stock precisely at M with harvest H_2. A more conservative approach would be to adopt a harvest slightly below H_2 and let the stock settle at a stable steady state slightly above M.

It is often taken to be self-evident that ideal management of a renewable resource implies harvesting at or near the maximum sustainable yield (H_2 in the diagram), and therefore requires maintaining a stock at or close to size M. This is not necessarily true, however. First, it is possible that a renewable resource may be uneconomic. For example, if harvesting costs are high and demand for the resource is low, then it may be good management to simply leave the stock alone, in which case it would grow to carrying capacity K and remain there.

Second, it is also possible that a resource should be fully depleted. If, for example, the current value of the resource product is very high, the harvest cost is low, and the growth rate is low, it might make sense to harvest all of the stock immediately, invest the proceeds, and earn more from the investment than could have been earned by managing the resource on a sustainable basis. It might seem like a dangerous policy to allow resource stocks to be eliminated in this way. However, this is what has happened to the forest stocks that used to cover many of Canada's major cities, and in most of these cases we would probably agree the city is a higher value use of the land than a forest.

Another important possibility is cyclical management, whereby the harvest level varies depending on economic conditions, subject to a requirement that the yield be sustainable on average. Thus, if prices of the resource good are high, a harvest exceeding the growth rate might be allowed. If prices are low, a harvest less than the growth rate would be called for, leading to a sustainable pattern of harvesting overall, even though in any one year the harvest might differ from the growth rate. There is also the possibility that optimal policy might call for variable harvesting, where the harvest would vary depending on economic conditions, but with no overall sustainability constraint.

Finally, it is possible that optimal management calls for annual sustainable yield management, in which case there should be a positive harvest equal to, on a year-by-year basis, the growth rate of the resource. The appropriate level of this yield may or may not be the maximum sustainable yield.

One difficulty of resource management is determining a fully optimal harvesting plan in a real situation, because such analysis requires knowledge of the future value of the resource. Given the high degree of uncertainty about future values, the sentiment in the resource management community is toward sustainable yield management that avoids the potentially serious mistake of depleting a resource that might become very valuable in the future. Thus, sustainable yield management can be seen as a type of insurance against uncertainty. Most major renewable resources are officially managed on a sustainable yield basis. However, as we shall see, sustainable yield is frequently not achieved, and in actual practice there are pressures that often cause excessive depletion.

10.3 Canadian North Atlantic Cod

For much of the past 500 years, the Canadian North Atlantic cod fishery has been one of the world's most productive fisheries. It is located in the Atlantic Ocean near Newfoundland and Labrador, and is officially designated as area 2J3KL by the Northwest Atlantic Fisheries Organization (NAFO). This fishery was a major source of income for Newfoundland and other parts of Atlantic Canada, and was also intensively fished by European nations, particularly Spain. The current international Law of the Sea (dating from 1977) recognizes that countries have a right to control fishing and other forms of ocean use within 200 miles of their shores. Most of this fishery lies within the Canadian 200-mile limit.

Until the 1960s, fishing in the Atlantic cod fishery was not closely regulated. The fishery was very abundant, although the stock did not seem as large as it once had been. During the 1960s, cod harvests rose sharply, reflecting progress in fishing technology and an increased number of boats. The harvest peaked in 1968 and then began to fall as a result of declining stocks. By the 1970s, serious concerns were being expressed about the future of the stock, and efforts were made both within Canada and internationally to reduce catches to sustainable levels. In particular, the 1977 extension of the nautical limit to 200 miles (from 12 miles) allowed Canada effective control over most of the fishery. Fish catches were sharply reduced in the late 1970s, and the cod stock began to recover.

The politics of this process led, however, to a bias in favour of overfishing. In Canada, it was always in the interest of politicians to use the most optimistic assessments of the stock in setting fishing quotas, and the fishing industry regularly complained that the quotas were too restrictive. In addition, various other Canadian policies, especially regional development policies, had the effect of subsidizing the Canadian cod fishing industry. Also, Spanish and Portuguese fishing vessels increased the intensity of their fishing efforts in areas outside the 200-mile limit.

As a result of overfishing, cod stocks started to fall again in the mid-1980s. The allowable harvest was reduced throughout the late 1980s as stocks fell, but the harvest consistently remained too high to allow stock recovery. The cod fishery remained commercially very important throughout this period, until 1992. In 1992, the stock had a dramatic further fall and was then less than 5 percent of its level only 20 or 25 years earlier—clearly in serious danger of extinction. In 1992, the fishery was closed for an indefinite period. This closure was a major economic shock to Newfoundland and also affected fishing fleets from other parts of Atlantic Canada and from other countries.

Initially, it was hoped that the stock would recover fairly quickly, over perhaps a decade or so, but the stock actually fell even further, raising the question of whether the stock had fallen below the minimum viable level. Fortunately, starting in about 2004, the stock did begin to recover. Although the basic moratorium on commercial fishing has remained in place since 1992, some fishing has been allowed in recent years, including recreational fishing, cod caught "accidentally" when fishing for other species (the *by-catch*), cod caught for purposes of scientific study, and a small amount of closely regulated commercial fishing. The problem is that even this small amount of fishing is of sufficient size to put the current stock at risk, and some Canadian regulatory authorities recommend a complete moratorium.

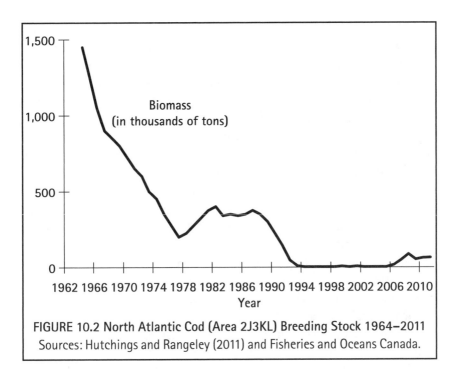

FIGURE 10.2 North Atlantic Cod (Area 2J3KL) Breeding Stock 1964–2011
Sources: Hutchings and Rangeley (2011) and Fisheries and Oceans Canada.

Figure 10.2 shows the evolution of the North Atlantic cod stock from 1964 to 2011. The stock did not fall to zero in 1994, but was close.

Overfishing of wild fish stocks is occurring all around the world. In recent decades, fishing fleets from some countries—particularly Japan, Taiwan, and South Korea—adopted drift net fishing, a process involving stationing large nets that catch everything, rather than tailoring them for specific types of fish. Drift nets, sometimes referred to as walls of death, represent a low-cost way of catching a lot of fish.

Drift nets create several problems, including the simple fact that current harvest levels are unsustainable. Another problem with drift nets is that they catch and kill a lot of species that are not commercially useful, including dolphins, a supposedly protected species. The fishing boats treat this extra kill as costless, but it may have substantial social costs due to its effects on the overall ecology of the oceans, and for other reasons as well. Ultimately, the United Nations imposed a partial ban on drift net fishing, making nets of more than 2.5 km in length illegal under international law. This law was originally enforced by patrols from the United States, Canada, Russia, and Japan. Subsequently, China and South Korea also joined the enforcement effort.

Despite efforts such as the moratorium on North Atlantic cod fishing and the ban on large drift nets, natural (wild) fish stocks have been declining worldwide. The global catch of wild fish peaked in 1988 and has been falling since then. To a large extent, natural (wild) stocks of fish have been replaced by farmed fish, which are fish grown in large enclosed pens, provided with food, and harvested much like domestic land animals, such as cattle and chickens.

Farmed fished are raised in crowded conditions, which increases the risk of disease. The disease problem is reduced in the short run by antibiotics, but overuse of antibiotics is leading to antibiotic resistant bacteria, which are a potential threat to the farmed stocks and also to wild fish stocks, and possibly to other species. Fish farming also results in a high density of biological waste, which often has a major, negative effect on the local ecology. In addition, farmed fish are often raised far from their natural habitats. For example, Atlantic salmon are raised in Pacific Ocean fish farms. Transplanting fish species in this way creates potential risks for local species. Using the terminology of the previous chapter, significant negative externalities are created through fish farming.

At present, in view of the continuing overfishing and depletion of wild fish stocks as well as the negative externalities of fish farming, this important renewable resource—fish stocks—is not being managed sustainably. It is likely that in the future humans will need to use the sea much more efficiently than it is currently being used, especially if sea levels rise (due to global warming) and if population grows significantly. Sustainable management of the world's fish stocks therefore remains an important objective.

10.4 Open Access Resources

Fish stocks are not the only renewable resources under pressure. Forests, soil, and wildlife species, such as elephants, are also being exploited at unsustainable levels. One reason for these problems is simple population growth: more people means more pressure on resource stocks. Population growth is discussed more fully later in this chapter. Another major issue for renewable resource management is market failure arising from the *open access problem* (sometimes referred to as the *tragedy of the commons*), which is actually a special type of externality problem.

The open access problem was first noted when sheep farming was a very important economic activity in England. Most towns had common areas where any sheep could graze. In addition, some individuals had private land. It was observed that common land was usually overgrazed: grazed to the point where the grass was damaged and its growth actually retarded, lowering the total yield from the common land. Why was the common being overgrazed when everyone knew that overgrazing was inefficient? Only an incompetent sheep farmer would allow his private land to be overgrazed. The answer follows from the basic theory of externalities. Grazing the common creates an externality.

Consider first the management of private land. If Farmer A allows his sheep to graze on his own land, there is a cost: the grass is eaten, so it cannot be sold to other sheep farmers or fed to other sheep. If the farmer is foolish enough to allow his land to be overgrazed, he will bear the full costs. As a result, he has an incentive to limit grazing to the efficient level.

Now consider the common. Suppose Farmer A observes that the common has already been grazed as far as optimal management would suggest. What should he do? If he does not allow his sheep to graze, he gets no immediate benefit at all. If he allows his sheep to graze, he will get some benefit. He will also bear some cost in that his sheep will have less effective grazing land in the future. However, he might conclude that if his sheep do not graze, someone else's sheep will, so he has nothing to gain by restraining his sheep. More generally, he has an incentive to allow his sheep to graze just up to the point where his (private) marginal benefit is equal to his (private) marginal cost.

The social marginal cost, however, is much higher than the sheep farmer's private marginal cost, because when Farmer A allows his sheep to graze the common, he is reducing the capacity of the land to support the sheep of other farmers who also use it. Therefore, the social marginal cost exceeds the private marginal cost, leading to excessive levels of grazing on the common. This conforms exactly to Figure 9.1 in Chapter 9.

The problem of common grazing land is dealt with fairly easily, at least conceptually. If grazing land is privately owned, a self-interested owner or user will have incentives to manage grazing efficiently. Thus, one solution is to convert common land to private control. This is in fact what happened to most common land in England. As population densities rose and the problem of the commons became more severe, particularly in the 17th and 18th centuries, common land was enclosed and converted to privately controlled land. This greatly increased agricultural productivity, although it also had the effect of reducing the real income of people without land who had formerly earned their living from the common land.

Other open access resources, such as ocean fisheries, are much harder to deal with, since it is often difficult to establish property rights. A fishing ground is like the common: in the absence of overall control, there is a tendency for waters to be overfished. There are really two externalities present.

First of all, since the total number of fish is fixed at any one time, a fish taken by one fishing boat is a fish that cannot be taken by another. The social cost of taking an extra fish includes the loss to the other boats, raising the social marginal cost of fishing above the private marginal cost. Therefore, a negative externality is created.

Secondly, as with the common, taking too many fish today reduces the number of fish that can be taken tomorrow. However, if there are fewer fish tomorrow, this is a cost borne by everyone who might fish, not just by the person trying to decide whether to take another fish. Thus, the social marginal cost exceeds the private marginal cost for this reason as well. This intertemporal externality leads to an inefficiently small fish stock.

Referring back to Figure 10.1, the open access externality can lead to a harvest level above H_2, creating possible extinction of the resource, when optimal management might call for a harvest level less than H_2. The response to externality problems in fishing has given rise to government regulation of the fishing industry in most countries. Canada has an active fishery management program in which governments appoint regulatory authorities to set catch limits (quotas), restrict fishing seasons, and carry out other regulatory actions. However, this system, intended to address the basic open access market failure, has not been up to the task in either the Atlantic or Pacific fisheries. In addition, as Section 10.3 emphasized, one problem is international externalities, as it is hard to develop international regulatory authorities. Such authorities do exist, but they have limited legal authority or police power to enforce adherence to their regulatory determinations.

10.5 Other Renewable Resources: Forests and Soil

In addition to depletion of fish stocks, there is considerable concern over depletion of other renewable resources, particularly forests and soil. To some extent, concerns in these areas also reflect externality problems. It can be argued that the destruction of the Amazon rain forest, for example, may have costly global effects on climate. Only a small fraction of such costs are borne by the farmers currently cutting down the forests. However, even in cases where externality effects are minor, such as in those parts of Canada's forests that are privately owned, it is alleged that forests are being depleted too rapidly. The basic argument seems to be that simple mismanagement and myopia are also important factors.

Soil depletion is also a very serious problem. One form of soil depletion is desertification—the transformation of fertile land into desert. About 40 percent of the world's surface area is defined as "drylands"—receiving less than about

50 cm of rainfall per year. Most of this land can be cultivated if managed well, but it is also vulnerable to desertification, during which standing water disappears, soil largely disappears, most vegetation disappears, and the land becomes mainly an infertile mixture of sand and rock.

Currently, deserts are expanding, and the desertification process is adding thousands of square kilometres to the world's deserts every year, significantly compromising the capacity of many countries to feed themselves. The full explanation for desertification is not well understood. It is due in part to changing rainfall patterns. In addition, loss of forest cover (deforestation) allows soil to blow away and wash into rivers. Poor agricultural practices also play an important role, particularly in Africa, where much of the land is treated as common land, subject to the tragedy of the commons described in the previous section. Also, using soil without replenishing important nutrients effectively "mines" it, and the soil ultimately loses its fertility. Even in Canada and the United States, where most agricultural land is privately owned, soil is being degraded or lost. Presumably, when soil and arable land begin to rise in value, more soil conservation will be undertaken.

10.6 Ocean Use

Oceans are common property and are subject to standard common-property problems. We have already considered the common-property problems associated with coastal fish stocks, and the same applies to ocean-going stocks. Each fishing vessel and each country has an incentive to take fish beyond the economic value–maximizing harvest.

Oceans are also used for transporting risky cargoes, particularly oil. We regularly read of oil spills. The basic point is that individual users of ocean transport have an incentive to underprovide safety. If an oil tanker spills its cargo, the owner of the tanker incurs some costs, but nothing approaching the full social cost of the spill. If owners of tankers did bear the full costs of oil spills, we would still have occasional spills, but far fewer than we have at present, since more resources would be devoted to prevention (stronger hulls, stricter standards about travelling in bad weather, etc.).

We do not have a good understanding of whether oil spills cause long-term damage. It is worth noting that about half of the 3.2 million tons of oil entering the ocean every year is natural seepage from offshore oil deposits. Oceans have apparently been handling this oil for many thousands of years. When oil is released into ocean waters, much of it evaporates, much of it is decomposed by bacteria, and the remainder eventually sinks to the bottom. There is no denying, however, that oil spills can have serious temporary effects on fish and other wildlife, not to mention lost human enjoyment of beaches where oil washes ashore.

A more serious threat to oceans comes from their use for garbage disposal. Huge quantities of garbage are towed out to sea and dumped. As a result, there are large quantities of long-lived plastics in the ocean. Plastic bags in the water look like jellyfish and are eaten by many animals, including sea turtles. Because plastic is indigestible, it gradually fills up a turtle's stomach, causing death by starvation. Balloons, plastic beads, and various other plastics either poison or starve much sea life. The plastic rings that hold together six-packs of canned beer and pop are particularly dangerous, strangling large numbers of birds, seals, and other animals. Medical wastes, including containers of infected blood, have occasionally washed up on U.S. beaches, and discharges of human sewage have made many beach areas around the world unsafe for swimming.

Because oceans are beyond the control of any one government, there are significant cross-country externalities in ocean use. Garbage dumped in the ocean by residents of one country might end up on the beaches of other countries. Such externalities make sustainable management at efficient resource-use levels hard to achieve, requiring significant international coordination.

10.7 Nonrenewable Resources and Intergenerational Equity

So far, we have discussed environmental problems arising from the open-access aspect of many renewable resources. Open-access externalities are less of a concern with major nonrenewable resources (although they can occur). The greater problem is simple resource depletion. Perhaps the most well-known example concerns oil, an apparently fixed resource that we are using up at a rapid rate. It has taken hundreds of thousands or even millions of years for oil deposits to accumulate, yet we could use most of them up in a matter of decades. At present rates of consumption, known reserves of oil will last for about another 52 years, and known reserves of natural gas for about another 64 years, as of 2012.[2] This problem arises even though oil production is not usually subject to externalities, property rights are well defined, and markets work well.

This time-to-depletion has, perhaps surprisingly, stayed very stable for about the last 50 years, and has actually risen in recent years as new reserves have been found more rapidly than old reserves have been used up. There are,

---

[2] See the BP Statistical Review: www.bp.com/sectionbodycopy.do?categoryId=7500&contentId=7068481.

however, several concerns. First, the new reserves are in locations that are increasingly difficult and dangerous to work with and more harmful to the environment, such as deep under water or in the Alberta oil sands in Canada. Second, there is reason to believe that current known reserves are overstated. And third, there is an upper limit to the potential amount of fossil fuels available in the earth's crust that can be used economically (barring unforeseen technological innovation), and sooner or later that limit will be approached.

It is difficult to incorporate sustainability requirements into the management of nonrenewable resources. Strictly speaking, nonrenewable resources cannot be used on a sustainable-yield basis. By definition, nonrenewable resources cannot be renewed on a time scale relevant to human economic activity. If the resource is used, it will gradually (or perhaps quickly) be depleted. A classic analysis of nonrenewable resource management carried out by Hotelling (1931) shows that efficient exploitation of a nonrenewable resource would, under otherwise stable economic conditions, lead to a gradual depletion of the resource. In addition, the real price would rise annually at a rate equal to the rate of interest, reflecting the increasing scarcity of the resource. This is known as Hotelling's Rule.

In 1973, a group of academics known as the Club of Rome published a widely read book called *The Limits to Growth* in which they argued that living standards would soon fall because we would run out of various nonrenewable resources, including oil. Their predictions, however, turned out to be very misleading, at least in the short run, for they failed to take into account the effect of changing prices. At present, even though current use levels suggest depletion of oil reserves in about 52 years, price increases would prevent such depletion even if no new oil was discovered. If oil becomes relatively scarce, its price will rise. The response will be just as it was in the early 1970s when oil prices rose sharply. Individuals will have economic incentives to economize on their use of oil, to develop new technologies that conserve energy, and to switch to other energy sources. Therefore, we will not "run out" of oil in 52 years, or in 152 years, even if no new oil is discovered. And, of course, significant new oil deposits will be discovered.

A more meaningful question than whether we will run out of oil relates to *peak oil*. The peak oil year is defined as the year when oil production reaches its maximum, after which oil production will have to decline. When we will reach peak oil production? Total production has been relatively stable for several decades, and output per capita has actually fallen from its peak in 1979. We must be close to peak production at present, although we may not have quite reached it yet. On the other hand, it is worth keeping in mind that countries with large oil deposits are concerned that alternative energy sources might render their oil reserves worthless. When two scientists claimed (falsely, as it turned out) to have discovered "cold fusion," oil producers feared it would be very damaging to their industry.

Resource depletion does not (necessarily) involve market failure. Given a particular population, and provided externality problems are either absent or appropriately addressed by policy, there is every reason to believe that fixed resources will be allocated efficiently by markets. As population grows, however, fixed resources tend to get used up at a faster rate and have to be spread over a larger population base. It is quite likely this resource depletion effect could lead at some point to declines in living standards. This is not a market failure, however, but simply the result of having to share a fixed pie among more and more claimants.

Another aspect of resource depletion is intergenerational equity. With any fixed resource, we have the option of using it now or saving it for future generations. We can, of course, substitute other things for used-up resources. As we use up oil, we can invest the resulting income in factories and other productive assets, including alternative sources of energy, that might be more valuable to future generations than the oil would have been. However, to the extent that current resources are simply consumed without a corresponding replacement investment, this is purely a matter of intergenerational distribution. Concerns about intergenerational equity are not easily dealt with and do not yield obvious answers. If we are concerned about future generations, using up resources is a legitimate problem, even if there is no market failure.

Intergenerational equity is a concern because the preferences of future generations do not enter into current prices. If future generations could bid for resources, current prices of exhaustible resources might be much higher than they are, and we would use them up much more slowly. This is not a market failure, but simply a question about whose welfare is to be considered in our objectives. One response is that governments should be the guardians of the future, but just as the future does not bid for current resources, it does not vote either, nor does it march in demonstrations or make campaign contributions. Governments might be more sensitive to posterity than are profit-maximizing firms, but we cannot expect such sensitivity to extend very far, as our experience with government debt accumulation and government fishery management suggests.

There are, however, some examples of government attempts to provide a sustainable benefit from current use of nonrenewable resources. After the substantial increases in oil prices that occurred in the 1970s, the government of Alberta set up the Alberta Heritage Savings and Trust Fund. The profits, or rents, from the government share of Alberta's many oil wells would be put into the fund and used for investments providing an ongoing stream of benefits to residents of Alberta. As of 2012, the fund had a value of $16.1 billion. However, the fund is not just a savings account. It also contributes to government programs on an annual basis. Between 1976 and 2012 it contributed approximately $34 billion to social initiatives in Alberta.[3] The Alberta Heritage Fund illustrates an approach to incorporating sustainability objectives into the management of nonrenewable resources. It is an attempt to ensure that a flow of benefits arising from oil is sustained into the future, even if the oil itself is gradually depleted.

In considering the management of resource stocks, we should keep in mind the discussions of transfer-seeking, or rent-seeking, discussed in Chapter 5. Resource stocks provide a pool of potential rents that many current claimants will compete for. Furthermore, since many of these resources are controlled by governments, there is a strong incentive for interest groups to lobby for public policies that will shift transfers in their direction. Future generations can be expected to have a hard time competing with current generations in this transfer-seeking game. Interestingly, however, some constituencies seeking to represent the interests of future generations have become very successful, including organizations such as Greenpeace (founded in Canada) and the Sierra Club.

10.8 Wildlife Conservation

Genetic diversity is being extinguished at a very rapid rate. Measuring species extinction is difficult, but it seems that the current extinction rate is between 1,000 and 10,000 times the natural extinction rate.[4] Most major mammals (except humans, our dog and cat companions, and farm animals such as cattle, pigs, and sheep) now have only trace populations compared to what they once were. Populations of large primates (such as orangutans and baboons), elephants, lions, tigers, whales, etc. are certainly no more than 10 percent of what they were a century ago, and they continue to decline.

Most people shake their heads when presented with such data. In the case of elephants, blame is usually fixed on the ivory trade, and the solution is seen as banning ivory markets. Unfortunately, this misses the main point. Major

---

[3] See www.finance.alberta.ca/business/ahstf/index.html.

[4] This information is available from a variety of sources. See, in particular, wwf.panda.org/about_our_earth/biodiversity/biodiversity/.

primates and other species, including elephants, are simply being replaced by humans. It is estimated that approximately 40 percent of the current biological capacity of the planet earth is devoted to the human consumption chain. If population doubles in the next 50 years, as it might, it is hard to see that much biological carrying capacity will be left for anything that does not enter the human food chain. In much of Africa, the human population has tripled in the past 30 to 40 years and animal populations have fallen correspondingly.

Forced to make a choice between saving the life of a human or a whale, human ethics would of course lead us to favour the human. However, saving existing lives is more compelling than trying to make room for large increments in population growth. We have to confront the issue of whether increases in human population are worth the opportunity cost of fewer animals and outright extinction of many species, including potential extinction of some of our near relatives such as (other) primates. In most economic analysis, we take human welfare as the objective we try to maximize. In such calculations, other animals enter only as tools, or instruments: their value is strictly related to their contribution to human welfare.

Some people will try to justify wildlife conservation on this instrumental basis: it is important to preserve major mammals so humans can enjoy looking at them, or it is important to preserve rain forests because we might discover medicines in them, and so on. There is, however, another point of view: animals have value in themselves. Under this view, chimpanzee welfare, elephant welfare, and dolphin welfare have significance that is quite independent of what these species might contribute to humans. Many environmentalists hold strongly to this view, and as we learn more about these particular animals, it becomes increasingly clear they share many of the attributes that we believe give humans intrinsic value.

A fairly extreme extension of this line of thought, referred to as the Gaia hypothesis, suggests treating the earth itself as a living entity with rights that humans should not be allowed to violate. While it is not entirely clear exactly what these rights might be, the idea has attracted considerable attention. Neither the Gaia hypothesis nor valuing animals for their own sake have, however, been embraced at the public policy level in Canada or elsewhere, and both would be difficult to implement.

10.9 Land Use, Waste Disposal, and Recycling

As mentioned at the beginning of this chapter, another major resource to consider is land itself. As populations grow, land becomes scarcer, housing becomes relatively more expensive, and congestion increases. One major problem associated with land use is what to do with garbage. In Chapter 9 we considered negative externalities associated with waste disposal, especially with hazardous waste. Here we consider the implications of waste disposal for management of land resources.

Current North American lifestyles generate a great deal of waste. The primary method of waste disposal is through use of landfills, but landfills are becoming harder to find. Cities such as Montreal, Toronto, and Vancouver have had considerable trouble in recent years finding new landfill sites in which to dump garbage, and they have expanded their use of incinerators. Incinerators create local negative externalities, however, and are subject to the NIMBY problem described in the previous chapter. Nevertheless, Canada is a large country, and by going far enough away from the cities (incurring high transport costs) it is still possible to find places to dump or incinerate garbage. As the costs of using landfill sites and other forms of waste disposal rise, it is natural to turn to recycling as a method of reducing waste.

Recycling is also made more attractive by the increasing scarcity of the materials we discard. As basic materials become scarce, their prices should rise and incentives to recycle should increase. This effect has taken a long time to emerge, but may finally be occurring. Over the past century, and especially in the past 50 years, technological progress has kept well ahead of resource depletion, with the result that the real cost of the basic materials making up most garbage, including paper, wood, plastics, and glass, has actually been falling over most of this period. However, such prices have firmed up in recent years, and there is a healthy market for many used and recycled items, including paper, metals of various types, plastics, and glass. In addition, more effective ways of handling recycled products have been designed. The easiest major waste item to resell and reuse is aluminum, followed by plastic. Traditionally, glass has been a difficult item to deal with, and much glass put in recycling boxes has ended up in landfills. However, at present, even reclaimed glass has a fairly active market in most parts of Canada.

Even so, the value of reclaimed products from recycling does not fully cover the cost of recycling in most areas. Much of the cost is still paid by taxpayers. There is an increasing attempt to use the polluter-pays principle by making producers of products that generate garbage pay for the cost of recycling, but this has not yet gone very far.

Efficient recycling is becoming an important area in corporate and public management. Designing products so they can be readily recycled is a particularly interesting technical problem, as is designing products that make use of recycled materials. As for public policy, designing efficient recycling systems is a considerable managerial challenge, and many early attempts were abandoned. Local governments have learned, however, to take advantage of incentive effects. Providing subsidized compost boxes and door-to-door pickup of recyclable materials have proved to be useful techniques. One very successful public policy measure is the use of deposits as an economic incentive to recycle. If we examine public garbage bins (and public streets, parks, and beaches), we will rarely observe bottles that carry a deposit, while non-deposit bottles and other materials continue to be a serious waste problem.

10.10 Sustainable Development

The modern concept of sustainability derives from renewable resource management. Sustainable management of a renewable resource means limiting the harvest so that the harvest rate can be maintained indefinitely. Extending this sustainable management concept to an entire economy is difficult. Applying sustainable yield on a resource-by-resource basis is not very satisfactory. As we have seen, the concept cannot apply to nonrenewable resources. Oil reserves that are used up cannot be replaced by new oil, at least not over relevant time scales.

However, we might try to apply a sustainable yield concept to the energy sector as a whole by requiring ongoing investment in appropriate infrastructure that can replace the energy yield of oil and other nonrenewable energy sources. Such infrastructure might include facilities to produce hydroelectric power, solar energy, wind energy, and so on. We might aggregate even further and not worry about sustainability in a particular sector (such as energy) and ask only that we be able to generate a steady or increasing flow of per capita consumption or utility. However, if we aggregate all the way to overall utility we tend to lose sight of the underlying ecological issues.

Another difficulty in applying sustainability as an objective is that it focuses attention on "conservation" or "maintenance" rather than on actual improvement in the human condition. For people in Canada, emphasis on maintaining the quality of life that we have seems important. However, for the many millions of people in much poorer regions of the world who wish to improve their lives, simply maintaining what they have is not enough. Reconciling the sustainability concept with economic development objectives has led to the concept of *sustainable development*, a concept that places emphasis on both sustainability and improvement through economic development.

Many definitions of sustainability have been suggested. One definition, developed by the United Nations Environmental Program (UNEP), suggests that sustainable development means "improving the quality of human life while living within the carrying capacity of supporting ecosystems." This definition has the advantage of being recognizable as a generalization of the original sustainable yield concept and is therefore related to underlying resource degradation issues. It also recognizes improvement in the human condition as an objective.

10.11 Population Growth and Environmental Sustainability

As is clear from other parts of this chapter, we might reasonably view the still rapidly growing human population as the underlying driving force behind many environmental concerns, and as a major threat to sustainable resource management. In the year 1 CE (or 1 AD), human population is thought to have been about 200 million, after which it required more than a millennium (about 1,200 years) to double to 400 million.[5] By contrast, the world's population doubled from about 1.5 billion to 3 billion in only 60 years, from 1900 to 1960, and then doubled again in only 40 years to over 6 billion by 2000. As of 2013, world population was over 7 billion.

The world population growth rate peaked in 1968 at 2.1 percent per year, implying a doubling time of about 35 years. The world population growth rate then fell gradually to about 1.1 percent as of 2012, implying a doubling time of about 65 years. Even at this lower growth rate, however, population growth is still very rapid by historical standards, and the world added about 80 million people in 2012. At present, a population the size of Canada is added to the world about every five months. Figure 10.3 shows the growth of human population over the last 500 years.

The tremendous increase in population that has taken place since the beginning of the Industrial Revolution (i.e., since about 1750) is due mainly to technological progress in food production and health care. This progress has also allowed living standards to improve dramatically for most of the world's people, despite the dramatic increase in population. Until the Industrial Revolution, the human impact on the global environment could reasonably be described as minor. Humans might have significant local effects, but the earth was very large compared to the rather puny efforts of human beings. Things have, however, changed very rapidly, and the human population has become so large it threatens to engulf most of the planet.

---

[5] Estimates of the history of world population are provided by several sources. The information here on world population is from the U.S. Census Bureau. See www.census.gov/population/international/data/. Early estimates are highly uncertain and might be off by 50 percent or more in either direction. Estimates covering the past 300 years are much more reliable.

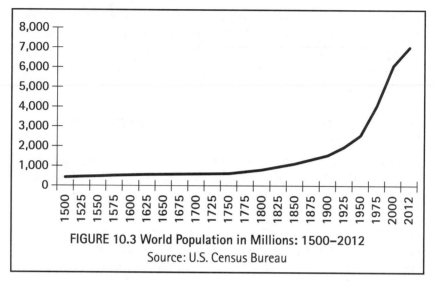

FIGURE 10.3 World Population in Millions: 1500–2012
Source: U.S. Census Bureau

Population optimists point out that many countries have gone through a demographic transition that has put zero population growth in reach for them. At low income levels, fertility tends to increase with income, but it seems that once a certain income threshold is passed, fertility tends to decline as income rises further, leading to sharp declines in fertility. Perhaps, therefore, if economic development can get sufficiently far ahead, populations will stabilize naturally at levels allowing attainment and sustainability of a high standard of living for entire world.

Figure 10.4 shows changes in the total fertility rate between 1972 and 2012 for the world's major regions and for the world as a whole.[6] The total fertility rate shows the number of children an average woman would have over her lifetime, given current birth rates of all age groups. Long-run stabilization of the population for the world as a whole requires a total fertility rate of about 2.3.[7]

The demographic transition occurred first in the wealthy countries of Europe and North America, and in Japan. As shown in Figure 10.4, by the early 1970s, fertility was already at or below long-run replacement levels

---

[6] The underlying data from the UN is actually provided for 5-year intervals. The value shown for 1972 is the 1970-75 value, and the value shown for 2012 is the 2010-15 estimated value.

[7] The replacement level of total fertility exceeds 2.0 for two reasons: a slight excess of male births over female births, and because some children die before growing up to child-bearing age. In high-income countries the replacement level is about 2.1, but in low income countries it is higher. For the world as a whole, the replacement level for the total fertility rate is about 2.3.

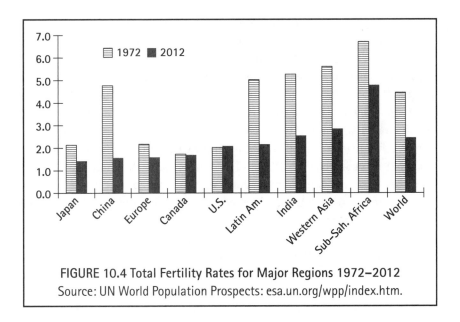

FIGURE 10.4 Total Fertility Rates for Major Regions 1972–2012
Source: UN World Population Prospects: esa.un.org/wpp/index.htm.

in Japan, Europe, and North America (although those populations were still growing, due partly to immigration and partly to the age structure of the population). In the past 40 years, there has been a dramatic decline in fertility in the world's two most populous countries—China and India, and also in Latin America. In all three of these regions fertility is now at a sustainable level; one that could be maintained in the long run without major problems.

Fertility in western Asia (the Middle East) is still too high to be sustainable, although it has fallen significantly. The region that has not gone through a significant demographic transition is sub-Saharan Africa (including Nigeria, Ethiopia, the Congo, and many other countries). This region has a much higher fertility rate than other areas. At present, its population is close to 1 billion, making it only a slightly smaller in population than China or India and comparable to Europe, or to North and South America combined. Population growth in sub-Saharan Africa is already causing significant shortages of food and conflict over resources in that area.

Even if replacement fertility is reached for the world as whole in the near future, it would still take several (perhaps three or four) more decades for population to stabilize, because population distributions are weighted toward the young. Population would grow significantly during that period, rising perhaps 40 or 50 percent above current levels.

If fertility does not decline further, in the absence of dramatic scientific and technological advances, population is very likely to be contained at some level less than twice the world's current population, because of resource constraints. What is at issue is whether this will be achieved in a reasonable way (declining fertility) or whether it will occur through nature's traditional methods of disease, malnutrition and outright famine, and war, all of which increase mortality. Disease is the probably the greatest immediate threat. After reaching an all-time low in the early 1980s, infectious diseases are making a comeback. AIDS and HIV get the most attention, but they are probably less important than the emergence of antibiotic-resistant bacteria and new respiratory viruses, which could well cause a major die-off in the 21st or 22nd century.

For any given population, we can manage environmental resources either poorly or well. We can attend to externalities and use the power of markets to promote efficient use of resources. We also need to understand the consequences of new technologies and deal with problems created through past ignorance, such as acid rain or toxic waste disposal. All of these things can make a huge difference, but ultimately our growing demands on a finite resource base will have to be stabilized.

This discussion is not intended to sound sensational. Ecological problems are very serious and are currently at dangerous levels in many parts of the world. These problems are not, however, technically insoluble, nor are they beyond the range of reasonable policy to improve. In fact, public policy has been very successful in dealing with the wave of environmental problems that emerged in wealthier countries in the early 1970s. In Western Europe and North America, air and water are both cleaner than they were 50 years ago. However, there is still relatively little explicit recognition of the fact that population growth is the main force underlying many environmental problems.

One also encounters simple denial of the seriousness of ecological problems, even in the face of overwhelming scientific evidence. During the 1981–85 period, the official position of the United States administration was that acid rain was not proven to have harmful effects. A (Canadian) National Film Board production on acid rain, entitled *Acid Rain: Requiem or Recovery*, which documented in rather conservative fashion much of the scientific evidence on acid rain, was temporarily banned in the United States during that period. That is ancient history now, but a similar pattern of denial has arisen over global warming in the 21st century.

On the other side, we sometimes encounter naive and emotional appeals to end pollution, occasionally in combination with a generalized attack on modern technology as the source of ecological evil. Some utopian notion of a natural lifestyle is sometimes held out as the objective. Unfortunately, humanity has had considerable experience with natural lifestyles, and they were not very pleasant. As Hobbes observed, a human being, in his or her natural state, lives a life that is "nasty, brutish, and short," and does not have much leisure for enjoying nature or anything else.

The best hope is to address environmental problems using tools that have proven successful in the recent past in raising the quality of human life. One important tool is the application of economic policy based on an understanding of incentive effects, harnessing market forces effectively. Perhaps even more important is ongoing development of scientific and technological knowledge. Furthermore, in some parts of the world, further reductions in fertility would be needed to achieve sustainable development.

11

Competition Policy

11.1 Introduction

The principle that competitive markets are important for good economic performance is one of the central themes in economics. This theme was first emphasized by Adam Smith (1776) and has been demonstrated repeatedly since then. For example, the recent transformation of China and India from economies based on government control and central planning to economies based on competitive markets has generated dramatic improvements in economic performance and quality of life in those countries.[1]

However, we have seen that competitive markets are sometimes subject to significant market failures, as when major externalities are present (Chapter 9). Governments have an important role to play in such cases, but good policy normally involves retaining the benefits of competition while incorporating some corrective action, such as a tax on the negative externality.

Sometimes, a market left to itself will not be sufficiently competitive and will therefore be prone to market failure based on market power—one firm or a small number of firms dominating the market and charging excessively high prices, or undertaking other anti-competitive actions. Governments have a role to play in limiting such abuses of market power, in promoting

---

[1] China's market-based economic reform began in 1978. The major shift toward market-based policies in India is normally regarded as having starting in 1991.

competition more broadly, and in preventing concentration of economic power in the hands of a few. In Canada, as in most countries, there is a body of legislation and a corresponding administrative apparatus charged with ensuring that markets achieve acceptable levels of competition. This area of policy is referred to as *competition policy*.

Canadian competition policy focuses on four major areas. First, it seeks to prevent firms from colluding (acting as a cartel) by fixing prices or entering into other anti-competitive arrangements. Second, it seeks to prevent undue reductions in competition arising from mergers—two or more firms combining into a single firm. Competition policy also focuses on the conduct of firms that do have significant market power, making sure that this market power is not abused. Finally, competition policy also seeks to protect consumers by preventing misleading advertising and other deceptive marketing practices.

11.2 A Brief History of Competition Policy
11.2.1 Early Legislation
The late 19th century is often described as a period of robber baron capitalism in North America. Several important industries were dominated by highly profitable cartels, sometimes called trusts or combines, in areas such as oil, steel, sugar, and various manufacturing industries. Furthermore, Canadian trade policies of the time included high tariffs designed to protect Canadian manufacturing, greatly restricting the ability of foreign firms to compete with Canadian firms, and therefore making it much easier for cartels in Canada to develop and exploit monopoly power.

By the 1880s, cartels and industrial collusion had become significant political issues in Canada and the United States. In reaction, governments in both countries adopted policies to deal with them, referred to as *antitrust* policy in the United States and *anti-combines* policy in Canada. In Canada the term "anti-combines policy" was later replaced by the term "competition policy."

Some limited policies seeking to reduce the power of monopolies and promote competition go back to the classical world (ancient Rome and Greece), and a few such policies had been occasionally applied in Europe from the Middle Ages forward. However, the world's first modern competition policy clearly specified in legislation is normally taken to be Canada's "Act for the Prevention and Suppression of Combinations Formed in Restraint of Trade," which passed through Canada's Parliament in 1889. The first U.S. antitrust law, the Sherman Act, was passed by the U.S. Congress in 1890.

11.2.2 Important Developments in Canadian Competition Policy

Initially, Canada's competition policy had very little effect, as no specific enforcement mechanism was created to accompany the new law. Police forces that normally dealt with crimes such as theft and assault were not likely to go out and arrest groups of executives for price-fixing. In 1910, new legislation, the Combines Investigation Act, replaced the earlier 1889 law and contained a variety of clarifications and extensions, including allowing for any six domestic residents to apply to a judge for an investigation into an alleged violation of the law. A 1919 amendment established a permanent investigative body, ultimately named the Competition Bureau, which plays a very important role in the administration of Canada's current competition policy.

A second weakness of the original law was its very limited scope, as it dealt only with cartels and the associated price-fixing or equivalent actions. Over time, the range of competition policy was expanded. Mergers were not mentioned in competition legislation at all, initially, and only in passing in the 1910 Act. In 1923, a new version of the Combines Investigation Act replaced the 1910 version, and it included explicit merger provisions, which were subsequently expanded. Various additional anti-competitive practices were made illegal in the Combines Investigation Act of 1923, as well as in amendments made in 1935 and 1952. Deceptive marketing practices, including misleading advertising, were included as anti-competitive practices in 1960.

Initially, Canada's competition law was part of criminal law. An alleged violation of competition law would be treated much like theft or assault. Thus, for example, executives convicted of price-fixing could, in principle, be subject to jail sentences. However, in addition to criminal law, Canada also has a system of civil law that deals with such things as contract disputes between firms, divorce cases, landlord/tenant disputes, etc. Civil law also deals with a variety of legal violations that are less serious than criminal offences (crimes) and do not lead to criminal records or to prison sentences.

On the surface, criminal law might seem a more effective vehicle than civil law for competition policy, as criminal code convictions must be a stronger deterrent to anti-competitive acts than findings of fault under civil law. However, criminal law requires a much higher standard of proof, as guilt must be established *beyond a reasonable doubt*, while in civil law the standard of proof is only the *balance of probabilities*. It is, therefore, much easier to obtain findings of fault under civil law than to obtain convictions under criminal law. For example, a criminal court judge should not convict even if the judge views the probably of guilt as 80 percent; the implied 20 percent chance of innocence is more than enough for reasonable doubt. But in a civil case, an 80 percent chance of wrongdoing is more than enough for a finding of fault. Also, while serious penalties were possible under criminal law, they were almost never imposed. Thus, under criminal law it was hard to get convictions, and penalties were light. Starting in 1976, parts of competition policy were moved to civil law, with further shifts later.

The Competition Act of 1986 provided a major revision and restructuring of competition policy in Canada, replacing the much amended Combines Investigation Act. One important change was to move significant sections of the law from criminal law to civil law, plus the associated creation of the Competition Tribunal to adjudicate civil law cases in place of the courts. One area of competition policy that was shifted to civil law was merger law. Thus, the Competition Bureau could bring a civil case before the Competition Tribunal, seeking to block a merger on the grounds that it would be likely to generate a substantial lessening of competition. The Competition Tribunal would then decide the case based only on the balance of probabilities standard rather than on the reasonable doubt standard.

Another major change in 1986 increased the importance of economic analysis in competition policy cases, as the Act explicitly recognized economic efficiency as an important factor in determining how cases should be decided. For example, a merger that would otherwise have been prevented might instead be permitted if it allowed for sufficient costs savings, generating a significant improvement in economic efficiency.[2]

The Competition Act of 1986 remains the foundation of current competition policy in Canada, although significant amendments to the law have occurred, particularly in 1999 and 2009. Important aspects of these amendments include a continuing shift from criminal law to civil law, increased penalties for civil law and criminal law violations, greater flexibility in dealing with anti-competitive agreements among firms, and adjustments to the merger review process.

---

[2] See Ross and Winter (2005) for a discussion of the efficiency defence in merger cases.

Important changes to Canadian competition policy are indicated in the following list.

1889   First Canadian competition law: An Act for the Prevention and Suppression of Combinations Formed in Restraint of Trade

1910   Complaint-based procedure established to initiate investigations; specific reference to mergers placed in the law

1919   First permanent investigative body established (subsequently renamed as the Competition Bureau)

1923   Many extensions, including substantive treatment of mergers

1960   Deceptive marketing practices included as anti-competitive practices

1976   Service industries included under competition law; some decriminalization (shift to civil law)

1986   Competition Act replaced earlier legislation; many changes, including expansion of civil law provisions and creation of Competition Tribunal

1999   Strengthened many areas of competition law, including applications to information and communications sectors, and more civil law provisions

2009   Increased penalties, more civil law provisions, more flexibility in handling anti-competitive agreements among firms

11.2.3 Objectives of Canadian Competition Policy

The economic interpretation of competition policy is that it should reduce the inefficiencies associated with market power and anti-competitive practices. This interpretation is a direct application of the analysis of monopoly power presented in Chapter 6. However, it gives an incomplete view of the historical source of competition law, which was largely based on fairness considerations. Specifically, the public sentiment against monopoly power was due primarily to the following two perceptions:

1. Cartels or combinations violated norms of procedural fairness in business practice. (For example, large firms conspiring to put a small competitor out of business might be viewed as simply unfair.)
2. The creation of market power through cartels led to the enrichment of a few owners of capital and the exploitation of consumers and smaller firms.

These two concerns are important, but they have little to do with the inefficiencies of monopoly power. Instead, they are based on notions of fairness or equity. The case against monopoly presented in Chapters 3 and 6 is primarily an efficiency argument—total economic surplus is reduced by monopoly power—and possible transfers of wealth associated with monopoly power are not part of this efficiency argument. These transfers may be undesirable, but that assessment depends on knowing who the shareholders in the affected firms are and who the affected consumers are, along with judgments of which individuals are more deserving than others.

Early perceptions of competition policy led naturally to a legalistic approach matching the criminal law system. In fact, the original form of competition law did not use the words "monopoly" or "efficiency" at all. Instead, the emphasis was on notions of conspiracy, by analogy with notions of conspiracy in crimes against the state or individuals. As time passed, however, the economic efficiency rationale for competition policy became more important, and the law moved away from a focus on conspiracy, although anti-conspiracy provisions still exist. Modern competition law is based primarily on promoting competition and on related issues of economic efficiency.

The stated purpose of Canada's competition policy is to "maintain and encourage competition in Canada," thereby achieving several objectives, including "to promote the efficiency and adaptability of the Canadian economy, to ensure that small and medium-sized businesses have an equitable opportunity, ... and to provide consumers with competitive prices and product choices."[3]

11.2.4 The Administration of Competition Policy

Most of the operations and investigations called for under the Competition Act are carried out by the Competition Bureau (referred to hereafter as the bureau) under the direction of the Commissioner of Competition. The bureau is part of Industry Canada (a department of the federal government). The position of the commissioner has been vested with considerable independence, much like that of the Governor of the Bank of Canada. The commissioner is, therefore, supposed to be largely free from political influences.

Both Criminal Code and civil matters are investigated by the bureau. In the case of Criminal Code offences, if a decision to proceed is made, the results of the investigation are communicated by the commissioner to the Attorney General of Canada for prosecution. Civil matters are referred to the Competition Tribunal for adjudication.

---

[3] This description is provided in the current version of the Competition Act at www.laws.justice.gc.ca/eng/acts/C-34/index.html.

The tribunal is composed of up to six federal judges and up to eight lay members, all appointed for terms of seven years. Most cases are heard by a panel of just three tribunal members, at least one of whom must be a federal judge. Thus, the tribunal acts as a substitute for the normal court system for civil law matters, while Criminal Code cases go through the courts.

The tribunal system has several advantages over the court system. First, the lay members of the tribunal are normally experts in appropriate areas of economics and business. The judges also are or become experts in competition law. A second advantage is that the tribunal is faster than the courts in dealing with cases (one of the objectives of the original legislation). A third advantage is the tribunal's greater flexibility in making decisions and facilitating negotiated settlements with firms accused of anti-competitive actions.

11.2.5 Anti-Competitive Practices

Most of the activities of the bureau are focused on a specific set of anti-competitive practices defined in the Act. These practices can be put in four general categories.

1. collusion
2. anti-competitive mergers
3. abuse of market power
4. deceptive marketing practices

Some practices within these categories (primarily in the collusion category) are part of criminal law and some are part of civil law. Furthermore, some practices are *per se* offences, meaning that simply carrying out the practice or act is illegal, regardless of the consequences. Other practices are subject to a *rule of reason*, meaning that the action may or may not be illegal, depending on its consequences. For example, collusion in the form of price-fixing is per se illegal. It does not matter whether or not significant damage is done by the price-fixing; the simple act of fixing prices is illegal. On the other hand, there is nothing illegal, per se, about undertaking a merger. Suspect mergers are evaluated on a case-by-case basis, applying a rule of reason. Only mergers that are judged likely to lessen competition substantially are violations of the law.

11.3 Collusion

Collusion refers to agreements among competitors over prices, quantities, market areas, or closely related matters. Such collusion is illegal under the

Competition Act, which refers to it as *conspiracy*. A collusive arrangement of this type is also commonly referred to as a *cartel*. The part of modern competition policy dealing with collusion is the descendant of the original legislation of 1889, which focused particularly on price-fixing conspiracies, or cartels. The Act also specifically prohibits bid-rigging, the analogue of price-fixing for bidding situations. Other prohibited practices include market-sharing arrangements (dividing a market along geographical or other readily identifiable lines), quota systems (limiting production to certain fixed amounts per firm), and agreements to deter entry of potential rivals.

The section of the Competition Act dealing with conspiracy remains part of the Criminal Code. Its basic intent is to prevent the formation of cartels and other kinds of anti-competitive collusion among firms. However, the Act explicitly allows coordination between firms for certain natural and obvious purposes, including defining product standards and industry terminology, standardizing packaging and measurement, and enacting measures to protect the environment. The Act also allows cooperation among firms to restrict advertising or for research and development.

Perhaps the world's best-known cartel is the Organization of Petroleum Exporting Countries (OPEC), which is made up of Saudi Arabia, Kuwait, and ten other oil producing countries. OPEC seeks to control, or at least influence, oil prices. It operates outside the legal jurisdiction of Canada or the United States or other countries where it could be prosecuted. It is, therefore, not doing anything illegal. However, in Canada, a cartel that acted like OPEC would be in violation of competition law.

Price-fixing or bid-rigging cases are brought before the courts quite frequently. One recent example, settled in 2012, was a price-fixing conspiracy among gasoline retailers in and around Kingston, Ontario. The retailers involved were Pioneer Energy, Canadian Tire, and Mr. Gas. The bureau was able to determine that representatives of these retailers were in regular telephone communication with each other for the purpose of agreeing on gas prices. The companies were fined a total of over $2 million. A more far-reaching recent example relates to the construction industry in Quebec,[4] where a large number of bid-rigging cases have gone before the courts in what is reported to be only the beginning of dealing with a large, overarching conspiracy involving organized crime and local politicians, as well as firms in the industry.

---

[4] See Banerjee (2012).

11.3.1 Incentives Under Collusion

The basic objective of collusion is to allow the firms involved to earn a monopoly-level profit, or close to it. Perfect collusion imitates the pure monopoly outcome: joint profits are maximized. In the days before the development of competition policy, collusion was sometimes maintained by explicit contract. Firms would sign contracts with each other, limiting the amount of output each would sell or the geographical area in which each would operate, or agreeing on prices directly.

Since the development of competition policy, collusive contracts are in violation of the law. Even if the legal system failed to actively prosecute a collusive agreement, no court would enforce such a contract. Thus, actual collusive contracts are of limited value to firms, as they are not enforceable and create a potential legal liability.

Firms engaging in collusion confront two basic problems: first, ensuring that the colluding firms maintain the agreement in the absence of a legally enforceable contract, and second, avoiding prosecution. These two problems present a trade-off to the firms involved, since actions that increase the chances of maintaining the collusive agreement typically make the prospect of prosecution more likely as well.

The basic incentive problem of collusion is as follows. The collusive agreement, by its nature, requires firms to restrain output below normal (non-collusive) production levels. Restrained output allows the industry to move up the industry demand curve and charge a higher price. The collusive price and output levels occur where industry marginal revenue is just equal to industry marginal cost, as with monopoly pricing.

From the point of view of any one firm, however, its own marginal revenue (i.e., the change in revenue from increasing quantity) is above marginal cost, meaning it has a unilateral incentive to expand output. This is best illustrated using the following equations, where the symbol Δ means "the change in."

$$MR^f = P + (\Delta P)q \tag{11.1}$$
$$MR^I = P + (\Delta P)Q \tag{11.2}$$

The price change, ΔP, from increasing quantity is negative, representing the price fall required if sales are going to increase by one unit. MR^f is a single firm's marginal revenue, MR^I is the industry's marginal revenue, P is price, q is the output of a single firm, and Q is the industry's output.

Recall from Chapter 6 that marginal revenue is the extra revenue resulting from a one-unit increase in output. If a single firm increases output, it gains the price charged for the extra unit of sales, but the industry selling price falls, reducing the revenue of the firm by the change in price, ΔP, times its output, q. These two effects are reflected in the two terms of Equation 11.1. Industry marginal revenue is similar, except the second term is industry output, Q, times the fall in price, as shown by Equation 11.2. Since industry output exceeds the output of any one firm, the effect of the price decline is larger for the industry than for a single firm. As a result, industry marginal revenue is less than the marginal revenue of the single firm that increases output.

An increase in output by one firm causes the revenue of other firms to fall. The industry marginal revenue associated with one firm's increase in output is that firm's marginal revenue minus the losses to other firms. Industry marginal cost is, however, just the same as a firm's marginal cost. If industry marginal revenue is set equal to marginal cost, the firm's marginal revenue must be above marginal cost. Consequently, the firm faces an incentive to expand output.

The following stylized example clearly sets out the incentive problem. Suppose there are several firms in an industry. In the absence of collusion, each would earn profit N annually. This level of profit might still exceed normal competitive profits, but it will be less than full monopoly profits. Profits under full collusion, if divided up among the firms, would yield an annual profit of M to each firm, where $M > N$. The annual benefit to each firm from collusion is $M - N$.

In effect, the colluding firms are in a prisoner's dilemma situation, as described in Chapter 6. If they cooperate, they all do well, but given the output levels of the other firms, any one firm has an incentive to defect by producing more output. A defecting firm raises its own profits but reduces the profits of the other firms by more than its own gain. By defecting, a single firm can earn even more than M, at least temporarily. In most cartels, sooner or later this proves to be an irresistible temptation.

Nevertheless, there have been periods of collusion in many industries. Cartels tend to be most stable when the firms involved can easily communicate with each other and when the relationship is likely to last a long time. If a collusive arrangement has been reached, and the firms are likely to interact for many years, the incentive to defect on the agreement is partially offset by the idea that defection today will be matched by retaliatory defection in the next period by the other firms. The defecting firm must trade off the short-term gains from defection against the long-term losses from disintegration of the collusive agreement: the firm will give up the benefits of collusion, $M - N$, for (at least some) future periods.

Economists have considered how firms can most effectively use this threat of retaliation in the industry to promote collusion. Like Ulysses confronted by the Sirens, the firms would like to collectively bind themselves to a course of action they would otherwise stray from; the firms would like to be able to commit themselves to the collusive agreement. One way to generate an environment that maintains collusion is by establishing the expectation that defectors will face damaging retaliation or punishment. The strongest form of punishment is that any defection will result in defection by the others, forever. Presented with such a prospect, firms have a strong incentive not to defect from collusion.

But what if defection did take place? Will the industry be locked forever in punishment mode, with firms foregoing potential monopoly profits? In fact, this so-called grim strategy of threatening permanent defection does meet minimal tests of consistency: it is what economists refer to as a Nash equilibrium, which means each firm is maximizing its profit, given the strategies selected by rival firms. In addition, these strategies are credible, or sequentially rational, in that it is not irrational for an individual firm to actually carry out the punishment threats if called upon to do so, given that it expects other firms to also do so. A more favourable outcome, however, from the firms' point of view, involves more limited trigger strategies of following a defection with only short periods of retaliation.

Axelrod (2006) has shown in laboratory experiments that so-called tit-for-tat strategies are good at maintaining collusion without sacrificing too much during retaliation. Tit for tat involves starting out by playing the collusive strategy (cooperating), but following any defection by a rival with a single period of retaliatory defection, then returning to the collusive strategy. Thus, if one firm raises its output and undercuts other firms in period 1, rival firms would respond by producing more, leading to further price reductions in period 2, reducing the profits of all firms. After this punishment period, however, the retaliating firms would return to the collusive output and price levels, expecting the initial defector to have learned its lesson. The firms' hope is that the expectation of such punishment, or the experience of punishment, will deter further defections.

Collusion is particularly difficult if there is considerable uncertainty in demand, so that firms have a hard time distinguishing between defection and bad luck. This increases any one firm's temptation to defect, because it may not even be found out.

Collusion is one way for a small group of firms to try to achieve monopoly profits (at the expense of consumers). Even in jurisdictions where collusion is illegal, and granting that collusion is usually unstable, it is still a significant business phenomenon and warrants public policy restricting it. The rationale for anti-collusion laws, therefore, has a solid normative foundation.

11.3.2 Enforcement

The conspiracy provisions in competition law are difficult to enforce. Explicit collusion over prices or quantities or market-sharing arrangements, supported by written documents, makes a strong case for prosecution. But what about cases where explicit collusion is maintained without written documents? Such agreements are clearly illegal, but hard to prove. Even more difficult to investigate are collusive arrangements based on a tacit (rather than explicit) understanding between competing business firms. Tacit collusion means that the managers of firms are aware of the advantages of collusion and maintain a collusive outcome without direct communication between them. If one firm in an industry always announces its price list first, and other firms follow with similar prices based on an implicit understanding that no one firm should rock the boat, is this conspiracy? Such cases fall in a grey area and would rarely be prosecuted.

11.4 Mergers

A merger occurs when two or more firms are combined into a single entity. Sometimes, one firm simply acquires another firm. A merger also occurs when one firm acquires only part of another firm. Sometimes, two or more merging firms create a new firm that acquires the assets of the merging parties. All mergers involve an acquisition of assets by the post-merger firm. Therefore, mergers are often called *acquisitions* (or *takeovers*), especially when the acquiring firm is much larger than the firm being acquired. When the two pre-merger firms are of similar size, the term "merger" is more commonly used. There is, however, no legal distinction between a merger and an acquisition.

A merger is a more direct method of trying to increase market power than is collusion. It brings control of previously independent operations under one management. Unlike collusion, however, mergers are not focused exclusively on increasing monopoly power. Most mergers, in fact, are based on potential efficiency gains—realizing economies of scale or other cost advantages.

The merger process is often referred to as the market for corporate control, reflecting the idea that the importance of mergers is the transfer of control of business units from one set of owners and managers to another. This buying and selling of business units is a market like any other. The standard normative economic analysis of markets can be applied to this market for corporate control. For example, if this market satisfies the conditions of perfect competition, then control over business units should wind up in the hands of those who can use the units most effectively. If, on the other hand, market imperfections are important in this market, then we might expect it to perform poorly from the public interest point of view.

Mergers often reduce competition. For example, if there are three firms in an industry and they merge to form a single firm, then a reasonably competitive market structure has been replaced with a monopoly. The Competition Act provides for taking action against a merger that "prevents or lessens, or is likely to prevent or lessen, competition substantially."

11.4.1 Types of Mergers

It is normal to distinguish between three types of mergers: horizontal mergers, vertical mergers, and conglomerate mergers. Horizontal mergers are those between two business units producing essentially the same or similar products—products that compete with each other in the marketplace. For example, a merger between General Motors and Toyota would be a horizontal merger. A vertical merger takes place between two firms otherwise in a potential buyer-supplier relationship—two firms carrying out adjacent steps in a production process. If, for example, a jet aircraft producer, such as Boeing, purchased a major airline such as Air Canada, this would be a vertical merger. A conglomerate merger occurs between firms carrying on different lines of business. For example, if Microsoft were to buy a hotel chain, such as Hilton Hotels, it would be a conglomerate merger. These definitions are conceptually useful, but many mergers have both vertical and horizontal elements, so the distinction among the three types is not always clear in practice.

The debate over merger policy is most acute with respect to horizontal mergers. The standard analysis of horizontal mergers focuses on the trade-off between the reduction in competition caused by a merger and the increase in efficiency due to economies of scale.

Consider an extreme case. Suppose there are two firms in an industry and production is characterized by very strong economies of scale (as in the production of wide-body jet aircraft), so that both firms have downward-sloping average cost curves over all reasonable ranges of production. Suppose one of the two firms acquires the other, creating a new, merged firm. The new firm could, if it chooses, produce the same output that the two firms had previously, and at lower average cost due to realizing economies of scale. Possibly, for example, the new firm could save money by having only one office building for its head office instead of keeping two buildings. There is an obvious efficiency gain arising from realization of economies of scale.

Unfortunately, the new firm would be unlikely to produce the old level of output. If the new monopoly firm wishes to maximize profits, it will restrict output, raise prices, and cause an increase in the standard inefficiency or deadweight loss associated with monopoly power. Depending on the nature of competition in the original duopoly situation, the monopoly outcome resulting from the proposed merger might be welfare improving or welfare reducing.

It is worth emphasizing that the firms themselves should do well. If stock markets behave rationally, and the purchase price of the acquired firm is appropriate, shareholders of both the acquired firm (the "target") and the acquiring firm should be able to get a financial benefit. That benefit may be based, however, mainly on a transfer from consumers, rather than on any improvement in efficiency.

Suppose, on the other hand that, despite substantial economies of scale, there were many firms in the industry, as if producers of wide-body jet aircraft were as prolific as corner groceries. At this extreme, it seems obvious that a few mergers would be in the social (and private) interest. Economies of scale would generate efficiency gains, and still the market would be highly competitive. Where should the line be drawn? Some countries have attempted to use concentration ratios as a guide. The four-firm concentration shows the fraction of sales accounted for among the largest four firms in an industry. A simple rule could be that a merger should not be allowed if, as a result, this ratio were to go above a certain level.

Unfortunately, the use of concentration ratios is not well grounded in economic analysis. Whether a horizontal merger improves or reduces welfare depends largely on the nature of demand in the industry, on the structure of costs, and perhaps most importantly, on the mode of competitive rivalry among firms in the industry. Interestingly, Canada's current Competition Act explicitly states that concentration data should not be the sole basis for finding that a merger substantially lessens competition.

Considerable research has focused on the gains to firms resulting from mergers, usually using financial stock market data. Unfortunately, most of this work does not directly address the social costs and benefits of mergers. These papers instead ask whether mergers generated net gains to the firms involved, as measured by changes in the stock market prices of the shares of bidder and target firms around the merger announcement date. The general conclusion of this work is that there are private gains to mergers, and most of the gains go to shareholders of target firms: there is a significant increase in share prices of target firms during the merger process, and a smaller increase in share prices of bidder firms.

The problem with using these results for an evaluation of merger policy is that, even if there are gains to firms involved in the mergers, it does not follow that the public interest is necessarily being served. As mentioned above, the gain to the firms might arise either from efficiency gains or from an increase in monopoly power, or from some combination of the two. If the gains come from an increase in monopoly power, then social welfare is probably being reduced, not increased.

The economic theory of vertical mergers is much less clear than the theory of horizontal mergers. The natural reaction to a proposed vertical merger is that it may reduce competition. There is, however, a well-known line of argument that runs in exactly the opposite direction. Suppose Firm A is a monopoly supplier of some important input to Firm B, which is in turn a monopolist in consumer markets. If the two firms are separate, then Firm A charges a monopoly markup on the input sold to Firm B, raising Firm B's costs. Firm B then charges a monopoly markup in the consumer market. Thus, a markup of price over marginal cost occurs twice, leading to the term *double marginalization* in describing this situation. If Firm A and Firm B were to merge, then the distortion associated with charging a monopoly price for the transaction between Firm A and Firm B disappears, and overall allocational efficiency may rise. In effect, vertical mergers reduce the number of steps at which monopoly power is used, and may, therefore, reduce the total social cost of monopoly power.

The case just described is the case of bilateral monopoly. Moving to other market structures greatly complicates the analysis. Public discussion of competition law and competition policy suggests that vertical mergers are of greatest concern in oligopoly situations. Suppose there is one firm in an upstream industry and several firms in a downstream industry. The downstream industry buys essential goods or services from the upstream industry. The fear is that if one downstream firm merges with the upstream firm, the merged firm will discriminate against the rival downstream firms. If it refused to deal with the downstream rivals altogether, then it could, in the absence of entry, establish a monopoly in the downstream industry.

In more complex situations, such as bilateral oligopoly (oligopoly in both upstream and downstream industries), economic theory is ambiguous concerning the effects of vertical mergers on performance. One important idea is that such mergers facilitate transferring assets that are difficult to transfer on an arm's length basis (i.e., through asset markets).

As for conglomerate mergers, economic theory has relatively little to say. Presumably, the basic rationale for such mergers is the advantage of carrying out two separate activities in the same firm, referred to as economies of scope. For example, the marketing network in place to market one line of products can be used to market another line of products acquired by the firm through a merger. Conglomerate mergers have no obvious effect on the competitiveness of particular markets because, by definition, they involve firms producing in different markets. As with vertical mergers, one of the gains might be an easier transfer of assets from low-value uses to higher-value uses.

Some critics have argued that conglomerate mergers lead to undesirable concentrations of political power. This concern focuses on aggregate concentration: the fraction of total economic power (usually measured by sales or total assets) accounted for by some small subset of large firms, such as the largest 10 or 50 firms.

11.4.2 Merger Review

The Competition Bureau reviews all large mergers. Large firms planning a merger transaction beyond a certain size ($77 million as of 2012) must notify the bureau before the merger takes place, and allow a review of the merger. Most corporate mergers fall below this threshold and are not reported or reviewed. Of those that are reviewed—between 200 and 300 per year in recent years—the vast majority are allowed to proceed without modification. In a typical year, a handful of mergers are restructured and allowed to proceed on a modified basis, often requiring some assets of the merged entity to be sold to potential competitors.

In addition, a few mergers are abandoned as a result or partial result of bureau concerns. For example, a major review of proposed mergers in the banking sector was undertaken in 1998. The Royal Bank and the Bank of Montreal planned to merge, as did the Canadian Imperial Bank of Commerce and the Toronto-Dominion Bank. The bureau recommended against these mergers. Because this involved the banking sector, the Minister of Finance had overall jurisdiction, and he decided to disallow the mergers, based largely on the bureau's recommendation.

Sometimes mergers fail to proceed even when approved by the bureau. In 2011, a very large merger was proposed between the TMX Group, owner of the Toronto Stock Exchange and other major exchanges in Canada, and England's London Stock Exchange. The bureau approved the merger but many other parties in Canada objected, arguing that a foreign enterprise, the London Stock Exchange, would, in effect, be acquiring Canada's major exchanges, and that this was against Canada's national interest. Ultimately, however, TMX shareholders rejected the merger and the TMX group merged instead in 2012 with a Canadian consortium of banks and pension funds called the Maple Group Acquisition Corporation, with the approval of the Competition Bureau. The merged entity operates under the name TMX Group (not under the name Maple Group), even though it was the TMX group that was acquired.

While the number of mergers directly affected by bureau activities is small compared to total merger activity, bureau activities have a significant impact on how firms approach large mergers. In particular, firms are more reluctant to undertake large mergers that have significant negative effects on competition.

11.5 Abuse of Market Power

Abuse of market power includes a category of conduct referred to as *abuse of dominant position*, along with several other types of anti-competitive conduct, including *resale price maintenance* and *exclusionary arrangements*.

11.5.1 Abuse of Dominant Position

Dominant position arises if a firm has a monopoly or near-monopoly position in a market in Canada. Abuse of dominant position can also be carried out collectively by a group of firms that, together, have a dominant position. A dominant position is not illegal in itself. However, taking advantage of a dominant position in certain ways—abusing that position—is illegal.

Such abuse arises when a dominant firm or a group of dominant firms takes certain actions to prevent entry or to damage rivals. Of course, many legitimate actions might prevent entry or damage rivals, such a producing a high-quality new product and charging a low price for it. For example, when Apple introduced the iPhone, its rival, the producer of the BlackBerry smart phone, was damaged. But there is nothing wrong with producing good products and charging attractive prices.

On the other hand, if a dominant firm persuaded a supplier of a critical input to withhold that input from a rival, such an action would be regarded as an abuse. For example, if Apple exploited its importance as a buyer of microprocessors and persuaded the producer of critical microprocessors not to sell to BlackBerry, such an action would be illegal.

It is not completely obvious which actions should be allowed and which should be prohibited. Economists, legal scholars, and others have devoted a great deal of effort to trying to answer this question. The Act includes many specific abuses, most of which fall into two general categories—attempts to deter entry by potential rivals and attempts to damage the competitive position of existing rivals. These possible abuses are handled on a rule of reason rather than a per se basis, and the Competition Bureau tries to assess on a case-by-case basis whether the abuse is sufficiently harmful to justify taking remedial action. The main specific abuses are as follows.

1. *Predatory pricing*, by selling articles at a price lower than the acquisition cost (or cost of production) for the purpose of disciplining or eliminating a competitor.
2. Use of *fighting brands*, introduced selectively on a temporary basis to discipline or eliminate a competitor.
3. *Pre-emption* of scarce facilities or resources required by a competitor for the operation of a business, with the object of withholding the facilities or resources from competitors.
4. Adoption of *incompatible product specifications* designed to prevent entry or eliminate a rival.
5. *Exclusive dealing* in the form of requiring or inducing a supplier to refrain from selling to an actual or potential rival so as to prevent entry or eliminate a rival.
6. Overpricing or *refusal to deal* by the upstream branch of a vertically integrated dominant firm so as to disadvantage a potential or actual rival at the downstream stage.

Determining when these activities cause market failure or economic harm is not easy. Winter (2009) provides a valuable economic analysis of such practices. The most extensively studied of these is predatory pricing.

11.5.2 Predatory Pricing

Predatory pricing is the practice of charging a low price with the intent of driving a rival out of the market and increasing monopoly power. Predatory pricing should be distinguished from a normal price war that may be the punishment phase of a generally cooperative industry, or from normal cost-cutting by an efficient firm that gradually drives less efficient firms out of business.

Some people have argued that predatory pricing would rarely, if ever, be undertaken by a rational firm—that the costs of predatory pricing almost always exceed the gains. If so, then competition policy authorities would not need to worry about predatory pricing, as it would almost never occur. The fact that, despite this argument, predatory pricing is sometimes apparently observed, especially in chain store situations, is sometimes called the *chain store paradox*.

However, the chain store paradox is not really a paradox any longer. Economists have shown that there are circumstances in which predatory pricing does make sense. One important part of the argument is that the predator must have some advantage, such as lower costs, over rivals, which make it better able to withstand a prolonged period of low prices. It would then be likely to win a war of attrition with rivals. Still, this period of attrition is likely to be very costly. In order to benefit from predatory pricing, the predator firm must enjoy a subsequent period of monopoly profits that is long enough to offset the losses incurred during the predatory phase. If the predator firm did successfully establish a lucrative position of market power, however, new rivals would then likely enter. In order for predatory pricing to make sense, entry would have to be sufficiently delayed that the predator would be able to recoup its earlier losses. Then, once entry occurred again, the predator would need to lower its prices again to compete with entrants or possibly engage in a new, costly round of predatory pricing.

A recent line of research has argued that predatory pricing is best viewed as a reputation-building exercise.[5] The basic idea is that certain attributes of the predator firm, such as its costs or the preferences of its managers, are unknown to actual or potential rivals. In essence, the firm might be either a tough firm (i.e., a firm with low costs and very aggressive management) or a weak firm (i.e., with high costs and an acquiescent management). Predatory pricing could be interpreted as an attempt to establish a reputation for being a tough firm. If successful, the firm may not only drive its current rival out of business, but it may also deter future entry, which is crucial to actually getting net benefits from predation.

However, even if we assume that predatory pricing does occur, the normative effects are ambiguous. Charging low prices is, in the first instance, good for consumers, and it is exactly what we want competition to achieve. If, however, the predator is able to drive competitors out of business, establish monopoly power for some period of time, and then raise prices, consumers may be worse off. It is necessary, therefore, to compare the benefits to consumers during periods of low price with the costs during the period of monopoly power. It is entirely possible that consumers might benefit on the whole from such pricing patterns.

Very few predatory pricing cases have been prosecuted in Canada. This probably reflects the reality that pure predatory pricing is not very common. In 1980, Hoffmann-La Roche (HL) became the first company convicted of

---

[5] See Kreps and Wilson (1982).

predatory pricing in Canada. HL is a large multinational pharmaceutical firm that dominates the world's vitamin market and is the developer and marketer of the tranquilizer Valium, which was for a number of years the world's best-selling prescription drug. As of 2012, Valium was still a major drug, although Xanax had taken over as top-selling tranquilizer by then.

HL had been charging $42.50 per 1,000 tablets of Valium on the basis of operating costs of about $3 per 1,000. A small competitor, Frank Horner Limited, began producing a generic substitute for Valium, as allowed by Canadian drug patent law, and offered it for sale to hospitals at a price of $6.90 per 1,000 tablets. HL's response was to give Valium to hospitals free of charge, forcing Horner out of the market. In addition to this prima facie evidence of predatory pricing, correspondence was obtained outlining the plans to drive Horner from the market. HL was convicted of predatory pricing. However, HL's penalty was only a relatively small fine. Only a few predatory pricing cases have been pursued by the bureau since then.

11.5.3 Resale Price Maintenance

Resale price maintenance (RPM)[6] is a vertical restraint—an arrangement between firms operating at different stages in an item's production process, and in different stages of a supply chain. Consider, for example, a producer of clothing that sells its product to retail outlets such as The Bay or Sears for subsequent sale to retail consumers. The retailer is the downstream firm and the clothing producer the upstream firm in this vertical relationship. Resale price maintenance arises when the upstream and downstream firms agree on how the downstream firm will price the product. Usually, such agreements specify only a minimum price. If the clothing producer enters into an agreement with The Bay and Sears that the clothing it supplies will sell for no less than some specific price, this is an example of RPM. Resale price maintenance might be a voluntary agreement between the two parties, or it might be essentially forced on the downstream firm by the upstream supplier as a condition of sale.

Any firm with market power, whether it is a dominant firm or not, might be investigated for anti-competitive resale price maintenance.[7] Resale price maintenance became illegal in Canada in 1952. From 1952 until 2009, it was a per se offence, meaning that the act itself was strictly illegal, regardless

---

[6] An excellent reference on resale price maintenance is Mathewson and Winter (1998).

[7] It is important not to confuse resale price maintenance with a "manufacturer's suggested retail price (MSRP)." There is no prohibition against a supplier "suggesting" a retail price, sometimes called a "list price," provided there is no agreement that forces a retailer to sell at that price.

of the consequences. It was also a Criminal Code offence. In 2009, RPM was moved to civil law and it became a *reviewable* act, subject to a rule of reason. Therefore, the Competition Bureau can investigate instances of RPM and bring a case against firms participating in RPM if it finds the impact to be anti-competitive. Thus, RPM is no longer illegal in itself, but only if it is judged to have significant anti-competitive effects.

RPM is often supported by *refusal to deal*—a supplier refuses to deal with a downstream firm that violates the agreed-upon pricing limits. For example, if The Bay decides to put the clothing in question on sale at a price below the RPM price, the producer might seek to punish The Bay by refusing to supply more clothing. Refusal to deal is itself a reviewable offence.

The intuition supporting laws against RPM is that RPM helps firms maintain market power. Restricting RPM, so the argument goes, should increase overall competition, and it should certainly lower retail prices. However, two counter-arguments have been presented.

One counter-argument relates to consumer search behaviour. If consumers see, or even hear about, a particular product being offered at a particularly low price, they will be unwilling to pay a higher price for the product at other retail outlets, possibly reducing overall sales. Firms involved refer to this as *spoiling the market*. If, furthermore, the discount price represented a marketing attempt to get people in the store and was not high enough to cover normal costs, overall sales at other outlets might fall to the point where the product could not be continued, and overall social welfare could decline.

A second, and more persuasive, argument in favour of RPM is that many products have a high service component, and the service will decline without RPM. The standard example is computers, as Apple Computer Inc. successfully fought an RPM charge in the United States. Personal computers are a product with a fairly high service component. Especially when personal computers were first introduced, most potential buyers knew very little about them. A buyer might spend several hours with a knowledgeable salesperson before making a choice. Furthermore, the buyer might expect to return for advice about software or hardware additions, for training, and, of course, for any repairs or other problems that might arise. The retail price of the computer must cover the cost of all these ancillary services, which were and are important to the product.

Consider the incentives facing a potential discounter. The discount firm can buy the product for the same wholesale price as the full-service outlet and offer it for sale for a lower retail price, but not offer much in the way of services. It might even operate as an online business, offering no ancillary services at all. Consumers would have an incentive to do all their learning at full-service outlets, essentially consuming costly services free of charge, and then buy from a discounter. Consumers would benefit initially, and discounters would benefit, but full-service outlets would suffer. Ultimately, full-service outlets would have to leave the market, with the result that consumers might well lose in the long run. This process has been a significant issue, as traditional retailers, such as Best Buy, have suffered while online vendors, such as Amazon, have expanded dramatically.

The question, of course, is not whether discounting is fair to full-service dealers. The public policy question is whether discounting is against the overall public interest. Apple was able to argue successfully that this discounting process would lead to the reduction, and in some areas, the elimination of full-service outlets, and that this was counter to the public interest. In effect, the argument is that there are positive externalities associated with ancillary services, and these positive externalities cannot be supported at socially efficient levels without RPM. (This argument presumes that the services in question cannot efficiently be priced and sold separately from the physical good.) On the whole the welfare effects of RPM are ambiguous, and the case for an active policy against RPM does not have a strong normative foundation.

11.5.4 Exclusionary Arrangements

The other major abuse of market power to consider is *exclusionary* agreements. Such agreements allow one firm (or a group of firms) access to a product or service, excluding other firms. For example, if a clothing manufacturer agrees to provide clothing only to The Bay, but not to Sears or any other retailer, such a contract would be exclusionary. Conversely, if The Bay agreed to sell clothing products only from this one supplier and not from other suppliers, that would also be an exclusionary contract. Like resale price maintenance, exclusive dealing is not per se illegal but may be judged illegal on a rule-of-reason basis if it has significant anti-competitive consequences.

11.6 Deceptive Marketing Practices

This area is the most recent major addition to competition policy, but it still has a long history, having been added in 1960. The Act contains both criminal law and civil law provisions intended to prevent or limit false or misleading advertising and other deceptive marketing practices. The Act specifies a wide range of prohibited practices, including the following.

- *False or misleading representations*: a representation (including but not restricted to advertising) to the public that is false in a material respect, including claims about warranties, servicing, testimonials, and product tests.
- *Double ticketing*: If a product is marked (by the seller) with two prices, the seller must sell at the lower price. Selling at the higher price is illegal.
- *Pyramid selling*: A pyramid selling scheme is one in which one person pays a fee to participate in the scheme and receives a fee for recruiting others to participate, in chain letter or pyramid fashion. Such schemes are illegal. This provision of the law is not intended to interfere with normal franchising operations. It is intended to prevent schemes in which recruitment commissions become more important than the underlying product.

In addition, there are various provisions about multilevel marketing, which is a slight variation of pyramid selling. The difference is that in multilevel marketing actual materials for sale are exchanged. For example, suppose person A obtains health food products and then sells a franchise to person B. Person B pays a commission to person A and receives the health food products. Person B then sells franchises to persons C and D, who pay commissions to B and, in return, receive the health food products. Thus, instead of the normal producer-wholesaler retail chain, there is a potentially much longer chain of transactions before the product reaches final consumers (if it ever does). Multilevel marketing is not illegal per se, but the law requires that potential participants be accurately informed about compensation levels of those already in the plan.

In assessing whether claims are misleading, the Competition Bureau and the Competition Tribunal focus on the overall impression given by product claims. Thus, for example, an advertisement featuring a large, misleading picture of the product accompanied by fine print saying "item in picture may differ from item on sale" would likely be a violation, despite the warning in fine print.

A significant deceptive marketing practices case was settled in 2012, resulting in a $9 million fine against a group of businesses and individuals.[8] The group of companies in the "scam" adopted names similar to the well-known Yellow Pages Group, which provides online and hardcopy directories of business contact information. The scam companies adopted names such as "Yellow Business Marketing" and "Yellow Page Marketing." These companies

---

[8] See Competition Bureau (2012).

produced promotional materials using symbols that closely resembled the trademarks of the Yellow Pages Group and sent these materials to thousands of small businesses via fax. The promotional materials created the impression that recipients of the materials were simply being asked to update their contact information for the online Yellow Pages directory. However, buried in the fine print was an agreement that by returning the form the victim was agreeing to a new two-year contract for a listing costing $1,428 per year with a scam company (such as Yellow Business Marketing). This activity was carried out in Canada, the United States, Australia, and other countries. Competition authorities in these countries cooperated in resolving the case. The fine of $9 million applied only to Canada, and additional penalties were imposed in other jurisdictions.

11.6.1 Economic Analysis of Deceptive Marketing

In Canada, misleading advertising and deceptive marketing practices have grown into a major area of competition policy. As a result, the marketplace is no longer dominated by the *caveat emptor* (buyer beware) philosophy. Sellers are responsible for ensuring that products meet advertised standards, as well as certain other standards that are not explicitly advertised but are taken to be implicit conditions of sale.

What is the normative economic rationale for such policy? Unlike the other anti-competitive practices, misleading advertising and deceptive marketing practices are not related to monopoly power. In fact, the industries where such practices occur most frequently are relatively competitive, such as general consumer retailing.

General public support for competition policy in this area is very strong, and very few complaints that enforcement should be reduced are heard, even among business lobbyists. However, as mentioned, such a rationale would have little if anything to do with monopoly power, and externalities and public good considerations do not seem relevant. Where then is the market failure?

The relevant cause of market failure is asymmetric information (Chapter 3). If buyers had full information about products and sellers, there would be very little need for legislation concerning misleading advertising and deceptive marketing practices, as consumers could not be misled or deceived. If a consumer had full information about, for example, a used car, it would not matter what the salesperson said. However, buyers are often less well informed about the nature of a product than the seller, so laws against misleading advertising can be justified on the basis of informational market failure.

11.6.2 Informational Market Failure: The Lemons Problem

The normal buyer-seller relationship is therefore one of asymmetric information. In the past fifty years, economists have come to understand that asymmetric information is an important source of market failure. Perhaps the most important implication of asymmetric information is the so-called lemons principle articulated by Akerlof (1970).

Akerlof first advanced the lemons principle to explain certain features of the used car market—in particular, why the market seems to be dominated by lemons, or poor-quality items. Akerlof considered a market with good used cars and lemons, and assumed that the good used cars and lemons do not look any different. He suggested that the essential characteristics of the car are hidden under the hood and can be inferred only by an expert or through experience. As a result, the buyer of a used car typically knows much less about it than the seller does. This is a situation of asymmetric information.

If an appropriate price for a good used car is P, and an appropriate price for a lemon is X, what price would the seller of a used car charge? The seller, Ava, of a good used car would certainly want to charge P. However, the seller of a lemon, Mason, also has an incentive to charge P! After all, the buyers cannot tell good cars from bad, so why should Mason reveal he has a poor-quality car? He has just as much chance as the owner of a good car of selling at price P. Buyers, however, realize that not all cars offered for sale at price P are worth P. A buyer expects there is some chance he or she will purchase a car of value X, and this will reduce his or her willingness to pay accordingly. In fact, if there are an equal number of good cars and lemons available, the appropriate market price is $(P + X)/2$, reflecting the average quality.

But owners of good used cars will be unwilling to sell their good cars for less than they are worth, so most owners of good used cars will then simply keep them, and the market will be dominated by lemons. The price will adjust accordingly so that, in the end, market price does not differ much from X, and very few good used cars will change hands. This is the lemons principle, sometimes called adverse selection: under conditions of asymmetric information, low-quality items will tend to dominate the market.

Market failure occurs because Pareto-improving transactions are foregone. There may be someone who would be very pleased to buy a good used car for price P, and someone else who would be very pleased to sell a good used car for price P. There are potential gains from trade if these two people could get together. However, in a market suffering from adverse selection, such trades will not take place. This is the market failure.

The lemons problem is very significant in many markets. Consider, for example, medical services. In the days before the medical profession was carefully regulated to maintain standards, it was plagued by quacks: doctors who promised much more than they could deliver. This was a successful strategy because patients had no way of judging quality of care, certainly not before treatment, and frequently not after treatment either. Standards regulation in many areas, including health care and other professions, can be viewed as a response to market failures caused by asymmetric information.

11.6.3 The Lemons Problem and Misleading Advertising

What do marketing and advertising have to do with asymmetric information and the lemons problem? Advertising is implicit in the lemons story. In effect, sellers of lemons are advertising their cars as high-quality cars. This is misleading advertising. In general, a buyer's main source of information about a product is what the seller says, either through advertising or directly. If the seller is free to misrepresent quality, then the lemons principle will apply. If, however, the seller is constrained to tell the truth, and has an incentive to tell the truth—created by the possibility of prosecution—then market failure will be reduced. In short, making misleading advertising and deceptive marketing practices illegal is an effective policy response to the market failure created by asymmetric information.

In addition, of course, such legislation appeals to notions of procedural fairness. Many of us regard misleading advertising and deceptive practices as unfair, quite apart from any associated market failure or efficiency losses.

11.7 The Evolution of Competition Policy

Since very limited beginnings in the late 1800s, Canadian competition policy has changed and expanded through an evolutionary process. Unsuccessful policies and practices have been discarded, new approaches have been tried, and policy successes have been retained and built upon. On the whole, competition policy became significantly more effective after the changes incorporated in the 1986 Competition Act.

Until 1976, the only legal approach to competition policy was through the criminal law system, and this limited its effectiveness. In trying to fit complex economic issues into the legal boxes of guilty or innocent as required by criminal law, fundamental economic considerations were often ignored. Economic considerations often involve trade-offs between degrees of competition, realization of scale economies, and other subtle but important aspects of business. A strictly correct legal decision could easily be a bad policy decision. At present, most competition policy activity occurs under civil law, which provides much greater flexibility. The Competition Bureau frequently reviews actions by firms and, if it sees a problem, seeks an agreement with the firm under civil law to stop the practice, often without penalty to the firm. Such an agreement is called a consent decree.

The range of business practices prohibited on the basis of anti-competitive effects or harm to consumers has expanded over time, which has also enhanced the value of competition policy. In addition, financial penalties for violations under both criminal law and civil law have increased dramatically in real terms, having been raised from levels that were little more than a "slap on the wrist," just part of the cost of doing business, to levels that provide significant deterrence. Fines in some areas have risen from thousands of dollars to millions of dollars in the past 30 years, a dramatic increase even after adjusting for inflation.

One major, gradual change in Competition Bureau practice has been a great increase in the emphasis on proactive rather than reactive actions. Instead of waiting for a firm to break the law and then seeking to punish it, the bureau now devotes much of its resources to communication and outreach—letting the business community know what the law is, and providing practical advice on how to comply. The bureau also spends a lot of time getting input on policy, and it has initiated many policy changes in response to input from the business community and the academic community. In addition, the merger review process now in place is proactive—it reviews mergers before they occur and seeks to restructure them where needed.

Another important change in Canadian competition policy is increased coordination with other countries, particularly the United States. Many of the firms under investigation nowadays are large multinationals whose entire international operations might be relevant in a given case. As a result, Canadian competition policy authorities have started to cooperate with their counterparts in the United States and Europe. There was a time when a lawyer or economic consultant working in Canada on competition policy cases would expect never to leave Canada. Today, such people might often fly to London or Washington or Tokyo (or elsewhere) to investigate cases.

There are also increasing attempts to harmonize competition policy across countries, and several countries that have lacked coherent competition policy in the past, especially in Eastern Europe and Latin America, are trying to develop competition policy institutions modelled partly on the Canadian standard. In addition, the World Bank has taken an interest in the development of competition policy infrastructure as part of the development process. There have also been suggestions in the World Trade Organization that competition policy issues might be linked to trade policy issues. Some of the changes that have occurred in competition policy have been intended to increase harmonization with the United States and with other countries more generally.

The economics profession and the law and economics community within the legal profession have also had a significant impact. Successive amendments to competition policy have gradually brought the law more into line with normative economic reasoning.

Has competition policy been successful? Without doubt, competition policy in Canada has had a restraining effect on price-fixing and overt collusion, and it has almost certainly more than paid for the costs of operating the policy on that basis alone. The operating budget of the bureau in the fiscal year ending in 2010 was about $51 million.[9] Fines and user fees generated revenues of about $44 million, leaving what is, by the standards of major agencies, a very small net cost to government. Furthermore, these explicit costs and revenues are negligible in comparison with the overall impact of competition policy. For example, a single merger might have a value in the hundreds of millions of dollars, and preventing one merger that would have negative effects on competition might more than offset the entire budget of the bureau for a full year or more. Similarly, the savings to millions of consumers otherwise harmed by misleading advertising and other deceptive marketing practices are very large compared to the operating costs of the Competition Bureau and the Competition Tribunal.

This section provides only a very brief account of the evolution of competition policy. See Ross (2004) for a more in-depth discussion of many of the associated issues, at least those up to 2004. Another very good source on the development of competition policy is the Competition Bureau website at www.competitionbureau.gc.ca/. This website also contains links to recent examples of Competition Bureau activity, including a discussion of recent cases, and is therefore an excellent resource for students.

---

[9] This information and much related information can be found in Competition Bureau annual reports. See www.competitionbureau.gc.ca/eic/site/cb-bc.nsf/eng/h_00169.html.

12

Regulation and Public Enterprise

12.1 Introduction

Most economic decisions are made in the private sector. Private individuals decide which products to buy and how much to buy, and firms owned by private investors make decisions about what to produce, how to produce it, what price to charge, and so on. These private-sector decisions are, however, made within a framework provided by government policy.

These framework policies cover a variety of policy areas, including international trade, the environment, competition policy, and tax policy, among other areas. Framework policies determine the "rules of the game," such as how much firms and individuals pay in taxes, or which competitive strategies are allowable and which, such as price-fixing, are not allowed. Furthermore, in some cases, governments take a much more active and direct role in business decisions, either through close regulation of firm-level decisions or through direct government ownership and control of productive enterprises, referred to as *public enterprises*. This chapter deals with both regulation and public enterprise.

12.2 The Meaning of Regulation

At the most general level, all business activity is regulated. Environmental and natural resource policy, discussed in Chapters 9 and 10, largely consists of regulation, and competition policy, discussed in Chapter 11, can also be viewed as regulation. However, as noted already, such regulation is simply part of the framework within which all private enterprises operate. When we speak of the regulated sector or regulated industries we mean something much more specific. We are referring to a group of firms or industries that are subject to price regulation or regulation of other important decisions normally made without government intervention, such as which product markets a firm is allowed to enter and which specific product characteristics the firm is allowed or required to provide. Such regulation is sometimes called close regulation.

Most closely regulated enterprises are private sector firms. However, public enterprises also make up a significant part of the regulated sector. Each closely regulated firm in the private sector is under the jurisdiction of some government appointed regulatory board or commission, as are many public enterprises. Some public enterprises are self-regulated, charged with pursuing a government objective and subject only to government oversight, without an intervening regulatory authority.

One important group of regulated firms consists of *public utilities*, which produce or provide important infrastructure, such as electric power, distribution of natural gas and heating oil, water, and waste disposal. Some transportation services, such as local buses and rapid transit, are also often included in this category. Because of the importance of public utilities, price regulation and related decisions are often referred to as public utility regulation. In addition to public utilities, other important regulated industries include telecommunications (telephone and Internet services), radio and television broadcasting, and parts of the agricultural, transportation, energy, and financial sectors.

It is important to note that when discussing regulation, the word *public*–as in public enterprise–refers to ownership by government. Public enterprise means the same thing as government enterprise, just as the terms "public policy" and "government policy" are equivalent. A private firm, or privately owned firm, is simply one that is part of the private sector (i.e., not government owned).

Unfortunately, this usage does not parallel standard financial sector terminology, where a public firm is one owned by the private sector but that is publicly traded. The shares of such a firm can be bought and sold on a stock exchange by anyone–by any member of the public. We can avoid confusion by referring to these firms as *publicly traded firms*, not simply as public firms. A private firm, or *privately held* firm, to follow this usage pattern, is one whose shares are not publicly traded: it is owned by a private group and others can be excluded. In policy discussions, confusion over this point can arise, although the context will usually make the meaning of the term "public" clear. In this book, we use the regulation terminology: public ownership means government ownership, and private ownership means ownership by the private sector, whether or not the shares are publicly traded. When we consider publicly traded firms or privately held firms, those terms will be used and not shortened to just public firms and private firms.

One other point of terminology is that many public enterprises are structured as corporations, with a government as the sole shareholder. In Canada, government-owned corporations are called Crown corporations. The term "enterprise" refers to corporations but also to other organizational forms. Thus, many public enterprises are not corporations, including government-owned schools, universities, and hospitals. Public enterprise refers to ownership by any level of government: federal, provincial, or local. A firm with significant government ownership *and* significant private sector ownership is referred to as a mixed enterprise or, in some cases, as a public-private partnership.

12.3 Natural Monopoly as the Rationale for Price Regulation

The most extensive level of price regulation and other types of close regulation is found in the public utility sector, and public utilities, such as producers of electricity and distributors of natural gas, are the industries we should keep most clearly in mind as we discuss price regulation. The basic rationale for price regulation in public utilities arises from market failure caused by natural monopoly.

Natural monopoly, as described in Chapter 6, is caused by economies of scale and economies of scope. Economies of scale are the advantages of producing a particular product on a large scale. Economies of scope are advantages from producing two or more related outputs in the same firm, as when a telecommunications provider sells access to both television signals and Internet connectivity. A *natural monopoly* arises when a single firm can produce an output, or a set of related outputs, at a lower cost for the relevant levels of output than two or more firms can. If the firm produces only one product, the definition implies that natural monopoly over a single product occurs when any feasible level of demand can be met at lower cost by a single firm than it could be by two or more firms.

For a single product, having a natural monopoly means the firm's average cost curve is downward sloping over most of the relevant range, as illustrated in Figure 12.1. The most common reason for this kind of cost structure is that fixed costs are very large compared to marginal costs. Fixed costs do not vary with amount of output produced. Sometimes, fixed costs are avoidable if the firm shuts down, but they must be incurred before any output is produced. Thus, to achieve efficient scale, the fixed costs must be spread over a very large output.

For example, there is room for only one James Bay hydroelectric project. The project consists of a system of interconnected hydroelectric power stations in the James Bay region of Quebec. The costs of the project were enormous, requiring large annual interest payments (a fixed cost) for many years on the construction loans taken out to finance the project. Even the annual fixed cost (overhead) of just maintaining the project is enormous. Since the project exists, however, adding a few more kilowatts (or even a few more megawatts) to the flow of electricity requires only flipping a few switches. Thus, marginal cost is very low until the maximum yield is approached. Average cost falls as output increases and the fixed costs are thus spread over a larger quantity. It would make no sense to have two separate firms trying to operate two James Bay projects, with two sets of transmission lines, etc. Having two firms would greatly increase the cost of generating any specific output level, given current technology.

Technologies do change, however. Long distance telephone service was once a natural monopoly, when long distance calls were sent through wires. Now that long distance calls are bounced off satellites, sent through fibre-optic cables, and received by smartphones and computers using wireless technology, this service is no longer a natural monopoly. In most parts of Canada, and in most other high-income countries, consumers now have access to multiple suppliers of long distance voice communication services.

An unregulated natural monopoly provides a worrisome opportunity for the exploitation of monopoly power, especially given the nature of demand for the services in question. Electric power and even telephone services are products with relatively inelastic short-run demand, meaning that if the price of power or telephone service were to rise sharply, most people would, in the short run, simply pay the extra cost rather than significantly reduce usage. Because of the dangers of monopoly exploitation and the resulting inefficiencies, most natural monopolies are subject to price regulation: they are not free to set their own prices. They must get permission for price changes either from a government-appointed regulatory board of some sort, or, in the case of some public enterprises, from Cabinet or legislative committees.

12.4 Types of Price Regulation

The first regulatory question to confront is simply, "How should the price be set?" There are several approaches that might be used, including average cost pricing, marginal cost pricing, nonuniform pricing of various types, rate-of-return regulation, and price-cap regulation.

12.4.1 Average and Marginal Cost Pricing

Two possible approaches to price regulation are average cost pricing and marginal cost pricing. Average cost pricing means that price should equal average cost at the output level chosen. Thus, the firm just covers its costs, including a normal rate of return on capital. Marginal cost pricing means that price should be set equal to marginal cost at the output level chosen. Output levels are determined by the amount demanded by buyers at the price charged.[1]

In general, just as marginal cost and average cost are not necessarily equal, marginal cost pricing and average cost pricing are not equivalent. It is possible that average cost and marginal cost prices could be the same, but depending on demand and cost, marginal cost pricing may lead to prices that are either higher or lower than those resulting from average cost pricing.

The rationale for marginal cost pricing follows from the application of the marginalist principle for the normative analysis of public policy, as described in Chapter 2. Recall that demand is a measure of marginal willingness to pay for the service, which we take as our best measure of marginal benefit. Therefore, price equals marginal benefit. The marginalist principle tells us that marginal benefit should be equated with marginal cost. Thus, setting price (marginal benefit) equal to marginal cost is the implied solution.

If the price exceeds marginal cost, then an extra bit of the service is worth more to some consumer (measured by his or her willingness to pay) than the extra (or marginal) cost of producing it. Net surplus can be generated (i.e., allocational efficiency can be improved) by increasing output. On the other hand, if price were below marginal cost, meaning the cost of producing the last unit was above the value of that unit, production should be decreased. Only when marginal cost is equal to price is allocational efficiency (i.e., Pareto efficiency) achieved.

This reasoning seems persuasive, and is logically sound. Marginal cost pricing is the efficient solution. Unfortunately, this is not the whole story, for marginal cost pricing can cause problems. More specifically, Figure 12.1 illustrates a situation in which marginal cost pricing causes the producer to incur losses. The cost curves reflect a common cost structure for hydroelectric power, with high fixed cost and low marginal cost. In this case, marginal cost is assumed to be constant. Cost, therefore, has the form $C = F + (MC)(Q)$, where

---

[1] Regulated firms are normally required to satisfy all demand forthcoming at whatever price is charged.

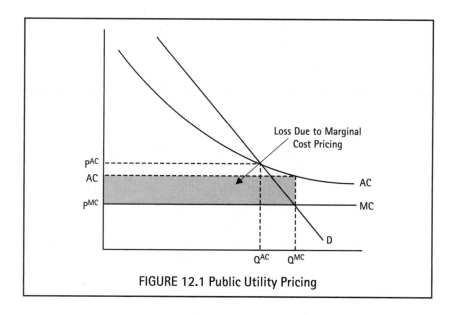

FIGURE 12.1 Public Utility Pricing

F is fixed cost, *MC* is the (constant) marginal cost, and *Q* is output. As drawn in the diagram, setting price equal to *MC* generates demand Q^{MC}. At that level of demand, the average cost, *AC*, exceeds *MC* and therefore exceeds price by the amount shown. The shaded region shows the firm's losses, indicating that the firm's revenues are not enough to cover its costs.

In order to cover its costs, the firm would need to charge a price of P^{AC}. At that price, the amount demanded is Q^{AC} and average cost just equals price, allowing the firm to break even. This is the average cost pricing approach.

If the firm shown in Figure 12.1 is to charge a price equal to marginal cost it would require a subsidy to stay in business, as its price would be less than its average cost. There are three objections to subsidies of this type. First, such subsidies can be viewed as unfair. If the services of public utilities are subsidized by taxpayers' money, this means that people who are heavy users of public utilities are, in effect, receiving a transfer from taxpayers at large, some of whom might hardly use the utility's services at all. Why should people who have a taste for goods produced by this public utility be subsidized by others?

The second objection is that the regulator is very unlikely to know what marginal cost is. Our previous argument for marginal cost pricing presupposes that the regulatory authority knows the level of marginal cost, so it can insist that the price be set at that level. If the regulator simply tells the firm, "Set price equal to marginal cost and the government will cover your losses," then very serious incentive problems are created. Specifically, if the firm's managers (and the unions representing the firm's workers) know that losses will be covered by taxpayers, and no one outside the firm has enough information to really understand the cost structure in detail, then the firm has very little incentive to keep costs down. If the firm is required to cover its costs, then at least some discipline is imposed on it. In short, after much painful experience, many people distrust any policy approach that involves having the government write blank cheques.

The third problem is that the cost of subsidies might be higher than is commonly understood. An extra dollar paid in subsidies has to come from somewhere: from current taxes, borrowing (creating a tax liability for the future), or "printing money" (which, as will be described in Chapter 15, tends to create an inflation tax). Furthermore, raising this dollar of extra revenue does not just take one dollar from somewhere else. The full opportunity cost of this dollar of revenue is more than one dollar. There are administrative costs in doing all the paperwork, and there are efficiency losses caused by the distortionary effects of taxes, not the least of which is all the effort that goes into tax avoidance and tax evasion by taxpayers.[2]

It is hard to get reliable estimates of the full cost of raising a dollar of tax revenue, but reasonable calculations suggest this cost could be as low as about $1.20 but could also easily be $2.00 or more, depending on the tax used and on other circumstances.[3] In short, the cost of a $1 million subsidy is much more than $1 million to the economy as a whole—at least $1.2 million and quite possibly close to $2 million. The implication of this extra subsidy cost is that we should be prepared to trade off inefficiencies in regulation (or in any policy area) against the inefficiencies caused by raising revenue. For this reason alone, a small departure from marginal cost pricing is perfectly reasonable, if it economizes on the use of government revenue.

These problems with marginal cost pricing all arise from a marginal cost that is below average cost. The opposite problem is less likely, but it can arise: a natural monopoly may have marginal costs substantially above average cost at the market-clearing output level. If so, then marginal cost pricing would

---

[2] Tax avoidance refers to legal actions taken by taxpayers to minimize or avoid taxes, such as investing in tax shelters or hiring tax accountants and tax lawyers to work the system in their favour. Tax evasion refers to illegal actions, such as hiding money in undeclared accounts.

[3] Dahlby and Ferede (2011) provide estimates of the marginal cost of tax revenue for Canada's federal government and provincial governments. The marginal cost depends in part on the type of tax used to raise revenue. Assuming the source of revenue is the income tax, they suggest a range from about $1.20 up to more than $2.00 per dollar raised.

generate large profits for the regulated firm. It seems inappropriate, on equity grounds, for shareholders or workers in public utilities to earn large, above-normal returns. If, on the other hand, these profits were turned over to the government, then consumers of the utility's services would be subsidizing general government programs, which might also seem unfair.

This brings us to the conclusion that if we were forced to choose between average cost pricing and marginal cost pricing, average cost pricing would be preferred. There are, however, more complex but very useful alternative pricing practices, which are described next.

12.4.2 Nonuniform Pricing

Regulators often allow regulated firms to use nonuniform pricing. The pricing we have considered so far assumes that the same price is charged for each unit of the product sold—the price is uniform. Most products are priced in this way; if one hamburger costs $5, then ten hamburgers cost $5 each, or $50 in total, and one hundred such hamburgers cost $500 (if anyone actually wants to buy that many hamburgers).

It is also fairly common, however, for products to be sold at nonuniform prices, which means that the price per unit is not always the same. There are several different types of nonuniform pricing. Such pricing is important in managerial decision making and is discussed in most managerial economics textbooks.[4] Nonuniform pricing is particularly important in the regulated sector.

The most common form of nonuniform pricing is *price discrimination*: charging different prices for the same good, based on the consumer's individual characteristics, on membership in an identifiable sub-group, or on the quantity purchased. The first of these types of price discrimination is sometimes called *individual price discrimination*. It is rarely used by regulated firms, but is sometimes used by other firms. For example, a car dealer might try to assess how much each potential customer is willing to pay for a particular car and adjust the price accordingly, with the result that the same type of car would be sold for different prices to different people, depending on their willingness to pay. *Perfect price discrimination*, sometimes called first degree price discrimination, means charging each consumer the maximum he or she is willing to pay for each unit of the product, thus extracting all consumer surplus from buyers.

We use the term *group price discrimination* when different groups of consumers are charged different prices. Group price discrimination is com-

---

[4] See, for example, Ch. 10 in Perloff and Brander (2013).

monly used by public utilities. For example, bus and rapid transit systems often charge higher fares for adults than for children, and electricity sellers often charge higher prices to commercial (business) customers than to residential customers. This type of price discrimination is sometimes referred to as third degree price discrimination.

When the price paid by a consumer depends on the quantity he or she purchases, we say the firm is using *nonlinear price discrimination*. The term "nonlinear" refers to the fact that the consumer's expenditure is a nonlinear function of the quantity purchased when price varies with quantity. If the price paid by a consumer does *not* vary—if it is constant—then expenditure, E, can be written as $E = PQ$, where P is the constant price and Q is quantity. This is a linear function.[5] Under nonlinear pricing, the price of an additional unit changes as we buy more. If the price, P, is not constant but varies with quantity, then expenditure will not be a linear function of quantity.

Nonlinear price discrimination arises if we have quantity discounts or surcharges. BC Hydro is a regulated public enterprise in British Columbia that produces electric power. As of 2013, BC Hydro charged residential consumers 6.8¢ per kilowatt hour (kWh) for the first 1,350 kWh per two-month period. For additional electricity in that period, the price is 10.19¢ per kWh. For use up to 1,350 kWh, expenditure is a linear function of quantity: $E = 6.8Q$. However, for quantities above 1,350 the average price paid increases as quantity increases. Therefore, expenditure is a nonlinear function of quantity for quantities above 1,350 kWh. BC Hydro's system exhibits the quantity-surcharge type of nonlinear price discrimination. The opposite pattern, quantity discounts, is also very common, especially in the non-regulated sector. With either quantity discounts or quantity surcharges, it is normal to price the product in blocks—one price for the first block, another price for a second block, and so on, an approach sometimes called *block pricing*. Thus, block pricing is a type of nonlinear price discrimination.

Another pricing method that might be used is *two-part pricing*, under which the producer charges a customer one fee for the right to buy the good, an access fee, and an additional fee for each unit purchased. For example, many telephone plans have this property—a consumer pays a monthly fee for access to the system and then pays extra for phone calls and text messages. While two-part pricing seems similar to nonlinear price discrimination, strictly speaking, two-part pricing implies that expenditure is a linear function of

---

[5] Recall that y is a linear function of x if $y = a + bx$, where a and b are constant. We call a the intercept and b the slope. For the expenditure function $E = PQ$, the intercept is zero and the slope is P.

quantity. If the access fee is A and the per-unit fee is P, then expenditure under two-part pricing is $E = A + PQ$, which is a linear function.

Why is nonuniform pricing used? In the unregulated private sector, firms presumably use it because they find it advantageous. But why do they find it advantageous? And what is the normative or public interest rationale for allowing nonuniform pricing in the regulated sector? Figure 12.2 provides an example in which nonuniform pricing, in this case simple two-part pricing, can improve efficiency.

In Figure 12.2, the average cost curve for the product, AC, lies entirely outside the demand curve, D. With uniform pricing, the firm cannot cover its costs, no matter what the price. The firm comes closest to covering costs by charging price P, producing quantity Q, and incurring average cost C. As average cost C exceeds price P, the firm would make losses equal to $(C - P)Q$. A private firm using uniform pricing could not stay in business, and a public enterprise would require an ongoing government subsidy.

Note, however, that this product is socially desirable, because the total value to consumers exceeds the total cost of production at output level Q. Recall (from Chapter 2) that the height of the demand curve shows the marginal value of the product as measured by willingness to pay. Adding up all those marginal valuations for each unit of output produced gives the total value of the product. This total value is given by the area under the demand curve, up to the production point. Thus, the total consumer value of Q is area $OAEQ$. The total cost is only $OCBQ$, which, as drawn, is clearly less than the total value.

One way of seeing this fact is to note that cost and total consumer value coincide, except that area ACF (vertically hatched) is part of consumer value but not part of cost, while area BEF (horizontally hatched) is part of cost but not part of consumer value. Therefore, consumer value exceeds cost if area ACF exceeds BEF, which is obviously true in this case.

The product is socially worthwhile in the sense that consumers are more than willing to pay for the cost of production, but the good will not be provided under uniform pricing if the firm must cover its costs. The value of nonuniform pricing is that it can extract more revenue from consumers without discouraging them altogether. If the firm charges P as a usage fee, and additionally charges an appropriately chosen access fee, it may be able to cover its costs. This access fee comes out of the consumer surplus that purchasers would otherwise enjoy at price P.

A private firm would want to maximize profit. A public enterprise should want to maximize social welfare, as given by total benefit minus total cost. In either case, the actual calculation of the appropriate usage and access fees is

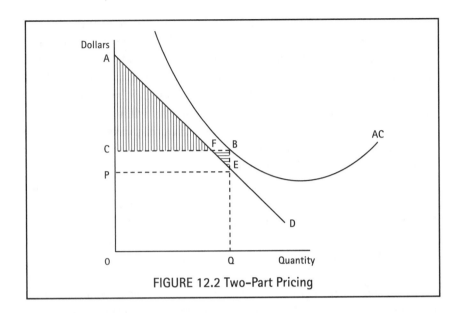

FIGURE 12.2 Two-Part Pricing

difficult, because increases in the access fee may induce some people to stop consuming. (They will do so if their personal consumer surplus after paying the usage fee and the access fee would be negative.)

Even for a regulated firm or public enterprise that could cover its costs with uniform pricing, a two-part pricing scheme allows it to charge a usage fee closer to marginal cost, and could increase efficiency. Being able to use nonuniform pricing does increase the ability of firms to extract surplus from consumers, and it can enhance the exploitation of monopoly power, if the firm wishes to use it for that purpose. Regulators should be alert to such possibilities.

Another form of nonuniform pricing is peak-load pricing, which is used for such products as electricity (as with Ontario's Smart Meter program), telephone services, and transportation services. Peak-load pricing involves charging higher rates during times of heavy use, and lower rates at times of light use. For example, in some mobile phone plans, long distance telephone rates are higher in the day than at night. The normative rationale for peak-load pricing is very clear: the marginal cost of telephone service at night is less than the marginal cost during the day. For example, as has already been mentioned, most of the costs of the telephone system are fixed costs, associated with the cost of the overall network. Given the network, the production cost of putting a call through is very low, until capacity is approached. As capacity is approached, however, sound quality declines, and when capacity is reached, no more calls can be handled and callers must wait, incurring waiting costs.

The main cost associated with a call during busy periods is the congestion cost imposed on the system, as manifested in delays and poor sound quality. This is part of the social marginal cost of the call, and it should be included in the price paid by the customer if efficiency is to be achieved. Put simply, if the network is at capacity, only those long distance calls that are most valuable, as measured by the amount people are willing to pay for them, should be made. If a higher price is charged, then only calls with a value at least equal to that price will be made. This is the peak-load principle, and it is important in achieving efficient use of scarce resources.

Looked at slightly differently, when a system is being used to capacity, the marginal cost of an extra unit of output is the cost of building and operating additional capacity. Therefore, the price charged in such periods should include a contribution to capacity costs. During periods of underutilized capacity, the only marginal cost is the marginal operating cost; no capacity charge should be levied.

Peak-load pricing bothers some people. More than one consumer advocate has complained that peak-load pricing is not very useful because the low prices are offered at inconvenient times. However, careful analysis suggests little conflict between any coherent idea of fairness and peak-load pricing. One reasonable idea of fairness is that users of economic services should pay in proportion to marginal cost, which implies that peak-load pricing is desirable, because marginal cost varies depending on the time when the service is used.

12.4.3 Rate-of-Return Regulation and the Averch-Johnson Effect

An important problem only touched on briefly so far is that regulators do not have nearly as much information about the firms they regulate as the firms themselves do. Even if the firms are required to provide large quantities of documentation, the regulators will not be able to interpret or appreciate what the documents say as well as the managers of the firm can. Specifically, the regulator cannot really be expected to know the cost curves or the demand curve of the firm as well as the firms themselves do. The managers of the firms do not know this information perfectly, of course, but they will have a better idea than others. Therefore, the regulator cannot directly impose the efficient pricing scheme. All a regulator can do is allow the firm to propose prices, and then either agree that the pricing proposal seems reasonable or reject it.

The basis for acceptance or rejection of pricing proposals is often a rate-of-return criterion. The regulated firm is allowed to set prices that earn a reasonable rate of return on a portion of its assets, referred to as the rate base and consisting of most assets.

Subject to the regulator's notions of fairness, and to the lobbying of interested parties, the firm will normally be allowed a considerable amount of latitude in determining the exact composition of its price increases. One hopes the firms will use this flexibility to maximize efficiency, given their budget constraints, through appropriate nonuniform price structures.

Unfortunately, there are several problems created by rate-of-return regulation, one of which is the Averch-Johnson (AJ) effect, first analyzed by Averch and Johnson (1962). They observed that the assets used to compute the rate of return consist mostly of physical capital: buildings, dams, nuclear reactors, etc. If the allowable rate of return is, say, 10 percent, and the firm has $1 billion in the rate base, then the firm is allowed to earn $100 million in net earnings, which is supposed to correspond to normal profits. However, the firm can increase its allowable earnings by increasing its asset rate base. If the firm doubled its rate base to $2 billion, it would be allowed $200 million in earnings rather than only $100 million. The firm may, therefore, have an incentive to make inefficiently large capital investments. The AJ effect is sometimes called rate-base padding.

A standing joke in some regulated utilities is that in instances of any unnecessary expenditure—if, for example, someone carelessly breaks a machine or buys expensive office furniture—someone else will just shrug and say "it all goes in the rate base." The basic message is that they do not need to worry about costs because unnecessary costs of this type still go in the rate base. Padding the rate base with wasteful expenditure actually allows the firm to earn more profit, because it will then be allowed to charge higher prices. In addition to the AJ effect, rate-of-return regulation also allows managers of regulated firms considerable insulation from market discipline. Management errors, inefficient labour contracts, thick carpets, or whatever, simply get reflected in higher prices.

In fairness to managers of regulated enterprises, we should assess the evidence before assuming that the incentives described in the previous two paragraphs lead to significant inefficiency. Managers of such enterprises understand that they are supposed to operate efficiently and many do. Overall, there is some evidence of rate-base padding. However, the overall inefficiency does not seem to be a major problem and, in particular, is not big enough to warrant giving up on rate-of-return regulation altogether.

12.4.4 Price-Cap Regulation

One successful alternative to rate-of-return regulation is price-cap regulation. The basic idea of price-cap regulation is that the regulated firm is allowed a certain maximum price increase each year. This price increase equals the relevant measure of inflation minus expected productivity improvements (which may be estimated using data from a range of jurisdictions). The firm may charge less than this price cap if it wishes. The advantage of this method is that the firm has an incentive to reduce costs and operate as efficiently as possible, because it will be able to keep the extra profits. The difficulty with price-cap regulation is that it may be difficult to determine an appropriate maximum price.

12.4.5 Multiproduct Firms and Cross-Subsidization

So far we have discussed price regulation as though each regulated firm produced only one product. In fact, many firms produce several products. For example, Canada Post, which is a Crown corporation regulated by Parliament, provides several classes of mail service and delivers mail between many sets of origins and destinations.

The following question has been posed: if a regulated firm has been instructed to set prices to cover its costs, how should those prices be set? In the case of a single-product firm, the answer is obvious: price must be set equal to average cost. (Even so, however, actually measuring cost can be difficult for a regulatory authority.) With a multiproduct firm, additional complications arise. For example, there may be several different ways of setting prices to cover costs. Trying to extend the idea of average cost pricing is not very helpful, because it is hard to assign the costs of general overhead to specific products. For example, how much of the cost of the giant mail-sorting machine in Toronto should be allocated to first class mail?

Accountants and economists have come up with various ways of making such shared cost allocations. Some of them could be (and are) used in actual pricing in both regulated and unregulated firms, but these average cost allocations do not maximize efficiency. The efficient solution, known as Ramsey pricing,[6] has been worked out, but it seems to violate norms of procedural fairness and, therefore, has not been widely used, although it has been applied in some cases. Actual regulatory practice makes fairly general use of cross-subsidization, which involves using revenues from one product

---

[6] The efficient solution was first determined by a young mathematician named Frank Ramsey in 1927. The basic formula is $(P - MC)/P = A/E$, where P is the price of a particular product, MC is the marginal cost of the product, A is a constant that is the same for all products produced by the firm, and E is the elasticity of demand. Not surprisingly, the formula links price to marginal costs. The additional element in the formula is that the markup of price over marginal cost is higher if the elasticity of demand is lower; that is, if demand is inelastic. This is a characteristic we associate with necessities. What the Ramsey formula says, therefore, is that markups should be highest for the most essential services! This is a situation where intuitive ideas of procedural fairness conflict with efficiency objectives.

or service to subsidize another product or service. For example, first class mail subsidizes other classes of mail.

12.5 The Capture Hypothesis: A Positive Theory of Regulation

So far our discussion of price regulation has been normative. We have focused on how regulation should operate, and looked at some of the nonuniform pricing techniques that might be used in the public interest. There is also a more cynical view of regulation, associated particularly with Stigler (1971) and Posner (1974) and known as the capture hypothesis. This hypothesis is a suggestion about the positive theory of regulation. It argues that regulators tend to be captured by the industry they are supposed to be regulating, and serve the interests of the industry at the expense of the public interest. Stigler and Posner maintain we would be better off doing away with most price and entry regulation.

Consider the case of a hypothetical young regulator, with business degree or public administration degree in hand, off to some unnamed regulatory agency, determined to serve the public interest. The young regulator is in for some hard years. The objective is to allow the firm a fair rate of return while ensuring it serves the public interest. But the young regulator finds that neither determining a fair rate of return nor identifying the public interest is easy. For one thing, the regulator never has enough information. The only source of information is, in fact, the regulated industry. Our regulator ends up spending a lot of time with industry people and finds they are not a bad lot. They treat regulators well, and frequently hire ex-regulators. Outsiders, such as politicians and consumer groups, on the other hand, do not understand the industry or the problems of regulators. In fact, after a few years on the job, our regulator is surprised by how frequently he or she sees things eye to eye with the industry, and is no longer disturbed by frequently taking the side of the industry when making regulatory decisions. Thus, the regulator is gradually captured by the regulated firm.

12.6 Major Areas of Regulation in Canada

The industries listed in Table 12.1 make up what might be described as the regulated sector in Canada. These are the industries in which price regulation and other types of close regulation are important. In some industries, such as electric power, nearly the entire industry is closely regulated. In others, such as the financial sector and agriculture, only part of the industry is closely regulated, and it is not completely obvious where to draw the line between closely regulated components and the other components of the industry.

TABLE 12.1 Major Regulated Industries in Canada

Industry	Regulatory Authority	Level of Government
Agriculture	Various marketing boards	federal and provincial
Electric power	Provincial agencies or self-regulated	provincial
Financial sector	Office of the Superintendent of Financial Institutions and provincial bodies	federal and provincial
Pipelines	National Energy Board	federal
Postal service	Self-regulated	federal
Radio-TV-Telecomm.	Canadian Radio-television and Telecommunications Commission	federal
Transportation	Various authorities	all
Water	Various authorities	provincial and local

Depending on how narrowly we define close regulation, the closely regulated sector has accounted for between 8 and 12 percent of GDP in recent years.

The primary rationale for regulation in electric power, pipelines, the postal service, and water is natural monopoly. And even in telecommunications, natural monopoly is traditionally the main reason for regulation, although technological progress, especially the development of the Internet and wireless communications, has reduced the relevance of natural monopoly in that sector. Two industries with a very different foundation for regulation are agriculture and the financial sector, as described in the following subsections.

12.6.1 Agricultural Marketing Boards and Supply Management

Agricultural industries are not characterized by natural monopoly and are normally highly competitive. In fact, they are often taken as the classic example of perfect competition. There are many producers, so no single producer has any influence on product prices but just takes the price as given by the market. As a result, there is little apparent reason for governments to intervene in agriculture. However, there has been extensive government intervention. Ensuring ample and secure food supplies and stabilizing farm incomes are the reasons normally given for regulation in agriculture.

The secure supply argument is based on concerns that war or natural disaster might disrupt food production and distribution. A government might, therefore, wish to have policies in place ensuring that domestic production would be sufficient to feed the national population even under such emergency conditions. However, since Canada is one of the world's most efficient and productive food producers and a large net exporter of agricultural products, it seems likely that Canada's food supply would be as secure as that of any country even without intervention.

The income stabilization motive arises from the high volatility of both world prices in agricultural products and farm output due to variability in weather patterns. Farmers have very uncertain incomes and, although crop insurance exists and agricultural futures markets are large and important, private markets have apparently not done an adequate job of insulating farmers from risk. There is, at least, significant political demand for government action in this area.

Marketing boards are formed by groups of producers for the purpose of marketing their products. Simply forming a marketing board confers no regulatory power and need not involve governments. However, governments have given some marketing boards broad powers of supply management and control over price and entry in certain areas. The discussion of regulation here is concerned strictly with marketing boards that have supply management powers. These supply management boards are similar in many ways to standard regulatory agencies: they are responsible to either the federal government or to a provincial government, and have broad authority to regulate the industry in question. The major supply management boards in Canada operate in milk, eggs, and poultry.

The most important economic function of the supply management boards is to restrict output through a quota system. The board allows a producer to sell milk only if that producer has a quota. If a producer wants to expand production, he or she must obtain more quota, usually either by buying or inheriting it. Quota systems are the perfect collusive arrangement. Entry is irrelevant because no one can enter and sell without a quota, and total output can be easily set. Total output is simply equal to the total quota. By setting the quota equal to the monopoly output, the industry can earn monopoly profits.

If quotas are set at the output level that would prevail in competitive markets they have no value. If quotas are set at the monopoly level, then the quota has value equal to the present value of the monopoly rent, because that is what someone would be willing to pay for the quota. This is illustrated in Figure 12.3.

Area *PEBC* is the monopoly rent created by the quota. The present discounted value of this monopoly rent is, therefore, the value of the quota, provided the market for quota rights is itself efficient. In Ontario, dairy

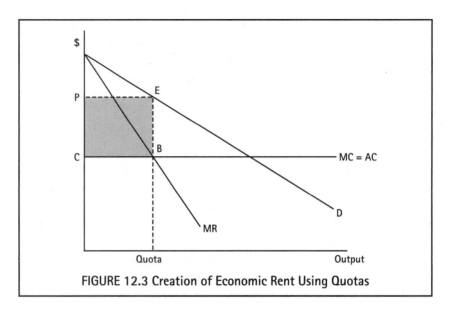

FIGURE 12.3 Creation of Economic Rent Using Quotas

quotas in January of 2013 could be purchased for about $25,000 for the right to produce and sell milk containing 1 kilogram of butterfat per day.[7] This translates to about $1,000 for the right to produce and sell one litre of milk per day on an ongoing basis. The total quota value of the average dairy operation represents several years of gross revenue that the quota allows the producer to earn. This implies that a substantial share of revenue (perhaps 25 percent) is monopoly rent.

The quota values represent the extra prices consumers pay for the products controlled by supply management boards. Farmers who received quotas free when they were first set up or farmers who realized appreciation on their quotas did well from the quota system, but farmers who must pay for the quota to enter the business receive no expected net benefit from supply management. The amount they pay is exactly equal to the expected excess return, so the two effects cancel each other out, leaving only normal profits. The new farmer would do just as well if there were no supply management. Prices for output would be lower, but this would be offset by lower costs, due to not having to buy quotas. The quota system is an example of the transitional gains trap discussed in Chapter 5.

In fairness to the quota system, it should be pointed out that, on average, the relative price of agricultural products fell through the 1960s, 70s, and 80s,

[7] Information concerning the price of dairy quotas on Ontario can be found at Ontario Dairy Quota Exchange website, www.milk.org/Corporate/View.aspx?Content=Farmers/QuotaExchangeInformation.

mainly because of technological improvement. The development of supply management systems dates principally from the 1960s, and it has helped ensure that farmers on the land at that time received some of the benefits of technological innovation in the industry.

12.6.2 Financial Regulation

The chartered banks are still the largest part of the financial sector. Among other functions, chartered banks accept deposits and make loans of various types and act as issuers of credit cards belonging to the Visa or MasterCard or, potentially, other networks. Other important parts of the financial sector include near banks (trust companies, credit unions, and the caisses populaires of Quebec), insurance companies, mutual funds, pension funds, securities dealers and exchanges, loan and leasing companies, and private equity firms (including venture capitalists).

Regulatory jurisdiction for the industry is divided between federal and provincial governments. Chartered banks are under the exclusive jurisdiction of federal legislation. However, insurance companies, trust companies, and loan companies are all subject to both federal and provincial legislative authority. Credit unions, the caisses populaires, and securities dealers are all under provincial jurisdiction. The outcome of this institutional background to financial regulation is a very complex regulatory system.

Chartered banks are regulated by the Office of the Superintendent of Financial Institutions (OSFI), which reports to the Department of Finance (Finance Canada), and by the Bank of Canada. Financial firms are subject to a wide variety of restrictions concerning the way in which they do business. Firms are supposed to avoid self-dealing, excessive risk taking, and taking advantage of inside information, and they are supposed to treat clients fairly. They are limited in the kinds of business they can undertake, and there are a variety of price-related regulations in the system.

The most important prices in the financial systems are interest rates–the price of money. Most interest rates are not directly regulated; however, the Bank of Canada (a Crown corporation owned by the Government of Canada) controls the overall pattern of interest rates through its own operations in financial markets.

All deposit-taking institutions (banks and near banks) may also belong to the Canada Deposit Insurance Corporation (CDIC), another Crown corporation owned by the federal government, which insures certain types of deposits up to certain limits. If the institution goes bankrupt, the insurance reimburses depositors up to the applicable limit. This is intended to eliminate the phenomenon of bank runs, which occur when many individuals try to simultaneously withdraw money from a single bank, rendering the bank illiquid.

Sometimes the need for regulation in the financial sector is taken as self-evident, arising from the importance of the financial markets. However, the implication that a sector should be closely regulated just because it is important has no basis in evidence or theory. The primary normative reasons for financial regulation relate, in part, to macroeconomic policy (described more fully in Chapter 15) and in part to market failure arising from information asymmetries.

Restrictions on excessive risk taking and self-dealing have their foundation in informational market failure. The idea that financial institutions might be prone to excessive risk taking arises from the following intuition. Because of high leverage, most of the money at stake in investments undertaken by financial firms is borrowed money. For every $1 of the owners' (shareholders') money at stake, there might be $25 of depositors' money at risk. High-risk strategies are attractive because the benefits associated with the strategy (i.e., the returns when things work out well) go to the owners, while the costs (i.e., the losses when things do not go well) are borne mostly by depositors, or by whoever insures the deposits, such as the CDIC in Canada. The incentive created by high leverage is sometimes described as "heads I win, tails you lose."

If depositors understand the environment in which they operate, and if they bear the downside risk of investment strategies, they will be reluctant to invest in an institution that does not have a safe, well-diversified portfolio. Unfortunately, for this "buyer beware" approach to work, depositors must be as well informed about investment opportunities as the managers of the financial firms, and this is unlikely. There is an inevitable informational asymmetry between customers and managers of financial firms. As discussed in Chapter 3 and elsewhere, informational asymmetries create market failure. This market failure is manifested in excessive failures of financial institutions and investments of time and energy by customers, in their attempt to monitor the decisions of financial firms, and in other ways as well. For example, these problems were an important cause of the financial crisis of 2008, which started in the United States, primarily due to excessive risk taking among banks and other firms making mortgage loans.

Because of informational asymmetries, there is a strong case to be made for having the government gather and provide much more information about the transactions of financial firms. Informational market failures could be reduced if monitoring agencies such as OSFI played a more active role in the financial sector and made frequent public reports of the activities of firms in the industry.

In addition, the legal power of government could be used to require disclosure of financial transactions by the firms involved. These are possible policy responses to market failures caused by informational asymmetries in the financial sector.

12.7 Public Enterprise

In Canada, as in most countries, an important part of business activity is carried out by public enterprises. Many of these enterprises are structured like private sector corporations, with boards of directors, chief executive officers, and so on. However, these firms are not owned by private shareholders, but by governments.

The term "public enterprise" lacks a precise definition. It is important to distinguish between public enterprises, which are owned by a government but operate at arm's length from the government, and actual departments of government. Thus, for example, the federal Department of Finance (Finance Canada) is part of government, not a public enterprise. On the other hand, BC Hydro is a public enterprise—a Crown corporation owned by British Columbia's provincial government. Many public enterprises are Crown corporations, but we will use the term "public enterprise" here.

A public enterprise has more autonomy than a government department, is technically responsible to Parliament or to a provincial legislature as a whole, and operates from a more specific mandate than a government department. Its employees are not part of the civil service, and its management is in the hands of a board of directors and a group of executives who are much more independent of government than are the senior bureaucrats who manage departmental affairs.

Public enterprises differ from the private sector in that their directors and senior management are normally appointed by government, they are exempt from many taxes paid by private sector firms, and their debt is ultimately a liability of the government and therefore no more risky than a government bond. Public enterprises will normally have a mandate that involves some objective other than profit maximization, and as such are instruments of government policy.

The public enterprise form can be thought of as an attempt to achieve some of the efficiencies of the private sector in the pursuit of government policies. Public enterprises are more important in Canada than in the United States, Japan, and even Australia, but are less important now than they were 30 or 40 years ago as a result of a significant "privatization" policy agenda in the 1980s and early 1990s which saw a number of public enterprises sold to the private sector (such as Air Canada and Petro-Canada).

12.7.1 Major Public Enterprises in Canada

The following two tables provide lists of the major public enterprises in Canada. Nonfinancial public enterprises are shown in Table 12.2 and financial public enterprises are shown in Table 12.3. The assets of the financial firms are not comparable to the assets of nonfinancial corporations. A central activity of the financial industry is creation of financial assets and liabilities. The firms borrow money (liabilities) from savers and loan the money (assets) to others. Consequently, the assets (and liabilities) of a financial firm will be very high in relation to shareholders' equity or fixed investment. Thus, an industrial firm with assets of $1 billion will typically be much larger in economic size than a financial institution with assets of $1 billion.

The largest nonfinancial public enterprises are in the electric power sector, and they account for over 95 percent of assets in that sector. Alberta is the only province served principally by a privately owned (but closely regulated) firm. The large electric power companies are among the largest firms of any type in Canada (as measured by assets). The other major public enterprises are largely in transportation, energy, communications, and financial services.

The larger financial public enterprises are of significant size and importance compared to most private sector financial institutions. The largest corporations

TABLE 12.2 Major Public Enterprises—Nonfinancial

Corporation	Assets (2011 $billion)	Ownership (Government of)
Hydro-Quebec	69.6	Quebec
Ontario Power Generation Inc.	32.1	Ontario
BC Hydro	19.5	British Columbia
Hydro One Inc. (Ontario)	18.4	Ontario
The Manitoba Hydro. Board	12.9	Manitoba
New Brunswick Power Corp.	5.6	New Brunswick
Saskatchewan Power Corp.	6.3	Saskatchewan
Canadian Wheat Board	4.2	Canada
Canada Post Corp.	6.7	Canada
Canadian Broadcasting Corp.	1.5	Canada
Saskatchewan Telecom.	1.6	Saskatchewan
Via Rail Canada Inc.	1.4	Canada

Source: Annual Reports.

TABLE 12.3 Major Public Enterprises—Financial

Corporation	Assets (2011 $billion)	Ownership (Government of)
Caisse de dépôt	191.3	Quebec
Bank of Canada	64.0	Canada
Export Development Corp.	33.6	Canada
Alberta Treasury Branches	27.4	Alberta
Canada Mortgage & Housing	19.0	Canada
Business Development Bank	18.2	Canada
Insurance Corp. of B.C.	12.9	British Columbia

Source: Annual Reports.

in Table 12.2 and 12.3 are all among the largest nonfinancial enterprises and financial institutions in Canada, respectively (as measured by assets).

Although Canada has a number of large and influential public enterprises,[8] they are less important in the Canadian economy than in they were in the 1970s and 1980s. Starting in the 1980s many countries, including Canada and the United States, began a process of privatization—selling public enterprises to the private sector. Deregulation, the process of removing close regulation in some industries, such as the airline industry, also got going in the 1980s. By the late 1990s, both the closely regulated sector and the Crown corporations had diminished significantly in relative size. The extent of public enterprise and regulation has been relative stable in Canada since then.

12.7.2 Normative and Positive Reasons for Public Enterprise

The most important normative rationale for public enterprises in the public utility area is natural monopoly. A public enterprise is an alternative to regulating the price and entry of a private sector firm, although public enterprises themselves are either regulated or have an internal regulatory process. There is, however, much more behind the development of public enterprise in Canada than just natural monopoly.

Some of the other reasons for public enterprise are related to more general problems of market failure. For example, even if the extent of economies of scale is not great enough to cause natural monopoly, an industry might

---

[8] The Treasury Board of Canada maintains summary information on federal Crown corporations. See www.tbs-sct.gc.ca/reports-rapports/cc-se/corporate-societe/ccp-pse-eng.asp for a list of Canada's major federal Crown corporations, with links to each one.

still be imperfectly competitive, and might be able to earn above normal or excess returns. Crown corporations have been introduced in such industries to try to reduce these rents, either by taking the rents themselves and turning them over to taxpayers, or by charging low prices and forcing the rest of the industry to compete, thus reducing its rents. This was part of the rationale for the development of Petro-Canada, which was ultimately privatized.

Another market failure reason for the development of public enterprise is the alleged inability of financial markets to finance very large-scale projects, even if those projects are worthwhile. Public enterprises are able to borrow more easily than private firms because their debts are assumed to be guaranteed by the government. In addition, the government can easily loan (or give) money to a public enterprise outright. This reason for the development of public enterprises has been important in the electric power industry, where the required investments have been largely compared to the size of any potential set of private financial sources.

Public enterprises may be used to supply public goods, although this is not a major activity of such firms. Public enterprises may also be used to subsidize the development of activities with positive externalities, and they may pursue distributional or equity objectives. In addition, some public enterprises, such as the CBC and the Canadian Film Development Corporation, are focused on other social objectives, particularly cultural objectives. Similarly, public enterprises have been set up in liquor distribution and to run lotteries, presumably to protect the public from anticipated excesses resulting from allowing liquor and gambling to be freely provided by the private sector. In short, public enterprise in Canada has been used to address almost the entire array of normative rationales for government intervention. Some people, moreover, would like to see public enterprises applied more as a tool of macroeconomic stabilization policy—essentially as employers of last resort.

Public enterprises have also been set up based on the following rationales: regional development, bridging gaps (undertaking economic activities that the private sector will not undertake), bailing out a failing firm, creating infrastructure, and outright nationalism (the desire to have a national presence in some industry). These rationales are at best questionable if taken as ends in themselves. They are valid only if they fit into the basic normative rationale for policy intervention.

For example, the bridging-gaps rationale can hardly be taken as a reason in itself for a public enterprise. There are many investments that the private sector will not undertake, and usually this is a good indicator that an investment is not worthwhile. The private sector does not grow bananas in the Yukon, but this is not a reason to create a Crown corporation to do so. If, on the other hand, the private sector fails to provide a service because of public good problems or externality problems, then public enterprise may be appropriate to fill the gap.

If the private sector is unwilling to finance a particular project, it is hard to tell whether this represents market failure, and therefore, justifies intervention by a public enterprise, or whether the project itself is not worthwhile. A politician's usual definition of a good project is one that helps win votes, and this also does not necessarily coincide with the market's definition of a good project, where people vote with dollars. There is, unfortunately, sometimes a strong temptation for politicians to use public enterprises to undertake economic adventures that the market would not support.

Another basis for the development of public enterprises is ideological. The basic ideology of socialism is that the state should own the means of production. Not many modern Canadian socialists would hold rigidly to this traditional ideal of socialism, and in 1991 the national NDP officially abandoned nationalization of key areas of the private sector as part of its policy platform. Still, many socialist elements in Canadian politics have been, and still are, very sympathetic to a general expansion of state ownership in the economy, and are happy to seize on any reason to promote the expansion of public enterprises. However, this sentiment has been much weaker in the first two decades of the 21st century than it was through most of the 20th century.

In addition, the creation and promotion of public enterprise is due in part to the (by now familiar) interest group activity described in Chapter 5. Public enterprises have constituencies. Many public enterprises, such as the Farm Credit Corporation and the Export Development Corporation, provide subsidies to interest groups. The subsidized groups then become voices in favour of expansion of the public enterprise.

12.7.3 Regulation, Public Enterprise, or Direct Government?
Direct government ownership and regulation of the private sector are alternative policy tools that can be used to respond to the same market failure that might justify public enterprise. The natural question that arises is, having identified a role for government intervention, should that role be assigned to a government department, to a public enterprise, or to a regulatory authority?

Unfortunately, although much has been written on this subject, we lack a clear consensus on what the important normative considerations are. All three types of government action involve what are sometimes called "agency" problems: some responsibility for the public interest is delegated to a particular set of people whose actions cannot be easily monitored and who have considerable discretionary power. Since the self-interest of such people may conflict with the public interest, we cannot always be confident the public interest will be served.

The theory of bureaucracy described in Chapter 5 is an example of the agency, or delegation, problems that can arise if tasks are allocated to a department of government (i.e., to the bureaucracy). The capture hypothesis described earlier in this chapter is an example of an agency problem arising with regulation. Public enterprises have similar agency problems, in that the managers of public enterprise and individual politicians can be expected to use public enterprises partly as tools of their own interests.

A public enterprise has several advantages over a government department. One advantage is that the functions of the public enterprise are insulated to a greater extent from day-to-day political pressures. It was argued, for example, that this was an important reason for setting up Canada Post as a Crown corporation in 1981, having been a department of the federal government before that. When postal service was under the control of a Cabinet minister, the principal objective of the minister was to survive the six months or one year in the portfolio without destroying his or her political career. In pursuit of this objective, it was much easier to provide subsidies to the post office than to make difficult management decisions.

The creation of a Crown corporation, on the other hand, allows someone (the CEO) to be held accountable for its long-run performance. This gives the CEO and the senior management an incentive to make decisions that are difficult in the short run, in the hope of getting long-run benefits. In addition, the government of the day is not held accountable at the political level for these decisions. A Crown corporation can take a tough line with its employees over some contract provisions without the government being accused of being anti-labour. It can more easily cut back uneconomic areas of service without being subject to the intensity of interest group lobbying that arises over department-level decisions in government.

A Crown corporation or other public enterprise has more flexibility in the use of its workforce (and in its ability to hire and fire) because its workers are not part of the civil service. Workers in Crown corporations feel, for the most part, that they are part of the business community, rather than part of government. The question, of course, is whether these differences have any effect. As the experiences of VIA Rail, the CBC, and other high-profile Crown corporations suggest, the activities of a Crown corporation do spill over into the political arena, and its managers are subject to at least some of the same pressures as civil servants to serve the short-term political interests of senior politicians.

The choice between a public enterprise and regulation of a private firm is somewhat arbitrary, since these two organizational forms are, to some extent, substitutes for one another. In the case of mixed enterprises, which are owned partly by government and partly by private investors, the distinction becomes blurred altogether. The presence of private shareholders should, in principle, impose additional discipline on a firm to make decisions on a business rather than political basis. But this may either enhance or impair the effectiveness of a corporation in pursuing a public policy objective.

12.8 Public Goods

Four main sources of market failure are described in Chapter 3. One of those sources is an absence of property rights, which can cause externality problems or public good problems. In this section we consider public goods and the role of public enterprises or other parts of the public sector in providing them.

12.8.1 Defining Public Goods

Public goods are not the same thing as publicly provided goods, although public goods are usually publicly provided. Normally, provision of public goods is carried out by government departments rather than by Crown corporations or other public enterprises. A public good has the following two characteristics:

1. A public good is nonrival in consumption: even though one person consumes the good, others may consume it also.
2. A public good is nonexclusive: it is impossible (or at least very costly) to exclude anyone from consuming the good.

In Chapter 3, this definition was illustrated using the example of a light-house. The services of a lighthouse are not used up when one ship is warned by the light; other ships will simultaneously receive the warning. Therefore, a lighthouse is nonrival. In addition, it is impossible to prevent anyone from seeing the light from lighthouses (without turning the light off). If anyone is to benefit from the lighthouse, all will have access. A lighthouse is nonexclusive.

It is possible to imagine goods that are nonrival, but at the same time, are exclusive. A painting is a good example. You may enjoy looking at a painting. Another person could simultaneously enjoy the painting (subject to limitations imposed by crowding). It is, however, relatively easy to exclude others from seeing a painting, simply by putting the painting in a room to which admission is controlled. Such goods, those that are nonrival but exclusive, are called *club goods*. Goods that are rival but nonexclusive are sometimes called open access goods or open access resources, which are discussed in Section 4 of Chapter 10.

Examples of public goods include national defence, public parks, police services, and the court system. Most public goods are provided directly by government. Construction or maintenance of a public good might be contracted out, but the payments and managerial decisions are made directly by government. Crown corporations and regulation of the private sector are rarely used for public goods.

12.8.2 The Efficiency Condition for a Public Good

The efficient outcome for a public good, as implied by the marginalist principle, is that a public good should be produced up to the point where the marginal social benefit equals the marginal social cost. Because a public good is nonrival, the marginal social benefit is equal to the sum of private marginal benefits. Equation 12.1 expresses this condition.

$$\text{SMB} = \Sigma\text{PMB} = \text{SMC} \text{ (efficiency condition for a public good)} \qquad (12.1)$$

12.8.3 The Free Rider Problem

The basic incentive problem of public goods resulting in market failure is that consumers of the good have no economic incentive to pay for the good, as they cannot be excluded even if they do not pay. They have an incentive to be free riders. This is the *free rider* problem.

For example, suppose a private organization proposes to provide a public good (such as public, non-commercial open access television), and asks for contributions. Many people will recognize that they would value such a service, but they also recognize that their own private benefit is small compared to the total cost of such an exercise. A contribution of $50 or $100 is not going to make much difference to the product delivered.

Furthermore, the consumer will be able to consume the good whether or not he or she provides a contribution. Many people intend to pay, of course, but just never get around to it. Each viewer has an incentive to be a free rider, to enjoy the product produced by the contributions of others. The Seattle station of the U.S. Public Broadcasting System (PBS) estimates that about 10 percent of its viewers contribute to the station, meaning that 90 percent are free riders. And this contribution rate of 10 percent is considered relatively high by the standards of other PBS stations.

Even when public goods are provided by the public sector, it is hard to determine the right amount of the public good, because the government does not know the marginal benefit placed on the good by consumers. Getting people to reveal their preferences is difficult and fraught with various preference revelation problems in that people have incentives to misrepresent their preferences.

If people think they will get something for free (i.e., that other people, or taxpayers at large, will pay for it), then if they place any positive valuation on the good at all, they have an incentive to overstate their preference for it. Conversely, if people believe they will be asked to pay in proportion to their announced interest, they will have an incentive to understate their preferences.

Because of the free rider problem, no private firm could make money from providing the service, even if the service is very valuable. Therefore, public goods need to be provided by collective action, normally through government. Much of what local governments do is provision of local public goods, such as roads, parks, streetlights, traffic lights, and so on. From a normative point of view, allocation of public good provision to a collective body, such a government, is usually the best approach. And one important principle of local government is that local public goods should be assigned to the level of government that coincides with the geographical range of the public good.

One interesting example of a public good problem arises in condominium (condo) developments, sometimes referred to as strata developments. A condominium is an apartment building in which the apartments or "units" are owned by private individuals instead of being rented. In a condominium, much of the infrastructure is a public good for the entire building. For example, the roof is a local public good. Everyone in a condo development benefits from the roof and no one in the development can be excluded. But if the individuals were left to themselves, no individual would have a sufficient incentive to repair or replace the roof on a timely basis. Such an expense would be very large for any one individual, and most of the benefit would go to others. To solve this problem, most jurisdictions have special laws for condo developments mandating the creation of a "strata council" or other governing body with the power to impose fees on all owners in a condo development, and with the responsibility to maintain the common infrastructure in the development. In effect, such a council is like a small government, and the main reason it is needed is to deal with public good issues.

13

Innovation Policy and Intellectual Property

13.1 Introduction

There is little doubt that technological innovation is the most important economic force underlying improvement in the human condition. Without technological innovation human beings would still be living short, harsh lives, spending most of their time just trying to get enough food to eat, and in imminent danger of death from any number of causes. Major innovations, from the discovery of fire and invention of the wheel through to modern medicine and telecommunications technology, have completely changed and greatly improved human lives.

Governments recognize the importance of innovation and have established a variety of policies intended to encourage it. One group of policies, which might be called *funding policies*, focus on providing financial resources for research and development (R&D). Such policies include tax concessions and subsidies for private sector research and development, as well as government grants and other funding for university-based research. Governments also provide funding for innovation through public enterprises that invest in innovative firms and through other mechanisms that support innovation finance.

A second group of policies seek to encourage innovation by treating successful innovations as *intellectual property* (IP) and granting innovators certain rights over that property. Intellectual property refers to creations of the mind rather than to physical property, and it covers three main areas:

inventions, such as new machines or new therapeutic drugs; literary and artistic creations, such as books, songs, and paintings; and trademarks and other symbols that identify particular products or organizations.

Intellectual property is often easy to copy. For example, once a new drug has gone through a pharmaceutical company's very expensive development process, it is normally relatively easy for other companies to determine the drug's formula. If allowed to do so, these other companies could easily make and sell the new drug relatively cheaply, thereby undercutting the original developer and making it difficult or impossible for that company to recoup its development costs. Such a process would greatly undermine the incentive to undertake drug development in the first place.

To prevent this problem, IP policy allows for the developer to obtain a *patent*, which gives the innovator exclusive rights over the innovation for an extended period (20 years in Canada). During this protected period of time, others cannot copy the innovation without permission from the innovator. The innovating firm can, if it wishes, retain monopoly power over the innovation and charge the associated monopoly price, or it can license the innovation to other firms and earn revenue from licence fees. This system is intended to strengthen the incentive to undertake inventive activity.

In addition, some IP protection is afforded to items deemed *trade secrets*. Literary and artistic creations are protected by *copyrights*. Also, *trademark protection* contributes to innovation incentives by making it easier for innovative firms to market their innovations without fear that other firms might use imitative marketing that would confuse consumers.

This chapter starts with a brief summary of the history of innovation, and then describes the market failures affecting the innovation process as well as the market-failure basis for innovation policy. We then consider the major innovation policies, starting with a description of patent policy, followed by a discussion of other forms of IP protection, and then by an overview of funding policies.

13.2 A Brief History of Innovation

Modern human beings (*Homo sapiens*) are thought to have emerged as a species about 200,000 years ago. For about 95 percent of the time since then, our species survived as hunter–gatherers, leading short and difficult lives.[1]

---

[1] A good general reference for human origins is the Smithsonian National Museum of Natural History. See humanorigins.si.edu/evidence/human-fossils/species/homo-sapiens. For life expectancy information regarding hunter-gatherers see Gurven and Kaplan (2007), who suggest that between a quarter and a third of all babies died in the first few years of childhood, and that those fortunate enough to survive the first few years had a life expectancy of only about 35 years.

Technology was primitive, although fire was in common use, as were crude stone tools. The rate of technological progress during *Homo sapiens'* hunter-gatherer period was very slow. For most of this period, if a typical hunter gatherer were transported forward or backward in time 100 or 1,000 or even 10,000 years from his or her actual lifetime, little if any difference would be observed in the state of technology, life expectancy, or real living standards.

13.2.1 Three Revolutions (Agricultural, Scientific, and Industrial)
The first great technological innovation in the history of *Homo sapiens* was the development of agriculture–the agricultural revolution. This revolution, sometimes called the Neolithic transition, began a mere 10,000 to 12,000 years ago, as human beings began to plant and harvest crops and raise domestic animals. Agriculture allowed for a substantial increase in population density, and hence in overall population. Over the subsequent millennia, innovations such as writing, the wheel, and the use of bronze and iron tools had a dramatic effect on much of the world, allowing for the development of true civilizations. Even so, technological change would have seemed almost imperceptibly slow to a typical individual. However, the development of civilization allowed small, privileged groups to pursue objectives other than just day-to-day subsistence.

One of the pursuits followed by (some of) the privileged few was intellectual enquiry, which gave rise to what many view as the second great innovation in the history of our species–the scientific revolution–often dated from 1543.[2] This revolution consisted primarily of the application of scientific methods to major areas of human interest, significantly altering the way humans viewed the world and greatly improving our ability to understand and control it.

The scientific revolution did not, however, have a major impact on economic activity until the Industrial Revolution, which began in Britain about 1760–more than 200 years later. The Industrial Revolution transformed the major industries of the time by allowing for the development of machines and industrial processes that relied on external forms of power (water, steam, coal, and ultimately oil) instead of on the raw muscle power of humans or animals, greatly increasing potential output. For example, a worker producing cloth using a water-powered or steam-powered loom could produce vastly more cloth per day than a worker using a hand loom. Similarly, steam locomotives could move far more material far more quickly than horse-drawn carriages could.

---

[2] This date is the publication date of the famous work by Nicolaus Copernicus on planetary motion. The scientific revolution was part of the broad cultural movement referred to as the Renaissance.

The design of machines to generate and use external power sources depended on the mathematical and engineering principles that had been one product of the scientific revolution. More importantly, however, the Industrial Revolution itself was based on the scientific mindset—a willingness to learn from experience, to try new things, and to go beyond traditional beliefs. Also, the modern discipline of economics, regarded as having started with Adam Smith's 1776 book, *An Inquiry into the Nature and Causes of the Wealth of Nations*, was motivated largely by the changes Smith saw around him arising from the Industrial Revolution. This revolution, which soon spread to North America and Western Europe and ultimately all around the world, also gave rise to modern market-based economies.

Prior to the Industrial Revolution, small groups of people were able to accumulate significant wealth and had the time to pursue leisure activities. However, the vast majority of the world's population lived at the margin of subsistence or not far above it. Life expectancy at the beginning of the Industrial Revolution was not much more than it had been at the start of the agricultural revolution over 10,000 years earlier. The Industrial Revolution allowed for both another great surge of population growth and, for the first time, for most people to enjoy a standard of living well beyond mere subsistence. It took another 100 years or so before these gains translated into significant increases in life expectancy, but such gains did eventually occur. Life expectancy at birth in Canada and many other relatively well-off countries is now 80 years or more, and most of those years are productive and healthy, thanks to modern medicine and other benefits of technological progress.

13.2.2 Major Innovations

Since the beginning of the Industrial Revolution, human beings have become accustomed to observing remarkable changes in technology over the course of their lifetimes. At no time has this been truer than during the past century. Many of us are amazed by how recent innovations such as personal computers and the Internet have changed the way humans live and work. And we can barely imagine life without technologies such as electric lights, telephones, and automobiles, all of which were invented less than 150 years ago and have become widely available only in the last 100 years.

The first telephone was patented by Alexander Graham Bell in 1876, the first electric light by Thomas Edison in 1880, and the first modern car by Karl Benz in 1885. The first powered heavier-than-air flight is attributed to Orville and Wilbur Wright in 1903, the first radios date from the early 1900s, and the first televisions from the 1920s. Even in the world's wealthiest countries, such as Canada, it is only in the last 100 years or less that most people have had access to such technologies and, in much of the world, widespread use has come only in the last generation—the last 30 years or so.

Perhaps the most important technological innovation of the last 150 years was the development of electricity generation and transmissions systems—the technology that makes it possible to use lights, radios, refrigerators, televisions, computers, electrical machinery, and other modern innovations in homes and businesses. Most of the necessary technology was developed in the late 1800s, but electricity networks were not generally available until the early 1900s in North America and parts of Europe, and later in other parts of the world. The first modern computers date from the 1940s, with the first personal computers appearing in the 1970s, along with the first handheld mobile phone networks. The Internet was introduced in the 1980s.

Recent improvements in health care are, if anything, even more strik-ing than these innovations in technology. For most of history, humans have been at the mercy of devastating outbreaks of infectious diseases, such as the bubonic plague, smallpox, and lethal flu strains.[3] However, modern vaccines and anti-infective drugs have dramatically changed the human experience. Diseases that were once a constant source of fear, and which usually claimed a few people from every extended family even only a hundred years ago, are now all but forgotten.

The first scientific application of the vaccination principle was due to Edward Jenner, a British doctor and scientist, in 1796. The idea that exposure to an infected person might prevent later disease had been known for many centuries. However, this is a dangerous practice, as the exposed person is also quite likely to contract a serious and sometimes fatal case of the disease. The innovation of the vaccination principle was to expose patients to a relatively safe agent that would provide immunity against a more serious threat. After exposure, the immune system generates antibodies and "remembers" the antibody template generated to fight the vaccine, and is then much more likely to be able to fight off infection by the live virus. Most modern anti-viral vaccines are based on inert (non-reproducing) forms of the underlying virus.

Jenner noticed that cowpox, a disease affecting cows, also caused a mild reaction in humans. He also noticed that people who milked cows rarely

---

[3] The "Spanish" flu of 1918-19 killed over 20 million people, and probably many more, and is thought to have sickened about 1 billion, approximately half of the world's then population. This flu mutated from an avian flu and is related to the H1N1 virus. While its origins are not entirely clear, it is now thought likely to have originated in either the United States or China, and not in Spain. See www.nature.com/nature/focus/1918flu/.

caught smallpox, one of the world's leading causes of death up to that time.[4] Jenner inferred that people who milked cows would normally catch cowpox early in their lives, and theorized that cowpox was like a mild version of smallpox that conferred immunity against smallpox. He turned out to be right, ultimately saving millions of lives. Due to smallpox vaccinations, the disease was ultimately eradicated entirely, although not until the 20th century.

Jenner was "lucky" in that a suitable vaccine for smallpox (the cowpox virus) existed in nature. Other successful vaccines required the ability to create inert versions of the infective agent and, therefore, did not emerge until the late 1800s, and most of the major vaccines were not developed until the 1920s. The first modern antibiotics (a type of anti-infective medicine effective against bacteria) date from 1928, when penicillin was discovered.

Surgery is medical treatment based on physical operations, often to remove or repair damaged tissue or organs. Surgery is among the oldest types of medical intervention—including practices such as setting and splitting broken bones. The very first known human writings (cuneiform writing from about 4,000 years ago in ancient Sumer, now part of Iraq) contain fairly sophisticated material about surgery. Surgery has advanced, primarily through small evolutionary steps, right up to the present. Perhaps the single most important innovation in surgery was the pioneering use of sterilization in 1865 by Henry Lister, a professor of surgery at the University of Glasgow in Scotland.

Lister had read about the latest work of Louis Pasteur on the "germ theory of disease," describing the role of microbes (germs) such as bacteria in causing disease and spoiling food. Suspecting microbes as a cause of post-operative infection, Lister started simple antiseptic procedures for surgical patients—washing wounds and instruments with a mild solution of carbolic acid that would kill microbes. Significant surgery was very risky at that time—a last resort. Using antiseptic procedures, Lister's surgical mortality rate dropped from about 45 percent, standard "best practice" of the time for significant surgeries, down to about 15 percent! The relatively simple change of implementing antiseptic procedures transformed the role of surgery, making it a realistic alternative for many more patients. Nowadays, problems such as a diseased gall bladder or appendix can be resolved with simple and virtually risk-free surgery. Before the development of antiseptic surgical techniques, such problems were life threatening and usually life ending.

---

[4] Mortality estimates for smallpox are uncertain and controversial. However, it is plausible to suggest that smallpox killed more than 30 percent of the population when it first entered Europe and, later on, the Americas. In the previously isolated Easter Island, smallpox killed fully 90 percent of the population within a few years of first exposure. See Brander and Taylor (1998).

Agriculture has also been an area of major recent innovation. For most of human history, food acquisition (hunting and gathering and then agriculture) occupied most of a society's available labour effort, and was by far the most important industry. Nowadays, in high-income countries such as Canada, agriculture is only a small part of economic activity. At present, agriculture accounts for approximately 2 percent of Canada's GDP and a similar share of the labour force, down from about 40 percent of the labour force as recently as about 100 years ago, reflecting the tremendous improvements in agricultural productivity arising from innovation. Important innovations have included new crop varieties, fertilizers, agricultural machinery, pesticides, and irrigation. The improvements during the third quarter of the 20th century (about 1950–75) were particularly significant and are referred to as the *green revolution.*

Not surprisingly, most of the literature on the history of innovation has a strongly optimistic tone. However, at this stage concerns have been raised that, after several centuries of accelerating technological innovation, we might be entering a period of diminishing returns in technological innovation. While innovation in information and communications technology continues at a rapid pace, there are indications that technological progress has slowed in other areas (as described in Brander [2010]).

13.3 Market Failure and Innovation

When people consider the recent record of innovation, it is normal to emphasize the dramatic progress of the past two centuries. However, we might take a different point of view and ask why innovation was so slow to get going even after the scientific revolution opened up so many possibilities nearly 500 years ago. Why did it take another 350 years or more to invent electric lights, telephones, modern cars, and other important technologies? And why, even then, was innovation so concentrated, occurring mostly in Britain and the United States and, to some extent, in a few countries in Western Europe? Market failure in the innovation process is one reason for this, and it is this market failure that provides a normative justification for the significant role of government policy in promoting innovation.

13.3.1 Innovations as Public Goods

The most important market failure affecting innovation is the fact that knowledge produced by innovation is a public good. As described in Chapters 3 and 12, a public good has two characteristics—it is nonrival and nonexclusive. For example, consider a drug company that develops a new drug. Each pill containing this medicine is an ordinary private good that is rival—if one person consumes the pill, no one else can do so. A single pill is also exclusive—it is easy to prevent others from taking that pill. However, without intellectual property rights, the knowledge required to make the new medicine is a public good. This knowledge is nonrival—if one person uses that knowledge to make pills, anyone else can use that same knowledge to produce more pills. Moreover, this knowledge is nonexclusive—once pills are available in the market it is easy enough for another company to buy a pill, determine its composition, and copy it. Imitators cannot be excluded unless they are legally prevented from doing so by intellectual property rights.

Almost all of the cost of a new drug is the development cost of discovering the new medicine and verifying its efficacy and safety. The cost of actually producing a pill or capsule is usually minor or even trivial in comparison. If other firms can free ride on the new knowledge and produce the same medicine, the innovator would have little chance of recovering its development cost. The free riders only have the small production cost of the pills to worry about and could, therefore, profitably sell the medicine at a relatively low price—a price too low for the developer to charge and still cover its development costs. This *free rider problem* would greatly reduce incentives to develop new drugs, as no one would have an incentive to do the expensive research necessary to produce new drugs or new smartphones or new crop varieties or other innovations that require a high level of initial investment but then can be easily "reverse engineered" and copied.

The public good problem can be viewed as a failure of property rights, as discussed in Chapters 3 and 12, and governments often take action to offset the potential resulting under-provision of public goods. Intellectual property rights, established by governments, are intended to reduce the problem of inadequate property rights. If a patent makes it possible for an innovator to treat the new knowledge embodied in an invention as intellectual property and can prevent others from using it, then the ability of potential rivals to free ride is greatly diminished and the incentive to innovate is enhanced.

13.3.2 Innovation Externalities
The externality problem, introduced in Chapter 3 and described in Chapter 9, is another form of market failure (based on incomplete property rights) that underlies innovation policy. In this chapter, we are primarily concerned with positive externalities generated by the R&D process. For example, when one firm carries out R&D, the researchers often present research papers at scientific conferences and publish in scientific journals. And they often

spend time simply discussing their work with other researchers. Also, if they do obtain patents, much information has to be disclosed in the patent application.

As a result, information that is helpful for other areas of research is provided to other researchers. For example, a researcher working on a drug to reduce high blood pressure might disclose information about biochemical processes that would be important for the development of other drugs, such as anti-infective drugs, or even for other product areas, such as medical equipment. This process generates positive externalities of the type sometimes called *knowledge spillovers*.

A second very important conduit for positive externalities is the movement of workers themselves. Researchers working for one firm will change jobs, moving to other firms, taking a lot of knowledge with them and benefitting the new firm. In effect, the training provided by any one firm to its researchers has a positive external effect on other firms.

As noted in Chapter 9, an activity with positive externalities will be under-provided by the private sector. We would, therefore, expect markets to under-provide R&D, and that some form of policy intervention could reduce or offset this market failure.

13.3.3 Informational Asymmetry in Innovation Finance

Informational asymmetries are a third form of market failure that influences public policy toward innovation. Informational problems were introduced in Chapter 3 and discussed further, as an explanation for certain areas of competition policy, in Chapter 11. In this chapter, we are concerned with problems that innovative firms might have in obtaining sufficient financing for innovation. While large innovative firms such as Apple or Microsoft are able to finance innovation using their own revenues, most entrepreneurial firms must obtain outside funding for the R&D process, and are therefore strongly affected by informational problems that make it more difficult to obtain innovation finance.

The problem is that outside investors typically know much less about the proposed innovation than the innovator does. This informational structure creates a market failure due to informational asymmetry[5] of the *hidden characteristics* type. We can understand this market failure by considering the situation from the point of view of an outside investor, such as a venture capitalist.

---

[5] An analysis of information asymmetries can be found in many microeconomics or managerial economics textbooks. See, for example, Chapter 15 in Perloff and Brander (2013).

Venture capitalists are specialized financial intermediaries who obtain investment capital from passive investors, such as through pension funds and wealthy individuals, and invest that money primarily in shares of entrepreneurial ventures. They will normally take a significant ownership stake in such a venture in return for providing it with a large contribution to its financial needs.

Suppose there are two types of innovators—high quality and low quality. If the venture capitalist can tell high-quality innovators from low-quality innovators, it can provide financing on a suitable basis to both types of firms, requiring a higher "price" (more shares per dollar) from the lower-quality venture to compensate for the lower chance of success. However, if the venture capitalist cannot distinguish high-quality from low-quality innovators, it will have to offer the same financing terms to both. In such a situation, high-quality innovators will be getting a less attractive "deal" than warranted by their underlying quality. The innovator knows this, with the result that high-quality innovators might turn down such offers, while low-quality innovators would accept, as the terms look attractive to them.

The process leads to a *lemons problem*—or, more formally, *adverse selection*—as described in Chapter 11. Specifically, we would expect the low-quality items (lemons) to dominate the market, as first described by Akerlof (1970) using the used-car market as an example. This is a form of market failure in which many high-quality innovators might be unable to obtain sufficient financing, or at least be unwilling to accept the unattractive terms on which such financing is offered.

Furthermore, once an investment in a venture is undertaken, it is difficult to monitor the activities of the innovator, making it difficult for an investor to determine whether appropriate decisions are being made and appropriate efforts undertaken. This creates an informational asymmetry of the *hidden action* type, a market failure called the *agency* problem, or *moral hazard*.

With established firms, potential adverse selection and agency problems are reduced by three important factors. First, in a traditional business, such as a new restaurant or a furniture factory, it is much easier for investors to understand the business and to assess the quality of a firm than they could in a new and untried business area. Second, established firms have a track record or reputation that investors might rely on. And third, established firms often have assets than can be used as collateral for an investment. New, innovative ventures lack such advantages.

Venture capitalists exist as specialized financial intermediaries precisely because they are good at assessing innovative firms, and they often employ industry specialists, such as people with PhD degrees or extensive experience in the areas of technology in which they invest. Even so, adverse selection and agency problems are often significant, and affect other potential investors and creditors (such as banks) to an even greater extent. Such market failures provide a strong motive for governments to become involved in innovation finance.

13.3.4 Effects of Market Failure on Innovation

The first paragraph of Section 13.3 asks why innovation in many areas took so long to develop. Innovation was very slow until the Industrial Revolution, and even then was much slower initially than it was from the late 19th century (i.e., the late 1800s) up to the present. What explains this pattern?

For successful innovation to occur, inventors need to have "four i's": intellect, information, incentives, and investment. The first "i" refers to the observation that inventors are, normally, highly intelligent and creative, which is not a surprise. The second "i," information, indicates that inventors require a base of relevant knowledge. Such information might be obtained through formal education or other forms of experience. The third "i," incentives, emphasizes that an inventor needs to feel that it is worthwhile to spend time on an invention rather than on more lucrative or more relaxing pursuits. And finally, the inventive process often requires the fourth "i," a significant investment of financial resources long before any financial returns materialize.

The first requirement, intellect, does not seem to be subject to any particular market failure, and it is hard to believe that the earlier, relatively slow pace of innovation was due to a lack of intellect among a society's most gifted members. The second item, information (and education) was, on the other hand, certainly a major problem until very recently. Throughout almost all of human history, the overwhelming majority of people have been poorly educated by modern standards—unable to read, unaware of basic scientific principles, capable of only simple arithmetic, and perhaps most importantly, confined by a world view that discouraged innovation and emphasized adherence to authority (political, religious, and social), leaving little room for individual initiative.

Lack of educational opportunity can be understood as a market failure. Specifically, education provides positive externalities, and we therefore expect private markets to provide too little of it. Educated people gain personal benefits from education, and that is not an externality. However, educated people also provide benefits for others. Doctors, engineers, accountants, and other professionals provide external benefits well beyond what others might pay for such services, and general education provides widespread community benefits, making for better informed and more capable parents, among other benefits. And people whose education helps them become successful innovators, such as Lister (antiseptic medicine) or Bell (telephones), provide enormous benefits—positive externalities—for others. These positive externalities provide a strong rationale for publicly funded, or at least subsidized, education. In any case, high levels of general education are important for innovation.

Incentives, the third "i," are also closely related to market failure. Inventive activity is often hard work, and a typical inventor has to persevere through much disappointment and failure before success is achieved. Inventors need incentives so that they are willing to incur such costs. Incentives might come from personal satisfaction or from intellectual curiosity, but financial incentives are very important. And without intellectual property protection, financial incentives are weak, as successful innovations will be readily copied, leaving little or no financial benefit for the inventor.

And finally, innovation often requires an investment of financial resources. It is rare that a person with the intellect and creativity, the education, and the personal incentive to undertake innovation also has enough money to finance it. It is important that a link be made between people able to innovate and those with the resources to fund innovation. This process, however, is subject to significant informational market failure, as described in subsection 13.3.3.

We can now understand why it was so hard for significant innovation to occur until recently, and we can also understand the forces that came together to start the Industrial Revolution in Britain. First, as already emphasized, the scientific revolution of the 16th century (the 1500s) provided the scientific method and principles needed for technological innovation. But this source of knowledge had limited influence at first, because relatively few people had the opportunity to learn about it. By the 18th century in Britain, however, scientific education was sufficiently widespread that a large potential pool of innovators was created. Early innovators were usually well educated, and their education and understanding of scientific principles were often essential to their innovations.

Britain was one of the few places in the world with a working patent system by this time, and it was also one of the few places where a successful innovator might hope to reap the rewards of individual initiative. The technological innovators of the Industrial Revolution were, in general, very interested in financial incentives.

Not all innovation is driven by financial incentives, however. Innovators such as Lister (antiseptic surgery) and Jenner (vaccines) did not seek financial gain for their contributions. Their primary objective was simply to save lives, and they were both very happy to have their discoveries widely copied and used. However, like modern researchers, they both certainly appreciated the boost that the great success of their work gave to their professional reputations. Such peer-group effects can act as important incentives, and Britain was among the first countries to develop an effective network of researchers, academic journals, research organizations, and universities that provided a suitable environment for such peer-group effects.

As for investment, financial systems everywhere at that time were crude by modern standards. However, Britain had what was then probably the world's most developed financial sector, including a functioning rule of law with meaningful contract enforcement and a well-developed banking system. As a result, investment capital to finance innovation was more readily available in Britain than in other countries.

This combination of relatively high levels of general education, strong financial and personal incentives for innovation, and a relatively good system of financial intermediation provides a good explanation for why the Industrial Revolution started when and where it did.[6] The British model took hold quickly in a number of other countries, particularly in the United States, which during the 19th century overtook Britain as the world's leading innovator. Through the 20th century, the essential components of a successful innovation system gradually spread throughout the world. These components largely depend on government policy, including policies regarding public education, a well-developed university system, intellectual property protection, and appropriate support and regulation of the financial system.

13.4 Patents

A patent is a right granted by a government, giving an inventor exclusive control over an invention. We often refer to a patent as intellectual property, although it is really the underlying invention that is the property, and the patent serves to protect it. Patents are intended to promote innovation, but they also create monopoly power, as the inventor is granted a monopoly over

---

[6] Historians have sometimes emphasized other factors, such as the availability of certain physical resources including coal, iron, and inland waterways, as well as sociological factors, such as a dominant religion that favoured thrift and individual initiative. These things certainly played a role and may have been necessary, but they do not explain the timing of the Industrial Revolution, nor do they explain why Britain was different from other countries with similar (or better) resource availability and sociological environments.

the patented invention. This section first describes the major rules of Canadian patent policy and then considers the basic trade-off or tension between the innovation benefits of patent policy and costs of monopoly power created by patents. We also consider whether other problems with modern patent policy might actually hinder innovation in some cases.

13.4.1 Canadian Patent Policy

Patent protection applies in the country that issues the patent. In Canada, patents are handled by the Canadian Intellectual Property Office (CIPO), an agency of the Canadian government.[7] However, before considering Canadian patent policy, it is important to recognize that patent policy in the United States is probably more important to Canadian inventors than Canadian patent policy is, due to the size and importance of the U.S. market. Patent policy in the United States is administered by the U.S. Patent and Trademark Office (USPTO), an agency of the U.S. government.[8] Fortunately for Canadian inventors, patent policy is very similar in the two countries and the patent systems are largely harmonized. In particular, an inventor who applies for a patent in Canada can easily apply in the United States, and vice versa.

Furthermore, significant international cooperation over patents is supported by the World Intellectual Property Organization (WIPO), a United Nations agency. WIPO administers the Patent Cooperation Treaty, allowing an inventor to apply for a patent in one signatory country, such as Canada, and have that application considered in up to the full 142 countries which have signed the treaty, including the United States. The criteria for patents and the judgment of patent officers vary from country to country, so an application might not be successful in all countries, but the major countries have a high degree of similarity in their approach to patents.

Technically, a patent is a right to exclude—to prevent others from using the patented invention. The owner of a patent may choose to be the sole producer of the product, may license others to produce the good for a fee, or may sell the patent. Thus, the patent can be treated like any other form of property. If a patent holder feels that a patent is being infringed—someone is using the invention without permission—then it is up to the patent holder to sue the infringing party. However, a patent holder also has obligations. In particular, patent holders are required to pay certain fees, and to make the invention available through production or licensing if there is demand

---

[7] Much useful information can be obtained from the CIPO website at www.cipo.ic.gc.ca.
[8] A valuable reference on U.S. patent policy is Gallini (2002).

for it.[9] And a patent holder must disclose a significant amount of information about the invention, which then becomes public information and may help other inventors.

In Canada, the United States, and most other countries, a patent lasts for 20 years from the date of filing an application. A patent holder may be an individual, a corporation, or another organization (such as a university). Not everything can be patented. To be patentable, an innovation must qualify as an invention. Inventions are defined by CIPO to be new and useful machines, new and useful compositions of material, other new and useful manufactured items, and new processes for producing particular products, along with improvements in any of these areas.

For example, a new *machine* used to produce screens for computer monitors might be patentable. A new cleaning spray (i.e., a *composition* of matter) for cleaning monitors might be patentable. A new type of screen might itself be patentable (a *product*), and a new *process* for setting up production of screens might be patentable. In addition, an *improvement* in any of these areas might also be patentable. The vast majority of patents (about 90 percent) are for improvements to existing inventions.

It is important to understand what is not patentable. Scientific theories or principles, basic laws of nature, mathematical facts or methods or algorithms, and abstract ideas are all not patentable. In short, basic research is not patentable. Also, in order to be patentable, a proposed product or process must be novel, useful, and sufficiently ingenious in the sense that it should not be "obvious" to someone skilled in the area. Judging novelty, usefulness, and ingenuity is often very difficult but, ultimately, CIPO (or the USPTO in the United States) makes these decisions. The next subsection describes a prominent example illustrating some of the challenges in making good patenting decisions.

13.4.2 The Amazon One-Click Shopping Patent

In 2012, the Canadian Intellectual Property Office, CIPO, granted a patent to Amazon for "one-click shopping." The original application was made in 1998 and close to 14 years of legal wrangling had followed. The ultimate decision was a surprise to many, as this case had become notorious in the United States.

---

[9] If there is insufficient demand for the innovation or for licences to use the innovation, a patent holder may allow the patent to be inactive, meaning that the patent is in force but no related production is taking place. Inactive patents require payment of an annual maintenance fee to stay in force. If the patent holder elects to stop paying the fee, then anyone can freely use the innovation—the patent protection lapses.

In the United States, Amazon was granted a patent for one-click shopping in 1999, shortly after the initial application. Amazon at the time was a pioneer in online sales of books and other products. It has since grown to enormous proportions, with 2012 revenues exceeding $50 billion, making it larger in economic size than many countries. The 1999 patent outlines the concept of having a single click of an online icon bring together product information with the customer's previously stored credit card and address information. Thus the primary purchase transaction was reduced to a single click. About three weeks after receiving the 1999 patent in the United States, Amazon brought a suit against Barnes & Noble, another online bookseller offering a one-click sales option to customers.

The Amazon suit created considerable controversy, including boycotts against the company. In light of the large amount of negative publicity, Amazon quickly reached a settlement with Barnes & Noble that was believed to impose little cost on that company. Rather than try to keep one-click shopping to itself, in 2000 Amazon began to sell licences to other online sellers, such as Apple's iTunes store.

Many observers, including Amazon programmers, expressed surprise that something as obvious as one-click shopping could be granted a patent. Other users of one-click shopping methods whose use, arguably, pre-dated Amazon's, did not apply for a patent because it seemed so obvious. After all, many things on the Internet are done with a single click and, presumably, making any online transaction as simple as possible is an obvious objective. Initially, both Canada and the European Union rejected Amazon's one-click patent application. However, Canada did ultimately grant the patent in 2012. The patent will expire in Canada in 2018, which is 20 years after the patent application was first filed in 1998.

Criticism of the Amazon U.S. patent was just a small part of a growing concern that the United States was not imposing strict enough standards, or that it was too easy to get a patent. In an April 2007 decision (*KSR International v. Teleflex*), the United States Supreme Court the found that the standard being used by lower courts for deciding on whether an innovation was "obvious" was too generous toward patent applicants. There has been a move to tighten up standards in the United States since that time.

13.4.3 Market Power vs. Innovation
So far, we have emphasized the role of patents in solving market-failure problems due to the public good and externality aspects of the innovation process. Left uncorrected, these market failures would result in inefficiently

low levels of innovative activity. By reducing these market-failure problems, patents are intended to increase innovation toward efficient levels.

However, patents also have an associated cost in that they create market failure in the form of monopoly power. A patent allows the holder to exercise monopoly power over the innovation. A stronger intellectual property right (IPR) might increase the incentive to innovate, but at the cost of greater inefficiency due to monopoly power. Getting this trade-off just right is the challenge at the heart of IP policy.

In practice, the strength of IPRs is determined by a variety of factors. In the case of patents, the most obvious variable is the length of the patent. However, patent breadth is also very important. A narrow patent allows limited monopoly power, as it would not preclude closely related innovations, thus enabling close substitutes in the product market. For example, the patent obtained by Karl Benz in 1885 on his original car was quite narrow, applying to a very specific design. Other people were able to develop and patent other types of cars, leading to a relatively competitive motor vehicle industry fairly quickly. On the other hand, Benz might have been granted a very broad patent, covering all potential motor vehicles. The consequences would have been very different. A broad patent provides more extensive monopoly power.

Another factor affecting the strength of patents is the ease of enforcement. If the courts are very sympathetic to patent holders when they sue alleged infringers, typically rendering quick positive decisions and imposing harsh penalties on infringers, then a patent gains strength. If, on the other hand, it is very difficult to sue infringers and the chances of success are low, then the patent offers relatively weak protection. Other relevant factors are the difficulty in getting patents approved, the nature and extent of compulsory licensing requirements, situations under which patents can be terminated, and various other factors. Thus, IPR strength is multidimensional, and getting the various aspects of patent policy set at appropriate levels is not easy.

There is a significant dynamic aspect to the trade-off between innovation incentives and monopoly power. Consider Charles, who belongs to the current generation of consumers, and Elaine, who belongs to a future generation. Specifically, suppose that Elaine has not yet been born but will be a consumer 30 years from now, while Charles, already fairly elderly, will have died by that time. What would happen if patent protection today were suddenly increased, assuming that this increase would have two effects—increased innovation of future products, and increased prices for currently available products protected by patents?

Charles would not like this change. He would pay higher prices today and would not expect to be around to enjoy the benefits of higher levels of future innovation. Elaine, on the other hand, would benefit from the change. She does not pay the higher prices on today's products, and by the time she is a consumer those products will no longer be covered by patents and will be available at competitive prices. In addition, she will benefit from an increase in innovation making additional products available to her in the future. Depending on whose welfare we care about more, we might favour either stronger or weaker patent protection. This potential trade-off between current consumers and future generations is not as severe as the generational conflicts of interest arising from environmental policy (Chapter 9) and natural resource policy (Chapter 10), but it is a genuine issue.

13.4.4 Can Patents Hinder Innovation?

So far we have considered situations in which stronger intellectual property protection would increase innovation. However, it is important to emphasize that this is not always the case. It is quite possible that stronger IP protection might reduce innovation, depending on the details of proposed changes.

We also need to recognize that more innovation is not always better. Most dictionaries define innovation simply as something new, and "new" does not necessarily mean better. A firm might introduce new products, but they could be innovations that are worse than the old products. Obviously, more innovation of this type could not be called good. However, in economics, the term "innovation" is usually taken to mean something positive—a change that constitutes movement toward better products or more efficient production processes.

Even if innovations represent product or process improvements, it does not follow that more is always better. For instance, if a society devoted most of its resources to research and development with the result that not enough resources were left over to properly feed, clothe, and house most of the population, we might conclude that the investment in innovation was excessive. In addition, it is quite possible that investments in innovative ideas might be wasteful, as when many firms carry out essentially the same or very similar research, causing duplication of effort. In general, there is an optimal or efficient level of innovation, and going beyond that level is possible but not desirable. More is not always better.

Now we can directly address the question of whether stronger IP protection might be harmful to innovation. Even if we want more innovation—if we think we are currently below the appropriate level of innovation—it does not follow that providing stronger IP protection will necessarily increase innovation. This can be seen using an extreme case. Consider a patent that is both very long (maybe 100 years) and, more importantly, very broad, ruling out any other innovation with any connection to the protected product. Suppose further that courts are very aggressive in protecting such intellectual property rights, making it easy for patent holders to sue and to win suits against alleged infringers of the patent, and imposing severe penalties on infringers.

Such a patent regime would be likely to sharply reduce and perhaps totally eliminate innovation in the area. For example, if Apple had received very strong patents on its iPad product, that could have precluded all other computer tablets.[10] More generally, such strong patents would make potential innovators recognize that existing patents held by incumbents would remain in place for a long time and that the risk of being sued and severely penalized for innovation was high. Such concerns would reduce or even eliminate their incentive to innovate. Even the firm holding the patent would have little incentive to innovate further, as it would be virtually immune to competition for a very long time.

Patent protection that is too strong will hinder innovation rather than promote it. Innovation would be maximized at an intermediate level of patent protection, not at the highest possible level. Some observers argue that the current level of patent protection in many areas is already too high.

A second way in which the patent system may hinder innovation is sometimes referred to as the "tragedy of the anti-commons." Just as the traditional tragedy of the commons (Chapter 10) is based on insufficient property rights, the tragedy of the anti-commons is based on excessive property rights. In this situation, a proliferation of patents creates so many rights holders over a potential new product that the associated transaction costs can delay or even prevent the innovation.

The iPhone, for example, was based on over 200 new patent applications[11] and draws on technology covered by hundreds of prior patents owned by a wide range of individuals and organizations. Furthermore, it is far from clear exactly which prior patents are sufficiently relevant to the iPhone to require explicit licensing. The large number of rights holders and significant uncertainty about which patents apply might be expected to encourage litigation or to lead to outright paralysis. Not surprisingly, Apple has been engaged in

---

[10] In fact, Apple did sue Samsung over alleged patent infringement regarding the Samsung tablet.

[11] This statement was made by Apple CEO Steve Jobs during his keynote address at the 2007 Macworld Convention. The transcript can be obtained from www.iphonebuzz.com.

extensive litigation with companies such as Nokia and Samsung over patent rights associated with the iPhone.

A third potential problem is rent-seeking. The patent system might be used by so-called "patent trolls" to, in essence, impose a tax on innovative firms. Patent trolls typically do little, if any, innovation of their own and have no serious plan to ever produce anything, but they acquire patent rights of marginal (or sub-marginal) technical relevance to the activities of other, active firms. Such patent trolls can threaten to use patent-related litigation to disrupt active firms, who often find it easier to pay off such claims rather than incur the expense and disruption of extensive litigation. By threatening such disruptions, these opportunistic patent trolls seek to obtain transfers or "rents" from genuine innovators.

One recent case involved BlackBerry Ltd. of Canada, then Research In Motion (RIM), the producer of BlackBerry mobile phones and associated services. In February 2006, RIM paid US$612.5 million to a small Virginia-based firm, NTP. The patents held by NTP were of questionable merit and some key patents were tentatively ruled invalid by the U.S. patent office after a review requested by RIM. However, NTP used sympathetic local courts in Virginia to threaten RIM with significant disruption and obtained a large settlement that many observers view as wholly unjustified.

NTP is a classic patent troll, consisting largely of lawyers and legal support staff. It does essentially no research and produces little, if any, tangible output. It simply acquires patents and seeks to earn returns from them, either by licensing them or by bringing lawsuits against successful innovators. This case illustrates the rent-seeking aspect of the patent system, as it highlights the significant shift in resources away from production of wealth (i.e., research and development) to fighting over the distribution of existing wealth (i.e., to rent-seeking through the legal system).

Both the anti-commons and rent-seeing problems suggest high levels of litigation (lawsuits). A number of CEOs of major technology companies have stated that they spend more on patent litigation than on R&D.[12] Certainly companies such as Apple, Nokia, Samsung, Microsoft, IBM, Intel, and others maintain very large legal departments dealing with intellectual property and are engaged in litigation on a continuous basis. Such costs can be expected to slow the pace of innovation. Companies without substantial resources to defend against legal predation might be deterred from innovating altogether.

---

[12] This assertion was famously made by Harold Goddijn, CEO of the European technology firm TomTom, and was immortalized on YouTube.

13.5 Other Intellectual Property Protection

Patents are the most important form of intellectual property protection. However, instead of seeking a patent, a firm might try to protect its intellectual property simply by keeping it secret, and such trade secrets are actually very important. Trade secrets are a recognized and legally protected form of intellectual property. In addition, Canada has two categories of intellectual property protection that are similar to patents—one for integrated circuits and one for industrial designs. The other major areas of intellectual property protection are copyrights, which protect literary and artistic works, and trademarks.

13.5.1 Trade Secrets

While new products or processes are often patented, an innovating firm might consider whether to just try keeping the technology secret instead of patenting it. Such a *trade secret* is a form of intellectual property, though it remains the exclusive property of the inventor only as long as it remains secret. Government policy does provide some support for trade secrets by allowing firms to enter into enforceable contracts with employees that prevent them from revealing trade secrets to others. Coca-Cola's formula is one of the world's most famous trade secrets. Not only has Coca-Cola kept the formula secret, it has used the existence of the secret formula as a marketing tool. And Coke has maintained this secret and the resulting market power much longer than a patent would have allowed.

Some industries, such as pharmaceuticals and consumer electronics, rely heavily on patents. However, survey data indicates that manufacturing firms in North America are actually somewhat more likely to rely on trade secrets than on patents for product and production process innovations.

There are several reasons why relying on trade secrets might be preferred to patents. First, trade secrets do not require disclosure of the technology while patents, on the other hand, do. Secondly, patents require considerable time and expense to obtain, and once granted, may require expensive litigation to protect, as it becomes necessary to sue others who seek to infringe the patent. It is often simpler and less expensive just to keep the technology secret. Also, trade secrets can usually be kept secret for at least some period of time and, even if the secret is eventually revealed, it would take still more time for imitators to begin production. Therefore, trade secrets are often preferred in situations where technology moves quickly and the innovator expects the advantage of one innovation to be displaced by another within a few years.

13.5.2 Integrated Circuit Topographies and Industrial Designs

Canada has a special category of intellectual property referred to as integrated circuit topographies (ICTs). An ICT is a configuration of semi-conductors, metals, insulators, and other materials used in a variety of technologically sophisticated products, such as computers and robots. The primary difference between protection of ICTs and patent protection is that ICT protection lasts for only 10 years rather than 20. Canada is one of many countries, including the United States, allowing a 10-year horizon for ICTs.

Industrial design refers to the shape, configuration, pattern, or ornamentation of some product whose use is not simply utilitarian but also includes an esthetic element. In other words, it is something people like to look at or experience. For example, a particular style of chair might be a protected industrial design. Because of the creative, esthetic element, protected industrial designs have something in common with copyrighted material. However, they also have something in common with patented items. Like ICTs, industrial designs receive protection for 10 years, during which time no one else may use the design without permission.

13.5.3 Copyright Protection

Copyrights provide intellectual property rights for innovative works in the creative arts, such as music, literature, painting, and related areas of activity. Copyrights also apply to computer programs and live performances. A copyright is, literally, a right to copy. If a songwriter has a copyright on a song, no one else is allowed to copy the song, not in written or audio form, without permission. A legal copy of the work can only be made with permission from the holder of the copyright. A songwriter might sell the right to record a song to a singer (a recording artist) who would then sell copies of the recording to consumers. The payment to the songwriter would normally be in the form of a share of the resulting revenues, referred to as a royalty.

The principles underlying copyright protection are similar to those underlying patent policy, as in the absence of IP protection, a free rider problem would arise. For example, the composer of a popular song faces the same free rider problem that the inventor of a new drug faces as the song is, essentially, a public good. Once a song is written it can be easily copied and used by any number of singers and enjoyed by any number of listeners unless it is protected in some way. Without copyright protection, it would be difficult for songwriters to earn a return on their songwriting efforts. It is true that many people would write music anyway, "for love not money." However, the incentive for highly talented artists to produce music would be much reduced, and they might be diverted to areas where they could expect compensation.

Copyright protection lasts much longer than patent protection as it remains in place until the death of the creator of the work, plus an additional 50 years. Creators often sell their copyrights to corporations or other organizations, which continue to receive royalties and other benefits from the copyright until 50 years after the death of the creator.

As with patents, copyrights are subject to extensive litigation. Many successful books or other works attract lawsuits. It is, therefore, not surprising that the Harry Potter series by J.K. Rowling, one of the most popular book series of all time, has attracted more than its share of litigation. One of the many cases was brought by American author Nancy Stouffer who had written two children's books, *The Legend of Rah and the Muggles* and *Larry Potter and His Best Friend Lilly* about 15 years before the first Harry Potter book appeared. Nancy Stouffer sued for copyright infringement on several grounds, including use of the word "muggle," a term used in the Harry Potter series, and over the name "Harry Potter" because of its similarity to "Larry Potter."

After many years of litigation and appeal, Nancy Stouffer lost her case. A simple word or name in common is not enough to trigger copyright infringement. There are, after all, many Larry Potters in the world (and many Harry Potters) and it would not make sense to give one person monopoly power over that name or any other name. Similarly, even a made-up word is regarded as part of the English language, and something that anyone is allowed to use. As it happens, however, "muggle" was a pre-existing English word in any case. In 2003, the Harry Potter usage of the word "muggle" was added to the Oxford English Dictionary to mean "a person who is not conversant with a particular activity or skill."

Ms. Stouffer might have had a case if her stories had some similarity in plot or character to the Harry Potter series, but there was very little similarity. And the author of the Harry Potter series, J.K. Rowling, convincingly denied that she had any knowledge of Ms. Stouffer's rather obscure stories when writing her first Harry Potter novels. Ms. Stouffer's case was further damaged when the courts determined that she had retroactively changed copies of her early manuscripts to increase use of the word "muggle" and enhance the apparent overlap with the Harry Potter series.[13]

Another interesting case is that of the Wyrd Sisters, a Canadian folk music band. One Harry Potter book has a scene in which the Weird Sisters play at

---

[13] See Grant (2011).

a school dance. When the existence of the real Wyrd Sisters came to light, they were offered $5,000, essentially as a courtesy payment. However, they tried to sue for $40 million instead. They lost the initial case but launched various appeals. Several years later, in 2010, the appeals were discontinued when the case was settled out of court. The details of the settlement are not known, but it is believed that the Wyrd Sisters received very little, apart from a lot of publicity.

One area of ongoing dispute in the topic of copyright policy is called *fair dealing*, which consists of exceptions to copyright for specific purposes. One fair use is for review or criticism. For example, someone writing a book review is allowed to quote passages from a book being reviewed in order to comment on those passages. Similarly, a student at a library would be allowed to photocopy a few pages of a book or journal for purposes of "private study." In addition to reviews and private study, exemptions are allowed for research, education, criticism, parody, satire, and news reporting. These exceptions to copyright protection do not give blanket authorization to use copyrighted works, however. The amount of material copied must be limited, the work must be properly cited, and the use must be "fair." An author who feels that his or her work has been unfairly used can sue the infringer and a judge would have to decide whether or not the use was fair.

One interesting point is that titles of books and songs are not in themselves protected by copyright. The title of this book is *Government Policy Toward Business*, but there is nothing to stop someone else from using the same title for a different book. And there are many books titled *Managerial Economics* or *Microeconomics*. In addition, concepts and ideas are not protected by copyright. For example, multiple textbooks on managerial economics or microeconomics contain many of the same main ideas and concepts. What is protected by copyright is the specific expression of those ideas and concepts. Thus, copying significant portions of this book or using very similar exposition would be a violation of copyright law. Deciding how similar a second work can be before it triggers a copyright violation is a difficult, subjective judgment that must be made by the courts when cases are litigated.

Unlike patent protection, copyright protection occurs automatically. While it is a good idea to register a work with CIPO, and publishers usually do, it is not legally necessary to do so.

13.5.4 Trademarks

A trademark is defined by CIPO as a word or design used to identify the product of a particular person or organization. Two of the most valuable and well-known trademarks are Google's multi-coloured name (with blue, red, yellow, and green letters) and the golden arches of the McDonald's chain of fast food restaurants.

Unlike the other types of intellectual property discussed here, trademarks are not primarily focused on promoting innovation, although they do have some role in protecting it. If, for example, Google produces a new online service and incorporates the Google trademark in it, it is easy for consumers to identify the item as a Google product, and other producers are limited in their ability to confuse customers by using similar trademarks.

The main rationale for trademark protection is not to promote innovation, but it is more like the rationale for preventing misleading advertising and deceptive marketing practices (Chapter 11). Specifically, protecting trademarks provides information to consumers. A hungry driver will catch sight of the McDonald's golden arches and immediately know what to expect if he or she stops for lunch.

More broadly, protecting trademarks reduces the informational asymmetries that can cause market failure. As mentioned in Chapter 11, building reputation is one way for firms to reduce informational asymmetries. Trademarks help in building a reputation and are useful in taking advantage of a positive reputation. Anyone who sees the McDonald's golden arches can immediately draw inferences about product quality due to McDonald's reputation. (And many people are very fond of McDonald's food.) The trademark helps limit the ability of rival firms to imitate McDonald's products or marketing in an effort to free ride on the company's reputation.

13.5.5 International Harmonization and Trade-Related Intellectual Property Rights

Over the past two decades, significant effort has been focused on the *harmonization* of intellectual property policy—seeking to make IP policies similar around the world. The international harmonization effort has been led, or perhaps pushed, by the United States, the world's largest producer of intellectual property. For many decades, U.S. producers and U.S. governments have been concerned about free riders on U.S. innovation, and have alleged that in some countries, particularly in Asia, products developed by American firms have been "reverse engineered" and copied with little regard for patents, trademarks, or other property rights. The United States has sought to bring intellectual property policy around the world into conformity with U.S. policy, although some modifications to U.S. policy have occurred as well.

One important step in the harmonization of IP policy was the World Trade Organization (WTO) agreement on trade-related intellectual property rights (TRIPS) that went into effect in 1995. This agreement significantly increased the level of harmonization across many countries, and generally raised the strength of IP protection in most regions of the world.

The distributional effects of the TRIPS agreement, the question of who gained and who lost through TRIPS, was studied by McCalman (2001), who focused on the effect of stronger patent rights. The United States experienced a large gain, reflected in the increased value of patents held by U.S. residents. A few countries in Europe also gained, but far less in total than the U.S. did (even on a per capita basis), and the European Union as a whole lost, as did all other major regions in the world.

The distributional effect of stronger patent protection and enforcement is not surprising. Patents are important in areas such as pharmaceuticals, telecommunications services and equipment, computing devices, medical devices, and various kinds of machinery. Many of the major producers are based in the United States. To obtain the associated products, other countries may import the products from the United States or they may pay licence fees to undertake local production. Or multinational enterprises based in the United States may undertake local production in those countries. All of these transactions imply a flow of earnings to the United States. McCalman (2001) did not consider the effect of improved copyright protection. If he had, he would have estimated an even larger gain to the United States, which is a major exporter of movies, TV shows, books, popular music, and other products protected by copyright.

From a global point of view, the main rationale for stronger and more standardized IP protection is not the distributional effect. The main intended effect is to reduce market failures that affect the innovation process, and thus increase innovation toward the efficient level. Have recent increases in IP protection around the world increased innovation? The empirical record on this point is unclear. The evidence certainly does not support any clear positive effect on innovation, and many observers argue that IP protection has gone too far.

It is also not clear that all countries in the world should have the same level of IP protection. Quite possibly it makes sense from an efficiency point of view (and from a fairness point of view) for low-income countries to have weaker levels of IP protection than the United States and other high-income countries have. If, for example, low-income countries in Africa do not honour U.S. patents for the purposes of local production and consumption in Africa, this is likely to have little effect on incentives to innovate in the United States, and it might do a lot of good in Africa.

13.6 Government Support for Research and Development

In addition to encouraging innovation through IP protection, governments also provide direct funding for various parts of the innovation process. Of particular importance is government support for research activities carried out at universities. In addition, there is an array of tax concessions and outright subsidies for R&D in the private sector, and governments also devote significant effort and resources to those parts of the financial sector that fund entrepreneurship and innovation.

13.6.1 University Research

Knowledge generated from university-based research is a public good, and both the research and teaching done at universities generate significant positive externalities that are important for innovation. University research and teaching would be under-provided if left to private markets, and this is a strong rationale for the extensive government support that exists. In Canada and most other countries, such funding policies have an important impact on innovation, as universities play a central role in the innovation process.

As noted earlier, the United States took over from Britain as the world leader in innovation during the 19th century. It maintained and even increased that lead for most of the 20th century, and it is still the world leader, although its dominance has been significantly reduced. As we look back over the 20th century, it is clear that a major reason for the dominance of the United States in innovation was its university system. And one major reason for the development of R&D capability in the U.S. university system was explicit government policy.

Perhaps the best-known example of university contribution to innovation is "Silicon Valley," the region south of San Francisco, California, that is centred on Stanford University and not far from the University of California at Berkeley, two of the world's leading universities. Silicon Valley, the centre of the microelectronics revolution, is the home of such iconic companies as Hewlett-Packard (started by two alumni of Stanford University) and Apple (co-founded by Steve Jobs and Steve Wozniak, a graduate of Berkeley). The technologies used in Silicon Valley are closely related to research conducted at Stanford and Berkeley, and most of the high-tech output of Silicon Valley comes from companies founded by Stanford and Berkeley alumni.

Stanford University, a private institution, does not receive significant government funding for its teaching activities. However, it is one of the largest recipients of research funding from the U.S. federal government, and this funding was fundamental to the development of Silicon Valley. Berkeley, a public university, was the recipient of large amounts of money from the state government of California *and* from the federal government. There is little doubt that the money invested by federal and state governments in these two universities has generated an impressive rate of return to the U.S. economy, and to the entire world economy.

Silicon Valley is just one example. More broadly, the United States was the first major country to create (starting in the 19th century) a large system of public universities that any intelligent and hard-working student could realistically hope to attend, regardless of family background.[14] Furthermore, this system was largely focused from the beginning on highly practical areas, particularly agriculture and engineering (and, later, business and economics), as well as basic science. In addition, the U.S. government pioneered the development of large national funding agencies that would support university research on a competitive basis. The dramatic improvements in global agricultural productivity in the third quarter of the 20th century known as the *green revolution,* and the development of modern computing, along with many other important innovations, are due in large part to the U.S. university system and its emphasis on applied research.

Governments around the world have learned from the U.S. experience, and many are following a similar model. The Canadian university system lagged behind the U.S. system during the 19th and 20th centuries, but it has followed a similar pattern of development and is now of comparable research productivity on a per capita basis. At present, the knowledge-based sectors in Canada's three largest cities—Toronto, Montreal, and Vancouver—are closely related to the universities in those cities, and some Canadian universities have become major contributors to the international research enterprise. The European university system has gradually reformed to become more like the U.S. model, and China is experiencing rapid growth of its university system, also using a similar model.

At present, the United States is no longer a leader in government funding for university-based research on a per capita basis, partly because other countries have expanded such funding and partly because funding in the United States has been cut due to budgetary problems for both state governments and the federal government.

---

[14] Not every student could expect to be admitted at a specific university. And some universities had racial, religious, and gender-based restrictions, but almost any student who qualified on academic grounds could reasonably hope to go to some appropriate university, and many did, giving the United States an advantage over other major countries where education was much more exclusive.

The role of government funding for university-based research is an important policy affecting industrial innovation. In addition to the funding levels, there are many issues that must be addressed regarding the design of such funding. One important issue concerns the relative weighting of applied research and basic research. Should, for example, universities such as the University of Calgary and the University of Alberta (based in Edmonton) make a large commitment to petroleum engineering, focusing on applied problems of direct interest to oil sands companies, if such commitments divert resources from basic research in areas such as physics or biology? It is sometimes tempting for a government to encourage a focus on very applied research of local interest—research that might generate direct local benefits. Basic research in physics or biology is pretty much a pure public good, and any benefits would accrue to the world as a whole.

We have learned from experience that it is important to get the balance right. A university that is too applied will soon cease to be a major research university, as its faculty will not keep up with developments in basic research, and such universities do not attract the most creative and effective researchers. Research-granting agencies that are too focused on applied research are following a short-sighted strategy. On the other hand, a university that disdains applied research is giving up the opportunity to make important contributions, as many applied problems can benefit from rigorous application of scientific research methods.

Another issue concerns how funds are allocated across fields. Should funding be focused on academic areas likely to contribute to industrial innovation, such as electrical engineering or computer science, rather than on disciplines such as law, sociology, and other fields that are less likely to produce such applications? And what about allocation across universities or regions? Should funding be based strictly on merit, even if the resulting allocation of research funds is highly concentrated? Or should funding agencies try to allocate funds more evenly between universities or regions? And to what extent should funding agencies encourage or even require collaboration between university researchers and industry?

Getting the right answers to these questions is not easy. In recent years, Canada has moved more in the direction of applied research, and granting agencies have emphasized collaboration between university researchers and industry. It is not clear what effect this shift in direction will have.

13.6.2 Tax Concessions and Subsidies for Private Sector R&D

There is a strong market-failure basis for government encouragement of innovation in the form of providing preferential tax treatment or subsidies to

R&D. The market-failure rationale for such policies lies in the public good nature of the knowledge generated by R&D and in the positive externalities or "knowledge spillovers" generated by the R&D process. To some extent, patent protection reduces the public good issues by limiting the extent to which the knowledge generated by R&D at one firm can be used by others. However, patents are not a complete correction even to the public good problem, and they do not address most of the externality issues. Therefore, even with a patent system in place, it is likely that R&D will be under-provided relative to the efficient level.

Accordingly, there is a strong normative basis for additional support for private sector R&D in the form of tax concessions and subsidies for R&D. The Canadian government is active in this area. The most important such program is the Scientific Research and Experimental Development (SR&ED) tax credit.[15] The program works by providing a corporation with a credit equal to some fraction of the money spent on R&D in a given year. (The fraction depends on the size of the company and other factors.) This credit can be deducted from any corporate taxes the firm owes. If the firm's tax liability is less than the credit, then the firm receives the difference as a payment from the government. If the firm owes no taxes (as is true for many firms) then the entire credit is paid to the firm as a subsidy. The total size of the credit exceeded $4 billion in 2012. There are also many other programs at both the federal and provincial levels that offer tax breaks or incentives for R&D, sometimes in particular areas, such as alternative energy.

The SR&ED program would seem to provide a strong incentive to undertake R&D in Canada, easing the effects of the externality-based market failure described earlier. However, this program also provides an incentive for firms to reclassify activities as SR&ED expenditures and to distort behaviour so as to increase SR&ED tax credits, even when such changes in behaviour have no positive effect on innovation. This is an example of moral hazard—and is a moral hazard created by government policy, which must be recognized as a cost of the program.

13.6.3 Financing Innovation

An alternative to direct tax concessions or subsidies for R&D is a subsidized or otherwise supported part of the financial system that provides innovation finance. Furthermore, as noted in subsection 13.3.3, innovation finance is

---

[15] See McKenzie (2012) for a detailed analysis of this tax credit.

itself subject to market failure based on informational asymmetries. Both of these factors contribute to a normative rationale for government contributions to innovation finance, particularly for entrepreneurial firms that do not have access to self-generated earnings that can finance R&D.

Innovation in entrepreneurial firms is funded in part by the financial resources of entrepreneurs themselves and by their friends and families. In addition, bank loans are important sources of finance. The primary additional sources of finance are venture capital and related forms of investment. Venture capitalists are financial intermediaries who get money from investors, such as pension funds and wealthy individuals, and invest that money in shares of young, privately traded, innovative firms. A related form of investment is *angel investment*, which refers to individuals or groups who invest their own money in such firms. In addition, there are *private equity* firms that are similar to venture capitalists but somewhat broader in their choice of investment targets. Also, some corporations maintain their own venture capital funds, and some large institutional investors, such as pension funds, invest directly in innovative privately held firms.

The Canadian Venture Capital and Private Equity Association (CVCA)[16] reports levels of venture capital investment in Canada of approximately $1.5 billion in 2011. As the United States is approximately 10 times as large as Canada in population and in economic size, it is useful to compare this amount with that of the United States, where total venture capital investment was approximately $28.5 billion in 2011—close to 20 times the Canadian level. Thus, the rate of venture capital investment relative to GDP or to population in Canada appears to be about one half that of the United States, a pattern that has held for a number of years.

One important difference between venture capital markets in Canada and the United States is that in Canada there is proportionately more government intervention in venture capital (and a larger net subsidy) than in the U.S. On the order of 10 percent of Canadian venture capital investment is due to governments, yet despite this government support, the Canadian venture capital market is considerably smaller in relative terms than in the United States.

Canadian governments at both the provincial and federal levels provide support to venture capital finance and other forms of innovation finance. In particular, the three largest provinces (Ontario, Quebec, and British Columbia) have all been very active, at different times, in supporting venture capital

---

[16] See www.cvca.ca/.

through a variety of programs. Among federal institutions, two major forms of government support for venture capital exist.[17] One is the Business Development Bank of Canada (BDC). The BDC, whose principal shareholder is the Government of Canada, is a major commercial lending institution, with considerable venture capital operations.

The second major form of government support for venture capital in Canada (and quantitatively the most important) until 2013 was the tax credit for Labour-Sponsored Venture Capital Corporations (LSVCCs). These venture capital funds were supported by both the federal and provincial governments. The LSVCCs contain "funds"–large pools of money–provided by private investors. Government involvement is in the form of tax credits for individuals who make investments in these funds. The federal government provided a 15 percent "refundable tax credit" until 2013 and some provincial governments provide an additional refundable tax credit of up to 15 percent. This refundable tax credit is, in effect, a subsidy to investment in such funds. The funds are called "labour sponsored" because each must be sponsored by an organized labour group–normally a labour union, but the sponsoring organization rarely has much effect on the fund. The funds' objectives include stimulating the growth of small entrepreneurial ventures with a focus on job creation.

The largest area of venture capital investment in Canada is information technology (computers, mobile phones, Internet companies, software, etc.), which accounts for about 40 percent of venture capital activity. Life sciences (drugs, biotechnology, medical devices, etc.) account for about 20 percent, as does "clean tech" (alternative energy). The other 20 percent covers everything else.

The overall record of government support for venture capital is somewhat mixed, as described in Brander, Hellmann, and Meredith (2012). Most labour-sponsored funds have generated relatively low returns for investors, and the firms they have invested in have not done particularly well. However, there is substantial variation among the funds and some have done quite well. Other forms of government support for venture capital in Canada and elsewhere in the world have shown reasonably strong performance, especially when the funded enterprises receive funding from both private sector venture capitalists and government-based venture capital.

---

[17] There are other types of support as well, including the Export Development Corporation of Canada (EDC), which is a federal Crown corporation, and direct investments in funds that also receive investments from private investors.

In summary, direct government funding support for R&D in private firms, for university research, and for venture capitalists has an important impact on Canada's business environment. Intellectually property policy is also very important. There is a strong consensus that such support is in the public interest. However, the particular design of both funding support and intellectual property policy in Canada, the United States, and in the world as a whole has been a contentious area in recent years, and it seems likely that policy in both areas could be more effectively designed.

14

Macroeconomic Policy

14.1 Introduction

This chapter focuses on one of the basic normative rationales for government intervention discussed in Chapter 3: macroeconomic stabilization. This is a very substantial topic in itself, about which many books have been written. Macroeconomic stabilization policies are very important in conditioning the general environment in which business firms operate. Interest rates, exchange rates, inflation rates, liquidity conditions, unemployment rates, the public debt, and other aspects of the macroeconomic environment are strongly affected, if not controlled, by macroeconomic stabilization policy.

14.2 Principles of Macroeconomic Stabilization

14.2.1 Objectives of Macroeconomic Policy

The basic objectives of macroeconomic policy are to stabilize the pace of economic activity and encourage economic growth. Before the development of active macroeconomic policy, market economies were subject to violent and damaging swings in overall activity, the most dramatic of which was the Great Depression of the 1930s. Because of this stabilization objective, the terms "stabilization policy" and "macroeconomic stabilization policy" are frequently used as synonyms for macroeconomic policy.

Part of the stabilization objective of macroeconomic policy is to keep the rate of unemployment low and stable. Another major focus of macroeconomic stabilization is inflation. As with unemployment, policy authorities would like to keep inflation rates stable, and beyond mere stabilization, they would like to keep them low. In fact, some economists and policy-makers view the appropriate target not as stabilization of inflation, but as stabilization of the price level, which would imply an inflation rate of zero! Canada last achieved zero inflation rates in the first part of the 1950s, although the inflation rate in 2012 in Canada was only 1.0 percent, which is close to zero.[1]

Macroeconomic stabilization policy has a major impact on the long-run growth path of the economy. One of the subtleties of macroeconomic policy is that it is often tempting to take actions that might increase the temporary growth rate of the economy and thereby redress short-run cyclical problems, even though such policies might be damaging to future growth. It is important for macroeconomic policy authorities to simultaneously consider the short-run (cyclical) and the long-run (growth) effects of their policy decisions.

Long-run economic growth is the most important measure of change in an economy's performance. A few decades of rapid economic growth can have a dramatic effect on human welfare. It can, for example, raise a typical person from near subsistence to comparative comfort, as we have seen in parts of Asia in the past few decades. Thus, for example, the general quality of life in economies such as Singapore, Taiwan, Hong Kong, and China has been completely transformed in the past 30 to 40 years. Even in Canada, which was already well-off 40 years ago and has had only modest growth in recent decades, the average Canadian was still considerably better off in the year 2012 than 30 or 40 years earlier.

14.2.2 Monetary Policy and Fiscal Policy

The basic tools of macroeconomic policy are monetary policy and fiscal policy. Monetary policy refers primarily to control over the supply of money, or more generally, over the general liquidity of asset markets. When we refer to the liquidity of a particular asset, we are referring to how easily it can be converted into cash or exchanged for some other asset. For example, cash itself is completely liquid, government bonds are quite liquid, real estate is less liquid, and machines in place in a factory are very illiquid. At the macro level, market liquidity refers to how easily credit can be obtained and the ease with which assets can be exchanged for other assets.

In most countries, it is a central bank's responsibility to control market liquidity. Central banks are part of the public sector, and are normally

---

[1] See Statistics Canada, CANSIM Table 326-0021 at www5.statcan.gc.ca/cansim/pick-choisir?lang=eng &tp2=33&tid=3260021.

structured as public enterprises. The senior officers of a central bank usually have considerable independence from the elected government of the day. In Canada, the central bank is the Bank of Canada and is a Crown corporation. In the United States, the central bank is the U.S. Federal Reserve System, usually called the Fed. The Fed is the most important central bank in global financial affairs, but it is now rivalled by the European Central Bank (ECB). The ECB is located in Frankfurt, Germany, and began operations in 1998. The ECB manages the euro, the European currency that was introduced in 1999 and is now used in over 20 countries. Other influential central banks include the Bank of Japan and the Bank of England. In the future, the Chinese central bank, the People's Bank of China (PBC), is likely to play an influential role in world affairs.

A central bank acts as a banker to other financial institutions. Thus, other financial institutions, such as commercial banks, can have accounts with the central bank and can make deposits in those accounts. Commercial banks can also borrow money from central banks. There are several ways a central bank can increase liquidity in the economy. One very direct method is by literally printing money. It can then give or loan the printed money to the government or to a client financial institution. An equivalent but more sophisticated alternative is for the central bank to create a deposit. If the central bank simply credits an account held by a commercial bank with an extra $1,000, it has just created $1,000. Similarly, a central bank can create money by writing a cheque drawn on a deposit it creates for itself. If the Bank of Canada writes a cheque, drawn on itself, for $1,000 and gives it to you, it has just created $1,000. The main recipient of central bank largesse is usually the federal government, which is able to use the central bank's power to create money as a way of (partially) financing government deficits.

When the Bank of Canada creates money, it increases the amount of money in the economy that can be loaned or used to buy other assets. This is why increasing the money supply causes market liquidity to increase. Aside from creating money directly, a central bank can also influence market liquidity by undertaking so-called open market operations, which involve the buying and selling of bonds in ordinary markets. Thus, for example, if the Bank of Canada purchases an outstanding government bond, it takes a moderately liquid asset (a bond) out of the hands of the private sector, and replaces it with a high-liquidity asset (money in the form of a cheque drawn on the Bank of Canada). This increases total liquidity in the system.

In addition, central banks provide loans to banks at a rate of interest known as the bank rate. Changing the bank rate also affects the amount of liquidity in the economy. For example, if the Bank of Canada lowers the bank rate, then commercial banks will be more likely to borrow money from the Bank of Canada and use this as a basis for loaning money to their clients, raising total liquidity in the system. The bank rate also acts as a signal of the Bank of Canada's intentions, and this signalling effect alone can often affect market liquidity.

The money supply is not a clearly defined concept. In fact, there are many different measures of the money supply. The monetary base is defined as the liabilities of the Bank of Canada, which consist mainly of currency and deposits in the Bank of Canada. This monetary base provides the foundation for a broader concept of money created through the banking system, according to the money multiplier process.

If, for example, the government is credited with an account with the Bank of Canada, and writes a cheque on that account, the recipient of that cheque will probably deposit it in a commercial bank, such as the Royal Bank of Canada or the Bank of Montreal. That bank, in turn, loans out most of that money to someone else, keeping only a small fraction of the deposit in the form of reserves. The recipient of the bank loan will then deposit that money in another bank. Most of this money is lent out again, except for reserves, and so on. At each step, liquidity is created. When the process ends, total deposits in commercial banks will have increased by several times and possibly by many times the initial increase in the monetary base. The sum of chequing account deposits in banks plus currency outside of banks is referred to as *M1*. If savings accounts and related accounts are added in, we have *M2*. And there are other, increasingly broad measures of the money supply that are sometimes used as well.

The important macroeconomic variable is market liquidity, but it is far from clear exactly how market liquidity should be measured. The total of bank deposits available to be loaned is very relevant, but so are deposits in other (i.e., nonbank) financial institutions, credit card lines of credit, and even short-term bonds. However, not all these financial instruments are of equal liquidity, so one cannot simply add them up. Whatever liquidity is, however, it is influenced by the monetary base, which is under the direct control of the Bank of Canada. If the monetary base increases, liquidity tends to increase; if the monetary base falls, liquidity tends to decrease.

Thus, the Bank of Canada has its impact by affecting the supply of liquidity through changing the bank rate, open market operations, creating money, and through other mechanisms. In addition, liquidity conditions are influenced by the demand for liquidity. We occasionally have situations when demand for new loans falls sharply and banks have trouble finding customers to take on loans. In such situations, we say that financial markets are highly liquid, meaning it is easy to borrow money. In these situations, the increase in net liquidity arises from a decline in demand rather than an increase in supply.

Fiscal policy refers to aggregate government expenditures, aggregate taxes, aggregate borrowing, and the net level of aggregate demand for goods and services that the government sector contributes to overall economic activity. One important fiscal indicator is simply the net deficit (or surplus) position of the government. For many purposes, we focus on the deficit position of all governments combined—federal, provincial, and local—although we also often consider just some sub-component, particularly the federal deficit.

If the federal government has a deficit, it has two alternatives: it can borrow from the public (domestic or international), or it can pay its expenses by having the Bank of Canada create money. Provincial and local governments can only borrow. Federal government expenditure is equal to revenues plus net borrowing plus net monetary base creation, and provincial government expenditure is simply equal to revenues plus net borrowing.

The overall budget deficit is not the only important fiscal indicator. Economists frequently subdivide the overall deficit into two components: a structural deficit and a cyclical deficit. The cyclical deficit is the component of the deficit attributable to the economy being in a cyclical downturn. The structural deficit is, therefore, the component that would remain even if the economy were performing at some neutral or reference level. The size of any cyclical deficit reflects what are sometimes referred to as automatic stabilizers, which are automatic changes in the tax-expenditure balance that occur as the cycle proceeds. For example, when the economy moves into a downturn and unemployment rises, income tax revenues will tend to fall and expenditures on employment insurance—government payments to unemployed workers—will tend to rise, causing the cyclical and overall deficits to also rise. Thus, the deficit will change over the cycle even without explicit government action.

14.2.3 Controlling Interest Rates

Interest rates are simply the cost of money. Consider the following example. Mei wants to buy a $500,000 townhouse but does not have enough money herself to make the purchase. She does have $200,000 on hand, but would need to borrow (i.e., obtain a mortgage for) the additional $300,000. Suppose that the interest rate she could obtain on a one-year mortgage is 5 percent. She would then need to pay $15,000 in interest during the first year of the mortgage. Now suppose interest rates suddenly rise and it turns out that the mortgage rate faced by Mei is 10 percent. In this case, she would need to pay $30,000 in interest in the first year of the mortgage. It is quite possible that Mei would find it feasible to pay $15,000 in first-year interest, but not $30,000. At an interest rate of 5 percent she would take the mortgage loan and buy the house, but at an interest rate of 10 percent she would decide not to take out the loan and, instead, defer her housing purchase. In effect, the interest rate is the cost, or price, of the loan, and if this price rises too high, people will demand fewer loans (i.e., less money).

Interest rates may be affected by both monetary policy and fiscal policy. If the Bank of Canada creates extra money, that additional supply of money puts downward pressure on the price of money, and interest rates tend to fall. Thus, expansionary monetary policy puts downward pressure on interest rates and contractionary monetary policy puts upward pressure on interest rates. If the government increases its deficit and does not cover the deficit with money-supply creation, it must borrow money. This increases the demand for loans and puts upward pressure on the interest rate. Holding monetary policy constant and decreasing deficits (or increasing surpluses) tend to make interest rates fall, and increasing deficits tends to make interest rates rise.

In public policy discussions, people often assume that low interest rates are good and high interest rates are bad, largely because low interest rates stimulate economic activity. It is important to recognize, however, that changes in interest rates have a significant redistributive effect, and some people are made worse off by interest rate reductions. Specifically, people who receive much of their income from interest earned on investments will have lower incomes if interest rates fall. More precisely, their real interest income will fall if the real interest rate, net of inflation, falls. The largest category of people who rely on interest income is retired people, most of whom depend heavily either on their own investments or on investments made on their behalf by pension funds.

Public policy discussions also sometimes exaggerate the extent of control the Bank of Canada has over the state of liquidity and interest rates. The Bank of Canada is a very important actor in the system, but liquidity conditions and interest rates are also affected by the actions and decisions of commercial banks, other financial institutions, investors, savers, and various foreign participants in financial markets, including foreign investors and foreign central banks. Suppose, for example, that the Bank of Canada wants some broad measure of money to increase. It can undertake an expansion of the monetary base, but unless commercial banks are willing to use that expansion as a basis for increasing loans, then broader aggregates will not be much affected. Similarly, the Bank of Canada cannot just choose appropriate interest rates. It can control the bank rate directly, but it cannot directly control mortgage interest rates or rates commercial banks charge for business loans. The Bank of Canada can usually pull enough levers to move interest rates up or down from current levels, but its influence is limited by all the other forces in the monetary system.

14.2.4 Aggregate Economic Activity and Keynesian Policy

In order to stabilize economic activity, the government would need to stimulate activity when the economy is operating too far below capacity and restrain activity when the economy gets overheated. As first emphasized by Keynes (1936), stimulating the economy requires increasing aggregate demand, which is the total demand for goods and services. Aggregate demand has four main components: consumer demand, investment demand, net exports, and government demand.

Increasing government spending tends to directly increase the government's demand for goods and services, but if the increased spending is financed by taxes, then consumers and businesses that pay the taxes have less to spend. If taxes are held fixed and government spending rises, then the government deficit rises and aggregate demand unambiguously increases. Consequently, net increases in aggregate demand are associated with increases in the deficit. Deficits therefore represent expansionary fiscal policy, and surpluses represent contractionary fiscal policy.

Investment demand—the demand for investment goods, such as new buildings, equipment, etc.—is responsive to interest rates. If a business has cash on hand, it can loan out the money, earning the going interest rate, rather than undertake new real investments. In this case, the opportunity cost of new investment projects is the interest rate. Most businesses must borrow to undertake new projects, in which case the interest rate is a direct, out-of-pocket cost associated with investment. In either case, if interest rates are high, the cost of investment is high, and less real investment will be undertaken than if interest rates were lower. The reasoning is very similar to that presented in Section 14.2.3, where we considered Mei's decision of whether to invest in buying a house. Higher interest rates lead to lower investment demand and lower aggregate demand.

Since both monetary policy and fiscal policy may influence interest rates, this is a second channel for aggregate demand to be affected by policy. (The first was direct government spending.) In particular, expansionary monetary policy puts downward pressure on interest rates, which tends to increase investment, which in turn increases aggregate demand and tends to increase economic activity. Contractionary monetary policy has the reverse effects.

Expansionary fiscal policy creates a complication, for while its direct effect on government demand is expansionary, it also tends to put upward pressure on interest rates. This is contractionary because investment tends to fall. In effect, government spending tends to crowd out private investment, referred to as the *crowding out* effect. If there is slack in the economy, the crowding out effect does not fully offset the expansionary effect of increased deficits, and so-called expansionary fiscal policy is indeed expansionary. However, if the economy is operating at capacity already, increased government spending must come at the expense of less spending elsewhere—usually by crowding out private investment.

Equation 14.1 summarizes this reasoning concerning the determination of aggregate demand.

$$AD = C + I\,(r(M,G)) + G + NX \qquad (14.1)$$

AD stands for aggregate demand, *C* for consumption demand, *I* for investment demand, *r* for the interest rate, *M* for the money supply, *G* for government spending, and *NX* for net exports. As indicated, investment demand depends on both *M* (monetary policy) and *G* (fiscal policy).

If the economy is operating at a low level, then it can be heated up by an expansionary monetary policy and/or an expansionary fiscal policy. Conversely, if the economy is expanding too quickly, it can be restrained with contractionary fiscal policy or contractionary monetary policy. This approach to policy was first systematically analyzed by Keynes (1936), and is therefore referred to as Keynesian policy. This view of policy contains considerable insight, but there are complications, as the following sections will show.

14.3 Macroeconomic Policy in an Open Economy
14.3.1 Effects of Exchange Rate Changes
So far, we have discussed macroeconomic policy without much discussion of the international environment. In fact, the international environment is very important for the conduct of macroeconomic policy. The starting point for discussing international effects is the exchange rate. Recall from Chapter 8 that the exchange rate is the rate at which one currency can be exchanged for another. Thus, if one Canadian dollar can be exchanged for 95 cents of U.S. currency, then the exchange rate is 0.95. If the value of the Canadian dollar were to rise to 98 cents per U.S. dollar, this would be an appreciation.

A decline in value, correspondingly, is a depreciation. There is an exchange rate between every pair of currencies.

The exchange rate is a very important variable to an exporter. If the Canadian dollar appreciates relative to the U.S. dollar, a Canadian producer who is selling in the United States and earning U.S. dollars suddenly finds that the Canadian-dollar value of those U.S. earnings has fallen. Typically, the producer's costs are primarily denominated in Canadian dollars. With stable Canadian-dollar costs and falling Canadian-dollar revenues, the producer's profit margin will fall and perhaps turn negative. The producer may raise U.S.-dollar prices to restore some of the lost Canadian-dollar value of the exports, but Americans would then purchase fewer goods, reducing the overall quantity of exports from Canada. Alternatively, the producer might simply cut back or even abandon exports to the United States.

From the point of view of an American importer who buys goods denominated in Canadian dollars and brings them to the United States, an appreciation of the Canadian dollar implies that the effective U.S.-dollar price of those goods has risen. This importer will also tend to reduce the quantity and value of Canadian goods purchased. Therefore, the Canadian-dollar value of export earnings and the real volume of exports will both tend to fall as appreciation occurs.

In addition, as American goods become cheaper to Canadians through appreciation of the Canadian dollar, Canadians will buy more of them. Thus, imports from the U.S. rise. When we consider the macroeconomic or aggregate effects of these individual incentives, we realize that the net export term in Equation 14.1 will tend to decline following this appreciation. Therefore, aggregate demand for Canadian-produced goods tends to fall, which is contractionary. Thus, exchange rate appreciation is a contractionary macroeconomic force, whereas depreciation is expansionary.

The exchange rate, especially the Canada–U.S. exchange rate, is an important macroeconomic variable for Canada. If policy authorities in Canada could put downward pressure on the Canadian dollar, this would tend to stimulate economic activity. However, a depreciating currency also has a cost. A country that lowers its exchange rate is just lowering the price at which it sells its goods, and is therefore lowering the return to the underlying factors of production that produce those goods. In effect, a depreciation is like a wage cut.

As Canadians, we can generate more demand for our services in the international marketplace if we collectively take a wage cut. Thus, if depreciation occurs, we find that the price of foreign goods rises relative to our incomes. Even domestic prices may rise as foreigners bid for our domestically produced goods. Domestic real estate looks increasingly like a bargain to foreign investors, and domestic residents may find it harder to buy homes as local currency prices of domestic real estate are bid up, etc. The wage cut makes us work harder to achieve a given consumption bundle. If we do not have enough work (i.e., if the economy has high unemployment and idle capacity), then a wage cut through depreciation may be a good response. However, being in a position where such wage cuts are needed is a symptom that the economy has not been performing well.

Canada has a flexible exchange rate. It is not targeted to any particular value in terms of another currency, but it can move in whatever direction international forces push it. Most countries have flexible exchange rates, although some countries peg their currencies to major international currencies (usually to the U.S. dollar or the euro). For example, Hong Kong pegs its currency, the HK dollar, to the U.S. dollar. This is referred to as a fixed exchange rate system. In fact, the rate is not strictly fixed but the currency is allowed to fluctuate only within a very narrow range. As of 2013, the allowable range for the Hong Kong dollar was HK$7.75 to HK$7.85 per U.S. dollar.

Prior to adoption of the euro in the European Union (EU) in 1999, the countries of the EU sought to keep currencies in close alignment with one another. This was not a pure fixed exchange rate system, but it was close. As of January 1, 1999, eleven members of the EU adopted the euro as a new common currency. The underlying currencies continued to exist, with a strict, fixed relationship to the euro. Initially, euro coins and physical currency were not introduced, but in 2002 they were introduced, completing a full replacement of individual, country-specific currencies. As of 2012, the euro had been adopted by 17 of the European Union's 27 members, including Austria, Belgium, Cyprus, Estonia, Finland, France, Germany, Greece, Ireland, Italy, Luxembourg, Malta, the Netherlands, Portugal, Slovakia, Slovenia, and Spain. In addition, several other small countries also use the euro, including Andorra, Monaco, San Marino, and the Vatican City.

14.3.2 Determinants of Exchange Rates

We have established that exchange rates are important macroeconomic variables, but how are they determined? And how can domestic policy authorities influence exchange rates? The answers to these questions are based on the idea that an exchange rate is simply a price. A currency is like any other asset, such as a bond, a stock, or a piece of machinery. Its price is, therefore, determined by supply and demand. Canada's exchange rates vis-à-vis U.S. dollars, Japanese yen, the euro, etc. are determined in international currency markets. If fewer people seek to buy Canadian dollars with Japanese yen, then demand for Canadian dollars in the yen-dollar market will fall and the Canadian dollar will tend to depreciate relative to the Japanese yen.

This pushes our question a step further back. We now know that exchange rates are determined by supply and demand in currency markets, but how are these supplies and demands determined? One source of demand for Canadian dollars in international currency markets arises from foreign consumers who want to buy Canadian goods and services. If a Japanese consumer holding yen wants to purchase Canadian-made furniture, somewhere along the line those Japanese yen must be exchanged for the Canadian dollars used to pay the furniture makers. Even more obviously, if Japanese tourists want to take vacations in Canada, they will need to buy (or will demand) Canadian dollars with their Japanese yen. These transactions contribute to the demand for Canadian dollars in the dollar-yen market.

Conversely, if Canadians wish to buy Japanese goods or take holidays in Japan, they will need to sell some of their Canadian dollars to obtain Japanese yen. This contributes to the supply of Canadian dollars in the yen-dollar market. Thus, part of the supply and demand for Canadian dollars arises from trade in goods and services.

However, only a small part of short-run fluctuations in exchange rates can be linked to changes in trade flows. A more important source of short-run variation in supply and demand for currencies comes from investment activities. For example, suppose a Japanese investor wishes to purchase a Government of Canada bond denominated in Canadian dollars. That investor must exchange Japanese yen for Canadian dollars before buying the bond. Investment demand of this type is an important part of the demand for Canadian dollars. Thus, the demand for Canadian dollars is determined in large part by the desire of foreign investors to make investments in Canadian investment instruments.

But what would make an investor want to purchase Canadian bonds? The return on holding a bond is the interest rate. If the interest rate is attractive, then the foreign investor will be more inclined to purchase the bond, and will, therefore, be more inclined to demand Canadian dollars on international currency markets. This creates an important link between exchange rates and interest rates. When Canadian interest rates rise, this makes Canadian bonds and other debt instruments more attractive. This, in turn, makes investors want to buy Canadian dollars to invest in these instruments. As these investors enter currency markets demanding Canadian dollars, they put upward pressure on Canadian exchange rates.

We can now infer one method by which Canadian policy authorities can influence the exchange rate. Specifically, by putting upward pressure on domestic interest rates through contractions in liquidity, it is possible for the Bank of Canada to put upward pressure on the exchange rate.

This interest and exchange rate mechanism strengthens the contractionary effect of tight monetary policy. Not only does the associated increase in interest rates tend to reduce domestic investment but, in addition, the exchange rate tends to appreciate, which puts downward pressure on net exports. Therefore, referring back to Equation 14.1, we can see that two components of aggregate demand fall—investment and net exports. This reasoning implies that if exchange rates are flexible (and provided investment can flow freely between countries), the international environment tends to strengthen the effect of monetary policy.

So far, we have identified two sources of supply and demand in currency markets. One source is the net effect of trade in goods and services; the other is the net effect of private investment flows. There is one other major source of demand and supply in currency markets: direct purchases and sales of currencies by governments. For example, the Bank of Canada maintains a large holding of U.S. dollars. If it wanted to put upward pressure on the Canadian exchange rate (on the value of the Canadian dollar) it could use some its holdings of U.S. dollars to buy Canadian dollars in world currency markets.

14.3.3 Fiscal Policy in an Open Economy

We have argued that the effect of international openness is to increase the influence of monetary policy on macroeconomic activity and to introduce a new instrument, direct currency transactions, as a tool of macro policy. What about the effect of fiscal policy? If international investment flows are highly mobile and exchange rates are flexible, we would expect the impact of fiscal policy to be weakened by open-economy considerations.

To see this open-economy effect, assume the government undertakes a pure fiscal expansion. That is, it increases government expenditures (as represented by G in Equation 14.1), using additional borrowing to finance the extra expenditures. As the government borrows money, it puts upward pressure on the interest rate. However, as interest rates rise, foreign investment flows in, attracted by these interest rates. Foreign investors must obtain Canadian dollars, so they enter currency markets, demanding Canadian dollars and putting upward pressure on the Canadian exchange rate. The rise in Canadian exchange rates, in turn, tends to reduce the net export component of Equation 14.1. This contractionary effect tends to offset the expansionary effect of the increase in government spending. Thus, fiscal policy loses some effectiveness in an open economy with flexible exchange rates and investment mobility.

We might note in passing that if there is a very elastic supply of foreign investment (i.e., if large investment flows will be induced by even small interest rate increases), then increased government borrowing will have little effect on interest rates. It is as if the government simply borrows directly from foreigners without disturbing domestic financial markets. Fiscal policy still loses its effectiveness in this case, because the highly responsive capital inflows put strong pressures on the exchange rate.

14.4 Inflation

14.4.1 The Meaning of Inflation

Inflation is the general rate of price increase. If all prices rise 5 percent per year, then the inflation rate is 5 percent per year. High and variable levels of inflation can be very damaging. In the first place, high inflation levels seem to be psychologically unsettling; most people simply do not like high inflation. In addition, high and variable inflation makes it more difficult for people to make good consumer decisions, since information about prices rapidly becomes out of date. Buying something means spending more time and effort searching the market to obtain price information than it otherwise would. In addition, high inflation rates seem to interfere with the operation of financial markets. For example, when inflation rates in North America were in double digits during the 1970s, long-term bond markets stopped operating.

We have discussed the inflation rate as though it were easy to observe. In fact, measuring the aggregate level of price change is not easy. In Canada, the principal measure of aggregate inflation is changes in the consumer price index (CPI) as calculated by Statistics Canada. Statistics Canada selects a representative bundle of consumer goods and services: food items, clothing items, transportation services, etc. The prices of these goods and services are then sampled over time in various locations in Canada. If all individual prices rise by 5 percent over a given year, then the CPI also rises by that amount, indicating 5 percent inflation.

The CPI slightly overstates increases in the cost of living (therefore slightly overstating inflation). One important reason for this is that the CPI does not fully adjust for changes in product quality or for the introduction of new goods. Thus, for example, it does not fully capture the idea that a laptop computer which cost $1,000 in 2012 was a much better product than a laptop computer that cost $1,000 in 2002. Second, the CPI also does not fully adjust for the fact that consumers change their consumption habits as relative prices change. Statistics Canada is always looking for ways to improve its procedures, and does make a reasonable but conservative attempt to deal with both of these effects. It is generally conceded that the upward bias still exists, but it is small. For the purposes of this textbook, we take the CPI as the appropriate measure of inflation.

14.4.2 The Fisher Effect

Inflation diminishes the value of money. If inflation is 5 percent per year, and Daniel has $100 under his mattress, then, by the end of the year, the value of that money has declined by about 5 percent. More to the point, if he loans $100 to someone else at the beginning of the year and is paid back $100 at the end of the year, he will have lost 5 percent of the value of that money. Daniel can, at the end of the year, purchase only 95 percent of what he could have purchased at the beginning. In order to protect the value of the money, Daniel would have to earn an interest rate of at least 5 percent. If the interest rate is exactly 5 percent, he is no further ahead at the end of the year than at the beginning. His real rate of return or real interest rate would be zero.

In general, the real interest rate is equal to the nominal or actual interest rate minus the expected rate of inflation. If expected inflation suddenly rises, then, to keep real interest rates constant, nominal interest rates must rise by the amount of the increase in the expected inflation rate. This is referred to as the Fisher Effect.

$$i = r + E\ (\text{infl})\qquad\qquad(14.2)$$

Equation 14.2 is the Fisher equation, which expresses the Fisher Effect in algebraic form. Variable i is the nominal interest rate, r is the real interest rate, and $E(infl)$ is the expected rate of inflation.

Focusing on the Fisher equation allows us to understand why government policy authorities may have only limited power to control long-run real interest rates. Specifically, if the government takes energetic policy action to change the nominal interest rate, it is possible that such changes might be offset by changes in inflationary expectations. The real interest rate may be harder to change, especially in the long run. The determinants of real interest rates include fundamental factors, such as individual attitudes toward time preference, the expected return on real investments, and, especially in an open economy, the willingness of foreigners to borrow and lend in domestic financial markets. Government policy can influence these things, but not always easily.

14.4.3 Inflation and the Money Supply: The Quantity Theory

The quantity theory of money starts with a relationship referred to as the *quantity equation,* which follows:

$$MV = PQ\qquad\qquad(14.3)$$

In the quantity equation, M stands for the money supply, P is the price level, and Q stands for the quantity of output. These are all variables we have discussed before. The other variable, V, is the *velocity* of money, and it is defined as being equal to PQ/M. Therefore, Equation 14.3 is true by definition.[2]

Conceptually, velocity reflects how many times a unit of money changes hands in a given time period to finance final-good transactions. If, for example, the total value of relevant transactions, PQ, is 1,000 and the total amount of money is 100 units, then units of money must have been used an average of 10 times each for such transactions. The velocity of money would be 10 in this case.

The quantity *equation* is not a theory; it is a tautology—something that must be true by definition. The quantity *theory* of money *is* a theory. It holds that output, Q, and velocity, V, are sufficiently stable that the price level is approximately proportional to the money supply. Thus, an increase in the money supply would cause an increase in the price level. A faster money supply growth rate would lead to higher inflation. In other words, inflation is created by money supply growth.

The basic logic of the quantity theory is as follows. Suppose that real output and velocity remain fixed, but the money supply doubles. This means that there are more dollars chasing the same goods. The real purchasing power of the expanded money supply cannot rise if real output is not rising. In order for real purchasing power to stay constant when the nominal money supply doubles, the purchasing power of each dollar must fall. An inflation rate of 100 percent will cut the value of each dollar by half, keeping total purchasing power constant, as required. Thus, if real output and velocity are fixed, inflation should equal the rate of growth of the money supply, other things equal.

The quantity theory can be wrong for two possible reasons. Either the quantity of output might change or velocity might change when the money supply changes. Either of these possibilities would cause inflation to be different from the rate of growth of the money supply. Consider first the role of output changes. Expansionary monetary policy increases aggregate demand. If the supply of goods and services can respond to the increase in demand, which will be possible if the economy is operating at less than capacity, then inflation need not increase commensurately with the increase in the money supply. If, however, the economy is operating at full capacity, aggregate supply cannot increase to match the increase in aggregate demand, and instead, inflation will result.

---

[2] To define the money supply in Equation 14.3 we can use any standard monetary aggregate, such as the monetary base or *M1* or *M2*. The velocity then refers to velocity of units of the monetary base, or of *M1* or of *M2*, respectively.

Velocity might also change. Particularly during a recession, when the money supply increases it is possible that a given unit of money will be used in fewer transactions. If people do not want to make additional purchases and the money supply rises, each unit of money will just be used less—for fewer transactions. This happened in the United States as it used aggressive monetary policy in an effort to recover from the recession of 2008–09. Money supply growth was quite rapid but inflation remained very low over this period because the velocity of money fell.

In practice, an increase in the rate of expansion of the money supply will often have output effects, velocity effects, *and* inflation effects. Some economists have argued that the inflation effects always dominate, at least in the long run. This is the long-run version of the quantity theory of money, which holds that monetary expansion has no long-run effect on real output, and translates directly into inflation. In this view of the world, monetary policy is described as neutral with respect to real output.

Real output will normally grow, and increases in the money supply will be required to accommodate this growth if deflation (a general decline in prices) is to be avoided. Additional monetary expansion, according to the quantity theory, will lead to commensurate increases in inflation. Table 14.1 shows recent inflation and money supply data from several countries.

It is clear from Table 14.1 that the correspondence between money supply growth (as measured by *M2* growth) and inflation is far from exact. Nevertheless, it is also clear that there is some positive relationship between money supply growth and inflation. Roughly speaking, single-digit money growth rates will normally produce low inflation, while money supply growth in the upper two- or three-digit range will produce high inflation. This lesson has gradually been absorbed into central bank practice, and many countries that had problems with inflation in earlier decades have managed to bring them under control in recent years.

Equation 14.3 implies that the percentage change in money supply must equal inflation (the percentage change in the price level) plus the percentage change in output minus the percentage change in velocity. If money supply growth goes from, for example, 3 percent to 10 percent, it is quite possible that inflation might not change much, because real output might increase a few percentage points or the change in velocity might fall by a few percentage points—enough to absorb the extra money. However, if money supply growth goes from 3 percent to 80 or 100 percent, there is no possibility that output could grow enough or velocity could change enough to absorb the extra money. High inflation would almost certainly result.

TABLE 14.1 Money Supply Growth (percentage change in M2 from the previous year) and Inflation

Country	1985		1995		2005		2011	
	M2	Inflation	M2	Inflation	M2	Inflation	M2	Inflation
Argentina	428	672	−3	3	22	10	26	9
Brazil	322	226	44	66	19	7	19	7
Canada	7	4	5	2	10	2	6	3
China	35	9	29	17	17	2	17	5
Israel	168	304	22	10	11	1	12	3
South Africa	15	16	16	9	21	3	8	5
Turkey	55	45	104	88	36	10	15	6
U.K.	11	6	20	3	14	2	−4	4
U.S.A.	8	4	7	3	8	3	8	3

Source: World Bank at data.worldbank.org/ and other official statistics.

14.4.4 Inflationary Expectations and the Effectiveness of Monetary Policy

Some economists argue that monetary policy is an ineffective tool for expanding output, even in situations of excess capacity, and that it should be targeted principally toward keeping inflation at low levels. Others have argued that monetary policy is very useful in influencing output. As mentioned earlier, we often observe that expansionary monetary policy has some inflationary effects, even in the presence of excess capacity. What determines the effectiveness of monetary policy as an output expansion tool?

One important determinant of the effect of monetary policy is the state of what economists refer to as "expectations." Recall that monetary policy has its expansionary effect largely by reducing interest rates, which increases investment. The first point to add is that the real interest rate is relevant for determining the real cost of investment. Expansionary monetary policy will increase investment demand only if it can decrease the real interest rate.

Suppose, however, that when an expansionary monetary policy is adopted, most people believe monetary policy is neutral and inflation will rise accordingly. If they believe this, then participants in financial markets will need to raise nominal interest rates to keep real interest rates at the going level, in accordance with the Fisher Effect. If nominal interest rates do rise to keep real interest rates constant, then no increase in investment demand is forthcoming, output stays constant, and inflation corresponding to the increase in the money supply results. Expectations turn out to have been correct and monetary policy has been neutral in its effect on output, translating only into higher inflation.

This description embodies consistent or rational expectations, and it demonstrates that monetary policy will be neutral if people expect it to be. People who hold this view are associated with a school of thought that goes by several different names: the monetarist school, the quantity theory school, the rational expectations school, and the policy neutrality school. Proponents of this view are opposed by Keynesians or neo-Keynesians, who believe the monetary policy mechanism described in Section 14.2.4 is very important.

Keynesian effects can arise if expectations differ from expectations of policy neutrality. Monetary policy can then have real output effects. In the early 1980s and 90s, both Canada and the U.S. embarked on tight money policies to try to reduce inflation, as have other countries in the early part of the 21st century. Economists of the rational expectations school argued that a reduction in monetary expansion could reduce inflation without much lessening of real economic activity.

In fact, real economic activity fell quite sharply when these tight money policies were used, and the expansionary monetary policy used in Canada and the United States after the 2008–09 recession did not lead to significant inflation. Therefore, the pure policy neutrality view has certainly been off target in recent decades. However, the monetary contractions of the early 1980s and 90s were something of a success for the policy neutrality school, for inflation was quickly brought down and was followed by long, sustained economic recoveries with lower levels of inflation. One interpretation is simply that the long run took a little longer to materialize than the policy neutrality school anticipated.

This discussion of expectations also suggests another point: the credibility of announced government policy has a major effect on the impact of government policy. Suppose, for example, the government announces that it will bring down inflation through contractionary monetary policy. If people believe this, then they will respond by lowering nominal interest rates, lowering wage demands, and so on, and the transition to lowered inflation will be achieved quickly and painlessly. If, however, people do not believe it, then they will not lower nominal interest rates or wage demands without a prolonged period of painful government restraint. Faced with such a prospect, the government might abandon the policy, proving the skeptics right. The effectiveness of government policy depends in part on credibility.

14.4.5 The Inflation Tax

As Table 14.1 indicates, some countries have experienced very high rates of money supply growth and inflation at various times. If, as argued earlier, inflation is costly, why do countries adopt such policies? The answer to this question is that inflation has value to governments, essentially as a tax. This is particularly true in many less-developed countries that do not have effective income tax systems.

To understand how the inflation tax works, consider the following thought experiment. Suppose real output in some country is 100, the money supply is 100, the velocity of money is 1, and the price level is 1. There is no income tax or sales tax, and all money is held by private citizens. The government wishes to consume real resources (presumably for public benefit). Suppose the government (through the central bank) creates 100 new units of money to be spent by the government. The government deficit is therefore 100, paid for by an expansion of the money supply. Assuming real output stays fixed at 100 and velocity stays fixed at 1, there is twice as much money demand as before for each unit of real output. At the old prices, both the private sector and the government could claim the entire GDP, but there would not be enough real output to go around. Prices must be bid up. The new equilibrium occurs after an inflation of 100 percent. The new price level is 2, in keeping with the larger money supply of 200.

Since the government has half the money supply (100), it can consume half the country's GDP. Private citizens are left with the other half for consumption and investment. What has happened? The real value of the private money supply has diminished by 50 percent, reflecting exactly the government's claim over resources. This government has, in effect, confiscated or taxed half of private sector income. This confiscation or taxation was achieved through inflation. The inflation was a tax on the private sector, just as if the government had taxed all citizens 50 percent of their income directly. This is described as the inflation tax, or seniorage.

In some countries, the inflation tax has at times been the most important single source of government command over resources. It is easy to collect and it is politically appealing, because most people do not understand it or even see it as a tax. When governments want to spend much more than they collect in direct taxes (i.e., when they run large deficits), the inflation tax is the tax of last resort. Most economists agree that the inflation tax is a very inefficient form of taxation, and is therefore indicative of bad government.

14.5 Unemployment
14.5.1 Types of Unemployment
So far, we have not discussed what is perhaps the major focal point of macroeconomic policy: unemployment. When politicians think about macroeconomic policy, they think first about unemployment, reflecting public concern. The first task in discussing unemployment is to be clear about terminology. The following list defines some of the relevant concepts.

> *Unemployed worker*: a person who is actively looking for work but not actually working, or who is on temporary layoff.
> *Labour force*: the sum of employed and unemployed workers.
> *Unemployment rate*: the ratio of unemployed workers to the labour force.
> *Participation rate*: the ratio of the labour force to the overall population.
> *Discouraged worker*: a person who would like to be employed but who is not actively looking for work, and who is therefore not counted as unemployed.

There will always be some people leaving old jobs and looking for new ones, or seeking first-time jobs. Similarly, there will always be some firms that find it necessary to reduce their labour force or go out of business entirely, releasing newly unemployed workers onto the labour market. Unemployment associated with normal job turnover of this type is called *frictional unemployment.*

In addition, some workers who would like jobs lack the skills necessary to make it worthwhile for a firm to hire them at going wage levels. Some workers live in regions of low labour demand, and might therefore be unable to find local firms to hire them, even if they have useful skills. Unemployment arising from the mismatching of skills or location is referred to as *structural unemployment.*

Finally, unemployment arising principally from swings in aggregate demand is referred to as *cyclical unemployment.* The distinction between frictional, structural, and cyclical unemployment is not absolutely clear in practice. In periods of low cyclical aggregate demand, the time spent between jobs for workers involved in normal turnover will increase, and the problems of regional and vocational mismatching will appear more severe.

14.5.2 The Natural Rate of Unemployment

Because of frictional and structural unemployment, even a perfect macroeconomic policy would not reduce unemployment to zero. Nor would we want unemployment to be zero. The task of matching workers to jobs is complex, and we can expect it to consume resources, including some time spent by unemployed workers searching for new jobs. Workers do not necessarily accept the first job offered to them, and firms do not always hire the first person to apply for a job. Similarly, it takes time for workers to realize that their skills might be out of date, or that they might have to move to find a new job. In any dynamic economy where skill requirements are evolving and the geographic pattern of activity is changing, there will be some natural frictional and structural unemployment.

There is, therefore, a natural rate of unemployment. This natural rate is determined in part by the size of new entry into the labour force, and in part by the rate of change of skill requirements and locational requirements in the economy. Most importantly, however, it is determined by the willingness of workers to be unemployed.

Most workers are voluntarily unemployed in the sense that they could find jobs at some wage. Understandably, however, a worker who has been earning $30 an hour or more might be unwilling to accept a job paying $12 an hour. Business executives who lose their jobs might be unwilling to accept jobs driving taxis (although some have), or working at Starbucks. In the short run, at least, they would prefer to look for a new job resembling their previous one rather than accept a much less attractive job. Such a situation is hard on the person involved, of course, but in a strict sense such unemployment is voluntary.

Time spent in job search will be higher if employment insurance is more generous, if family income is higher (e.g., if there is a working spouse), or if the worker retains some hope of direct government policy to save his or her job. The natural rate of unemployment is sensitive to all these factors.

It is a mistake to try to use macroeconomic policy to reduce the natural rate of unemployment. If we incorrectly judge the natural rate to be lower than it actually is, and try to use increased aggregate demand to lower the imagined cyclical unemployment, then, instead of reducing unemployment and raising output, we will tend to induce inflation and increase the government debt. Macroeconomic stabilization policy is best in dealing with cyclical departures in unemployment from the natural rate. It is not effective in pushing the natural rate down.

It should be emphasized that there is nothing particularly good about the natural rate of unemployment. The natural rate may well be too high, as it certainly is in Canada. The point being made here is simply that macroeconomic policy is not a good tool for dealing with the natural rate. If the natural rate is too high, this is most likely due to government policy itself, which has created too much rigidity in labour markets. For example, the policy of supporting depressed regions through money-losing public enterprises, rather than reducing unemployment, actually increases the natural rate. This arises because the policy prevents workers in those regions from recognizing the market's signal to change their skills and/or locations.

Similarly, a policy of generous employment insurance increases the natural rate. For example, in some communities in Canada it has become common practice for many workers to work for the minimum time required to be eligible to receive employment insurance benefits, and then to give up the job to someone else who will do the same thing. In this way, two or three people can be employed doing the work of only one full-time worker, receiving a subsidy from the rest of Canada to support them when they are not working. Such problems were at one time more common than they are now, as Canada has significantly tightened the eligibility requirements for receiving employment insurance. In particular, this practice now requires the compliance of employers as workers who simply quit their jobs do not qualify for benefits. To qualify, workers must be fired or laid off. The official rule is that workers qualify for employment insurance if they lose their jobs "through no fault of their own."

The more generous employment insurance is, the less likely people will be to take low-paying or unattractive jobs. Inevitably, the policies that we use to cushion the cost of unemployment and to allow people to live decent lives even if unemployed must make unemployment less unpleasant than it would otherwise be. Most Canadians favour such policies, but we should recognize that they do tend to raise the natural rate of unemployment because of the associated incentive effects, as higher benefits reduce the incentive to accept low-wage employment opportunities. There is an inescapable trade-off between providing higher benefits and reducing the unemployment rate, and it is not obvious exactly where the balance should be struck.

If we are convinced that government policies have generated an excessively high natural rate of unemployment, then the appropriate response is to modify those policies. For example, instead of subsidizing uneconomic industries, it would make more sense to subsidize the acquisition of new skills, or to subsidize relocation costs, or even to subsidize the job search process itself.

14.6 The Public Debt

It would not be appropriate to discuss macroeconomic policy without considering the public debt. The public debt acts as a constraint on the major tools of macroeconomic policy. A government's debt is nothing other than the accumulation of (properly measured) net fiscal deficits. The amount of aggregate debt a government can accumulate is limited; therefore, its capacity to carry out fiscal policy is also limited. In addition, the aggregate level of public debt may have an impact on economic growth and may, therefore, be viewed as an instrument of macroeconomic policy itself.

As of 2013, Europe is once again in recession. Like Canada, the United States, and many other countries, Europe went into recession—declining GDP growth—in the 2008–09 period.[3] The normal prescription for the "great recession" of 2008–09 would have been for European governments to spend money, running deficits to boost aggregate demand and stimulate the economy. The problem was that European governments, especially Greece, but also Italy and several other countries, had already been running significant deficits

---

[3] The U.S. recession is officially dated as starting in December 2007 and ending in June 2009. In Canada the recession was much shorter, going from the final quarter of 2008 through the second quarter of 2009. In the eurozone the official dates are the first quarter of 2008 through the second quarter of 2009.

in the preceding economic expansion. When the recession hit, the deficits quickly got worse, and Europe was in the position of suffering a debt crisis and a failure of aggregate demand at the same time.

As a result, Europe was not able to establish a strong recovery. A tepid recovery began in late 2009 but by 2011 some countries were already slipping back into recession, and by 2012 it became clear that the European Union as a whole was in recession again—a double-dip recession. The major fault lay not with the finance ministers and other leaders in place at the time. The fault lay primarily with the irresponsible policies of the earlier boom period. Instead of saving money during a boom, some governments were already pushing their borrowing to the limit.

The experience in the United States was not as bad as in Europe, but a similar problem had emerged. The United States budget was in deficit for most of the boom period just prior to 2008—running a deficit every year from 2002 through 2007. Therefore, as the recession became severe in 2008 there was not enough room for an aggressive stimulus program. As a result, the United States recovery was weaker than it should have been, although it looks like the United States has avoided the double-dip recession experienced by Europe. Canada was one of the few countries to run a responsible fiscal policy over this period and has suffered less from the economic downturn of 2008–09 than other high-income countries. In any case, the main point is that the overall public debt is an important factor that can limit a country's ability to conduct macroeconomic policy.

14.6.1 Sources of the Public Debt

Using fiscal deficits to stimulate economic activity, and therefore expand employment, has an important budgetary consequence: it tends to lead to an accumulation of debt. In principle, application of Keynesian macroeconomic policy should not result in increasing debt. The original idea was that governments would run deficits in times of low aggregate demand and surpluses in times of high aggregate demand. While there was no absolute requirement that deficits and surpluses would be exactly offsetting, it was presumed that no large net accumulations of surplus or debt should result. Roughly speaking, the basic innovation of Keynesian policy was that budgets should be balanced over the business cycle, rather than insistence that budgets balance in each year.

Rather than achieving budget balance over the business cycle, virtually all governments that have applied Keynesian principles have experienced a bias toward deficit spending. In Canada, the federal government ran a surplus in the 1973–74 fiscal year. It then ran 34 consecutive annual deficits, creating a major debt problem in Canada. However, through aggressive action the Canadian government was able to post a small surplus in 1997–98, followed by small surpluses every year until the recession of 2008–09 pushed the federal government into deficit again. As of 2012–13, Canada's federal government continues to run a small net deficit but has claimed that it is on track to eliminate the federal deficit by 2015. Among the world's high-income economies, Canada has arguably the strongest budgetary position.

There are two basic reasons why deficits are more common than surpluses. The first relates to the positive theory of government. It is very easy for governments to spend money and very hard for them to reduce expenditure. Citizens want expensive social programs such as universal health care, subsidized higher education, generous welfare programs, and universal pensions. They also want low taxes. The benefits of higher spending come immediately; the costs come later, to be dealt with by other governments. For these reasons there is a natural bias toward excessive spending.

Second, there has been a systematic under-assessment of the natural rate of unemployment. Throughout the last five business cycles, even at the most vigorous peak of the cycle, unemployment has seemed too high and was a policy priority. There have been strong calls for expansion of aggregate demand throughout the cycle.

Canada's relatively responsible approach to federal budgets dates from the 1990s, when the federal government sought to establish fiscal responsibility as a top priority, and as already noted, succeeded in running small budget surpluses until the recession of 2008–09. This required significant political courage, although enough concern about mounting debt had been expressed to make the policy politically successful in the end. The basic argument made by the finance minister who orchestrated the policy, Paul Martin (who subsequently became prime minister), was that fiscal responsibility actually did more to promote improved real incomes and employment opportunities than deficit spending did. From an economist's perspective, it made sense for the government to run surpluses in the late 1990s and early to mid-2000s in view of the robust performance of the economy, but it is not an easy political achievement in a democratic country whose voters want benefits now.

So far, we have focused mainly on the Canadian federal government. However, it is really the consolidated budgetary statements of the federal government, the provincial governments, and local governments that is relevant when assessing the overall sustainability of government programs. Regrettably, the budgetary positions of the provincial governments appear less healthy than that of the federal government. As of 2012–13, most provincial governments were running significant deficits, although much of the combined deficit was cyclical rather than structural. The consolidated position including all governments (federal, provincial, and local), seems reasonably sound, but some restructuring is likely needed to the financial structure of several provincial governments.

14.6.2 The Burden of the Public Debt

One reason for concern about the public debt is Keynesian. We want governments to have enough money saved or at least have enough budgetary room to increase spending and run deficits during recessions. This seems to require that governments run surpluses in good times.

However, as a point of arithmetic, if an economy is growing it is not strictly necessary to run surpluses to remain solvent. The primary variable to focus on in assessing solvency is the debt-to-GDP ratio. GDP determines ability to pay. As long as the debt-to-GDP ratio is falling, a government's budgetary position is improving in the sense that the ability to pay (GDP) is rising faster than the amount that is owed (debt). A deficit implies that debt is growing, but if GDP is growing faster than debt, then the debt-to-GDP ratio is falling, which indicates a more comfortable budgetary position.

However, relying on economic growth to allow for continuous deficits is a dangerous policy as it is very easy to slip from sustainable to unsustainable deficits. And of course, the debt-to-GDP ratio falls much faster for any given GDP growth rate if the government can actually run surpluses. Reducing the debt-to-GDP ratio is the very least a government should do in good times. However, we usually take a surplus as the appropriate target during boom times, even though a budgetary structure can survive without surpluses if the economy is growing fast enough.

In countries that have experienced continuing deficits, as Canada did in the 1975–96 period, the result has been a rapidly accumulating national debt. In 1974, interest on Canada's federal debt used up about 9 percent of federal revenues and was much smaller than government expenditures on goods and services. In 1996, interest on the federal debt peaked at 36 percent of federal government revenue and, at over $45 billion, was greater than expenditures on goods and services. Interest on the debt, over the single decade from the mid-1970s to the mid-1980s, changed from being a modest portion of revenue to being the single most important broad category, taking dollars away from government services such as health care and education. In the years following 1996, debt charges (i.e., interest) have fallen as a share of revenues, and were about 9.5 percent in the 2011 fiscal year. Table 7.8 provides some basic data on deficits and debt service for all levels of government combined.

It is important to have a clear understanding of exactly what the burden of the debt is, especially since this subject is the source of much confusion. To start with, there is an important distinction between an internally held debt and an external debt. The easier subject is the external debt. An external debt is an amount owed by a domestic government to foreign entities, such as foreign individuals, foreign businesses, or foreign governments. This debt has two significant characteristics. First, it is owed to people or organizations that are not subject to taxation by the domestic government, and second, it is usually denominated in a foreign currency.

An external debt is much like a debt owed by one individual to another. If large debts are undertaken now, this represents a burden in that the debts must be paid back later. If the debts are used to finance projects with a higher rate of return than the interest rate, then the benefits will exceed the burden. If not, the burden will exceed the benefits. During the early 1980s, an international debt crisis arose because many countries, especially in South America and Africa, undertook debts that could not be easily repaid. Much of this borrowing was used to pay for sharply increased international oil prices (that occurred in 1973–74 and again in 1979) and therefore reflected current consumption. Similarly, during the 1990s and 2000s, a variety of individual countries (particularly Greece) found themselves unable to pay owed interest on their international debts accumulated to finance current consumption. The problem was that few long-term real assets whose earnings could be used to repay the debt were put in place.

In any case, an external debt represents a clear burden or liability for future taxpayers. Even if a country defaults on the debt, there are very high costs, since this will compromise the ability of a country and its citizens to participate in international financial markets. Specifically, if a national government either fails to pay or is late in paying it debts to international creditors, then firms and citizens in that country will typically find it difficult to borrow money in international markets. This is because lenders fear that the government's financial problems might reduce the prospects for private borrowers to repay loans. Even if these private borrowers earn enough foreign exchange to pay back these loans, they might find the government wishes to tax or simply confiscate a large share of it. Also, a government that cannot pay its debts creates uncertainty about the long-run economic climate, and increases the likelihood that domestic businesses will fail.

A domestically held debt is somewhat different. In fact, there was a considerable controversy in the 1960s over whether a domestically held debt was a burden at all. The basic argument supporting the idea that an internal debt imposes no burden on the future is that an internal debt is a debt "we owe to ourselves." The future reshufflings of income between taxpayers and bondholders are just transfers and, so the argument goes, do not impose real resource costs on the economy. Unfortunately, however, this argument is false.

Speaking pragmatically, if a debt is denominated in domestic currency and is owed to domestic residents, the government always has two feasible options that it does not have with external foreign currency debt. It can simply print money to pay off the debt, or it can tax recipients of interest income a substantial part of that income.

Common sense, however, suggests there is a burden on the future created by a public debt, even if it is internally held. Common sense is sometimes wrong in economic matters, but in this case it is right. The burden arises because when the government borrows money it exchanges something of equal value: a bond promising command over resources in the future. This is a liability on taxpayers at large. Non-bond-holding taxpayers in particular suffer an increased future liability with every extra dollar the government borrows. While it is true that the government will not go bankrupt over an internal debt, it is also true that someone will bear the burden.

If the government prints money to pay off the debt, then inflation will result, and, in effect, an inflation tax will extract wealth from citizens. If, alternatively, the government taxes interest income at high rates, it is confiscating from bondholders some of the payment that had been promised to them. In short, the government has sufficient power over internal debtholders that it can always find a way to meet its budgetary requirements by imposing the burden of the debt on them if it chooses to. With external debts, the burden cannot be imposed on the recipients of the interest payments, short of actual default. Thus, while an internal debt can be dealt with more easily than an external debt, it is no less a liability for future taxpayers.

Debts may still be worthwhile. If the debt is used to pay for an asset that generates returns in excess of the interest payments, then the burden of the debt should be gladly accepted, for this burden will be less than the benefits. If borrowed money is used to pay for schools and hospitals that greatly increase the quality of life and/or increase the productive capacity of the population, or if it is used to pay for roads and bridges that greatly improve private sector productivity, then this borrowing is a good investment. Public borrowing must, however, be viewed as an investment. If government borrowing is used to fund uneconomic public enterprises, or if it is spent on current consumption that does not generate future benefits, then that borrowing will impose a net burden on the future.

It is possible for governments to get into a situation where they need to borrow money primarily to pay interest on previously accumulated debt. The cascading effect of borrowing money to pay interest on previous borrowings creates an obvious potential sustainability problem, as some lenders may get nervous and refuse to lend more, at which point the government would default on its debts. This is much like the problem confronted by insolvent individuals or private firms who find themselves borrowing money just to pay interest.

If it is possible to turn the corner and get to a point where debt actually starts to fall, then this "vicious cycle" can be reversed. As debt levels fall, less money has to be spent on interest payments on that debt, and more money is available to pay off the underlying debt principal and, of course, more money is available for other uses. The federal government and Canada as a whole (i.e., the federal government plus the provinces) apparently turned this corner in the late 1990s, although it would be easy to reverse this effect, as happened in the early 2000s in the United States.

There is a strong political incentive in favour of deficit spending, as the benefits occur in the short run and the costs are long-run costs which be faced by future governments. However, governments in many regions, including most Canadian jurisdictions, have learned the lesson that these costs are usually not worth incurring. Another short-run incentive that governments face is to attempt to present misleading information about the budgetary position. In contrast, at the federal level and in most provinces in Canada, changes have been in the direction of providing more accurate and more helpful information.

14.6.3 Government Deficits and Current-Account Deficits

One noteworthy aspect of Canada's recent experience with deficits is that the pattern of government deficits is similar to the pattern of something called the current-account deficit. The current account consists essentially of the sum of export earnings on goods and services, plus Canadian earnings from foreign investments, minus imports of goods and services and investment earnings flowing to foreigners from Canadian investments. If this account is in surplus, Canada would be building up financial claims on the outside world, because earnings from the outside world would exceed payments to the outside world. Conversely, if the current account is in deficit, this means Canada is becoming increasingly indebted to the rest of the world.

In fact, the current account in Canada was in very substantial deficit from the early 1980s through the late 1990s, but it turned positive in 2000. It turned negative again when the U.S. entered its recession in early 2008, and it has remained large and negative since then, through 2012. The main reason for the large deficits is the slow pace of economic recovery from the recession in the United States leading to lower exports from Canada to the United States than would otherwise occur. Current-account deficits imply that foreign claims on Canada are growing; foreigners are earning Canadian dollars from exports to Canada and from repatriated interest payments and profits from Canadian investments that, in total, exceed the amount Canada earns from foreign sources. Thus, if Canada converted its foreign earnings to Canadian dollars in international markets, foreigners would still have Canadian dollars left over. What happens to those extra dollars?

The answer is that foreigners invest them in Canadian assets, including direct loans to the federal government and provincial governments. Thus, a current-account deficit is exactly offset by a capital-account surplus, which is an excess of investment inflows over investment outflows. In fact, the current-account deficit must always equal the capital-account surplus, because of the following accounting convention. If foreigners earn excess Canadian dollars, there are two things they can do with them. They can invest them in Canadian assets such as corporate stock, government bonds, Toronto real estate, etc. Alternatively, they can simply hold the Canadian dollars in bank vaults or under mattresses, or whatever.

Both of these uses of Canadian dollars are counted as capital inflows to Canada. If a foreigner simply holds Canadian $100 bills under a mattress, this is an example of the second type of use—holding Canadian money. Thus, currency is itself viewed as an investment asset, and holding currency counts as making an investment in Canada. In fact, very little of the accumulated earnings by foreigners from Canadian sources are held as currency, but this accounting convention ensures that the capital-account surplus always exactly offsets the current-account deficit (or vice versa).

A substantial part of the investment inflow (or capital-account surplus) represents foreigners loaning money to (i.e., investing in) Canadian governments by purchasing interest-bearing government bonds. Therefore, the current-account deficit and government budget deficits are related, and are sometimes referred to as twin deficits.

14.7 Macroeconomic Stabilization and Market Failure

In keeping with traditional discussions of public policy, this book has distinguished among four types of normative rationale for policy: efficiency (or market failure), fairness, macroeconomic stabilization, and other objectives. As some critics have pointed out, however, it is not obvious that stabilization policy should be regarded as an independent motivation for policy. According to this view, macroeconomic policy is properly viewed as part of the efficiency, or market failure, rationale for policy. After all, if workers and equipment that could be productively employed are standing idle, this is a clear example of economic inefficiency. Pareto improvements could be made by putting those resources to work.

In short, macroeconomic stabilization is not an end in itself. It is useful to the extent that it reduces or corrects market failure. The attractiveness of this idea is best appreciated by considering what we would recommend for policy if stabilizing some economic variable actually reduced economic efficiency. Suppose, for example, we observe that unemployment is higher in January than in June. Suppose further that the main reason for this is that many industries, such as construction, are less productive in January than in June because of weather conditions. We could, at some cost, stabilize employment between the two months by undertaking large amounts of employment-generating deficit spending every January and restraining economic activity every June.

Such a policy would likely reduce real annual incomes, implying that it is (Pareto) inefficient. Would we advocate this efficiency-reducing policy? Obviously not. Macroeconomic policy is useful only to the extent that it serves either the efficiency rationale for intervention or, possibly, the fairness rationale for intervention. It is not really an end in itself. Macroeconomic failures are really microeconomic market failures writ large.

Why, then, do we distinguish between macro stabilization and efficiency rationales for intervention? In part, this reflects the history of economic thought and of actual policy, which have tended to separate micro-based policies, which focus on individual markets, from macro-based policies, which focus on aggregate business activity. Also, although stabilizing economic activity does not necessarily always improve economic efficiency, it usually does. It seems reasonable therefore, as a practical matter, to isolate stabilization as a specific subsidiary objective.

Conceptually, however, macro and micro policy principles cannot be logically different. To be logically complete, macro policy analysis must be based on the behaviour and efficiency properties of individual markets, just as micro policy analysis is. The Keynesian approach to deficit spending and stabilization is based on the idea of significant failures in labour markets and financial markets, and possibly on simple failures on the part of individuals to make correct optimizing decisions. Under such conditions, active monetary and fiscal policy can have significant positive effects, if skilfully applied.

14.8 Long-Run Economic Growth

Public policy tends to focus on short-run macro stabilization, perhaps to an excessive extent. Long-run economic growth is more important; after all, it has dramatically improved the material standard of living in most of the world in just the past century (or less). Cross-country comparisons of economic growth have been particularly striking in recent decades. While virtually all countries go through business cycles in which the pace of economic activity rises and falls, some countries have performed consistently better than others.

Much of the relevant data has already been presented in Table 7.10, which shows that a number of countries, mostly in Eastern Asia, have gone through truly transformative growth in per capita income over the past few decades. The leader is China, where per capita real income (as measured by GDP per capita, adjusted for purchasing power) was, in 2011, an astonishing 17 times its 1975 level. South Korea is not shown in the table but had a per capita income in 2011 over five times as great as in 1975—performance that would in itself be astonishing if not for China's.

Other countries in this fast-growing group of East Asian economies include Singapore, Taiwan, Hong Kong, and, more recently, Indonesia, Malaysia, and Thailand. Japan would be part of this group as well except that its rapid growth occurred in the 1950s and 1960s; it was really the pioneer of the rapid Asian economic-growth experience. India has also had a transformative growth experience since about 1990. Changes of the magnitude experienced by these economies are so dramatic that quantitative comparisons lose some of their meaning. It is accurate to say, however, that the quality of life was totally transformed in the space of about 35 years, or less. A young adult in Singapore or South Korea today would find the living experience of his or her grandparents at a similar age so much poorer in material terms as to be difficult to comprehend.

On the other hand, there is a large group of countries, including much of sub-Saharan Africa and parts of Latin America and the Caribbean, where real incomes have stagnated or grown only slowly despite starting at very low levels. Some countries have even experienced sustained declines in per capita real income. Most of these countries are not shown in Table 7.10, but one example, the Congo, is shown.

As for Europe and North America, most countries have turned in strong performances over the 1975–2011 period compared with long-run historical standards. The wealthy countries of 1975, countries such as Australia, Canada, France, Norway, and the United States (all shown in Table 7.10), experienced a near doubling of per capita real income with growth ranging from about 70 percent to about 110 percent over that time period. Such growth rates seem, however, somewhat anemic compared with the East Asian experience. Among European countries, the poorer ones have grown the fastest, so that Spain and Italy, in particular, have substantially closed the gap between themselves and the other European countries. In East Asia, Europe, North America, and a few other countries, the period 1980–2011 was one of convergence, with all these countries experiencing rising real incomes, but with the poorer ones growing fastest. However, in other parts of the world, the poorest countries have remained very poor.

It is important for policy-makers in any one country, such as Canada, to understand the causes of growth, and it is particularly important for development of the low-income countries. The puzzle is far from being completely resolved, but the following general statements can be made.

First, the basic type of economic system seems to be very important. Central planning under state socialism or communism did not perform well, whereas market-based economies have performed well. There were centrally planned economies that produced quite good standards of living, such as the former East Germany, but compared to West Germany, East German performance was very poor. Another striking comparison is between centrally planned North Korea and market-based South Korea, as North Korea is far, far worse off. In East Asia, the comparison in the 1970s and 1980s between market economies, such as Japan and Singapore, and centrally planned or state socialist economies, such as Vietnam and Cambodia were at that time, is overwhelming. As the former centrally planned economies changed over to market-based systems, many very quickly began dramatic improvements in economic performance. This group includes China and India, which reinforces the point that central planning appears to be vastly inferior to market-based systems.

It is apparent that the very rapid growth in East Asia, India, parts of Europe, and elsewhere is largely the result of technology transfer. Firms in these countries have rapidly adopted technologies developed mostly in other countries, particularly in the United States, although domestic innovation and R&D are starting to become important in these other countries as well. This technology transfer has resulted in greatly improved worker productivity and real incomes.

However, one important question is why technology transfer occurred in some places but not others. Economists argue that successful technology transfer is related to human capital or workforce skills, but we still have to ask why the relevant human capital is available in some areas but not in others. One possible explanation is that human capital might be closely related to years of schooling, but it turns out that variation in years of schooling does not explain much of the variation in apparent technology transfer. Education is no doubt important, but quality of education, which is very hard to measure, appears to be more important than mere years of schooling.

This is a book about government policy toward business. A natural question to ask is how such policies affect growth. Policies are important, although we would not get unanimous agreement on the growth consequences of some of them. Evidence suggests that having an open economy with few trade barriers and high capital mobility contributes to strong economic performance, as is consistent with the ideas discussed in Chapter 8.

Appropriate regulation is important. Some potential market failures, especially in industries with significant economies of scale, such as electric power generation, should be regulated. In addition, informational asymmetries create a strong rationale for significant regulation in the financial sector. However, excessively high levels of regulation can be a problem.

In a revealing experiment described in de Soto (1989), a group of researchers tried to obtain permission to open a small clothing factory in Peru. Registering the factory took 289 days and required the efforts of several skilled people. Bribes were solicited on ten occasions, but paid only twice, when the process would otherwise have been stopped. The total cost, not including the value of time spent by the researchers, was the equivalent of roughly three years' wages at Peru's minimum wage. Clearly, just getting permission to start the factory, let alone equipping it with machinery and workers, would be beyond the means of most potential entrepreneurs. Incidentally, at no time during the 289 days did any of the regulatory authorities realize they were dealing with a completely fictitious simulation. This suggests the regulatory structure in Peru was incapable of accomplishing any substantive objective, but acted mainly as a source of income for government workers and an impediment to private sector activity.

Provision of government infrastructure, much of which has public good characteristics or generates positive externalities, is also important. Such infrastructure includes roads, communications facilities, ports, educational facilities, and so on. The conduct of macroeconomic policy itself seems to be of some importance. The uncontrolled deficit spending and resulting hyperinflations that have occurred in much of Latin America at various times would, for example, seem to go a long way toward explaining poor performance in these countries. After they improved their monetary and fiscal policies, their economic performance greatly improved. Successful performance seems to be related to fiscally conservative deficit and demand management policy, which should serve as a warning for the United States and for European countries currently living beyond their means.

The role of research and development is subject to some debate and is difficult to estimate, partly because research and development itself is so difficult to measure. It is clear that at a world level economic growth depends upon technological progress, as described in Chapter 13. It is far from clear, however, that it is in a single country's interest to subsidize research and development by public policy. Research results are often freely available, and even proprietary research can be readily licensed. The rapidly growing economies of East Asia have, for the most part, purchased or borrowed technology rather than produce it themselves. The same is true of Canada, although Canada is a significant producer of innovation relative to its size.

Perhaps the most important government policy is simply a matter of having a stable, functioning government. Countries that experience civil wars and religious conflict do not do well. Nor do countries where government leaders are concerned principally with enriching themselves rather than in providing good government. In this book we have covered many of the policies that are associated with good government. Perhaps the central principle is that governments should respect and harness markets and market-based incentives, but should also be alert to significant market failures and seek to correct them.

15
Corporate Social Responsibility

15.1 Introduction

We frequently assume that governments seek to maximize overall well-being for society at large, whereas firms seek to maximize profits. However, this is an incomplete description of what governments and firms actually do. In practice, as emphasized in Chapter 5, we should expect decision-makers in government to pursue their own self-interest as well the broader social interest. Correspondingly, we should understand that managers in the private sector, in addition to trying to earn profits for their firms or for themselves, often pursue social objectives, even at the cost of lower profits.

Managers may of course make private contributions of their own time and money to charities or other social causes. Such actions are not the subject of this chapter. In this chapter we focus on the pursuit of social objectives using resources that belong to the firm and might otherwise be used to increase the firm's profits. Decisions over such activities are normally made and implemented by the firm's managers, although shareholders and boards of directors may also play a role.

This pursuit of social objectives by private sector firms is commonly called *corporate social responsibility* (CSR).[1] The world's largest developer of voluntary

---

[1] These objectives are not confined to corporations but apply to any business, so the term "business social responsibility" would be more accurate. However, it is the term *corporate social responsibility* that *has* become widely accepted.

international standards, the International Organization for Standardization (ISO), has attempted to provide standards for corporate social responsibility.[2] ISO defines social responsibility as "acting in an ethical and transparent way that contributes to the health and welfare of society." It identifies several major areas of corporate social responsibility, including the environment (or sustainability), treatment of employees, consumer issues, community development, and internal governance.

Probably the quantitatively most important CSR policies relate to the environment, and include such things as reducing pollution (including greenhouse gas emissions), using recycled materials, manufacturing products that can be readily recycled, using renewable resources on a sustainable basis, and economizing on the use of nonrenewable resources. Community development is also a major area and may include corporate policies such as donations to hospitals, universities, and other charitable causes, along with programs for helping groups of disadvantaged people. Consideration of CSR is closely related to the study of *business ethics*. The basic normative question in studying CSR or business ethics is, "What is the social responsibility of business?"

A striking feature of the literature on CSR is that a single very short article by Milton Friedman (1970) is a focal point for much of the debate on this topic. The title of Friedman's article, "The Social Responsibility of Business is to Increase its Profits," clearly states its main point. Most other commentators argue that profit maximization by itself is not sufficient for socially responsible corporate behaviour. In this chapter, we start by setting out Friedman's basic argument, and then consider that alternative view—that ethical principles require broader social objectives for business.

15.2 Social Responsibility and Profits

Friedman (1970) provides several arguments in support of his view that the ethically correct objective for managers of firms is to maximize profit. The two most important of these are a responsibility to the owners of the firm and the efficiency effects of competitive self-interest—the invisible hand. In addition, he suggests several other reasons.

Before considering Friedman's arguments in more detail, we should note that his position is not quite as extreme as the title of his paper suggests. Specifically, he does recognize two managerial responsibilities in addition

---

[2] A description of ISO standards for corporate social responsibility can be found on the ISO website at www.iso.org/iso/home/standards/management-standards/iso26000.htm.

to maximizing profit: legal constraints and what he calls "ethical custom." Thus, Friedman accepts that it is not socially responsible (that is, it would be ethically wrong) for a corporation to increase its profits through illegal acts such as theft or fraud. He also acknowledges that it would be wrong to violate ethical custom, but he does not state which ethical customs he has in mind. Much of what is considered corporate social responsibility could be viewed as ethical custom; for example, helping the disadvantaged or respecting the environment.

However, Friedman does provide several examples of CSR programs that he opposes. One example is the reduction of pollution beyond what is required by law. Another example is hiring chronically unemployed people beyond the employment needs of the firm so as to reduce poverty. He also opposes profit-reducing corporate charitable donations.

15.2.1 Responsibility to Owners

The argument that managers have an ethical obligation to maximize profits derives in part from the responsibility managers of a firm owe to its owners. To understand the point, consider the following example. Suppose Sonya, a university student, has been asked to "house sit" for some friends of her parents who own a very nice home. Sonya is to stay in the house and take care of it for two weeks while the owners are away on vacation. Sonya is very concerned about the welfare of homeless people. Without telling the owners, she invites a group of homeless people to live in the house while the owners are away. When the owners return the home is dirty and much of the food is gone. Was Sonya's decision to invite homeless people into the house ethical (socially responsible)? Would it have been ethical even if no food had been eaten and the house was clean when the owners returned?

For most of us, the answer to the house-sitting questions is that it was wrong for Sonya to invite the homeless people to live in the house while the owners were away. The situation is worse if the home was dirty and the food eaten when the owners return, but just letting people into the house seems wrong, even if they do no harm. Furthermore, even if the owners of the home were very wealthy and the homeless people were poor, it seems wrong for Sonya to use her control of the house in this way. Most of us accept that she has a duty to the owners of the asset (the house) to manage that asset in their interests. Even if we believe that the owners of the house should do something to help the homeless, it nevertheless seems wrong for Sonya to use (or misuse) her position of trust in this way—imposing her own social judgment on the owners.

Friedman views managers of a corporation in the same way. The managers are taking care of the corporation on behalf of its owners, the shareholders. Even if we think that the shareholders should do more to help the poor or to help the environment, the managers' role is to carry out the legal wishes of the shareholders, not to indulge their own social views at the shareholders' expense. Friedman (1970) writes as follows:

> In a free-enterprise, private-property system, a corporate executive is an employee of the owners of the business. He has direct responsibility to his employers. That responsibility is to conduct the business in accordance with their desires, which generally will be to make as much money as possible.

15.2.2 Efficiency (the Invisible Hand)

Friedman also reminds us of the concept of the *invisible hand* first articulated by Adam Smith (1776) and described in Chapter 3. Smith emphasizes that society is much better off if we can rely on the self-interest of the "butcher, baker, or brewer" to provide us with food rather than relying on their "benevolence." Nowadays, we can substitute the term "social responsibility" for "benevolence."

The invisible hand is competitive markets guided by self-interest. By pursuing their self-interest in competitive markets, firms achieve something they did not explicitly intend—they maximize the economic benefits (total surplus) available. By maximizing profit, the producers will maximize economic benefits for society overall, even if that is not their objective. If managers abandon their pursuit of profits in favour of vaguely specified social objectives, they are likely to be inefficient and cause a net loss in economic benefits to society as a result.

For example, one social objective commonly suggested when Friedman was writing his article was that firms should avoid raising prices so as to restrain inflation. We now understand that such an approach would likely be harmful. As described in Chapter 14, the main cause of high inflation is rapid money supply growth, which stimulates demand for goods and services. Prices rise because demand rises. If firms fail to raise prices, the result will simply be excess demand at the old prices—resulting in costs of delay, failure of the goods to be allocated to their highest-value uses, and other problems. Society would likely be worse off under such a system than if firms simply tried to maximize profits, allocating goods to people who value those goods most through increased prices.

15.2.3 Legitimacy and Expertise

In addition to the responsibility of managers to the owners of the firm and the efficiency arising from the pursuit of profits in competitive markets, Friedman also emphasizes several other benefits of profit maximization, or disadvantages of alternative CSR policies.

One such concern relates to the *legitimacy* of managers' decisions regarding CSR expenditures. Suppose a firm decides to contribute to disadvantaged groups. Which group should it help: sick children? long-term unemployed? poor elderly people? And what about other groups that are not necessarily disadvantaged, such as Boy Scouts, immigrant groups, sports teams, particular religious or ethnic groups, and university students, all of which have been recipients of substantial gifts from corporate donors? Some people might think such groups are very worthy, but others, including many shareholders, might think they should not be subsidized. What provides legitimacy for the decisions of corporate executives to help or subsidize such groups using shareholders' money?

The question of legitimacy is closely related to the concern that pursuit of CSR can amount to *taxation without representation*. Suppose, for example, that senior managers of a large firm decide to make generous donations to the United Way—a large general-purpose charity. These donations are costly to the firm, which can fund them by raising prices, which harms consumers; by reducing dividends, which hurts shareholders; or by reducing wages, which hurts workers. One or more of these groups will, in effect, be taxed to support the United Way without their explicit approval—without representation.

Any shareholder, consumer, or worker who wanted to contribute to the United Way could do so directly. Why then should the corporation's senior executives presume to make that decision for them? Similarly, we should not expect or want business executives to decide which cultural activities to support using money that would otherwise go to shareholders. Business should, under this argument, supply goods and services that people are willing to pay for, and not paternalistically decide on social policy.

And even if there is agreement on a target group, it is far from clear that the money will be well spent. Managers who make such decisions might lack *expertise*. Suppose, for example, that a toy company decides to help sick children. What should the toy company do? It could donate money for a children's wing in a hospital, it could fund research into treatments for certain childhood diseases, or it could pay for trips to Disneyland after treatment. Lacking expertise in dealing with sick children, even well-intentioned executives might have very little idea of how best to spend the money, and might allocate it very wastefully.

15.3 Social Responsibility Beyond Profits

Much of the rationale for corporate social responsibility can be viewed as a rebuttal to Friedman's arguments. A major alternative to the shareholder responsibility argument for profit maximization is referred to as *stakeholder theory*. And the major problem with the efficiency (invisible hand) argument is *market failure*. In addition, the legitimacy and expertise issues can be appropriately dealt with.

15.3.1 Stakeholder Theory

The argument that managers of corporations should seek to maximize profits is based largely on an assumed exclusive responsibility of managers to shareholders—the owners of a corporation. Alternatively, shareholders can be viewed as just one group of stakeholders—just one group to whom managers have obligations. This alternative perspective, referred to as stakeholder theory by Freeman (1984), is that managers have obligations to several groups in addition to shareholders.

In particular, managers might have obligations to workers. In many countries, including Canada, there is widespread acceptance of the view that firms have responsibilities to workers, including a responsibility to provide a safe working environment. This requirement is understood, even in the absence of its specific inclusion in labour contracts and in the absence of specific laws or public policies regarding industry practice. If, for example, a worker is told to clean up a construction site, that worker would expect that the site would be free of toxic waste which would be hazardous to the worker's health, or that the company would take proper precautions for dealing with hazardous materials. Employees have a reasonable expectation that the employer would take preventative measures, not wait to be sued by employees.

Similarly, firms could be viewed as having obligations to their customers. Many such obligations are now embodied in law, such as requirements for truth in advertising (Chapter 11) or product safety regulations. However, many philosophers and others argue that firms might have an ethical obligation to go beyond minimal legal or regulatory requirements. For example, some firms develop products, such as voice-activated appliances, tailored to the needs of consumers with physical disabilities, even when little or no profit is available and when not required by law to do so.

Another important stakeholder group might be neighbours—people who live near a production facility. It is fairly common for conflicts to arise between late-night bars and nearby neighbours who object to noise late at night. Some bars close earlier than legally required out of a sense of responsibility to their neighbours. And, of course, environmental damage in the neighbourhoods surrounding production facilities has often been a major concern.

The view that only shareholders count and that other stakeholder groups have no standing is rejected by most philosophers and by most business executives. Ownership and stewardship of assets are not the only relationships that induce responsibilities. Responsibilities to workers, consumers, neighbours, other firms, and to governments are also widely accepted. If these other responsibilities are ethically significant, then single-minded pursuit of profits is not necessarily the ethically correct objective for managers. Managers have some obligations to shareholders, but those are not their only obligations.

15.3.2 Efficiency, Market Failure, and Corporate Responsibility

Even if we reject the shareholder responsibility argument for single-minded pursuit of profits, as suggested by the previous section, it is still possible that profit maximization might be ethically justifiable. Specifically, if profit maximization really does maximize economic benefits—if the invisible hand really does work—then profit maximization might still be appropriate. To paraphrase Smith (1776) and Friedman (1970), we might say that maximizing profits is the best way to meet our ethical obligations to *all* stakeholders, not just to shareholders.

The problem with this efficiency argument for profit maximization is market failure, as explained in some detail by Arrow (1973). (See also Chapter 3 in this book.) Private markets governed by self-interest do not always maximize surplus. For example, problems might arise because of market power, externalities (or other forms of incomplete property rights), and informational asymmetries. In such cases, simple profit maximization will not be efficient.

Externalities, analyzed in some detail in Chapter 9, are particularly important. For example, consider a factory that emits pollutants damaging to the health of nearby residents. This health damage is a negative externality. To address this problem, the government could impose a tax on emissions from the factory. If the tax was set at the right level, a profit-maximizing factory would cut back emissions by the just right amount in response to the tax, and profit maximization by the factory would be efficient.

However, many externalities, especially small ones, are left uncorrected. For example, many businesses generate a lot of waste, some of which goes into landfills, and much of which ends up on the street. In either case, the waste creates negative externalities by using up valuable space (in landfill sites) and causing littered streets and sidewalks. This is a negative externality that causes inefficiency. However, if businesses adopt a norm that everyone picks up their garbage and recycles it when appropriate, then we would all be better off. In short, norms of corporate social responsibility can increase efficiency.

Transparency and honesty are important aspects of CSR. Failures of transparency and honesty create informational asymmetries. As described in Chapter 3, informational asymmetries can cause inefficiency, and they are common. Firms often know the quality of their products better than consumers do. A firm engaging in a business negotiation knows its capabilities better than the firm it is negotiating with does. And a manager knows whether he or she intends to actually follow through on an agreement while the other party does not. Such informational asymmetries can cause market failure. Suppose, however, that business executives generally subscribe to a policy of honesty in communicating with each other, thereby removing informational asymmetries. Agreements could be made over the phone, contracts would not have to be written down, lawyers would not have to be consulted, and transactions could be concluded quickly. Much business is in fact conducted in this way, which is very efficient if business partners can be trusted.

If, on the other hand, dishonesty is the norm, then oral agreements would never be sufficient and written contracts would be required for everything. Furthermore, if contracts are violated, then redress through the court system is required, which would be very expensive for all parties, including for society at large which pays for the courts. Many Pareto-improving transactions would be foregone altogether, simply because the two parties could not trust each other to fulfill the terms of the transaction. It is frequently alleged that such problems are an important reason why some poor countries remain poor. A corporate social responsibility norm of honesty can be regarded as a solution to potential market failure due to asymmetric information. If people simply tell the truth, then asymmetric information is not a problem, as credible information can be readily transmitted to the uninformed party.

This trust or honesty issue is also an important explanation for why, in certain countries, business is dominated by a particular ethnic group or even by a few families. People trust each other within the group, and it is much more efficient to do business with people you can trust than with people you cannot trust.

Business honesty also generates positive externalities. Honesty may be a good policy for the person in question because of reputation effects, but in addition, his or her honesty creates benefits for others as well, including for business associates and third parties. Because honesty is associated with positive externalities, there is reason to believe that private incentives will provide too little of it. The standard policy solution of subsidies seems impractical, however, in the case of honesty.

However, social values and personal ethics can be an important substitute for government policy. If business executives are honest because they have a personal commitment to honesty or because their friends will ostracize them if they prove to be dishonest, then honesty will be promoted without the need for active public policy. Business will run much more efficiently as a result. Many sociologists have linked the 18th- and 19th-century economic development of England and the United States to the rise of the Protestant religions and their emphasis on the values of honesty, thrift, and hard work.

Honesty is only one example of an ethic that is important to general business efficiency. Thrift and hard work are also important, as are loyalty and altruism. A business enterprise in which employees are willing to help each other, even when no direct credit is forthcoming, will generally operate more effectively than one in which employees engage in backstabbing.

In addition to promoting business efficiency, business ethics also have a direct effect on the psychological well-being of the population at large. Most people simply feel better when they are in an environment where they believe they can trust others, and where they believe they are contributing to something worthwhile. They are also more likely to emulate such behaviour if they observe it in others. For example, as experiments have shown, a motorist is much more likely to stop to help someone with a flat tire if he or she has recently seen someone else stop to help a motorist in distress.

The main point of this section is to show that we cannot assume that profit maximization is necessarily efficient for society as a whole, despite the invisible hand principle. The invisible hand applies when markets are perfectly competitive and market failures are absent. In the presence of market failure, CSR has an important normative role. Society as a whole is better off if managers accept an ethical obligation to do something other than just maximize profit, such as pollute less, invest in worker safety, or be honest in dealings with consumers and with other firms, even when it is not in their immediate financial interest to do so.

15.3.3 CSR Legitimacy and Expertise
Section 15.2.4 raises concerns about the legitimacy of CSR policies adopted by managers, and about managers' ability or expertise in carrying out the policies. It is possible for a firm to adopt CSR policies in a way that lacks

legitimacy. It is also possible for firms to be very inefficient in implementing the policies, using more resources than necessary to achieve a given outcome. Such problems were common in the early days of CSR policies. However, it is also possible for these policies to have legitimacy and to be implemented effectively. Furthermore, such positive outcomes are not difficult to achieve.

The implicit argument made by some critics of CSR is that because some CSR programs have been arbitrary (lacking legitimacy) and poorly implemented (inefficient) it follows that all CSR policies should be rejected. This is what logicians call a *false dilemma*. The implied dilemma arises from presenting only two options: accept bad CSR programs or reject all CSR programs. Therefore, if we do not like the first option we are pushed toward the second. However this is a false dilemma because these are not the only two options. Another option is to improve the design of CSR programs so that we can reject bad programs but accept good ones.

We can start by considering an example of the wrong way to approach CSR, loosely based on a real situation. Suppose that Jack, the CEO of a major corporation, likes golf and meets some friends to play golf one weekend. After playing, Jack's friend Ravi asks if Jack's corporation might support a summer program to give disadvantaged teenagers an opportunity to learn golf and help keep them off the streets. Jack likes golf, feels that helping disadvantaged teenagers is a worthy cause, and therefore signs up his cor-poration as a sponsor of the program, providing a CSR grant of 200,000.

This approach lacks legitimacy. The CEO has just agreed to spend share-holders' money without consulting them, making an arbitrary decision based largely on his own preferences. If the firm studied alternative ways to help keep disadvantaged youth off the streets they might find that golf programs are very inefficient. Golf fees are expensive, as are golf clubs, and the courses are often a long way from where disadvantaged teenagers live. And most kids in the target population are not very interested in golf—their friends and families don't play, they can't play it at school, and it is not particularly good exercise in any case. It might turn out that a soccer camp is much more efficient, with inexpensive facilities readily available at most schools during the summer, generating much higher benefits per dollar.

A firm that is adopting a CSR program should not rely on the CEO or other senior executives to make arbitrary decisions of this type. Most cor-porations running such programs have a professional CSR officer or team whose job it is be well informed about efficient ways of achieving potential CSR objectives. Furthermore, once a policy has been designed it should be clearly described to and voted on by shareholders, at least in broad outline form. A CSR plan voted on by shareholders has just as much legitimacy as a tax policy implemented by a democratically elected government.

As with tax policy, a CSR policy might not be unanimously supported, but we do not require unanimous support for legitimacy. And a shareholder who does not like a corporate CSR policy can always just sell his or her shares. Similarly, a customer who does not like the policy can stop buying the product and a worker who does not like the policy can find a new job. All of these ways of escaping a CSR policy are much easier to carry out than escaping taxes. Therefore, if anything, CSR policies voted on by shareholders are less coercive than tax increases voted on by voters.

As for expertise, it is easy enough to gain (or hire) expertise in implementing CSR programs. There is no reason to believe the firm would be less capable than governments in running youth programs. And in many areas of potential CSR activity, a firm has a big advantage in expertise over government programs. For example, a firm has a much better idea of how to reduce pollution coming from its factory or how to make its workplace safe than do government officials. Overall, we can conclude that legitimacy and expertise issues need not be major problems in adopting and implementing CSR policies.

15.4 Feasibility

So far, we have focused on the basic ethical or normative question, "Should firms adopt CSR objectives aside from maximizing profit?" We have asked the question, "What is the right thing for a manager to do?" Our tentative answer, so far, is that while we need to be careful to avoid arbitrary or badly designed CSR policies, there is an ethical case for such policies. However, we must still address the crucial question of feasibility: Is it possible for firms to follow meaningful CSR policies and survive, or even prosper? It is not very helpful to tell managers that they should follow CSR policies if the effect is to drive them out of business.

We might even accept a feasibility constraint on some ethical obligations—allowing that particular CSR policies are appropriate only if the firm can carry them out without going out of business or losing its competitive position. However, in some cases we might agree it is better to go out of business rather than engage in ethically unacceptable practices (such as using slave labour or exploiting children).

15.4.1 Survival Bias

The feasibility problem for CSR policies arises because of *survival bias*. Suppose that we rely on CSR policies as the main tool for fighting pollution. Firms that reduce pollution emissions by using expensive filters and other costly pollution-reduction technologies would earn lower profits than firms who do not bother to reduce emissions. Quite possibly these socially responsible firms would incur significant costs in reducing pollution and would not even survive, making large enough losses to ultimately go out of business entirely. Firms that did not spend money reducing pollution would earn higher profits and could charge lower prices and offer higher wages. These "irresponsible" firms could expand. Ultimately, the firms following the desirable policies would lose and the firms that continued to pollute would win. This survival bias leads to a kind of negative or adverse selection—the market would select the undesirable outcome in the form of rewarding the firms that continue to pollute.

Critics of CSR would argue that we are much better off with systematic government policy that requires all firms to reduce pollution (or that taxes emissions from all firms) instead of relying on each corporation to reduce pollution according to its own sense of social responsibility or "benevolence." Not only is it naive to expect sufficient voluntary reductions in pollution, it would also be counterproductive by inducing undesirable survival bias in favour of polluting firms.

15.4.2 Doing Well by Doing Good

A response sometimes given by CSR proponents to the survival bias problem is that firms can often "do well by doing good." In other words, a firm adopting a CSR policy might find that profits go up rather than down, enhancing rather than reducing its chances for survival and expansion.

For example, a restaurant might, as a matter of corporate social responsibility, provide printed and online information about the nutritional content of its menu items. At first glance this policy seems likely to reduce profits. Obtaining the information is costly, as is printing it. And customers might be dissuaded from many items that are tasty but that have some negative nutritional feature, such as high calorie content. However, it might turn out the customers like having the information available, with the result that demand and profits go up, not down. Similarly, firms that produce products using recycled materials might find that customers are willing to pay more for those products. Or a firm that makes donations to a university might find that the goodwill generated helps the firm in recruiting students for jobs, or in other ways. And firms that adopt sustainability policies often emphasize those policies in their advertising and find that customers respond positively.

If it is possible to "do well" (make more profits) by "doing good" (using CSR policies) then we do not need to worry about survival bias. Firms adopting such policies will survive and prosper. Unfortunately, however, this is far from a complete response to the selection (or survival) problem.

First, to the extent that a CSR policy increases profits, it is not clear why we need to talk about CSR at all. Firms have an incentive to pursue such policies just as a matter of profit maximization. They do not need, additionally, to be instructed to design CSR policies. Such policies will presumably be implemented if managers simply follow Friedman's prescription to maximize profits. It is possible that CSR policies might suggest creative ways of maximizing profit that managers would not otherwise discover, but that it is not likely to be a common occurrence.

Arguably, CSR objectives have relevance as distinct objectives only if they reduce profits. Otherwise profit-maximizing firms would do them anyway, and the CSR categorization would be redundant or unnecessary. Thus, either CSR policies are those that would be conducted anyway, or they reduce profits and raise the survival bias problem. And what do we do about survival bias? If expecting firms to reduce pollution through voluntary action would only succeed in making socially responsible firms go out of business, we need an alternative.

15.4.3 Responses to Survival Bias

In many cases, CSR cannot be a substitute for government action. With environmental protection, for example, it seems clear that efficiency requires government policy, such as pollution taxes or standards. Similarly, while we hope that most firms provide honest advertising, we do not rely only on CSR; we also have laws that require truth in advertising and active enforcement mechanisms for those laws.

Broadly speaking, it is unlikely that CSR can resolve major market failure problems, such as the externalities that underlie environmental problems or the asymmetric information problem that is the basis of truth in advertising laws. Furthermore, CSR is unlikely, by itself, to deal with the major fairness or discrimination concerns. Thus, for example, we have public policies that provide economic aid to the disadvantaged rather than relying purely or even substantially on CSR or other forms of private charity. And we have laws against certain types of discrimination (such as workplace discrimination based on gender) and certain types of labour practices (such as child labour) that would violate widely held values regarding fairness. While we expect firms to treat people fairly, we would not expect that CSR would be sufficient by itself.

In all these areas, public policy provides a level playing field that allows firms to carry out socially desirable policies, even when those policies impose some cost on the firms. If all firms face the same costs, then no one firm suffers a competitive disadvantage. However, we cannot expect public policy to redress all market failures or deal with all fairness issues. Business norms, including CSR practices, also play a very important role. How do we avoid survival bias—rewarding of irresponsible practices and punishment of responsible practices—in such cases?

Often the CSR issues are too small to seriously jeopardize a firm's survival. For example, if a large company with hundreds of millions of dollars in revenue per year allocates a budget of a few hundred thousand dollars to support educational programs for young people, this is not likely to put the firm's survival or even its competitive position at risk. Many CSR policies have very low costs and can be implemented without concern about survival bias.

However, there are some cases in which CSR programs are potentially important from a social point of view, are not covered by government policy, and are large enough to impose a significant financial disadvantage on firms that adopt them. Such situations could lead to survival bias if some firms, but not all, adopt these CSR programs. Sometimes this problem cannot be avoided, and a firm that wants to survive and compete effectively cannot afford the luxury of CSR programs.

For example, in Chapter 4 we considered the role of bribery. Basic CSR practice, taken for granted in Canada, is that firms should not pay bribes. Such things do happen in Canada, as recent scandals in Montreal indicate,[3] but instances are relatively rare. In some countries, however, bribes are normal business practice.[4] Firms will argue that they cannot compete without paying bribes. As a result, often a contract for a new road or bridge, or a permit to open a new business will go to the firm willing to pay the highest bribe to the decision-maker rather than go to the firm that can do the best job.

It is sometimes possible that a given economic structure might potentially support two outcomes or equilibria, one with a high level of corporate social responsibility and one with a low level. For example, we can imagine business operating without bribery (high CSR) or with bribery (low CSR). The high-CSR outcome, where no firms engage in bribery, will be more efficient

---

[3] See, for example, Les Perreaux, "Corruption inquiry told Montreal Mayor's circle allegedly took bribes," *Globe and Mail*, October 22, 2012 at http://www.theglobeandmail.com/news/national/corruption-inquiry-told-montreal-mayors-circle-allegedly-took-bribes/article4628693/.

[4] The organization *Transparency International* assesses the corruption levels on a country by country basis. In 2012 it rated Denmark, Finland, and New Zealand as the least corrupt countries, while Afghanistan, North Korea and Somalia were the most corrupt. Canada was among the least corrupt, being rated in 9th place for freedom from corruption. See cpi.transparency.org/cpi2012/results/.

and better for all firms than the low-CSR outcome, where all firms use bribery. With high CSR the same opportunities are available as with low CSR, and no costly bribes have to be paid. The problem is that one firm might perceive an advantage in "defecting" from the high-CSR equilibrium—offering a bribe to solicit a contract. Even a small bribe might work if the other firms are not using bribes.

This situation is much like the prisoners' dilemma game described in Chapter 6. With such games, if the basic interaction is repeated, it is possible that the high-CSR outcome might be supported as an equilibrium, although the low-CSR solution is also a possible equilibrium. The important mechanism that can support high CSR (no bribery) is firms' ability to punish a firm that defects and resorts to bribes, perhaps by refusing to do business with that firm, undercutting it when it bids on other projects, or ostracizing the senior managers of the defecting firm, not inviting them to social events. Of course firms have to observe the bribery or other questionable practices in order to take such action, but often they do have a very good idea, even if the evidence falls well short of what would be needed for legal proof.

If a high-CSR equilibrium has been established, it would be very costly for a single firm to defect and incur the associated punishment. Therefore, the high-CSR equilibrium can be maintained. Conversely, if a low-CSR equilibrium is in place, there is very little a single firm can do to change things, as a firm that refuses to pay bribes when everyone else does simply won't get any business. Such low-level outcomes can exist for a long time. Even within Canada and the United States we can see significant business differences from city to city, with significant corruption in some cities, but very little in many others. We see even larger differences across countries, including much-publicized endemic corruption in countries such as Afghanistan and Somalia.

From the public policy point of view, one important question is how to move from a low-CSR equilibrium to a high-CSR equilibrium. An intense legal enforcement effort might be helpful, although it might be prohibitively costly to maintain surveillance and enforcement for long. Sometimes a change in business culture will be generated from within the firms themselves, if a few people take a leadership position in trying to change the business culture.

Public awareness of the issues can play an important role. For example, if senior executives in many corporations are keeping corporate and personal funds in tax havens such as the Cayman Islands or the Bahamas to avoid paying taxes, then no firm is likely to suffer from doing the same. However, if most firms pay their taxes honestly, then a firm that defects by avoiding or evading taxes by using tax shelters might be harmed if that knowledge becomes public. Many consumers might prefer not to buy products produced by such a firm.

Feasibility is a genuine problem. In some situations, a firm that adopts a CSR policy consistent with current Canadian norms would not be able to survive. For example, a firm trying to operate in Afghanistan while maintaining gender neutrality in human resource policies and refusing to pay bribes might not be able to operate. However, in Canada, the United States, and much of world, the use of broad CSR standards has become common, suggesting that the potential survival bias problem is not too severe, and that it is possible to get out of the low-CSR equilibrium and move to a high-CSR outcome.

15.4.4 A Case-Study: CSR at McDonald's

One of the first major companies to adopt explicit CSR policies was the McDonald's fast food empire. Its best known and most successful venture in this area is the network of Ronald McDonald Houses that provide accommodation for families of children undergoing medical treatment at hospitals. This is an example of the "community development" type of CSR.

The Ronald McDonald House concept did not originate with McDonald's but is credited to Fred Hill, an American football player. While playing football in Philadelphia, Hill and his wife spent a lot of time at the hospital where their 3-year-old daughter received treatment for leukemia. They noticed many other families in the same situation, including many families that travelled long distances to get to the hospital but could not afford hotel rooms. Hill approached the Philadelphia Eagles football team about setting up a charity to provide a temporary residence for families of children being treated at the Philadelphia Children's Hospital. The Eagles approached McDonald's, which decided to support the concept.

Today, there are over 300 Ronald McDonald Houses around the world providing accommodation and other services for sick children and their families. In Canada, there were 14 Houses as of 2013, providing temporary accommodation for well over 10,000 families each year. The Ronald McDonald Houses are highly visible, and are viewed as a very successful charity.

The Ronald McDonald Houses are not managed by McDonald's but run as a separate charitable organization, the Ronald McDonald House Charities. The largest single donor to this charity is the McDonald's Corporation, but most of the money comes from a wide range of other donors, including corporations and individuals.

The Ronald McDonald Houses have been a tremendous marketing success for McDonald's, which is probably a good example of a corporation that "does well by doing good" through a CSR policy. Very likely, the expenditures by McDonald's on these houses are good investments even from a purely marketing point of view. And every time there is a local campaign to raise money for a Ronald McDonald House (which is a frequent occurrence in Canada's major cities), significant media exposure is generated for McDonald's as well. McDonald's makes explicit marketing use of the houses. It currently runs a program of donating 10¢ to Ronald McDonald Houses for every "Happy Meal" purchased, and this fact is prominently displayed on Happy Meal packaging.

This example illustrates some interesting points about CSR. First is the connection between the product and the program. The program is targeted at families with young children, which also makes up the primary consumer base for McDonald's. This is a common theme among CSR programs—firms often focus CSR efforts on issues closely related to their own products or their primary consumers. This practice reflects the idea that a firm's consumers are an important stakeholder group for the firm.

Second, the example allows us to focus clearly on the question of whether such CSR expenditures are good expenditures. Specifically, if we look at all the money spent on Ronald McDonald Houses, we can ask the question as to whether it would be better if that money were spent somewhere else. For example, would be it better to spend the money on actual health care facilities? And if residential facilities for families are the best use of money, why doesn't the health care system make those investments without the need for CSR?

Supporters of the Ronald McDonald program would make the following points in answer to these questions. First, they would say that the same amount of money would not be available without the Ronald McDonald program. Furthermore, the additional money is not a tax imposed on consumers or shareholders of McDonald's without representation. When consumers buy Happy Meals at McDonald's they know they are, in effect, contributing 10¢ per Happy Meal. And shareholders buy and hold McDonald's stock in full knowledge of, and in some cases because of, the connection with Ronald McDonald Houses. Consumers and shareholders might feel much better about their contributions than they would about a general increase in taxes used to fund health care. Arguably, the Ronald McDonald program is also more effective than a publicly funded program would be. Possibly, for example, the connection with McDonald's allows the Ronald McDonald program to take advantage of the positive reputation and high visibility that McDonald's has with children. And children just feel good being in a Ronald McDonald House; better than being in an anonymous government facility.

In addition to its relationship with Ronald McDonald House Charities, McDonald's also has a substantial in-house CSR program, which it refers to as "Global Corporate Social Responsibility, Sustainability, and Philanthropy."[5] In 2012, McDonald's Canada was recognized as marketer of the year by *Marketing* magazine, in large part because of its CSR activities. (Among other things, McDonald's Canada runs a youth hockey program called the AtoMc program.) McDonald's has apparently turned CSR programs to its advantage. Critics have suggested that McDonald's is simply using CSR to maximize profits, but there is little doubt that the CSR programs developed by McDonald's also do considerable good, and that most people approve of and appreciate those contributions.

15.5 Government Policy and CSR

This textbook is primarily about government policy. We should, therefore, ask about the connection between government policy and CSR, or business ethics more broadly. There are three important aspects of this relationship to emphasize.

First, if government policy was perfect there would be no need for CSR policies aside from profit maximization. Government policy would correct the market failures and would make the distributional transfers required by fairness. Managers could then just focus on maximizing profits. However, government policy is far from perfect. It is not possible for governments to observe every market failure and correct it, or to take care of every disadvantaged person. CSR polices can be very effective in filling in some of these gaps. If we ask the question, "What is an ethically correct action for a manager?" we conclude that the manager has an obligation to do more than simply maximize profits. Managers also have responsibilities to other stakeholders of the firm, including society at large, and can take actions that offset some market failures and promote fairness in business dealings.

Second, while CSR can fill in some gaps, it is not a complete substitute for government action. It is still important for government policy to address major market failures and to deal with major redistributive policies. Relying on voluntary action by corporations and other firms would not be enough. CSR policies are best viewed as a complement to government policy, not as a substitute for it.

Third, we should be aware of the effect government policy has on business ethics. If, for example, the tax system is so full of loopholes that it encourages

---

[5] A description of these programs can be found at www.aboutmcdonalds.com/mcd/sustainability.html.

business decisions to be made principally for reasons of tax avoidance, not only does this have direct efficiency costs, but also it undermines the business ethic that business is supposed to produce value for money, not defraud taxpayers. Similarly, if governments are seen to reward successful lobbying by bailing out failing businesses or, even worse, to solicit bribes in return for favourable treatment, this has the indirect cost that all citizens, including business managers, become more cynical. They will tend to modify their behaviour accordingly, reducing their willingness to pay taxes and contribute to the general public welfare. Conversely, it is possible for government policy to promote and support corporate social responsibility. For example, governments can work with firms to develop CSR initiatives and can run complementary public awareness campaigns.

For these reasons and others, CSR policies and government policies have developed together. For example, corporate responses to environmental problems and government environmental policies have emerged over the same period of time and have served to reinforce each other. Ultimately, both business ethics and government policies reflect the underlying values and changing circumstances of an evolving society.

References

Akerlof, George. 1970. "The Market for Lemons: Quantitative Uncertainty and the Market Mechanism." *Quarterly Journal of Economics* 84: pp. 488–500.

Anas, Alex and Robin Lindsey. 2011. "Reducing Urban Road Transportation Externalities: Road Pricing in Theory and Practice." *Review of Environmental Economics and Policy* 5: pp. 66–88.

Antweiler, Werner and Sumeet Gulati. 2012. "Reducing the Environmental Impact of Transportation – British Columbia's Tax Policy Initiatives." *Canadian Tax Journal* 60: pp. 869–880.

Arrow, Kenneth J. 1951, 1963. *Social Choice and Individual Values* (revised ed.). New York: John Wiley & Sons Inc.

_____. 1973. "Social responsibility and economic efficiency." *Public Policy* 21: pp. 303–317.

Averch, H. and L. Johnson. 1962. "Behaviour of the Firm under Regulatory Restraint." *American Economic Review* 52: pp. 1058–1059.

Axelrod, Robert. 2006. *The Evolution of Cooperation* (revised ed.). Perseus Books Group.

Banerjee, Sidhartha. 2012. "Federal Competition Watchdog Hopes to Sink Teeth into Quebec Corruption Actors." *National Post* online Nov. 11, 2012.

www.news.nationalpost.com/2012/11/11/federal-competition-watchdog-hopes-to-sink-teeth-into-quebec-corruption-actors/.

Barstow, David. 2012. "Vast Mexico Bribery Case Hushed Up by Wal-Mart After Top-Level Struggle." *New York Times* online April 21, 2012. www.nytimes.com/2012/04/22/business/at-wal-mart-in-mexico-a-bribe-inquiry-silenced.html.

Boardman, Anthony, Ruth Freedman, and Catherine Eckel. 1986. "The Price of Government Ownership: A Study of the Domtar Takeover." *Journal of Public Economics* 31: pp. 269–285.

Brander, James A. 1995. "Strategic Trade Policy." *Handbook of International Economics* 3: pp. 1395–1454. New York: North-Holland.

_____. 2010. "Innovation in Retrospect and Prospect." *Canadian Journal of Economics* 43: pp. 1087–1121.

Brander, James A. and Steve Dowrick. 1994. "The Role of Fertility and Population in Economic Growth: Empirical Results from Aggregate Cross-National Data." *Journal of Population Economics* 7: pp. 1–25.

Brander, James A., Thomas Hellman, and Tyler Meredith. 2012. "What Ottawa Can Do – Venture Capital." *Policy Options*, 33(10) November: pp. 42–44.

Brander, James A. and Barbara J. Spencer. 1985. "Export Subsidies and International Market Share Rivalry." *Journal of International Economics* 18: pp. 83–100.

Brander, James A. and M. Scott Taylor. 1998. "The Simple Economics of Easter Island: A Ricardo-Malthus Model of Renewable Resource Use." *American Economic Review* 88 (March): pp. 119–138.

Carlton, Dennis W. and Jeffrey M. Perloff. 2005. *Modern Industrial Organization*, 4th ed. Boston: Addison Wesley Longman.

Christensen, Jen. 2012. "The Billion Dollar Election: Who Got Paid." CNN online Nov. 9, 2012. www.cnn.com/2012/11/09/politics/election-who-got-paid/index.html.

Clark, Colin W. 1990. *Mathematical Bioeconomics: the Optimal Management of Renewable Resources*, 2nd ed. Toronto: John Wiley & Sons Inc.

Coase, Ronald H. 1960. "The Problem of Social Cost." *Journal of Law and Economics* 3: pp. 1–44.

____. 1974. "The Lighthouse in Economics." *Journal of Law and Economics* 17(2): pp. 357–376.

Competition Bureau. 2012. www.competitionbureau.gc.ca/eic/site/cb-bc.nsf/eng/03439.html.

Cournot, Augustin. 1838. *Recherches sur les principes mathématiques de la théorie des richesses.* Paris: Hachette.

Dahlby, Bev and Ergete Ferede. 2011. "What Does It Cost Society to Raise a Dollar of Tax Revenue? The Marginal Cost of Public Funds." *C.D. Howe Institute Commentary* 324, online March. www.cdhowe.org/pdf/Commentary_324.pdf.

de Soto, Hernando. 1989. *The Other Path.* New York: Harper and Row.

Downs, Anthony. 1957. *An Economic Theory of Democracy.* New York: Harper and Row.

Frank, Kenneth. T., Brian Petrie, Jonathan Fisher, and William C. Leggett. 2011. "Transient Dynamics of an Altered Marine Ecosystem." *Nature* 477 (01 September): pp. 86–89.

Freeman, R. Edward. 1984, 2010. *Strategic Management: A Stakeholder Approach.* Cambridge, U.K: Cambridge University Press.

Friedman, Milton. 1968. "The Role of Monetary Policy." *American Economic Review* 58: pp. 1–18.

____. 1970. "The Social Responsibility of Business Is to Increase Its Profits." *New York Times Magazine* September 13: p. 32.

Gallant, Roy A. 1990. *The Peopling of Planet Earth: Human Population Growth through the Ages.* New York: Macmillan.

Gallini, Nancy. 2002. "The Economics of Patents: Lessons from U.S. Patent Reform." *Journal of Economic Perspectives* 16: pp. 131–154.

Goldman, Jason G. 2012. "How Democracy Works in Nature." BBC online November 14, 2012. www.bbc.com/future/story/20121114-election-day-animal-style/1.

Gordon, Stephen. 2012. "Subsidies Put the R&D Horse before the Innovation Cart." *The Globe and Mail* online February 21. www.theglobeandmail.com/ report-on-business/economy/economy-lab/subsidies-put-the-rd-horse-before-the-innovation-cart/article547671/.

Grant, Drew. 2011. "10-Year Time Capsule: 'Harry Potter' Feeding Frenzy Leads to Glutton Punishment." *Salon* online April 12, 2011. www.salon.com/ 2011/04/12/10_year_time_capsule_harry_potter_greed/.

Gurven, Michael and Hillard Kaplan. 2007. "Longevity Among Hunter-Gatherers: A Cross-cultural Examination." *Population and Development Review* 33: pp. 321–65.

Hahn, Robert W. 1989. "Economic Prescriptions for Environmental Problems: How the Patient Followed the Doctor's Orders." *Journal of Economic Perspectives* 3: pp. 95–114.

Hamermesh, Daniel. 2010. "When Your House Is Burning Down, How Good Is a Public Good?" *Freakonomics* online. www.freakonomics.com/2010/10/06/ when-your-house-is-burning-down-how-good-is-a-public-good/.

Hardin, G. 1968. "The Tragedy of the Common." *Science* 162: pp. 1243–1248.

Harris, Richard G. 1985. "Why Voluntary Export Restraints Are Voluntary." *Canadian Journal of Economics* 18: pp. 799–809.

Harvey, Charles M. 1993. "The Reasonableness of Non-Constant Discounting." *Journal of Public Economics* 53 (1994): pp. 31–51.

Head, Keith. 1994. "Infant Industry Protection in the Steel Rail Industry." *Journal of International Economics* 37: pp. 141–166.

Head, Keith and John Ries. 2010. "Do Trade Missions Increase Trade?" *Canadian Journal of Economics* 43(3): pp. 754–775.

Hotelling, Harold. 1929. "Stability in Competition." *Economic Journal* 39: pp. 41–57.

———. 1931. "The Economics of Exhaustible Resources." *Journal of Political Economy* 39: pp. 137–175.

Hutchings, Jeffrey A. and Robert W. Rangeley. 2011. "Correlates of Recovery for Canadian Atlantic Cod." *Canadian Journal of Zoology* 89: pp. 386–400.

Jensen, Michael C. and William H. Meckling. 1976. "Theory of the Firm: Managerial Behaviour, Agency Costs and Ownership Structure." *Journal of Financial Economics* 3: pp. 305–360.

Keynes, John Maynard. 1936. *The General Theory of Employment, Interest and Money.* London: Macmillan.

Kahneman, D., J. Knetsch, and R. Thaler. 1986. "Fairness as a Constraint on Profit Seeking." *American Economic Review* 76: pp. 728–741.

Kirkpatrick, David D. and Kareem Fahim. 2012. "Egypt Islamists Expect Approval of Constitution." *New York Times* online December 15, 2012. www.nytimes.com/2012/12/16/world/middleeast/egypt-draft-constitution-vote.html?pagewanted=1&thpw.

Kitzmueller, Markus and Jay Shimshack. 2012. "Economic Perspectives on Corporate Social Responsibility." *Journal of Economic Literature* 50: pp. 51–84.

Kreps, D. and R. Wilson. 1982. "Reputation and Imperfect Information." *Journal of Economic Theory* 27: pp. 253–279.

Krugman, Paul R. 1986. *Strategic Trade Policy and the New International Economics.* Cambridge, MA: MIT Press.

____. 1987. "Is Free Trade Passé?" *Journal of Economic Perspectives* 1: pp. 131–144.

Lind, R.C. 1982. *Discounting for Time and Energy Policy.* Washington, DC: Resources for the Future.

Lindsey, Robin. 2010. "Reforming Road User Charges: A Research Challenge for Regional Science." *Journal of Regional Science* 50(1): pp. 471–492.

Locke, J. 1939. "An Essay Concerning the True Original Extent and End of Civil Government." Reprinted in *The English Philosophers.* New York: Random House.

Lucas, R.E. 1981. *Studies in Business Cycle Theory.* Cambridge, MA: MIT Press.

Luk, Vivian. 2012. "Disabled woman Wants Punishment for Vancouver Cop Who Pushed Her." *The Vancouver Sun* online August 24, 2012. www.vancouversun.com/health/Disabled+woman+wants+discipline+Vancouver+pushed/7142717/story.html.

Lynn, Jonathan and Anthony Jay. 1984. *The Complete Yes Minister.* London: BBC Books.

Magee, Stephen. 1991. "A Taxing Matter: The Negative Effect of Lawyers on Economic Activity." *International Economic Insights 2* (January/February): pp. 34–35.

Mathewson, G.F. and Winter, R.A. 1998. "The Law and Economics of Resale Price Maintenance." *Review of Industrial Organization* 13: pp. 57–84.

McCalman, P. 2001. "Reaping What You Sow: An Empirical Analysis of International Patent Harmonization." *Journal of International Economics* 55: pp. 161–186.

McKenna, Barrie. 2011. "Flawed R&D Scheme Costs Taxpayers Billion." *The Globe and Mail* online April 27, 2011. www.theglobeandmail.com/report-on-business/flawed-rd-scheme-costs-taxpayers-billions/article1939418.

McKenzie, Kenneth J. 2012. "The Big and Small of the Tax Support for R&D in Canada." *SPP Research Papers* 5(22) online. www.policyschool.ucalgary.ca/sites/default/files/research/k-mckenzie-rd-tax-final.pdf.

McVeigh, Tracy. 2012. "Saudi Arabian Women Risk Arrest as They Defy Ban on Driving." *The Observer* online June 17, 2012. www.guardian.co.uk/world/2012/jun/17/saudi-arabian-women-risk-arrest-ban-driving.

Moore, Dene. 2012. "Pipeline Pitch: Registry Reveals Enbridge's Heavy Presence in Halls of Power." *The Canadian Press* online August 23, 2012. ca.news.yahoo.com/pipeline-pitch-registry-reveals-enbridges-heavy-presence-halls-183523758.html.

Nemetz, Peter. 1986. "Federal Environmental Regulation in Canada." *Natural Resources Journal* 26: pp. 551–608.

Niskanen, William A. 1971. *Bureaucracy and Representative Government.* Chicago: Aldine-Atherton.

Posner, R.A. 1974. "Theories of Economic Regulation." *Bell Journal of Economics* 5: pp. 335–358.

Perloff, Jeffrey M. and James A. Brander. 2013. *Managerial Economics and Strategy.* Boston, MA: Pearson.

Rawls, John. 1971. *A Theory of Justice.* Cambridge, MA: Harvard University Press.

Rhoads, Steven E. 1985. *The Economist's View of the World Government, Markets, and Public Policy.* Cambridge: Cambridge University Press.

Ricardo, David. 1817, 1971. *The Principles of Political Economy and Taxation.* Baltimore: Penguin.

Ries, John C. 1993. "Windfall Profit and Vertical Relationships: Who Gained in the Japanese Auto Industry from VERs." *Journal of Industrial Economics* 41: pp. 259–277.

Romero, Simon. 2012. "Brazil Enacts Affirmative Action Law for Universities." *New York Times* online August 30, 2012. www.nytimes.com/2012/08/31/world/americas/brazil-enacts-affirmative-action-law-for-universities.html.

Ross, Thomas W. 2004. "Canadian Competition Policy: Progress and Prospects." *Canadian Journal of Economics* 37: pp. 243–268.

Ross, Thomas and Ralph A. Winter. 2005. "The Efficiency Defense in Merger Law: Economic Foundations and Recent Canadian Developments." *Antitrust Law Journal* 72: pp. 471–504.

Samuelson, P.A. 1954. "The Pure Theory of Public Expenditure." *Review of Economic Statistics* 36: pp. 386–389.

Schelling, Thomas. 1981. "Economic Reasoning and the Ethics of Policy." *Public Interest* 63: p. 40.

Smith, Adam. 1776. *An Inquiry into the Nature and Causes of the Wealth of Nations.* Dublin: Printed for Messrs Whitestone, Chamberlaine, etc.

Spencer, Barbara. 1980. "Outside Information and the Monopoly Power of a Public Bureau." *Southern Economic Journal* 47: pp. 228–233.

Stigler, G.J. 1971. "The Theory of Economic Regulation." *The Bell Journal of Economics and Management Science* 2 (Spring): pp. 3–21.

Sutter, John D. 2012. "The Woman Who Defied Saudi's Driving Ban and Put It on YouTube." CNN online June 10, 2012. www.cnn.com/2012/06/10/world/meast/sharif-saudi-women-drive/index.html.

Tirole, Jean. 1988. *The Theory of Industrial Organization.* Cambridge, MA: MIT Press.

Tullock, G. 1967. "The Welfare Costs of Tariffs, Monopolies, and Theft." *Western Economic Journal* 5: pp. 224–232.

_____. 1976. "The Transitional Gains Trap." *Bell Journal of Economics*: pp. 671–678.

Vitousek, Peter M., Paul R. Ehrlich, and Anne H. Erlich. 1986. "Human Appropriation of the Products of Photosythesis." *BioScience* 36: pp. 368–373.

Weiss, Marissa. 2012. "Is Acid Rain a Thing of the Past?" Science Now, *Science* online June 28, 2012. www.news.sciencemag.org/sciencenow/2012/06/is-acid-rain-a-thing-of-the-past.html.

Winter, Ralph A. 2009. "Antitrust Restrictions on Single-Firm Strategies." *Canadian Journal of Economics* 42: pp. 1207–1239.

Index